Macbeth before Shakespeare

Macbeth before Shakespeare

BENJAMIN HUDSON

OXFORD
UNIVERSITY PRESS

Oxford University Press is a department of the University of Oxford. It furthers
the University's objective of excellence in research, scholarship, and education
by publishing worldwide. Oxford is a registered trade mark of Oxford University
Press in the UK and certain other countries.

Published in the United States of America by Oxford University Press
198 Madison Avenue, New York, NY 10016, United States of America.

© Oxford University Press 2023

All rights reserved. No part of this publication may be reproduced, stored in
a retrieval system, or transmitted, in any form or by any means, without the
prior permission in writing of Oxford University Press, or as expressly permitted
by law, by license, or under terms agreed with the appropriate reproduction
rights organization. Inquiries concerning reproduction outside the scope of the
above should be sent to the Rights Department, Oxford University Press, at the
address above.

You must not circulate this work in any other form
and you must impose this same condition on any acquirer.

Library of Congress Cataloging-in-Publication Data
Names: Hudson, Benjamin T., author.
Title: Macbeth before Shakespeare / Benjamin Hudson.
Identifiers: LCCN 2022040757 (print) | LCCN 2022040758 (ebook) |
ISBN 9780197567531 (hardback) | ISBN 9780197567555 (epub) |
ISBN 9780197567562
Subjects: LCSH: Macbeth, King of Scotland, active 11th century. |
Macbeth, King of Scotland, active 11th century—In literature. |
Scotland—History—To 1057—Historiography. | Shakespeare, William, 1564–1616.
Macbeth. | Scotland—Kings and rulers—Biography. | Kings and
rulers in literature. | Scotland—History—To 1057. | Scotland—Inliterature.
Classification: LCC DA778.8 .H83 2023 (print) | LCC DA778.8 (ebook) |
DDC 941.101/092 [B]—dc23/eng/20220922
LC record available at https://lccn.loc.gov/2022040757
LC ebook record available at https://lccn.loc.gov/2022040758

DOI: 10.1093/oso/9780197567531.001.0001

1 3 5 7 9 8 6 4 2

Printed by Sheridan Books, Inc., United States of America

For Ben and Will

Contents

Note on Methodology	ix
List of Abbreviations	xi
Acknowledgments	xiii
Preface	xv
Introduction: A Man and a Legend	1
1. Macbeth: Place and Past	10
2. Macbeth Emerges	34
3. King of All the Scots	58
4. Fame and Defamation	83
5. Not the Beginning of the Legend	102
6. Weird Sisters and the Prior of Loch Leven	124
7. Macbeth and Renaissance Scotland	144
8. The Literary Scot in Tudor England	165
9. Macbeth before Shakespeare	190
Conclusion	205

viii   *Contents*

Appendix 1. The Children of Macbeth?	213
Appendix 2. Andrew of Wyntoun's Macbeth Episode: A Translation	219
Notes	231
Selected Bibliography	255
Index	287

Note on Methodology

FEW PEOPLE KNOW all of the half dozen languages spoken in early Scotland or the dialects in which the Macbeth legend was composed. Although the spelling of personal and place names has changed since the Middle Ages and Renaissance, often the pronunciation is not too different. Throughout this narrative, with a few well-known exceptions, names are given in modern English and, for Gaelic and Norse names, the original language is given in round brackets (). Gaelic is used here as a generic term for the language spoken from what is now southwest Ireland to northeast Scotland; the written forms are known as Old Irish (to about the year 900) and Middle Irish (to about the year 1200). The English translations of texts strive for intelligibility rather than strict definition. Unless otherwise stated, all translations are by the author.

Usually there is little controversy among scholars about the chronology of events. Scottish incidents have been collected in two old, but still valuable, source books by A. O. Anderson: *Scottish Annals from English Chroniclers* and *Early Sources of Scottish History*. In order to keep citations manageable, dates are cited only if they are controversial or little known.

The author is cheerfully aware that absolute uniformity has not been achieved.

Abbreviations

§	section
CDIL	*Contributions to a Dictionary of the Irish Language*
CIH	*Corpus Iuris Hibernici*
ES	Anderson, *Early Sources of Scottish History*
ed(s).	editor(s)
f(f)	folio(s)
ff	following
fl.	*flourit*
HMSO	His/Her Majesty's Stationery Office
Lat.	Latin
LL	Book of Leinster
l[l]	line[s]
MI	Middle Irish
MS(S)	Manuscript(s)
NLS	Edinburgh, National Library of Scotland
no.	number
ODNB	*Oxford Dictionary of National Biography*
OI	Old Irish
ON	Old Norse
p[p]	page[s]
PRO	Public Record Office
r.	*recto*
rev.	revised
s.a.	*sub anno*
trans.	translator
v.	*verso*
vol(s).	volume(s)

Acknowledgments

I HAVE INCURRED many debts during the writing of this book, and it is a pleasure to acknowledge them while thanking those individuals and institutions. For permission to read manuscripts in their care and for the courtesies they extended to me while consulting their collections, I thank the librarians and staff of the Aberdeen Municipal Archives, the Queen Mother Library of the University of Aberdeen, the Royal Irish Academy, the Bibliothèque nationale de France, the Bodleian Library, the National Library of Scotland, Perth Municipal Archives, Dundee Municipal Archives, Trinity College (University of Cambridge), Trinity College (University of Dublin), and the Paterno/Pattee Library of the Pennsylvania State University.

Some ideas and analysis that appear here were refined in other venues. The problem of the historical prince as distinct from the literary anti-hero was the topic of several lectures delivered at the Smithsonian Institution, first in the talk "Macbeth the King" and then four seminars under the collective title "Macbeth: King and Play." The intersection of history and fiction was the topic of my *Léacht Mháirtín Uí Bhriain* (Máirtín Ó Briain Memorial Lecture) presented at the National University of Ireland—Galway. Additional research was undertaken while I was holding a Benjamin Meaker Distinguished Visiting Professorship at the University of Bristol.

Turning to individuals, I thank my son Robert Hudson for permission to use his photographs of the places he was led to by an overenthusiastic parent. For discussing aspects of Macbeth and Scottish history during the course of many years and for the insight provided by their work, I thank Alison Hudson, R. Andrew McDonald, and Susan King. The late James Campbell discussed aspects of Macbeth and Scottish history with me during many years; his kindness, critical sense, and penetrating intelligence are all gratefully remembered. My wife Aileen is once again the unsung heroine, not only living with Macbeth and his entourage for years, but also for all her encouragement and labors on the manuscript. Susan Ferber has been a laudatory editor.

Any errors are, of course, my own.

Preface

MACBETH IS A name that sets its own tone. While the literary character is familiar throughout the English-speaking world and beyond, few realize that he was based on a historical prince. Both the actual king and the fictional monarch have fascinated writers for centuries, beginning with the poets who recited their verses at the medieval monarch's court. The historical Macbeth lived in the eleventh century, a tumultuous period of European history that was an age of change in statecraft, worship, and literary culture. The real Macbeth was an avid adopter of new ideas, but his behavior and views were shaped by a culture that looked back centuries earlier for its inspiration and vocabulary. Sovereignty goddesses, saintly men, and legendary heroes populated the cultural memory of his society.

Almost immediately after his death in 1057, Macbeth's legend began to form. The historical king became intertwined with a literary character developed and embroidered by Medieval and Renaissance writers to suit their own political and cultural agenda. For two centuries, beginning with the fourteenth-century Scottish scholar John of Fordun until the sixteenth-century English historical popularizer Raphael Holinshed, the literary Macbeth was discovered, lost, and altered to accommodate supporting characters, different locales, and changing motivations. To the saintly King Duncan were added the malevolent weird sisters while the murderous Lady Macbeth was confronted by the stalwart Lady Macduff. Macbeth's fortress at Lumphanan was overshadowed by a royal court of crime at Dunsinane.

The process of transformation was completed in the seventeenth century by a London playwright named William Shakespeare whose play called *The Tragedie of Macbeth* became one of his most popular works. Samuel Johnson and his biographer John Boswell remembered act I. 3 as they rode through the woods outside the town of Forres (where it was believed that Macbeth and Banquo met the witches) and Abraham Lincoln, in a letter of 1863 to the actor James Hackett, wrote that *The Tragedie of Macbeth* was his favorite play. Adaptation continued as Macbeth has been played, among others, as a cook in *Scotland, PA* while his queen became the heroine of Dmitri Shostakovich's opera *Lady Macbeth of the Mtsensk District*.

This book studies the man and the legend that preceded William Shakespeare's play. Two key questions are prominent. First, who was this eleventh-century prince and why did his career attract historians and playwrights? Second, how did his history become legend and how did the legend develop during the more than five centuries between his reign and the early seventeenth century? The search for answers leads to a fresh examination of historical and literary texts from medieval to seventeenth-century Scotland and to its neighbors. Understanding Macbeth and his legend leads beyond northern Britain. The historical prince fought and allied with Vikings and Normans, while he traveled the length of Europe to make a pilgrimage to Rome. Creators of the literary character found inspiration in Irish, French, and Old Norse literature as well as in motifs circulating around continental Europe. When the literary Macbeth moved south to England in the sixteenth century, his reception must be placed within the theatrical treatment of the Scots even as political events were bringing a Scots monarch onto the English throne. A few years before Shakespeare is believed to have written his tragedy, two versions of the Macbeth legend apparently were circulating around London. William Shakespeare was not alone in his fascination with a king from the Middle Ages.

Divergence between historical fact and literary invention is a familiar feature in connection with the famous or infamous; Macbeth was no exception. The solution to the puzzle of why a successful, but commonplace, prince became the central figure in a legend that grew and developed over centuries might never be found. There are works claiming to find the "real" Macbeth. This is not one of them. Too few records, however defined, have survived from this period to permit the illusion that the individual prince can be discovered. While William Shakespeare's *The Tragedie of Macbeth* is one of the justifications for this study, the book does not concern itself with an analysis of the drama. There are many other works that deal with his literary creation, and the mountain of Shakespearean criticism grows every year. When William Shakespeare wrote his tragedy of Macbeth, he used a legend that had evolved during several centuries with many of the elements that he would rework and make uniquely his own. This study is concerned with that real and fictitious individual.

Macbeth before Shakespeare

Introduction

A MAN AND A LEGEND

BOOKS RARELY BEGIN at the end, but this study finishes at the point where the Macbeth legend is generally believed to have started, in an important town during a noteworthy year. The year was 1605 and the town was Oxford, home to the ancient university. In August, the Scots King James VI, who had recently added England to his domain (becoming King James I of that realm), visited the university in the company of his Danish-born wife Queen Anne and their son Prince Henry Frederick. James was one of the new breed of European monarchs: well educated, cosmopolitan in outlook, and inquisitive in intellect. He had received a classical education from some of Europe's finest scholars, but his particular interests were Scottish history and the occult. The king was also an author who had written several books, including one on the occult called *Daemonology*. Most famously, a decade later he was the patron of what became known as the King James Version of the Bible.

Oxford's scholars were determined to make the royal stay memorable. Preparations had been ongoing for months, and events were planned that reflected King James's interests. The detailed schedule for the royal visit included lists of who was to be at which event as well as thorough instructions on the expected standards of behavior.[1] Students and faculty were reminded to wear academic robes while in public, to attend their lectures, and not to shout or complain if there was not enough room for them at the theatrical performances. In an age that believed in a divinely ordered division of society, the members of the ancient seat of learning were conscious of their special identity. When King James arrived at the entrance to the town, the scholars of the university were directed to stand on one side of the street while the "strangers," those who were not part of the university, were confined to the other side.

His Majesty's entrance into the town was greeted with a dramatic performance, but the Oxford presentation was muted and historical. At the gates of St. John's College, a brief poem called the "Three Sibyls" (*Tres Sibyllae*), composed in Latin by alumnus Matthew Gwynn, was spoken by youths dressed as the prophetesses of the ancient world. The king was hailed as a descendant of Banquo and saluted with three titles: first as king of Scotland, then as king of Ireland, and finally as king of England. The title "king of Ireland" was especially timely, since on March 11 of that year a royal proclamation had declared that all the inhabitants of Ireland were the direct subjects of King James and not their clan chief or local lord. The selection of Banquo to represent the ancestors of James's family, the Stewarts or Stuarts, might have been made because of the narrative of Banquo's career from a book His Majesty owned called *Holinshed's Chronicles*: there a threefold greeting is given by three women in a scene with Banquo and his companion Macbeth.

For the royal entertainment there were tours of the colleges, debates between the university's scholars, and theatrical productions. King James enjoyed the tours and especially liked the debates. Scholarly disputation had been developed in the medieval universities and remained an important part of the advanced education with which James was familiar. Topics for the Oxford debates reflected the king's wide range of interests: theology, medicine, law, philosophy, and science. The topic for one debate was the question "Was it possible for the imagination to produce real effects?" During the disputation, the king became so excited that he abruptly joined the contest. Possibly he was inspired by a similar scene in *Holinshed's Chronicles* when Banquo and Macbeth discuss whether the women who had hailed them were real or imaginary.

Less successful, however, were the theatrical entertainments. Despite being the patron of his own troupe—the King's Men—James was not fond of long plays late in the day because he arose early in the mornings. At Oxford the performances began at 9 PM and could continue until 1 AM. Four plays were chosen to be performed and their reception was tepid at best. The first play was *Alba*, and James was persuaded to remain for the entire performance by the pleading of the university's chancellor. The king was audibly bored during the second play, *Ajax Flagellifer*. Disaster struck in the midst of the third, especially long, play called *Vertumnus sive annus recurrens* (written by Matthew Gwynn) when His Majesty fell asleep. King James then took matters into his own hands and refused to attend the last play; he preferred a tour of the university library.

Those little difficulties did not disturb the king's hosts who, the following October, published *Oxfordes triumphe in the Royall entertainment of his most excellent maiestie the Quene and the Prynce 27 August 1605 With the Kinges oration Delivered to the universitie and the incorporating of Diverse noblemen Maysters of Art*, written by Anthony Nixon. Less flattering details were noted by Philip Stringer from the University of Cambridge, which was next on the king's academic tour. Stringer had arrived in Oxford on the first day of the royal visit on an administrative matter and stayed until the king departed. The University of Oxford's rival did not wish to make the same mistakes.[2]

Why is 1605 considered to be the year when Shakespeare began to write the *Tragedie of Macbeth*? Mainly because in 1950 a patent attorney from Philadelphia named Henry Neill Paul published *The royal play of Macbeth: when, why, and how it was written by Shakespeare*. Paul proposed that Shakespeare wrote *The Tragedie of Macbeth* during the winter of 1605/1606 and that the play was first performed at Hampton Court in August 1606, when King James entertained his brother-in-law King Christian of Denmark. He based the chronology on his claim that the *Tragedie of Macbeth* contained references to events of 1605, especially the infamous Gunpowder Plot of November and its aftermath. He also suggested that among the "strangers" in the crowd at Oxford during King James's visit was an actor and playwright named William Shakespeare. Shakespeare is known to have been well acquainted with Oxford because the university lay along the route from London to his home at Stratford-upon-Avon. His journey occasionally was interrupted in Oxford because a London friend named John Davenent had opened a wine bar there and Shakespeare lodged with him. As a member of James's theatrical troupe, the King's Men, Shakespeare would have taken more than a casual interest in the University of Oxford's choice of entertainment for the king.

Henry Paul's speculative reconstruction of the chronology has become generally accepted scholarly opinion. There is, however, no direct evidence for that date, and the first reference to the play is five years later in the diary of a part-time magician cum physician named Simon Forman who attended a performance of the *Tragedie of Macbeth* on April 20, 1611. His summary of the play differs somewhat from the first known script of the play, which appeared in 1623 when, seven years after Shakespeare's death in 1616, two of his colleagues, John Heminges and Henry Condell, published *Mr. William Shakespeare's Comedies, Histories, & Tragedies* in a volume now known as the *First Folio*.

———

There are many controversies connected with *The Tragedie of Macbeth*, but on one point scholars agree: William Shakespeare did not invent Macbeth. How much his drama owes to earlier writers and/or to his own genius is not the concern of this study. This book studies the evolution of Macbeth from the historical Scots king to the character selected by Shakespeare to be the anti-hero of his tragedy. There were five and a half centuries between the reign of the historical prince and Shakespeare's literary creation. Macbeth did not emerge from a vacuum, and it is important to place him in the culture and history of the society that produced him. That includes the historical story tradition that would have explained the past to Macbeth and his contemporaries. This cultural and political world from which the stories emerged spanned the northeast Atlantic, from southwest Ireland through what is now Scotland to Scandinavia. Fantasy and fact combined in the intricate symbol stones that dotted the Scottish countryside and in the retelling of tales of heroes battling supernatural foes and human enemies or prophecies of the imminent end of the world.

Fantasy and legends were a part of Macbeth's world, but so too were the harsh realities that awaited even a king. From the assassination of his father to the climactic battle with his predecessor Duncan, Macbeth's early career saw him as both the hunter and the prey. His accession to the kingship on August 16, 1040, brought a new unity to the Scots as well as a new type of monarch. That was useful, since Macbeth had to face new circumstances. When he battled with the Norwegian king's subjects, the Vikings of the Orkney Islands, for control of Caithness and Sutherland, for example, they were fighting over tax revenues. His pilgrimage to Rome, the only one known to have been undertaken by a medieval Scots monarch, in 1050 was made in the middle of a vigorous reign. Finally, he was the first Scots king to invite Norman knights to his domain after they had been expelled from the England of the half-Norman King Edward the Confessor. Yet there was more to his career than politics and warfare. A fresh analysis of the surviving records indicates that he had children, in addition to a stepson from his wife's previous marriage.

Macbeth's legacy was a legend that has had a resonance for generations of historians, authors, and theatergoers. After his death, the physical destruction

Introduction 5

of Macbeth's dynasty was completed in a couple of generations on the battlefield by the armies of his rival Malcolm Canmore and his descendants. The devastation of his reputation was a longer process, taking more than three centuries, but the literary partisans of the House of Canmore were no less thorough. The biographical and fantastic elements connected with Macbeth were becoming part of the Scots' literary horizon in the twelfth and thirteenth centuries. Macbeth was remembered as a good king, although he was little more than a name in the historical king lists. When he reappears in narrative histories in the fourteenth century, the depth of his fall is visible in the *Chronicle of the Scottish Nation* written by a priest from Aberdeen named John of Fordun. Assembled in the aftermath of the Great Plague and at a time when Scottish armies had been unsuccessful against the English for a generation, Macbeth's clan had vanished as a political force, and his image as a good king had been replaced by that of a tyrant. John's narrative was as much a morality tale as a history, and Macbeth appears as the caricature of an unreasoning monster. He is not the main character but merely a one-dimensional villain and foil to the hero of the piece, Malcolm Canmore. The literary Macbeth was a malleable villain and, while subsequent treatments of his legend in the hands of later writers brought variations in appraisals of his character, John of Fordun's villain would be the foundational character.

The real father of the Macbeth legend as it appears in Shakespeare's drama was a fifteenth-century Scottish prior named Andrew of Wyntoun who had a taste for the supernatural. Andrew shifts the emphasis from Malcolm to Macbeth as his partially successful effort to conflate two versions of the Macbeth story reveals the circulation of different legends. The first has Macbeth kill Duncan, who is described as his uncle, and marry his aunt due to his interpretation of a dream. The second legend turns Macbeth into a semi-demon as his devil-father seduces his mother with promises of their son's invincibility. Andrew's inclusion of weird sisters from Old Norse legend, magic rings, and ethereal dogs produces a more developed character of Macbeth. While using themes in common with European medieval literature, he also used ideas, symbols, and tales found throughout the northeastern Atlantic.

As the Middle Ages were followed by the Renaissance, the legend of Macbeth gained a revival in the hands of Hector Boece, a sixteenth-century university lecturer and administrator. Boece's career at the new University of Aberdeen placed him on the border of Macbeth's home region and in his *History of the Scots* a new Macbeth is created. The medieval fiend is replaced by a stylish monster whose personality was similar to princes such as the English king Henry VIII and the French king Francis I. Boece's version of the legend was copied, at second hand, into William Shakespeare's main source, Raphael Holinshed's *Chronicles*. Despite criticisms by fellow historians, Boece's history became the accepted interpretation of the Scottish past. *History of the Scots* was used by the political and religious rivals George Buchanan and John Leslie, spiritual duelists in the confrontation between Catholicism and Protestantism, to justify their views of the present. At the same time, the question of succession to the English throne, for which King James VI of Scotland was the leading contender, meant that by the late sixteenth century the Scots were especially interesting to their southern neighbors. Theater was one place where this fascination with the Scots could be seen. During the last decade of Queen Elizabeth's reign, several plays feature Scots kings to greater or lesser degrees. At the beginning of the seventeenth century, apparently there were two performance pieces in London about Macbeth. Neither survives, unfortunately, so they must be reconstructed from asides in other documents.

———

This book presents the background to the historical Macbeth, the actual prince and his career, and the development of the legend. The general progression is chronological with the occasional digression. In the midst of this narrative the pertinent events are assembled and analyzed.

The narrative begins with an examination of the background to the genuine prince. The first chapter looks at the circumstances of the appearance of Macbeth's ancestors, the Scots of Dál Riata in the north of Britain, probably during the fifth century. Reasons are suggested for their initial success in settlement and later expansion into the lands of the neighboring Picts; from greater ferocity to changing patterns of land use. The arrival of the Vikings in the ninth century added a new layer of complexity to an already complicated situation. The collapse of the Pictish kingdoms and the continuing military ascendancy of the Scots meant the subsequent hostilities between the Vikings and the Scots must be viewed within the context of fights for resources as much as battles for movable wealth.

In the second chapter, the beginning of Macbeth's career is the topic. This involves the reign of his father Findlay whose fights with the Viking settlers in the Orkney Islands would be bequeathed to his son. Intermarriage between Scots and Scandinavians provides a subtext to events as family connections had their own influence on the behavior of individuals. An unexpected source of information is a gospel now called the "Book of Deer" that has charter notes of benefactors to the church of Deer, located somewhere in the vicinity of the medieval Deer abbey. They include members of Macbeth's extended

Introduction

family and the notes give some information about their regions of authority as well as the basis of their wealth. Macbeth needed rich relatives as, at the beginning of his kingship, he was pulled into the political affairs of Scandinavia. Danish efforts to maintain lordship over Norway had led to internal conflict among the Norwegians, who were divided in their support of King Óláfr "the Stout," better known as St. Olaf. The king of the Danes, Cnut the Great, made a famous journey to eastern Scotland, to Fife, in order to secure the allegiance of Macbeth and two other princes. His place in the Danish scheme of affairs brought Macbeth into conflict with his cousin Jarl Thorfinn of the Orkneys. The ensuing battles were for lumber and the collection of taxes, rather than the ill-defined lootings of popular literature.

Macbeth's reign as king of all the Scots began in August 1040 and is the theme of the third chapter. From challenges by rival clans to donations to churches to his final embroilment in English political affairs, he had a busy reign. Macbeth's rule was marked by an internationalism not found among previous kings. He made a pilgrimage to Rome and employed mercenary soldiers from Normandy. During his reign, information is learned about his wife Gruoch, the famous Lady Macbeth. She was wealthy in her own right and was a benefactress of the Church of St. Serf at Loch Leven. Her family line continued with her son Lulach, and for the next centuries her descendants would battle the clan of Malcolm Canmore. At the end of his reign, Macbeth became involved in the political turmoil at the English court.

The fourth chapter studies the events after Macbeth's death as his rival Malcolm Canmore becomes the patriarch of a family that dominated Scottish history for the following two and a half centuries. Malcolm's clan was the beneficiary of a good report after his marriage to the future St. Margaret of Scotland. Her support for the reformed religious orders was crucial for their successful settlement in Scotland. The goodwill extended to her children, especially to her daughter Queen Matilda of England and son King David of Scotland. Malcolm's family became more involved in the French-speaking elite that was dominating Britain; they benefited from having their story presented in the best possible terms while their rivals failed to enjoy similar indulgence. Even popular literature such as Geoffrey of Monmouth's *History of the Kings of Britain* had an episode in which Macbeth's homeland was considered a wilderness. As the aristocracy of both England and Scotland become increasingly francophone, the monarchs were judged on how closely they adhered to a French model. Anything else was dismissed as primitive or even barbaric. Literary assassination went together with military defeat. When Lady Macbeth's great-grandson's infantry attacked King David's horse-mounted nobles at the battle of Strathcathro, the former's defeat was hardly surprising. The consequences were marked by a note in the Book of Deer in which David allows the clergy to keep their benefits. When a possible descendant of Lady Macbeth was executed at the beginning of the thirteenth century, an era had passed.

By the fourteenth century the fights and competitions of Macbeth and his contemporaries were relics of ancient history. There remained, however, a curiosity about the past. When the Anglo-Scottish wars began in the late thirteenth century, propagandists on either side brought history into service for their cause, which is the theme of the fifth chapter. There are pieces of antiquarian interest before this, but the hostilities led to a spate of historical writing. Foremost among the Scots were two clergymen: John Barbour and John of Fordun. The latter wrote the influential *Chronicle of the Scottish Nation*, an account of the Scots from their settlement in Britain to the High Middle Ages. Within this chronicle was a history of Malcolm Canmore that contained the basic legend of Macbeth. There is little character development; Malcolm is all good and Macbeth is all bad. Nonetheless, that narrative continued in the versions of the Macbeth legend to the seventeenth century.

More talented as a writer was John of Fordun's younger contemporary Andrew of Wyntoun, the subject of chapter 6. Andrew was less a controversialist and more a collector than John. Where he found many of his materials is not now known, but Andrew tapped into a rich vein of folklore/popular history as he gathered information. Some of the new information about Macbeth came from the archives at St. Andrews cathedral, such as the grants to the church, while the demonic origins of Macbeth are obscure. Nonetheless, Andrew adds the occult to the legend, with the first appearance of the Weird Sisters, prophetic dreams, and magic rings. Many of the novelties can be traced back to Celtic literature or the ancient beliefs of Scandinavia. They also reflect the concerns of society at the close of the Middle Ages. Andrew was writing at the beginning of a period when these items were considered increasingly menacing by the authorities. Simultaneously, more popular entertainment is appearing in the records, from plays to tales. Amusement then, as now, could be expensive and many of the notices appear in financial records.

While John of Fordun and Andrew of Wyntoun were pioneers in the development of the Macbeth legend, the real forerunner of Shakespeare's Macbeth was a university administrator named Hector Boece; his contribution is the topic of chapter 7. Boece presented a multi-faceted king, an advance on the nondescript scoundrel. The occult is pushed to the margins as Macbeth appears as a Renaissance prince both as a law giver and a successful

Introduction 9

commander. There is more elaboration to the actual legend as Macbeth and a new character called Banquo defeat invaders from Scandinavia. Diplomacy and court politics in addition to murder become rungs up the ladder of Macbeth's ambitions. Boece's work was harshly criticized by other historians, but it quickly became the accepted version of the past. Two reworkings of the legend were commissioned by King James V and his mother. More important, Macbeth became embroiled in the religious controversies of the day.

Chapter 8 moves the inquiry to England where a writer named Raphael Holinshed was composing a history of Britain. His version of the Macbeth legend is the direct ancestor of William Shakespeare's drama. Holinshed and his work have been studied intensively, so only a brief overview is given. That leads to the question of how were Scottish kings portrayed in the English theater prior to the first decade of the seventeenth century, when the *Tragedie of Macbeth* is thought to have been first performed. Not surprisingly, in the years before the death of Queen Elizabeth I, interest began to increase in the Scots in some surprising forms.

Was William Shakespeare the first to use the legend of Macbeth as a performance piece as distinct from literature? The question is investigated in chapter 9. There is evidence of certainly one and probably two works in which the character of Macbeth appears. The first is mentioned by Shakespeare's sometime acting colleague and occasional business partner, Will Kemp, while the other is a reference to a play about a king called Malcolm. This leads back to the question of when was *The Tragedie of Macbeth* first performed? The first record of a performance is almost half a dozen years after the date of 1606, generally believed to be the date of the completed composition. The conclusion offers a summation of the life of the real prince and the creation of a legend.

When William Shakespeare began to write the *Tragedie of Macbeth,* he had at his disposal a legend that developed over centuries as well as a topic that had been presented to the public in a different form a few years earlier. Macbeth had made the journey from historical prince to literary character, together with his contemporaries Duncan, Malcolm Canmore, and Edward the Confessor. Their stories went from historical records to historical recreation to political theory to popular theater.

I

Macbeth

PLACE AND PAST

AFTER SEEING WILLIAM Shakespeare's *Tragedie of Macbeth*, the audience can be excused for thinking that they have seen medieval Scotland. Much of the play is historical after all. Macbeth was a real king of Scotland who did kill his predecessor Duncan. Duncan did have two sons named Malcolm *Canmore* ("Big Head") and Donald. Contemporary with them were Lady Macbeth, Siward, and the English king Edward. The ruins of a fortress on Dunsinane Hill are still visible, and it is possible to walk in a day from there to what had been Birnam Wood. Shakespeare, however, used those historical tidbits to create a Scotland that was a flight of imagination. It is a tribute to his genius that the play is so convincing.

Few pieces of evidence survive for the historical king whose name was spelled Mac bethad, although a timeline can be extracted from the surviving chronicles. He attended a royal meeting with the English king Cnut in 1031, killed his predecessor named Donnchad (modern Duncan) in 1040, put down a rebellion by Donnchad's father Crinan in 1042, made a pilgrimage to Rome in 1050, lost a major battle against the earl of Northumbria in 1054, and was slain in 1057 by Malcolm Canmore. Those half dozen items are supplemented by genealogies, church records, and some miscellaneous pieces. Taken as a whole, however, a vista opens on a time and place quite different from the theatrical setting. Medieval Scotland cannot be recaptured in all its complexity, but it is worth trying to discover how much the mists of time can be parted. To learn more about the real Macbeth it is necessary to set him in his world.

The Land beyond the Wall

Macbeth's kingdom had two names. To the Irish and Scots it was Alba, which formerly had been the name for all of Britain until the tenth century when (in the form of Gaelic spoken at that time, Middle Irish) it was limited to the land north of the firth and river Forth. The English knew it as Scotland, which first appears in the *Anglo-Saxon Chronicle* (in the version now known as the Parker Chronicle) for the year 934 when the Anglo-Saxon king AEthelstan led an invasion of the Scots. The difference is important because the names disguise two different views. Alba refers to a place while Scotland designates a territory where a people—the Scots—happened to be located at the moment.

Whether Alba or Scotland, a distinguishing feature was its situation in the north: north of the fertile lands of southern Britain, north of the great waterways—the firths of the Forth and the Clyde—that almost divide Britain in two, and north of the walls—the Hadrian and Antonine—of the most successful conqueror, Rome. A century after their first conquests, when they decided to set a limit to the colony of Britannia, the Romans built, c. 142 AD, a turf barrier called today the Antonine Wall, extending from Bo'ness on the Firth of Forth to Old Kilpatrick on the Clyde estuary. To observers, such as the third-century Roman historians Herodian and Dio or a fourth-century panegyrist on the emperor Constantius, the land beyond the wall was a wilderness of hills, trees, and wetlands.[1] Little had changed four centuries later when the Anglo-Saxon historian Bede, who lived near the other Roman barrier now known as Hadrian's Wall, also remarked on the steep and rugged mountain chains.[2] Within those hills was the mysterious Caledonian Forest, a place of legend. The ninth-century *History of the Britons*, attributed to a priest named Nennius, claimed that the seventh of twelve battles fought by Arthur of Britain had been in the Caledonian woods (*in silva Celidonis*).[3]

The coastline surrounding the mountains and woods is broken by numerous waterways and could be as dangerous as the interior. In addition to expected perils such as submerged rocks there were the dangers of tide and current. One of these is the infamous Corryvrekan (Gaelic *Coire Breccain*, "speckled cauldron"), the world's third largest whirlpool, located between the Isles of Jura and Scarba. Two important water entrances into the interior are the afore-mentioned Firth of Forth on the east coast and the Firth of Clyde on the west. During Macbeth's reign, the Forth marked the southern bound of the Scots people as distinct from the Scots domain.[4] Equally important, on the west coast, north of the Firth of Clyde, is the Firth of Lorn, named after Macbeth's clan, which is the southern extent for a series of inland lakes or lochs that include Loch Lochy, Loch Oich, and Loch Ness in the valley known as the Great Glen, extending northeast to Inverness. This seems to have been the route taken by Macbeth's ancestors as they immigrated into the lands around another major waterway: the Moray Firth. At the river Ness, between Loch Ness and Inverness, the seventh-century writer Adomnán of Iona claims that St. Columba confronted a monster, today called the Loch Ness monster, which attempted to kill one of his monks.[5] Columba overcame the beast and forced it to flee. The obstacles of the firths and rivers were militarily important. According to the historian Orderic Vitalis, the invasion of southern Scotland in 1091 by King William II of England was halted on the southern shore of the Forth because there were not enough vessels to ferry his troops across.[6]

There were few land routes in Macbeth's Scotland. The Romans built a military highway along the southern side of the Antonine Wall and it intersected another Roman supply road running south to the former legionary camp at Carlisle, close by Hadrian's Wall. Hadrian's Wall had its own service road that ran along its length. Malcolm Canmore used the western way in 1070 when he led his army for a surprise attack on the English settlements in the vicinity of Hadrian's Wall.[7] Another Roman supply road, now known as Dere Street, ran along the eastern coast as far as the river Forth. When the Anglo-Saxon King Edmund went to meet the Scots king Malcolm I in 945, he paused his journey along this route to visit the community of St. Cuthbert at Chester-le-Street.[8] King William I sent his eldest son Robert along this route as far as Falkirk to attack the Scots in 1080.[9]

Hindrances from both geography and water explain why invasions of Scotland often came from both land and sea; if one route was blocked the other might be open. When Earl Siward of Northumbria attacked Macbeth in 1054, the *Anglo-Saxon Chronicle* notes that he used both ships and infantry.[10] A century earlier, the Anglo-Saxon king AEthelstan attacked by land and sea in 934, according to the *Anglo-Saxon Chronicle,* while a similar tactic was used later by King William I in 1072.[11]

Early in Macbeth's life, the Scots annexed two southern territories. The first, south of the Firth of Forth and north of the river Tweed, was called Lothian. This was completed c. 1018 at the battle of Carham.[12] According to the *Scottish Chronicle,* the Scots had begun to seize territory as far south as the fortress of Edinburgh in the tenth century. The second addition, southwest along the river Clyde, was the kingdom of Strathclyde. King Malcolm "the Bald" had been the ally of the Scots at the battle of Carham, but he died shortly afterward and his kingdom was annexed.

Immigrant Warriors

Macbeth's ancestors arrived in Britain around the year 500 from an Irish kingdom called Dál Riata. Located on the eastern border of modern county Antrim, Dál Riata extended from the northeastern corner to the river Bann. An anecdote about the emigration concerns Macbeth's paternal ancestor Loarn and the Apostle of Ireland, the famous St. Patrick. The saint was traveling round Ireland and, after crossing the river Bann, he entered the inconsequential kingdom of Dál Riata where he met a prince with a proposition:

> Patrick was welcomed in the land by Erc's twelve sons. Erc's son Fergus the Great said to Patrick: "If my brother [Loarn] respects me in dividing his land, I would give it to you." . . . Patrick said to Fergus. "Though your brother does not respect you today, it is you who will be king. The kings in this country and over Fortriu [south-central Scotland] will be descended from you forever."[13]

Aggression and morality combine in this episode. Fergus observed the hierarchy of his society by asking the saint to bless his endeavor with an offer of land taken from his brother. Patrick's response was a prophecy that promised royal status for Fergus and his descendants if he led his people across the thirteen miles of the North Channel separating Ireland from what is now western Scotland and into the region of the river Forth. There were, however, no sympathies spared for the intended victims and no doubts about the fitness of the enterprise. This was a brutal world where the strong took what they could, and the weak hoped for the best.

This anecdote is found in the tenth-century collection of materials about the saint known as the *Tripartite Life of Patrick*. The story was compiled by a man with an immediate interest in it: Joseph son of Fáthach (d. 936) of the Clan of the Rough Kinsfolk (Cland Gairb Gaelta) of Dál Riata. The name of his clan suggests that his home was the Rough Bounds (Garbh-chríocha) which extend from Morvern in Scotland. He was the "heir" of Patrick and that meant he was head of the church of Armagh and leader of all the churches in Ireland dedicated to the saint.[14] Joseph believed that he was writing history, not legend, and that the St. Patrick anecdote was correct or he would not have included it in his dossier. The anecdote of Patrick and Fergus is a type of historical remembrance intended to answer the question "why" more than simply the "how" or the "where." The society that produced Macbeth wanted to know the reasons for past actions.

The story of Patrick and Fergus took place during a desperate time for the people of Dál Riata.[15] The withdrawal of the Roman administration left a power vacuum even in the regions beyond the walls and, sometime before the end of the fifth century, colonists from Dál Riata sailed eastward to annex lands in Argyllshire on the northwestern coast of Britain. Their emigration to Britain appears to have coincided with the movement of other clans out of the west of Ireland, from Donegal and the region of Sligo Bay, who were known collectively as O'Neill (MI Uí Néill). They dominated the north of Ireland and occasionally claimed suzerainty over all Ireland for the next thousand years. Their origins are obscure although later legends look to a common ancestor called Niall "of the Nine Hostages."[16] Dál Riata was not alone in

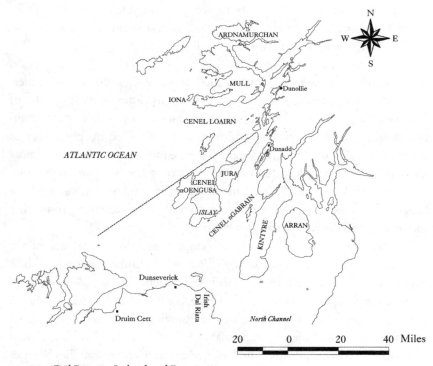

FIG. 1.1 Dál Riata in Ireland and Britain.

Macbeth: Place and Past

its danger, as other kingdoms in the northeast region, known as the province of Ulster, were trapped between the new expanding power and the sea. Compared with the situation in Ireland, a new home in Britain might have appeared to be a safe haven.

Clans from Irish Dál Riata might not have been the first to hold land in Britain, and there are legends of Irish kings holding some type of lordship, such as the tale "How the Kingdom of Scotland was given to Fiachna."[17] They did not believe themselves to be the first to arrive in British Dál Riata. A convoluted piece of geographical lore in the *History of the Britons* claims that Dál Riata was first settled by a legendary figure named Istoreth, son of Istorinus, and later it was the first landing place in Britain for the descendants of Scotia, the daughter of Pharaoh who was believed to have given her name to the Scots.[18] Not a state in the modern sense of the word, Dál Riata was the collective name for a group of clans that found it convenient to cooperate against a common foe or, when it suited, to fight among themselves. As inhabitants of Ireland they were called Scotti, which had been used by the Romans to identify the Irish. Whether or not Fergus led the first group, by the sixth century Dál Riata was a bi-coastal kingdom whose domain spread from Ireland to Britain.[19] The territory in Ireland had been small, but in Britain it eventually extended from the Mull of Kintyre as far north as Ardnamurchan and, according to the "Tale of Cano son of Gartnán" (OI *Scéla Cano meic Gartnáin*), it eventually extended as far north as the Isle of Skye.[20] Even after the royal families had moved to Britain, for several centuries they continued to control their Irish homeland.

Macbeth's ancestors were not the first colonists to sail from Ireland to Britain. Irish immigrants had been arriving before St. Patrick supposedly approved the royal exodus from Dál Riata.[21] Initially they were raiders, not peaceful farmers, and the threat existed for a long time. The Romans set up forts at what are now Chester and Carlisle as well as a naval base on the Isle of Anglesey in order to intercept marauding bands from Ireland. The raids seem to have increased after 300 AD when there are reports of attacks by large Irish fleets. The Scotti had allies among the people who lived north of Hadrian's Wall, called Picti, "the picture people," now known as the Picts. The Picts were actually the native Britons who lived outside Rome's immediate control, and they were so named by the Roman soldiers because of their body art. After Rome's legionary forces were withdrawn from the island in the first decade of the fifth century, the Picts and Scots intensified their attacks on the crumbling defenses of Roman Britain.

Picts and Scots

The Picts were to learn that having the Scotti as neighbors was different from having them as allies. The circumstances of settlement are obscure, and it is unclear whether the immigrants from Ireland won the lands in battle or were settled there by the Picts themselves. The uncertainty extends to literary history. The *Tripartite Life of Patrick* can be set beside a tale well known to the storytellers of Ireland and Scotland called "The Coming of Dál Riata into Britain" (OI *Tochomlud Dáil Riatai i nAlbain*) that survives only in fragments copied into later tales. This was a "Learned Tale," a story from the classical literary canon of the Gaelophone world, recited by every historian or *senchaid* (now popularly known as the "senachie"). Through the centuries the *senchaid* became a popular entertainer, eventually developing into the professional storyteller of Gaelic-speaking Ireland and Scotland. The "tales"—divided into categories such as raids, destructions, voyages, elopements, and wooings—were considered to be suitable entertainment for royal feasts or recitations at festivals.[22] In addition to "The Coming of Dál Riata into Britain" there was "The Coming of the Picts from Thrace to Ireland and their coming from Ireland to Britain" (OI *Tochomlod Cruithnech a Tracia co hÉrind ocus a Thochomlod ó hÉrind co Albain*). The list of "Learned Tales" was periodically revised, with the last one made during Macbeth's lifetime.

A summary of "The Coming of Dál Riata into Britain" is found in John of Fordun's fourteenth-century *Chronicle of the Scottish Nation*. His account of the Scottish emigration into Britain shows how extravagant legend was blended into sober history. The thirty-first chapter of his first book (or section) has the title "About the cause of the first coming of the Scots to the island of Alba" (*De causa prima Scotorum aditus ad Albionem insulam*), where "Scots" has been substituted for "Dál Riata" of the "Learned Tale," and it tells how Fergus with his brothers Loarn and Oengus sailed from Ireland to Britain in the year 403 AD in one of several waves of emigrants.[23] The Picts were so terrified at the prospect of fighting these warriors that they opened the gates of their fortresses in surrender rather than meet Fergus and his siblings in battle. Fergus reigned for sixteen years and was the first Scot to rule west of Drum nAlban (Ridge or Backbone of Britain), the mountain range that extends from Sutherland to the Firth of Clyde and divides the western coastal regions from the rest of the island. The tale continues with the Picts and Scots making common cause and gathering allies—Vespiliones and Huns—across the sea for an attack against the Romans. Regardless of allies and prestige, the Romans were not easily cowed. When they faced the Scots in battle at

Carriden (east of Bo'ness and site of a Roman fort), Fergus and his followers were annihilated.

Fordun's story provides another example of how fact and fantasy complemented one another in the literature about early Scotland. Even though individual details are historically correct, the chronology is askew and the elaboration cannot be proved. For example, the historical event that is listed second, the alliance among the Scots, Picts, and Germanic peoples, actually occurred first. This was the *barbarica conspiratio*, otherwise known as the Pictish Revolt of 367, when the Roman administration in Britain was briefly overwhelmed by attacks from the Scots, Picts, and Anglo-Saxons that led to mutinies among the legions. Conversely, a demonstrably false item is the alliance with the Vespiliones and Huns. Vespiliones, correctly *vispiliones*, were not a people but a class of criminal; they were grave robbers. To compound the error, the Huns never were in Britain, and their attack on the western lands of the Roman Empire occurred two generations later, in the mid-fifth century. Fordun's third point, the battle among the Romans, Picts, and Scots at Carriden, apparently occurred a generation later in the waning years of the fourth century when the Roman general Stilicho led an expeditionary force against the Picts and Scots.[24] The first item of Fordun's list—the movement of the royal Dál Riata dynasties to Britain—seems to be a conflation of several attacks on Britain from Ireland that had been occurring since the fourth century with the movement of the royal families from Ireland to Britain at the end of the fifth century. In short, Fordun's synopsis shows that the information in a "Learned Tale" could be confused, but the individual items could also be correct.

The Clans of Dál Riata

Dál Riata was a kingdom or *túath*. Within Dál Riata there were different levels of kingship. The local ruler was a "king of a people" (*rí túaithe*) while above him was a regional overlord (*ruire*) and, at the highest level, the king of kings (*rí ruirech*).[25] There were similar duties among the kings of various levels. Although first and foremost a war leader, a king at all levels also had spiritual responsibilities. Like the pharaohs of Egypt, the king maintained the cosmic balance within a kingdom. So long as he was a fair ruler, then there would be plenty to eat and victory in battle. If the king became unjust, then there was disaster.

Within the kingdom, the society of Macbeth's ancestors was organized around family groups such as the *cenél* (kindred or extended family) or *clann* (descendants) now shortened to the more familiar "clan."[26] Dál Riata had four primary *cenéla*—Cenél nGabráin, Cenél Loairn, Cenél nÓengus, and Cenél Comgaill—of which the first two were the most important. The kin groups provided physical and legal security for the individual, where its members could be provided with medical care or food. Ferocity was proclaimed in their names; *gabrán* means "rough" while *loarn* means "wolf."

Members of the *túath* observed certain ceremonies such as the king-making ceremony called the "wedding" (OI *banais*). This was literally a marriage between a royal human bridegroom and a bride who was the sovereignty-spirit of the land. Conversion to Christianity added a few more elements to the ritual, including a brief invocation from the clergy asking for prosperity to accompany the new reign. A survival of this appears in the *Prophecy of Berchán* in some lines of verse referring to a tenth-century king named Constantine: "With fruit on slender branches, with ale, with music, with good cheer, with grain, with milk, with well-grown cattle, with pride, with fortune, with worthiness."[27] Hills were used as king-making sites. Although there was room on the hilltop for only a few people, the ceremony could be seen below by a larger audience. For Dál Riata the inauguration site is believed to be the hill of Dunadd in the Crinán Moss, at the head of the Kintyre Peninsula.[28] On the summit of Dunadd is a stone with a carving of a boar and, nearby, a foot-shaped depression in a rock. Both the boar and the foot are mentioned in literature. Throughout the British Isles, the boar was a symbol of ferocity and intelligence, the traits expected of a successful king. The boar is one of the beasts on the so-called Pictish Symbol Stones, where geometric designs combined with animal, human, and fantastic beings to produce mysterious, but artistically brilliant, scenes. A main character in the medieval Welsh tale "How Culhwch won Olwen" is the boar Twrch Trywth, who is powerful, clever, and fierce. The foot-shaped rock cavity is mentioned in Irish tales as a part of the tradition of magical stones. On the inaugural site in Ireland at Tara were two flagstones called Blocc and Bluigne. They were in front of the famous standing stone known as the "Stone of Destiny" (OI *Lia Fáil*) that would "scream" when struck by the chariot hub of a true king.[29]

These warrior clans inhabited distinct areas. Information about the internal organization of the clans within Dál Riata, together with some genealogical information about the princely houses, is found in a tract known as *The History of the Men of Britain* (OI *Senchus Fer nAlban*), which is a miscellany of genealogies, political geography, and a naval muster roll. Although originally composed c. 700, material was added to it in the tenth century and that text survives in a seventeenth-century copy.[30] *The History of the Men of Britain* gives the location of each clan, together with the number of its households. Macbeth's clan of Cenél Loairn was the largest, with seven hundred houses divided among three subgroups; it was located in the north of Dál Riata, extending from the coast of the Ardnamurchan Peninsula to Knapdale in Kintyre, and included the islands of Mull, Tiree, Coll, and Colonsay.

The main fortress was at Dunollie, just north of modern Oban, and all that survives is the ruin of the later medieval castle. The fort seems to have been named after an otherwise unknown individual called Ollach son of Brian who is mentioned in the Old Irish tale "The Cattle Raid of Fráech" (OI *Táin Bó Fráich*).[31] With five hundred sixty houses, Cenél nGabráin was the next largest, and it encompassed the area from Knapdale to the Mull of Kintyre, together with the islands of Jura, Arran, and Bute as well as parts of the Cowal Peninsula.

Fighting was the main business of the aristocratic male, which justified his leadership and the accumulation of privileges.[32] Training began with children's games, which developed boys physically and taught them how to perform as a unit. When the Irish St. Berach traveled to Scotland for adjudication of a land dispute, he came to the fortress of the Dál Riata King Áedan son of Gabrán during a feast, where boys were playing games in front of the stronghold.[33]

FIG. 1.2 Dunollie Castle, site of Cenél Loairn Fortress.

Berach's rival Diarmait urged the children to assault the holy man, but when they attacked him with their clubs and stones their feet miraculously were unable to move. The lack of organization was typical. Ambushes, sorties, and battles were elaborately organized, but grand plans quickly degenerated into clashes between small groups or individuals. Local leaders were expected to direct their men as well as they could. Warriors took advantage of the chaos to settle scores with personal enemies and, calling to each other by name, they fought duels in the midst of the combat.

Boats were an important means of transportation for troops. Macbeth used them, as did his ancestors. The sixth-century British writer Gildas in his sermon "Concerning the Ruin of Britain" (Lat. *De Excidio Britanniae*) claims that Irish invaders arrived in coracles (*de curucis*); those vessels survived into the twentieth century as fishing boats.[34] Medieval images of these vessels show them to be oval in shape and lightly constructed with a wooden frame over which were stretched the hides of animals, to provide a waterproof covering; in the last century, tarred cloth was commonly used. The boats were propelled by both sails and oars, with the oars used to maneuver and to move the vessel when the wind died. Only one sail was used and professional sailors manned the ships.[35] The importance of the *curach* is reflected in the position of the builder, who had the rank of an aristocrat (OI *aire déso*) in Irish law.[36] To ensure that these sea-going expeditions had sufficient crews, a quota of men was established, with each clan of Dál Riata obligated to furnish men according to its population. According to the *History of the Men of Britain*, twenty houses were obliged to furnish the crew for two "seven-bench" boats in the kingdom's flotilla. There were two rowers to a bench, so each vessel had a crew of at least fourteen men.

While territorial aggrandizement was outwardly the mark of a successful prince, success was measured internally by holding the kingship and keeping it from other (or even their own) families. The result, not surprisingly, was frequent warfare. Tales of fights within families became a staple of literature and, like the murder of Duncan by Macbeth, they often ended tragically. A popular romance that begins with warfare within the clans of Dál Riata is the "Tale of Cano son of Gartnán" (OI *Scéla Cano meic Gartnáin*). The story tells how Cano, a member of the royal dynasty, and his family emigrated from Dál Riata to the Isle of Skye.[37] They were successful and brought the island under their control, but this achievement was envied by their kinsman Áedán son of Gabrán. He ordered the killing of Cano's father Gartnán and forced Cano to flee to Ireland where he found employment as a mercenary. While employed by a king named Marcán, Cano fell in love with his wife Cred. In the best tradition of romantic tragedy, all ends badly for the thwarted lovers. Moving from literature to history, a famous feud in the late-seventh to early-eighth century was between Macbeth's ancestor Ainfcellach son of Ferchar "the Tall" (Ferchar Fota) and his brother Selbach. After the death of their father, Ainfcellach ruled for a year until Selbach forced him into exile in 698. Ainfcellach returned twenty years later, but was killed during a fight between the brothers at the battle of Finglen (in the Braes of Lorne).

Warriors for God

Warriors were not the only people moving around Britain and Ireland. By the fifth century there were also Christian missionaries. The establishment of Christianity in the British Isles is an obscure topic. There had been Christians in Britain possibly since the first century AD. The church of Glastonbury (in Somerset) claimed Joseph of Arimathea (who provided the tomb for Jesus's body after the crucifixion) as its founder.[38] Emperor Constantine I issued an edict of toleration giving legal status to Christianity after his victory at the battle of Milvian Bridge in 312; that included all parts of Britain under Roman control. Moving across the Irish Sea, St. Patrick is popularly famous as the man who brought Christianity to the Irish, but there seem to have been Christians on the island before his mission. A note in the fifth-century chronicle of Prosper of Aquitaine claims that a missionary called Palladius went to Ireland to minister to its Christian community early in the century.[39] As the story of St. Patrick and Fergus shows, the royal families of Dál Riata had converted to Christianity before leaving Ireland, and their travels were accompanied by priests and monks who preserved their story in written form such as chronicles. When missionaries found a place for their labors, they dedicated their chapels to the patron saint of their home church, which gives an approximate indication of the ties among the religious houses on two islands.[40]

The tide turned after the fifth century as missionaries from Ireland labored in Britain. Among them was an O'Neill aristocrat named Crimthann whose name in religion was Columba (Latin for "dove"). St. Columba (521–597) became one of the most famous religious leaders in early medieval Europe. Ironically, he became the patron saint of the peoples of Dál Riata (who had fled Ireland to escape his clan) when he founded a church on the tiny island of Iona in the Hebrides, only one mile wide and two miles long, lying at the southwesterly tip of the Isle of Mull. This was within the territory of Macbeth's ancestors Cenél Loairn. Iona became the head of churches dedicated to

Columba in both Ireland and Britain. Artifacts associated with him became famous. His crosier, called "Battle-triumph" (OI *Cathbuaid*), led the Scots, possibly including Macbeth, into battle while the sixth-century copy of the Psalms called "Battler" (OI *Cathach*) that the saint might have copied is in the library of the Royal Irish Academy.[41]

Adomnán son of Rónán (c. 628–704), the ninth abbot of Iona, is responsible for supplying much of what is known about Dál Riata and its neighbors in his *Life of Columba* (Vita Columbae). While he was writing a religious biography of Columba and the church on Iona a century after the saint's death in 597, he was aided by his own knowledge of the area and by informants who had known the saint. Adomnán was, however, a child of his age and his *Life of Columba* is divided into three sections: miracles, prophesies, and angels. A modern reader is occasionally bewildered by the juxtaposition of the ordinary with the divine. Some miracles are underwhelming, such as Columba's warning to the copyist of a manuscript that he was about to spill his ink. Others are astonishing, such as the column of angels extending from Heaven into the church where the saint was praying.

Three examples of Columba's powers are pertinent in connection with Macbeth. The first was Columba's reluctance to make Áedán, son of Gabrán, king of Dál Riata, preferring his brother.[42] Only after an angel showed him a list of kings with Áedán's name among them and then beat him with a book made of heavenly glass, did he comply. There is an echo in Shakespeare's drama when Macbeth sees the shadows of Duncan's descendants emerging from the smoke of a cauldron. The second example is Columba's afore-mentioned missionary journey up the Great Glen to Inverness (the region round the Moray Firth, where Macbeth's clan would eventually settle), where he encountered the sea beast who has become identified with the Loch Ness monster. The lake dwelling fiend tried to eat one of his monks, but the saint stopped the beast with the sign of the cross.[43] Finally, humans could be just as unwelcoming as monsters. When Columba eventually arrived at his destination, the Pictish king named Brude, whose citadel was somewhere in the vicinity of modern Inverness Castle, closed the fortress gates against the saint, which miraculously swung open at Columba's prayer.[44]

As the head of the church of Iona, Adomnán controlled an important archive with chronicles and lists of kings that were periodically updated.[45] The clergy took an interest in political affairs and had their favorites among the princely dynasties of Dál Riata. Adomnán, for example, mentions people and events connected with Cenél nGabráin frequently, but Cenél Loairn only once, and then in an aside as the place where monks were delayed from sailing back to Iona by contrary winds.[46] Animosity between the community of Iona and Macbeth's ancestors is suggested by a story in the sixteenth-century compilation *Life of St. Columbkill* that was commissioned by the Donegal lord Manus O'Donnell (d. 1564). The subjects of Loarn were reluctant to pay tithes to Columba. He eventually told them to render their tithes to the saint, but Columba rebuked Loarn by telling him that if the order to pay had been obeyed more quickly, then his descendants would have ruled in Ireland as well as Scotland.[47]

Macbeth's clan had its own holy individuals. The pedigrees of Dál Riata saints preserved in the seventeenth-century collection compiled by the great Irish antiquarian Duald Mac Firbis (Dubhaltacht Mac Fhirbhisigh) are almost exclusively connected with Cenél Loairn through Macbeth's ancestor Loarn. One of them is Berchán of Clonsost on whom was fathered the *Prophecy of Berchán*, a pseudo-prophecy on the kings of Ireland and Scotland from the ninth to eleventh centuries.[48]

Macbeth's Family Moves North

Like the Irish, the Britons living north of the Forth (i.e., the Picts) were divided into separate kingdoms called (with the modern equivalent in parentheses): Cath (Caithness and Sutherland); Fiddach (Ross, Moray); Ce (Banff, Buchan, and Mar); Circenn (Angus and the Mearns); Ath Fotla (Atholl and Gowrie); Fib (Fife); and Fortriu (Strathearn, Meneth, and parts of Clackmannan). In the second quarter of the eighth century was the career of the powerful king of the Picts called Angus son of Fergus (OI Óengus mac Fergusso). His home was the kingdom of Circenn and he began his career by defeating the neighboring princes before turning his attentions to Dál Riata, particularly Macbeth's ancestors in Cenél Loairn. Although never able to overcome the clans of Dál Riata decisively, his assaults were so relentless that by the year 740 the chronicles merely record "the hammering of Dál Riata by Angus." Within a decade, Angus's attentions had turned to the kingdom of Strathclyde, but, as was true of lands ruled by many charismatic leaders, the empire did not survive his death in 761.

Angus's contemporaries, however, did not have the advantage of hindsight. Either during his reign or shortly thereafter, there is evidence that Macbeth's ancestors moved north. First, place names around the Moray Firth suggest the presence of Gaelophone speakers in the middle of the eighth century.[49] Second, a now lost version of the vita of the Scottish St. Catroe, surviving in a seventeenth-century copy, states that the Scots who lived around the island of

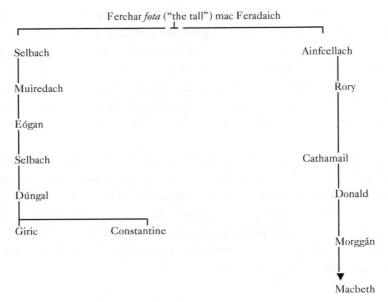

FIG. 1.3 Macbeth's Ancestors, Seventh to Tenth Centuries.

Iona moved north into Ross where they settled: in the early medieval period Ross was linked with Moray.[50] The clans of Cenél Loairn lived around Iona, and a move toward the northeast along the Great Glen, following the major waterway of Loch Ness, leads to the fertile lands surrounding the Moray Firth where Macbeth's ancestors later are found in the rich farm lands of Banff and Buchan.

Why were the Scots able to move into the lands of the Picts when they had so recently been powerless in the face of them? One possible reason was the weather.[51] The Scottish clans moved east during a period of climate change that had been going on for some time. Northern Europe had reached a nadir of cold, leading to movement of communities. Settlements in southern Sweden, for example, moved from the interior closer to the coast by the late eighth century. Pictish society might have been in crisis because they were farmers who grew grain. Cultivation of grain so far north was a risky business, and farmers would have been most susceptible to the vagaries of weather. A growing season that increased or decreased by a few days meant the difference between feast and famine. In contrast, the Scots of Dál Riata were mainly fishermen and herdsmen. Weather influenced these occupations but not so dramatically as it did grain farmers. More important, their lands lying on the northwestern coast of Britain came into direct contact with the warm waters from the extension of the Gulf Stream, which protected them from extremes in temperature. When the Scots moved eastward they had to face the same problems as the Picts. Late in the ninth or early in the tenth century, the church dedicated to St. Serf on the island in Loch Leven surrendered its lands and goods to the bishop of St. Andrew. Religious establishments valued their independence, but according to a charter note, the monks were facing famine and were so poor that they could not afford warm clothing. They gave up their freedom in return for food and clothes.[52]

The New Land

Emigration merely exchanged one problem for another, as Macbeth's ancestors were to learn. Another group moving into northern Scotland was the Vikings. The debate continues as to whether the Vikings oversaw the destruction of the old British society or were simply high-spirited visitors who occasionally roughed up the natives, but their impact on European history is undeniable.[53] Centuries after the last Viking sailed, they achieved immortality as literary villains. Macbeth's victory over them, which first appears in the sixteenth-century history of Hectore Boece, established his reputation as an intrepid warrior.

The Vikings moved into the islands north of mainland Scotland probably around the same time that Macbeth's clan moved east. A contemporary account of the arrival of the Vikings around Scotland is given by the Irish geographer Dícuil who wrote *The Book about the Measure of the World* (Lat. *Liber de mensura orbis terrae*) around the year 825. He reminisced that, thirty years earlier, he had been told that six days sailing beyond Ireland was an island (almost certainly Iceland) where the light lasted so long during the summer solstice that it was possible to pick lice off one's clothes at midnight. He also wrote of islands—probably the Shetland and Orkney Islands, and possibly the Outer Hebrides—where religious hermits from Ireland had lived for a century until they left rather than live with "North men."[54]

Despite the popular image of the Viking as fiend, Vikings could live peacefully with their neighbors. In the Shetland Islands, at the famous site of Jarlshof (a name that owes much to Sir Walter Scott and little to the Middle Ages), a Viking settlement was placed literally on top of a subterranean Pictish village, The Picts lived in dwellings known as wheel houses because the rooms or chambers opened onto a central circular living area. In a land this far north, living below ground was more comfortable than above, and their houses would have enjoyed a constant temperature of about 50 degrees

(a)

(b)

FIG. 1.4A AND B Jarlshof: Pictish Wheelhouse (a) and Viking House Foundation (b).

Fahrenheit. Above them were the rectangular houses of the Vikings who would have found the climate beside the sea mild. The two groups lived together, one atop the other, apparently for more than two generations. Pictish subterranean wheel houses were remembered in a curious fashion in Old Norse literature and from there made their way into modern literature. The twelfth-century *History of Norway* (Lat. *Historia Norvegiae*) states that the Picts were magical pygmies who disappeared into their houses beneath the ground at noon. The theme was taken up in the twentieth century by the novelist John Buchan in his story "No Man's Land," where a young Oxford scholar meets a clan of Picts who had survived by living in remote caves.[55]

When the classical Viking Age began at the end of the eighth century, the raiders initially busied themselves with attacks on churches conveniently located on the coasts. The church of Iona, for example, was raided four times in thirty years. Constant fear of attacks led to the abandonment of some churches or at least a dwindling of their population. Even before the most famous attack on Iona in 825, administration of the churches dedicated to St. Columba outside Britain was moved to Kells in Ireland. The move was probably encouraged by killings. When a monk named Blathmac learned that marauding Vikings were approaching, he hid a valuable reliquary (container for sacred objects). Eager for martyrdom, according to his vita, he refused to tell the marauders where it was. The Vikings admired Blathmac's courage and loyalty to his faith before killing him.[56]

Scandinavian settlers began to establish outposts throughout the Northern Hebrides, and medieval Icelandic works such as the *Book of the Icelanders* (ON *Íslendingabók*) and *Book of Settlements* (ON *Landnámabók*) give brief accounts of some settlers such as Ketil "Flat Nose." His daughter Auð "the deep-minded" was married to a Viking chieftain named Olaf "the White" (also known as Olaf of Dublin). Olaf and his brother Ívarr came close to establishing a Viking kingdom stretching from Ireland to Britain in the wake of raids across Northern Britain c. 869 to c. 875. Place names help to give a chronology for settlement as the Scandinavian names in the Hebridean Isles outside of Dál Riata—for example, on the Isle of Lewis—are older than the Scandinavian names in the Hebrides that were part of Dál Riata, such as on the Isle of Arran.[57]

All ranks of society took part in the colonization, such as the powerful family of Rögnvald Eysteinsson of Møre, from what is now Norway, who settled in the Orkney Islands during the reign of Rögnvald's kinsman and ally Harald "Fair-haired" who is credited with the unification of the Norse.

Rögnvald had little interest in the region and the family's fortunes were unsteady until command was taken by his son "Turf" Einar, so-called because he convinced his followers to burn turf or peat for fuel instead of the scarce wood. Despite Einar's ability, his father despised him because his mother was a slave. So Einar offered his father an arrangement that would suit both of them: he would go to the Orkneys and never return. From his family came a policy and a person to dominate Macbeth's life: control of the timber resources and tax revenues from the regions now known as Caithness and Sutherland, and Macbeth's tenacious foe the Orkney *jarl* (earl) Thorfinn the Mighty.

Cenél Loairn and Cenél nGabráin in the East

The eastward movement of Macbeth's ancestors from Dál Riata was followed by the territorial expansion of their rivals Cenél nGabráin. Located in the Kintyre Peninsula, Cenél nGabráin had been shielded from the full fury of Angus son of Fergus by Cenél Loairn. After the death of Angus, two brothers, Áed and Fergus the sons of Eochaid, were successively kings of Dál Riata and they began an offensive against the Picts. This continued into the next generation when Ferguss' son Constantine led a successful invasion of the Pictish kingdom of Fortriu in 790, the same kingdom that St. Patrick supposedly promised to Fergus of Dál Riata. For the next fifty years Fergus's sons Constantine and Angus and their sons ruled Fortriu with the kingship passing from brother to brother and nephew to nephew. They made an alliance with the church of St. Cuthbert and their names are commemorated in its *Book of Life* (Lat. *Liber vitae*) kept by the community to remember their patrons.[58] Disaster struck, however, in 839 when Constantine's son Éoganán was killed during a battle with Vikings sailing from Ireland.

Now it was the turn of Áed's descendants, who had remained in the Kintyre Peninsula, to move eastward. They seized their chance and quickly moved into Fortriu, led by the famous Kenneth I son of Alpin (OI *Cináed mac Alpín*). He, not Macbeth, was the great legendary figure of Scottish history during the Middle Ages. His reign and his descendants are mentioned in various records, the most important one being a contemporary account called the *Scottish Chronicle* that was begun during Kenneth's reign, probably at the church of Dunkeld c. 849, and continued to the late tenth century at St. Andrews. This important history was modeled after the fifth-century chronicle of Prosper of Aquitaine, and it might not be coincidence that a volume called simply "Prosper" was in Scotland, in the library of the church of St. Serf's at Loch Leven in the twelfth century.[59] The *Scottish Chronicle* is

Macbeth: Place and Past

important because it was not completely edited in favor of Cenél nGabráin, as were many other records of early Scotland, so it provides a more nuanced record of the ninth to tenth centuries.

There is little indication of competition between Cenél Loairn and Cenél nGabráin as they moved into the lands of the Picts. The rivalry reappears, however, late in the ninth century when Giric son of Dúngail (a dynast of Cenél Loairn and descendant of Selbach, the brother of Macbeth's ancestor Ainfcellach) confronted his Cenél nGabráin rival Áed son of Kenneth I (Áed mac Cináeda) and killed him in battle in 878. Giric's fortress of Dundurn was a former Pictish stronghold about sixty miles east of Cenél Loairn territory in Dál Riata. By the fourteenth century he was remembered as a successful king who had freed the church from the unjust extractions of the Picts. What exactly that meant is unclear, possibly that the Pictish aristocracy were levying taxes on church property. Regardless of the precise practice, the clergy were not ungrateful. A prayer specifically for his safety is preserved in the "Dunkeld Litany": "We ask You to hear us so that You defend and protect our King Giric and his army from all ambushes of his enemies."[60] The clergy needed the king to protect and enrich them, while the king needed the clergy to endorse his rule and contribute some of their wealth to the royal treasury. Clerical support included prayers for the royal family and their ancestors, such as the prayer for Giric in the "Dunkeld Litany."

Giric's career is also revealing for the political importance of family constructions—especially the synthetic one of fosterage, when a child was sent to live with an important family where he would remain until adulthood. According to the *Scottish Chronicle,* Giric was the foster father of Eochaid, who was a grandson of Kenneth I and the son of King Rhun of Strathclyde.[61] Fosterage was an important tool in the delicate weaving of alliances between families. At the highest social levels these alliances were matters of importance to the entire kingdom. Relations between foster parents and foster children often were closer than those of children with their biological families. Eochaid's family history illustrates why artificial connections might be more important than biological ones. He had few reasons to love the family of his grandfather Kenneth. Eochaid's paternal grandfather Artga had been killed on the orders of his mother's brother Constantine. No details have survived concerning the fosterage or the relations between the two men. All that is known is that after Giric defeated and killed Eochaid's Uncle Áed, he placed Eochaid in the kingship.

Eochaid ruled under the supervision of Giric for about eleven years. According to the *Scottish Chronicle,* the two men were expelled from the kingship on the feast of the martyr Ciriacus (August 8) during a solar eclipse. There was a solar eclipse on that date in 891, with its path of totality south of Scotland.[62] Giric's eventual fate is unknown, although the *Prophecy of Berchán* claims that his brother, called Constantine in king list I, succeeded him briefly.[63]

Giric's supremacy over Cenél nGabráin was ended by Kenneth's grandson Donald, the son of Constantine. Known as "Crazy Donald" (Domnall Dásachtach) he devoted his days to patrolling the borders of his kingdom and attacking his own people when it was too quiet. His subjects returned the compliment and killed him at his fortress of Dunnottar. Cenél Loairn was unable to take advantage of the turmoil. One of the reasons was the dynasty in the Orkney of the previously mentioned "Turf" Einar, son of Rögnvald Eysteinsson of Møre; he was the ancestor of Macbeth's rival the Orkney *jarl* (earl) Thorfinn the Mighty.

"Crazy Donald" was succeeded by Constantine son of Aed whose nickname was the "Middle Aged." He married an Anglo-Saxon noble-woman and their son was called Eadwulf, which was transliterated into Middle Irish as Idulb or Idulf. During the first quarter of the tenth century, he battled a trio of Viking brothers: Reginald, Sigtrygg, and Godfrey (Rögnvaldr, Sigtryggr, and Guðrøðr) who were the sons of a previous king in Northumbria named Godfrey Hardacnutsson (d. 896) and described by later Irish writers as the descendants of a man named Ívarr (MI Uí Imhar).[64] Reginald died in 921 and Sigtrygg in 927, after which Constantine tried to prevent the expansion of the Anglo-Saxon family of Alfred the Great of Wessex into the region. His defeat by Alfred's grandsons AEthelstan and Edmund at the battle of Brunnanburh in 937 (the location of which remains open to speculation) was the beginning of the end of his supremacy. He abdicated the kingship for a life of religious retirement at St. Andrews, where he died in 952.

The competition between the rival families of Cenél nGabráin resumed with Constantine's successor Malcolm I. He was a son of "Crazy Donald" and his name in Middle Irish, Máel Coluim, means devotee of Columba of Iona. Three other kings of Scots had this name and they were all his descendants, including Macbeth's rival Malcolm Canmore. Columba of Iona was considered a patron saint of the descendants of Áedán son of Gabrán, and this ensured that the churches dedicated to him throughout Scotland and Ireland would look kindly on Malcolm and his family. Augmenting spiritual support was an equally useful military alliance. In 945 Malcolm became "the helper by land and sea" of the English king Edmund, the half-brother of AEthelstan. Edmund had defeated the kingdom of Strathclyde and discovered that holding onto conquered territory was harder than fighting the battle. He made the alliance with Malcolm who received the tax revenues from Strathclyde as payment for the alliance. Even though both parties probably intended to discard the treaty at the first convenient moment, the collaboration was continued by Malcolm's son Kenneth II, his grandson Malcolm II, and his great-great-grandson Malcolm Canmore. The English alliance changed the balance of power in the north and emboldened Malcolm to revive the feud with his hereditary enemies of Cenél Loairn. Around the year 950 Malcolm led an army north into Moray and killed its king, an otherwise unknown prince named Cellach. The lack of evidence forbids conclusions, but the English support for Malcolm's family was a disaster for their cousins as well as the Scots in the north.

Just as a golden age for the southern Scots appeared to be beckoning—with the Viking menace vanished and a new friend in the English king—Malcolm was assassinated in 954 by his own subjects in the "sword-land" (i.e., land won by conquest that did not pay tax) at Fetteresso, just beyond the fortress of Dunnottar.[65] He was succeeded by Constantine's son Idulb (d. 962), who added what were probably his mother's family lands in Lothian (including the fortress of Edinburgh) to his domain. The Scots had always been their own most dangerous foes, and conflict within the royal family became easier as clans made their homes in different parts of the kingdom. Malcolm's family lived in the Mearns at Dunnottar, while Idulb's family lived in Fife. The children of Malcolm and Idulb began a cycle of murder and retaliation. A vicious civil war erupted in 962 between Malcolm's son Dub ("the Black") and Idulb's son Cuilen ("the Puppy"). For a couple of years an uneasy accommodation had the two men sharing power as joint kings. The truce did not endure, and Dub was hard pressed by Cuilen who wanted sole rule. So Dub went north to Cenél Loairn to find allies. Unfortunately for him, the invasion led by his father had taken place barely fifteen years earlier and its memory had not faded. Dub was killed in obscure circumstances and his body was hidden under a bridge at Kinloss near the town of Forres. Popular legend connects the discovery of his body with a solar eclipse. If there is any truth behind the legend, then it seems to refer to the solar eclipse of July 20, 966.[66] Dub's murder began a bloody feud that raged for the next two generations, ending in the eleventh century. Chaos now became normal among Duncan's ancestors. Cuilen had only a few years to savor his triumph before he and his brother Eochaid were killed in a burning house by the men of Strathclyde.

FIG. 1.5 Dunnottar Castle. Photograph by Robert Hudson.

To add to the excitement, Vikings reappeared on the west coast. Two brothers, Magnus and Godfrey Haraldsson, began to assemble an empire that eventually was known as the Kingdom of the Isles.[67] As part of their kingdom-making, they attacked the church of Iona and raided Dál Riata. Godfrey died in 989, just in time for the appearance in the British Isles of two of the most important captains of the Viking world: the Danish king Swein Forkbeard; and the Norwegian prince Olaf Tryggvason, who married into the royal Viking family at Dublin. The Vikings of the Orkney Islands joined in the fray. By the end of the tenth century, their goal had changed from loot in the form of jewelry or slaves to tax revenues paid by the population and, almost as important, timber from harvesting the oak forests that grew along the river valleys. Europe's great forests were disappearing, but its need for timber was increasing.

At the beginning of the eleventh century the jarl of the Orkney Islands was Sigurd "the Stout" (ON Sigurðr inn digri) son of Hlǫðvir a descendant of "Turf" Einar; his family fought Macbeth's ancestors for possession of Caithness and Sutherland. In common with many Viking nobles, Sigurd was the product of a mixed-marriage. His father Hlǫðvir had married an Irish woman named Eithne who was reputedly a witch. According to legend, she wove for Sigurd a magical banner that had the image of a raven.[68] The banner brought victory to all who followed, but death to the man who carried it. Behind his fatal banner, Sigurd extended his authority from the Orkney

Islands to the Irish Sea. When it came time to look for a wife, Sigurd turned to his enemies, the Scots. He married Macbeth's second cousin, a daughter of Malcolm son of Máel Brigte, the man who succeeded Macbeth's father as king of Cenél Loairn. Although her name is unknown, her son was famous. He was Thorfinn and was remembered as an ugly man, but one who was born lucky. His Scottish grandfather gave him the province of Caithness as a birthday present, temporarily ending the dispute between the Scots and Vikings.

Sigurd had little time to savor this triumph, and when Thorfinn was five years old, he was killed in Ireland at the battle of Clontarf in 1014. According to the legend in *Njals Saga*, his death was connected with the disclosure among his troops of the secret about his mother's raven banner. Eventually it was noticed that any man carrying the fatal raven banner was killed and no one else would pick up the cursed cloth. When Sigurd ordered one of his soldiers to pick up the banner, he was curtly told to carry his own devil. He hid the banner inside his shirt and died when a sword pierced his heart through the cloth.[69]

The Wild North

Macbeth's ancestors were violent and tenacious from necessity. They were unwelcome newcomers to northern Britain but found that a fast sword and a little luck could yield a kingdom. Missionaries jostled with mercenaries to make their respective conquests. In either case, the victors were more ferocious, cunning, and tougher than their opponents. Nor did this situation change quickly. As the Scots triumphed over the Picts, they had to face a new foe in the Vikings. When a third enemy, the English, reappeared in the tenth century, it was only one more complication in a dangerous region.

The importance of family ties in the preservation of history at this time is clear and it went beyond genealogical vanity. The privileges and positions enjoyed by one's ancestors determined if someone would have a life of wealth and comfort or one of poverty and hardship. They extended to the kingship, and success was much more difficult for someone without the necessary pedigree. That explains why lineages were so carefully copied and recopied for centuries after the individuals were no more than names. This also explains why information about some individuals could be so radically different from one story to another. This hyper-competitive world was the heritage of Macbeth. The rewards for success were great: high office, wealth, and prestige. The penalty for failure was simple: death.

2

Macbeth Emerges

THE YEAR 1000, the famous millennium, marked a watershed in the cultural transition of the Scots. The earlier "heroic" age of small-scale clan warfare and idiosyncratic expressions of religion and culture still dominated as the glorious heroes of the past continued to be celebrated and their legends recopied. The earliest surviving manuscript with tales about heroes such as Cú Chulainn, *Lebor na Huidre*, is from the eleventh century. A man's (but not necessarily a woman's) identification was submerged in his ancestral clan. All this, however, was beginning to change as the small kingdoms, individualistic warriors, and itinerant saints became anachronistic curiosities. One organization driving change was the Church, which wanted a united Christendom modeled on the Roman Empire. Small kingdoms became targets for larger neighbors, and a successful king was one who expanded the boundaries of his kingdom by conquering his neighbors and destroying rival royal families. Dynasties jostled for power, and royal families attempted to keep their independence. Safety within the glorious isolation of a clan was ending.

The victors in this competition enjoyed the spoils of tangible wealth and intangible prestige. The latter included the privilege of rewriting of history. Verses and stories provided by the poet (MI *fili*) or historian (MI *senchaid*) glorified the winners and vilified the losers. Sober history was rarely interesting to those who demanded exciting stories in tales told on long evenings. Dynastic crowing was tempered, however, in the records maintained by the clergy, whose written documents preserved a longer memory. They show the ebbs and flows of power, although few have a continuous record. Entire kingdoms mysteriously appear and disappear in the few documents that survive for this early period. Any appearance in those documents depended on family connections, the goodwill of the church keeping the records, or how noteworthy events were believed to be.

The obscurity in the surviving records of Macbeth's family ends in the year 1020.[1] For the next half-century events connected with Macbeth and his family were recorded in a variety of surviving documents. Why? Had Macbeth's clan of Cenél Loairn become too powerful to be ignored any longer? Or was it connected with a marriage that some medieval writers claimed to have been made between Macbeth's father and the daughter of King Malcolm II of the southern Scots?

Macbeth's Family

The question "Who was Macbeth" would have been answered in a different way during his own time than today. Modern answers begin with his career, but medieval replies started with his family. The importance of ancestry is clear from the many medieval stories that begin with lists of pedigrees and genealogies. These lists were more than antiquarianism or sops to vanity; they were important for a person's standard of living. The right to own land, the opportunity to contest for high office, and even the status of whether one received or paid taxes were all connected with pedigree. Lineage determined whether one lived a life of comfort or endured an existence of hardship. Gaelic society was obsessed by status and ancestry, so it is not surprising that genealogy and lists of kings were among the most popular types of entertainment. Recitation of names was accompanied by peripheral information such as nicknames, outstanding deeds, or notable events. Many of these lists now survive only in later copies, such as the lineages of the kings of the Scots.[2]

Two genealogies, both surviving in twelfth-century Irish manuscripts, give Macbeth's lineage. The earlier, held by Oxford's Bodleian Library, was written between the years 1125 and 1130.[3] The information is repeated in a later manuscript, the encyclopedic *Book of Leinster* written in the last quarter of the twelfth century, and in the library of Trinity College, Dublin.[4] Macbeth's genealogy is found almost at the end of the catalogue of lineages. In the earlier manuscript, it is the third of the lists of "Scottish Kings" (*Ríg Alban*), and immediately following it are the genealogies of the *Fomore*, the giants of Irish mythology. The information is limited to Macbeth's male ancestors on his father's side (his patrilineal ancestry)—"Macbeth the son of Findláech the son of Ruaidrí the son of Domnall the son of Morggán"—before referring to another list and back through the generations to Loarn son of Erc.

Macbeth's clan lived in northeast Scotland, in the regions of Buchan and Mar. The region of Mar is roughly the area between the river Dee on

FIG. 2.1 Regions.

the south and the river Don to the north, extending somewhat like a triangle from a point at the city of Aberdeen. Buchan is the district immediately to the north. The twelfth-century geographical tract called *Concerning the Situation of Scotland* (Lat. *De Situ Albanie*) connects the two areas together as its fifth of seven parts of Scotland. Within Mar is Lumphanan, the fortress that is associated with Macbeth throughout the Middle Ages; it is now called the Peel of Lumphanan (a "peel" is a fortified stone house). All that remains of the stronghold is an earthen foundation on the north side of the river Dee in Aberdeenshire. This is a good location with convenient access to navigable water as well as proximity to land routes. Nearby is a cairn, known locally as "Macbeth's Cairn," in which was discovered a small cavity, eighteen inches by nine inches, excavated in a rock.[5]

Lumphanan is also on the edge of one of Scotland's most famed farming regions. Prior to the agricultural improvement efforts of the eighteenth to twentieth centuries there were small pockets of land suitable for arable farming north of Hadrian's Wall, but only a few extensive areas such as this corner of land jutting into the North Sea. Macbeth's family lived in one of the largest

FIG. 2.2 Peel of Lumphanan. Photograph by Robert Hudson.

areas of productive arable farming and livestock grazing in Scotland. This is the region that extends from just south of the city of Aberdeen northwest to Elgin. From there it follows a coastal strip to Inverness where it widens again round the Moray Firth and the river Ness as far north as Dornoch. The region is warmed by the North Atlantic Drift, a branch of the Gulf Stream that brings the warm water from the Gulf of Mexico to the British Isles and then round the Pentland Firth down the eastern coast of Scotland. Throughout history this region has been important agriculturally and was famous for its grain fields. The relationship of agricultural produce to political power in the Middle Ages was simple. The richer or more productive the farmland, the greater the yield of crops or the larger numbers of livestock it could support. More food meant a larger population. More people meant more tax revenues and a larger army. Wealth and troops were two important components of power in early medieval Britain.

Lumphanan appears to have been the southerly extent of Macbeth's clan. The reason for the speculation comes from information found in the notes copied into a small Gospel known as the *Book of Deer*, which was written sometime in the ninth century.[6] It contains parts of the Gospels of St. Matthew, St. Mark, and St. Luke, the entire Gospel of St. John, and also part of the Office for the Ill. As its name suggests, the little volume belonged to the monastery of Deer in Buchan, the Celtic monastery that predated the religious house of the High Middle Ages, located north of Lumphanan. No one knows precisely where this house was situated, but recent excavations have found evidence for a structure contemporary with the community within the ruins of the later Cistercian abbey, so the latter might be atop the site of the older church.[7] Of particular importance in the *Book of Deer* are the story of the church's foundation and its charter notes.[8] The history of the church's origins claims that its founder was Saint Columba of Iona. While this kind of material is hardly historical fact, the *Life* of Columba does claim that he traveled around this region. During a journey through Buchan, Columba saw a place where he wished to build a monastery. The owner of the land, named Bede, refused to give it to the saint. He changed his mind after one of his children became ill, and he asked Columba to heal him. The latter agreed, on the condition that Bede donate the land for a church/monastery. Columba, in turn, gave it to his companion Drostan. As Columba was preparing to depart, Drostan began to cry. The saint considered this to be a divine sign and said that the monastery was to be named *déra* (tears) and it became known as "Deer" in English.

More important than the veracity of the origin legend are the charter notes written in the margins of the *Book of Deer*. These record gifts made to the community by pious benefactors from the tenth century to the middle of the twelfth century. These notes were meant to remember those devout individuals whose gifts often came with the stipulation that the church community say prayers on their behalf. They also provided evidence for possession of land or claims of privilege because the descendants of religious benefactors might be less interested in charity and more concerned with retrieving valuable farms. Church records are full of stories, from an ecclesiastical point of view, of fights to keep land that had been donated to them.[9] Among the individuals mentioned in the charter notes from Deer are members of Macbeth's family such as the sons of his great-great-grandfather Morggán.[10] Morggán's son Muiredach gave Mac Garnat's farm to the church. One memorable gift came from another of Morggán's sons, Macbeth's great-uncle Cathal, who stipulated that a banquet for all the members of the religious community be held every Christmas and Easter. Later benefactors included Macbeth's cousin Malcolm son of Máel Brigte, who donated the village of Elrick. Macbeth's step-grandson Máel Snechtai, the son of Lulach, bestowed the farm of Mac Dub on the church.

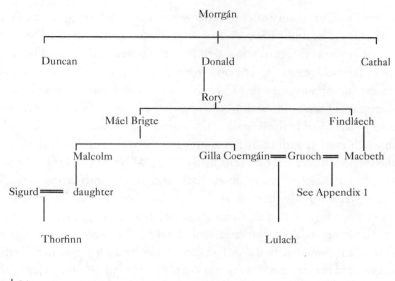

FIG. 2.3 Genealogy of Macbeth's Clan.

Macbeth's Father

The first member of Macbeth's immediate family to appear in the written records is his father Finlay son of Rory (MI Findláech mac Ruaidrí). Finlay's death at the hands of the sons of his brother Máel Brigte (Servant of [St.] Brigit"), was recorded in the contemporary record preserved in the *Annals of Ulster* for the year 1020 as "Findláech son of Ruaidrí, a Scots king, was killed by his own people."[11] The so-called *Annals of Tigernach*, preserving a later and less accurate record, note that he was killed by the sons of his brother Máel Brigte" but incorrectly identify him as a *mórmáer* (great steward) of Moray.

Finlay's relations with his Viking neighbors were little better than with his family according to the history of the jarls of the Orkney Islands, now known as *Orkneyinga Saga*, which records a fight between the Orkney Jarl Sigurd "the Stout" and a Scots prince named Finlay.[12] There is an episode, apparently late in the tenth century, when Finlay the *jarl* or earl (ON Finnleik Jarl) challenged Jarl Sigurd of the Orkneys to combat at Skíðamýrr (now Skitten in Caithness). The Scots had lost lordship over this area in the previous generation to Sigurd's father Hlöðvir, and Finlay wanted it back. The precise date is unknown, but this battle is placed before the events of 995, when Sigurd converted to Christianity after the Norwegian king Olaf Tryggvason offered him the choice of immediate conversion or immediate execution. The battle between Finlay and Sigurd was a set-piece encounter, really a duel between armies. The belligerents agreed on a time and place for a battle. This gave everyone the opportunity to gather their troops and soothe their fears. In this mixture of scheming and dread appears the legend of the famous raven banner of Jarl Sigurd. The heavily outnumbered Sigurd was comforted by his Irish witch-mother Eithne. She gave him a magical banner that had a design in the shape of a raven, the favorite bird of the Old Norse god Oðin, the lord of the slain. Banners were not uncommon, and the eleventh-century tract *In Praise of Queen Emma* (Lat. *Encomium Emmae Reginae*) recalled that King Cnut of England also had a banner upon which a raven appeared in time of battle; if victory awaited, the raven would have its beak open and talons extended. Sigurd's banner, however, had special powers. Eithne told her son that death awaited the standard-bearer, but victory went to those who followed the banner. Her prediction was proved correct in the battle of Skíðamýrr as three men died carrying the raven banner, but Sigurd won the fight. The author of *Orkneyinga Saga*, however, was skeptical about tales of enchanted banners or Irish witches. He claimed that Sigurd won because his troops fought exceptionally well after he had agreed to return the ancestral (ON *óðal*) rights to their lands. Although the Scots were defeated, they did not abandon all hope. The contest continued after the deaths of Finlay and Sigurd when their sons Macbeth and Thorfinn fought for possession of the region.

Finlay's murder at the hands of his kinsmen, the sons of Máel Brigte, secured his place in the Irish annals. The names of two of Máel Brigte's sons are preserved: Malcolm and Gilla Cóemgen (servant of [St.] Kevin). Malcolm succeeded Finlay as king and reigned from 1020 to 1029. This Malcolm should not be confused with his contemporary in the south, Duncan's grandfather Malcolm II. The northern Malcolm was elderly when he became king, with an adult daughter who had been married to Jarl Sigurd of the Orkneys and at least one grandchild, the future jarl of the Orkney Islands Thorfinn, then about eleven years old; *Orkneyinga Saga* claims that he was five years old when his father Sigurd died at the battle of Clontarf. Malcolm might have been an old man in a hurry, which explains why he was willing to murder in order to become king. His desperation would have been great if his uncle Finlay were the younger man. Significant differences in ages among siblings are a feature of polygamous societies such as the medieval Gaels, with easy divorce and frequent remarriage. The higher a person's position on the social scale, the more likely were multiple marriages. If Malcolm realized that, in the natural course of events, a younger uncle would outlive him, then he would not hesitate to attack him. The murder of Finlay by a member of his family is a depressingly commonplace example of succession within the royal dynasties of the period. Clergy attempted to impress on their flock the cooperative nature of families and gave sermons on forbearance, but the motivation of ambition undid their best efforts. Warriors amused themselves in evenings with heavy drinking to the accompaniment of poets singing the praises of their ancestors and reminding them of ancient grievances.

Macbeth's Mother

Finlay might have been just another footnote to history were it not for his famous son, but more obscure is Macbeth's mother. Only the sixteenth-century historian Hector Boece gave her a name: Doada. If Boece is accurate, this is probably a variant spelling of the name Duada from MI *dúad* meaning "hardship, toil" with the extended meaning of "hard worker." Several texts imply that she was a kinswoman of Finlay's southern rival, Malcolm II.[13] A thirteenth-century collection of historical materials from the church of St. Mary's, Huntingdon, describes Macbeth as Malcolm's "grandson."[14] The earldom of Huntingdon had been in the possession of the Scots kings beginning in the twelfth century, so its churches had particular interests in the genealogy of the royal family. A confused confirmation of some family relationship was given by the fourteenth-century Augustinian historian Peter Langtoft, who claimed that Macbeth was Malcolm's brother.[15]

The ambiguity surrounding Macbeth's mother is less surprising in light of the vague information about the king of the southern Scots named Malcolm II. For such an important man, his family life is unclear. He had at least one daughter named Bethoc whose name means "young life" or "babe." She married Abbot Crinán of Dunkeld and they had two sons named Duncan and Maldred. A monk of Cluny named Ralph Glauber, an exact contemporary, claims that Malcolm also had a son whose godfather was Cnut the Great, the king of the English.[16] If so important a child as a royal son and heir could be remembered only in an aside, there is little surprise that a daughter was less known. Diplomacy, not romance, dictated the life of a princess.

King Malcolm II of the dynasty of Cenél nGabráin is one of history's frustratingly mysterious famous people. He was widely admired, especially by the Irish literati who rarely had a good word for any foreign prince. The *Annals of Tigernach* describe him as the preeminent king of western Europe. Among the few known personal facts about him is his mixed parentage: his father was

Scots, but his mother was Irish. The contemporary *Prophecy of Berchán* claims that Malcolm's mother came from the southeastern Irish kingdom of Leinster, from one of the northern branches of the royal line that controlled the lands south of the Viking town of Dublin. The poet described her, in terms that were intended to be flattering, as "the cow who grazes on the banks of the Liffey."[17] Apparently his father Kenneth had looked for an Irish treaty and Malcolm was a product of the diplomatic marriage.

Malcolm II, son of Kenneth, or more precisely Máel Coluim mac Cináeda, was the driving force in northern Britain in the early eleventh century. He had grown up during the ferocious civil war of the tenth century when branches of his clan battled for supremacy. Cousin fought cousin, and Malcolm II battled King Kenneth III (Cináed mac Duib), whose nickname was "Grim," the son of his Uncle Dub. Malcolm killed him in 1005 and began a reign of almost thirty years that ended with his own death in battle in 1034.

Malcolm became the head of a kindred reeling from ruthless fighting within the royal family, in addition to the usual battles with their neighbors. The circumstances of his succession did nothing to ease fears. Taking the kingship by murdering a cousin was not unknown. But while much was forgiven (or overlooked) in a prince, fratricide was a serious crime in a society in which the family was one of the few stable institutions. Under the circumstances, Malcolm needed some type of triumph at the beginning of his reign. A quick, successful plundering of the neighbors, for example, would demonstrate that he was a competent captain, and rivals would be wary about challenging him. An additional benefit was the loot. Few things soothed uneasy minds as agreeably as an addition to their treasure chest. Malcolm had much to gain from an easy triumph. And at the very first hurdle in his career as a king, he stumbled.

The intended victim was the cathedral community at Durham. For a prince looking for easy prey, Durham had much to recommend it. It had a cathedral barely ten years old, and bishops were wealthy. The bishop and his community had spent years roaming throughout northern England trying to find refuge from the Vikings. After leaving their home at Lindisfarne in the middle of the ninth century, they had wandered through northern England and southern Scotland before settling at Chester-le-Street c. 883 and then moving to Durham c. 995. The church buildings at Durham were probably still under construction, including the all-important wall. At first glance, an attack seemed to be an uncomplicated matter. It was not.

The little that is known about this raid comes from a tract called "The Siege of Durham" (Lat. *De Obsessione Dunelmi*), which was written a generation later.[18] According to its report, the Scots' attack was a fiasco in almost every respect. Setting aside the notion of whatever "luck" one believed came from an inaugural raiding expedition, there was no divine benefit to be gained from attacking a house of worship. This was particularly true for one like Durham that is situated on a massive outcropping where only one side is suitable for an army's advance. The Scots were slaughtered, and the heads of the slain were placed on stakes in front of the church. Each woman who washed a head received a cow as her payment.

The true measure of the man becomes visible after this disaster. Malcolm was able to maintain his grip on the kingship while looking for a new enterprise. He learned from his mistakes and avoided attacks on well-defended places. Malcolm also understood that a prince needed wealth to pay for his government as well as for distribution among his supporters. Turning his gaze south, he saw the rich lands south of the Firth of Forth beckoning in the fertile fields of Lothian. Scottish interest in the region dated from the ninth century when his ancestor Kenneth, son of Alpin, raided it, and the region around Edinburgh had been annexed by Malcolm's distant cousin Idulb in the tenth century according to the *Scottish Chronicle*. So when Malcolm struck the English again in little more than a decade, c. 1018, he went into Lothian. This time the attack was much better planned. The English were in disarray after the Danish prince Cnut celebrated his conquest of them with selected executions that included the earl of Northumbria, the overlord of the region. Malcolm fought the Anglo-Saxons outside the town of Carham, beside the river Tweed. He was victorious and annexed the remainder of Lothian; the Tweed remains the boundary between Scotland and England.[19]

Malcolm's opportunism knew no limits, as his allies discovered. When his ally at the battle of Carham, Owain "the Bald" of Strathclyde, died, Malcolm rewarded the men of Strathclyde for their alliance by annexing their territory.[20] Malcolm wanted to extend his control throughout northern Britain and was willing to use any method to gain it. Looking northward, royal pedigrees reveal that while war might gain a kingdom, marriage helped to keep it. Perhaps that was the background to any possible marriage between one of Malcolm's daughters and a northern Scots king such as Finlay. There were benefits for both parties. The bridegroom gained a powerful ally who could help him seize and hold the kingship. The father-in-law gained a son-in-law whose kingdom was one less potential staging area for an invasion. More important, any grandsons would bring their maternal grandfather's line to the throne.

Macbeth's Early Years

The year of Macbeth's birth is unknown, but there is one slight reason to place it c. 1010. When his father Finlay was slain in 1020, there was no recorded response. Macbeth clearly was not old enough to succeed his father or take revenge for his murder. On the other hand, he was old enough to seize the kingship when his cousin died in 1029, the time his reign began, according to the chronology provided by the contemporary *Prophecy of Berchán*. If he had been about ten years old on his father's death, any demonstration in his favor would have been wasted. Boys came of age in Gaelic society when they were about sixteen years old, and there was no provision for rule by a minor. Nine years after his father's death, however, Macbeth would have been considered an adult who could keep his cousin Gilla Cóemgen from seizing the kingship.

The correct Gaelic form of Macbeth's name is Mac bethad, a compound of two elements: *mac* (son) and *bethad* (life). By extension a "Son of Life" meant Christian. Macbeth's name was uncommon but not unique. Macbeth, a wise man of Munster, died in 728. A Macbeth was one of three Irishmen who set themselves adrift in a coracle with no oars in 891 to go where the Lord directed; they landed in England and were taken as curiosities to the court of Alfred the Great. King Macbeth from northern Kerry died at the battle of Clontarf in 1014, while one of the foremost poets of Ireland named Macbeth died at Armagh in 1041. During his lifetime the name Mac bethad began the process of contracting into the more familiar form Macbeth.

The spelling of Macbeth's name seems to have been a problem for non-Gaelic-speaking scribes.[21] In England, the biographer of his contemporary Edward the Confessor, writing c. 1065, eight years after Macbeth's death, did not even attempt to spell it but referred to him simply as the king with the "outlandish name" (*barbarus nominus*). He was not alone in his bewilderment. Scribes in Scotland who were not Gaels, such as the French-speaking clergy spilling into the kingdom during the twelfth century, spelled Macbeth in various ways. An amusing variety is found in twelfth-century Scottish charters for a noble named Macbeth of Liberton (which lies about two and a half miles southeast of Edinburgh Castle). He appears in a half dozen charters between 1127 and 1147 because his house was a local landmark and boundary marker. In the first extant charter, c. 1127, a grant made by King David to St. Cuthbert's, Edinburgh, his name is spelled Malbead de Libertone. Name of both person and home change in the royal grant to the Abbey of Newbattle, c. 1142, where Macbeth is called Makbet de Libertona. The great charter with which King David founded Holyrood Abbey remembers him as Macbetber.

Macbeth's name is given again as Malbeth de Libertone in a later grant of fifty-two acres in Dalkieth to Holyrood by King David. Macbeth was a witness to the charter of David's son Earl Henry to the Abbey of Kelso, issued sometime between 1141 and 1147. There his name is spelled Malbeth, but a confirmation of that charter by Henry's son Malcolm IV in 1159, spells it Machbet. A re-confirmation of the Kelso grant by Malcolm's brother and successor William spells Macbeth's name Machebet. The grants of Macbeth's lands to Geoffrey and, later, Richard de Melville preserve the spellings Malbet and Malbet Bere. The variety of spellings would continue to be found in the legend of Macbeth as late as the seventeenth century.

His Christian name prompts a question: was Macbeth originally intended for a career in the church? The name Macbeth is found in association with one particular group of clergy called the Céli Dé (Servants of God). While some scholars hesitate to describe them as a religious order, the Céli Dé subscribed to a common code of conduct that emphasized attention to spiritual exercises.[22] They were organized by Máel Tuile late in the eighth century at the church of Tallagh in Ireland (today a neighborhood of Dublin) for the express purpose of resisting laxity in religious life. This was no idle concern. For many of the clerics in the great monasteries, their behavior was little different from that of the nobles who patronized them. The powerful churches were even indulging in warfare with each other. The Céli Dé lived simply, with a stress on prayer and private devotions. A peculiarity of the Céli Dé was their habit of referring to themselves as *maccu bethaid* (sons of life), a poetic way of calling each Christian. There was a Céli Dé community at Monymusk on the river Don, not far from Lumphanan, the fortress traditionally associated with Macbeth. The only known bequests of King Macbeth are to the community of Céli Dé, which served the church dedicated to St. Serf on an island in the midst of Loch Leven in Fife.

High Office

Nowhere was the necessity for the "correct" pedigree more important than in succession to high office where business and politics combined. Even the property transactions found in the *Book of Deer* show the layers of royal authority among the Scots as well as their economic importance. While there are similarities with contemporary society among the Gaels of Ireland, the Scots had a slightly different organization. When they moved into the lands of the Picts, they eliminated all kings except the leader of their *cenél*. The local and provincial princes were denied royal status as the former became known as the *toísech* (leader) and the latter were called the *mórmáer* (great stewards)[23] Offices could be combined, and the notes in the *Book of Deer* state that Macbeth's great uncle Muiredach, son of Morggán, was both *toísech* and *mórmaer*.[24]

The head of society was the king or *rí*. Why did anyone want to be king? In addition to the constant danger of death in battle (Scots kings always led their troops from the front) there was the even greater danger of murder by a disaffected relative, as the fate of Finlay demonstrates. Denied a private life, a prince was constantly surrounded by people who wanted something such as preferment or patronage. Any personal matter such as marriage was directed for the good of the kingdom rather than his own inclination. More persuasive, however, were the two familiar reasons for wanting the position: power and wealth. The king could do anything because he was "above the law." Restraints on his behavior were few. If the acts were managed properly, a prince could take his subjects' goods, invade their homes, and put them to death. Moreover, he directed the affairs of the kingdom, declared war on his neighbors, was remembered in the prayers of every church throughout his realm, and had the constant flattery of poets.

If power was not a sufficient incentive, there was wealth. This was spelled out by an Irish priest with a taste for political science named Fothad "the Canon" (in the sense of a member of the clergy) who wrote a treatise on the privileges of power called "The Rights of Every King" (*Cert cech ríg co réil*).[25] Although the original claims to have been written in the ninth century, it was relevant enough to be recopied (if not composed) in the twelfth century and so it describes the situation during Macbeth's lifetime. The king received wealth from the taxes known as *cáin* (often spelled *can*) paid by his subjects usually in the form of food as well as customs duties. For goods brought into the kingdom, the prince could choose either the goods or payment at a set rate. When one of his subjects died, he received a portion of his goods. An important revenue producer was a prince's private business enterprises. The royal "trade" was livestock rearing and a lord had grazing rights over the lands of his people. This was a remunerative enterprise largely because a proportion of his animals had to be maintained by his subjects through pasturage. In theory, all the landowners had to allow the prince's livestock to roam over their land. In this way a king could own a vastly greater number of animals than his personal farms could accommodate. These became more extensive because there were also lands reserved for the king that provided the means to pay his officials. Whoever held the kingship had exclusive access to resources denied to everyone else.

Macbeth and His Family Earn a Living

Most people spent their time earning a living and carrying out mundane daily activities, as did Macbeth and his clan. The notes in the *Book of Deer* show that the gifts to the church were the generous actions of wealthy individuals who could afford to give fields, farms, and relief from taxes. They also reveal what was valuable to Macbeth's society. The donations of land brought the fuel, food, and clothing that sustained the clergy. There were also grants of privileges or "reliefs," usually in the form of tax rebates. While the tax was intended for the king, the nobles who had authority over the region—the *mórmáer* and the *toísech*—and collected those taxes were compensated for their labor by keeping a percentage of the levy for themselves. An act of piety was to return their portion to the religious community. Any or all three dignitaries could give up their share of the taxes as a donation to the community. When they gave up their share of the tax revenue in favor of the community, they were surrendering part of their income.

Taxes were paid in various ways. Sometimes it was in movable goods such as grain or livestock. At other times the payment was in processed food such as bacon or cheese. Grain seems to have been the main currency in the vicinity of Deer. Payments were assessed in multiples of a *davoch*, which was a vat or cauldron. Malcolm, for example, gave two davochs from a place known as Ros Abard.[26] Payment in this fashion was ancient. The Romans had used measuring vats to collect their dues as did the Irish. People tried to cheat on their taxes by filling the cauldron slowly so that there was a lot of air in the grain.

While Celtic society prized the possession of livestock, this was not true for arable agriculture, although it was a lucrative occupation. Grain growers were prospering at this time, because of the weather. Beginning in the tenth century, the cold period in Europe had given way to a warming trend that extended to the start of the fourteenth century. This period, sometimes called the European Climatic Optimum, witnessed a dramatic rise in temperatures, which benefited agriculture throughout Britain. Crop yields increased and that, in turn, contributed to a rise in the population. The population in Britain seems to have quadrupled during the period from circa 1000 to 1315. Those who gained the most would have been grain farmers such as Macbeth's family.

Beginning a Career

Macbeth succeeded his cousin Malcolm as king of Cenél Loairn in 1029. The *Prophecy of Berchán* states that the "Red King" (Macbeth) was a king for thirty years. This is slightly generous because Macbeth was actually king for only twenty-eight years, but numbers were habitually "rounded up" in poetry.

At the beginning of his reign, Macbeth became embroiled in Scandinavian affairs, particularly Norwegian affairs. There was a Norwegian colony in the Orkney Islands; therefore, the kingdom was Macbeth's neighbor. After the death of Olaf Tryggvason in 999, Norway came under the control of the Danish king Svein "Forkbeard," Olaf's former ally. Circumstances changed c. 1014 when one of Svein's former soldiers named Olaf Haraldsson or Olaf "the Stout" converted to Christianity in Normandy and returned to Norway. As a descendant of Harald "Fairhair," he declared himself king. His reign was difficult, not least because his efforts to convert the Norwegians to Christianity met resistance from powerful members of the aristocracy, who were encouraged by Cnut, the son of Svein "Forkbeard" and king of Denmark and England. Although initially forced to flee England, Cnut returned and, after defeating Edmund "Ironside," son of King Aethelraed, Cnut was declared king in 1016; he added Denmark to his realm in 1018 after the death of his elder brother. He also inherited his father's claims over Norway. In 1028, King Olaf Haraldsson was expelled from his kingdom. He returned in 1030 but was slain by the Norwegians themselves at the Battle of Stiklestad, fought on July 29. A year later, Olaf was declared a saint by Bishop Grimkell of Nidaros. Fighting for a dead saint was easier than fighting for a live king, and among the supporters of Olaf were the sons of Jarl Sigurd "the Stout" of the Orkneys. Thorfinn's relations with the king had been unsteady, but his brother Brusi and nephew Rognvald had been prominent allies. After the death of Olaf, Cnut had his son Svein installed as his representative in Norway, under the regency of his mother Ælgifu of Northampton.

As well as furthering Cnut's interests in Scandinavia, the death of Olaf of Norway provided an opportunity for him to establish his authority in the north of Britain. A display of power could deter any opposition coming from that region. The first mention of Macbeth as king is in the *Anglo-Saxon Chronicle* for 1031 when Cnut traveled to Scotland where he met three kings: Malcolm, Macbeth, and Echmarcach the lord of the Isles:

> [Cnut] went to Scotland and a Scottish king Malcolm submitted to him and two other kings: Macbeth [MS Mælbæþe] and Echmarcach [MS Iehmarc].[27]

The third king was Echmarcach, son of Ragnall, the lord of the Isles. By the eleventh century, the kingdom of the Isles extended intermittently from the Isle of Man in the Irish Sea to the Isle of Lewis in the Outer Hebrides; Echmarcach had ascended to its lordship in 1029.[28] Another record of the meeting comes from a contemporary poem by the Icelandic skald (ON *skáld*, poet) Sigvatr the Black. He was no friend of Cnut, whom he blamed for the death of his hero King Olaf, yet a poet had to earn a living, so Sigvatr amused himself by slipping in a reference to Olaf:

> The heads of famous foreign lords journey to Cnut, from Fife in the midst of the north, a peace buying was that. Olaf never sold himself in this world to anyone in that way; often was victory to the Stout.[29]

Cnut had no desire for Olaf's supporters to establish a base in northern Britain where the annexations of Lothian and Strathclyde by Malcolm II had upset the political balance. For his part, Malcolm appears to have chosen his retinue with the intention of making Cnut aware of two realities. First, the master of northern Britain was Malcolm. Any diplomatic business the Dane wanted to conduct had to be negotiated with him. Second, any effort by Cnut to weaken Malcolm by turning his subordinates against him (one of the Dane's favorite tactics, which had served him well in Norway) was doomed to failure. Malcolm had nothing to fear from the northern Scots or the Vikings of the Isles. While Cnut's supporters tried to put the best interpretation on the meeting by claiming that Malcolm became Cnut's "man," it is obvious that the Dane's effort to frighten the northern prince failed. The *Anglo-Saxon Chronicle* notes that Malcolm adhered to his agreement only so long as it suited him. Apparently both parties got what they wanted at this Danish-Scots meeting. Cnut left satisfied that there would not be any aid forthcoming from the Scots to his foes in Scandinavia. The Scots were convinced that after this show of power (such as it was) Cnut had no interests in northern Britain.

Cnut's meeting with Malcolm, Macbeth, and Echmarcach provides the background to the appearance of Macbeth, called Karl Hundson, in an episode in *Orkneyinga Saga*.[30] The author seems to have relied heavily on a poem in praise of the Orkney jarls composed by an Icelandic poet or *skáld* named Arnórr "Jarls' Poet" (Arnórr jarlaskáld Þórðarson, c. 1012–c. 1075), who was a member of Thorfinn's retinue. After Macbeth succeeded his cousin Malcolm as king, he fought with Malcolm's grandson Thorfinn for control of Caithness and Sutherland; the saga explicitly places the conflict between the years 1029 and 1035.[31] According to the saga, Karl demanded, in his capacity as king, that Thorfinn give to him tax (ON *skattr*) from Caithness. Thorfinn refused, claiming that since the district had been given to him by his grandfather, he did not have pay. Karl sent his nephew Moddan to collect the taxes. Thorfinn gathered a force to attack Moddan, who fled. In retaliation, Karl then led a fleet of eleven ships to attack Thorfinn in the Orkney Islands while Moddan returned to Caithness with an army. According to Arnórr's verses, Thorfinn took five ships from Caithness to Deerness in the Orkneys, where Karl launched a surprise attack, but Thorfinn was victorious. A period of warfare followed. The prose narrative claims that Karl and Thorfinn fought round the Moray Firth. Arnórr claims that Karl recruited troops throughout northern Britain and Ireland for a confrontation at Tarbat Ness on the Moray Firth, which he claims was a victory for Thorfinn. Moddan returned to Caithness where Thorfinn's ally Thorkel "The Fosterer" ambushed and killed him by setting alight the house where he was sleeping. Moddan was decapitated as he attempted to escape by leaping from the balcony. Despite the claims of his supporters, Thorfinn's attempt to seize the region around the Moray Firth failed. That he died as the Orkney jarl rather than Scots king testifies to the success of Macbeth at repelling boarders from his ship of state.

Interpretation of a text such as *Orkneyinga Saga* is difficult, and scholarly opinions on the historical reliability of Old Norse sagas have been divergent. Nineteenth-century scholars believed the sagas were eyewitness transcriptions of historical events, while many twentieth-century scholars disregarded all of them as historical fiction. When their information can be checked independently, the truth is somewhere between the two extremes. Among the historical sagas for events after the year 1000, when they can be compared with other historical documents, the main facts are often correct. Arnórr's verses are especially important because they supply the source material the saga writer used in fashioning the narrative as well as giving a sequence of events. Misinterpretation by later historians also plays a part. For example, Moddan is said to have met the king at Beruvík, which is usually translated "Berwick" and identified with the town on Scotland's southeast border. The actual place seems to have been the river Barbeck in western Scotland, which would have been called Berubrekkr in Old Norse; the name for where it flows into Loch Craignish, in the Cenél Loairn homeland in Argyll, would have been *beru vík*, "bay of Beru."[32] Thorfinn was also a Christian who had made a pilgrimage to Rome and seems to have been the founder of a bishopric, with a cathedral possibly at Birsay. Churches kept records, and a prominent benefactor, such as Thorfinn, would have the outlines of his career remembered.

This chapter in *Orkneyinga Saga* was composed independently of the materials preceding and following it, which solves some problems.[33] Why did the author of *Orkneyinga Saga* not call Macbeth by his name since the Old Norse version, Magbjóðr, appears earlier in the saga? The answer is simple; the two pieces were composed independently. Why do some scholars identify Karl as Macbeth? When the name Macbeth is substituted for Karl Hundason, then this episode fits intelligibly in the historical record so far as it is known. The Karl Hundason episode in *Orkneyinga Saga* describes the continuation of the feud between Macbeth and the family of his cousin Malcolm. In this instance, however, Malcolm's family was a part of the Scandinavian world. Often overlooked, from the Middle Ages to the present, is that the Scots lived on the edge of the Scandinavian diaspora. In light of Cnut's visit to Scotland, the fights between Macbeth and Thorfinn were about more than taxes. The two men supported two different sides in the Norwegian succession struggle. Of course, no political excuse was necessary for a fight over the taxes of the region, but the quarrel could become more intense with support for different causes.

The Karl Hundason episode in *Orkneyinga Saga* shows that, like so much else, the behavior of even the Vikings had changed by the eleventh century. The descendants of pirates were now landed proprietors. The right to collect taxes from a particular region rather than conducting raids had become one of the most important ways of ensuring financial prosperity. That wealth paid for political causes, and the lords of the Orkneys had supported Olaf. After Olaf's death, the Orkney jarls were among the leaders of opposition to Danish overlordship. A question is how much did Macbeth's subsequent career owe to the support of the Danes? Cnut died in 1035, after which St. Olaf's illegitimate son Magnus "the Good" became king of Norway and Cnut's son Hardacnut succeeded his father in Denmark. Even though Cnut had clearly desired Hardacnut to succeed him in England, the son's fear of a Norwegian invasion of Denmark prevented him from sailing to England where his half-brother Harold ruled until his death in 1040.

His Cousin's Keeper?

Support from the Danes would have emboldened Macbeth. In 1032, the year after the meeting with Cnut, Macbeth's cousin Gilla Cóemgen son of Máel Brigte and the *mórmáer* of Moray, died in a burning house, together with fifty of his men. Killing people inside a burning house is usually considered a Viking tactic, but the Irish and Scots were no strangers to it. A banqueting hall or a fortress could have accommodated fifty men. The scene around the conflagration must have been one of mayhem as Gilla Cómgen and his entourage tried to find an escape without being killed the minute they were on the open ground. The victims were perfect targets for the attackers as glare from the flames ensured that any one of the choking men who did get out of the house was practically blind if he tried to fight. Those inside the house died from smoke inhalation before their bodies burned.

There are several points to be observed from this record of Gilla Coemgáin's death. First, this was no casual killing but premeditated murder designed to be carried out with the maximum amount of public attention. Execution by burning on this scale was an act of violence that required elaborate planning. Second, the leader of the attackers had to have enough wealth and prestige to rally a large body of men to his cause. The killers needed roughly twice the number of men who were inside the house to ensure that their victims did not escape. Finally, many of the attacking party must have thought that the leader of the attack had a just motive, for a *mórmaer* was an important person. He was the chief noble in the province after a king, and his family would be expected to seek revenge. Therefore the attacking party had to have a leader who would be able to protect them because their identities would be well known. There was no anonymity in the glow from a burning house.

The chief suspect must be Macbeth. If, as seems almost certain, Gilla Coemgáin had been one of the murderers of Finlay, then, in the eyes of his contemporaries, Macbeth was entirely within his rights to avenge his father. As king, he could command the resources. As king, he could endure the legal consequences, and, since the king was the government, any retaliation against him would be treasonous. There was an additional practical aspect. Macbeth needed to make a public statement that anyone who harmed him would suffer. If he did not make such a statement, his kingdom would be harassed continually by his enemies.

Perhaps the most convincing reason to see Macbeth's hand behind the death of Gilla Coemgáin is a marriage. Even the approximate date is unknown, but Macbeth married Gilla Coemgáin's widow named Gruoch; she is better known today as Lady Macbeth. Her name means "tresses" and, later, it meant "enchantress." To place her in the context of this period requires the correlation of several sources. This will be examined in detail later, but briefly, her marriage to Macbeth is confirmed from a grant to the church of St. Serf's at Loch Leven, where they are called the king and queen of Scots, and Gruoch's father is specifically named as Buide. Her connection with Gilla Coemgáin is seen through the pedigrees for her son Lulach. His patrilineal genealogy is found in the twelfth-century Irish collections mentioned earlier. His matrilineal line is given in the fourteenth-century work known as the

Poppleton manuscript, which reads "Lulac nepos filii Boide" (Lulach the nephew of Buide's son.)[34] Lulach's father had no known connection with any Buide, so the reference must be to his mother.

Macbeth was not alone in his murderous industry. The next year Malcolm was making his own fatal decisions on the behalf of Duncan. By now he was aware that Duncan would be his successor and this presented a problem. Succession among the Scots was patrilineal, passing from father to son. This could skip a generation, but the farther in kinship one was from a previous king, the more precarious were the chances for succession. Duncan had a link to the kingship only through his mother Bethoc. Since his father Crinán was a clergyman, he might not have been able to call upon the loyalties of a band of warriors.

FIG. 2.4 Glamis Symbol Stone 2. Photograph by Robert Hudson.

All those problems were compounded by the presence of another man who was also the grandson of a king, but his connection ran through the male line. This was the son of the son of Buide, the son of Kenneth (mac meic Boete meic Cináeda). His sole memorial is the bleak announcement in the *Annals of Ulster* that Malcolm had him killed in 1033. The grandson of Buide was the great-grandson of the previous King Kenneth III, who was slain in 1005 by Malcolm II. Kenneth's family would want revenge, and one of them was the murdered man's aunt (and Macbeth's wife) Gruoch. The practice of eliminating rival cousins could be described, with grim jocularity, as pruning the branches of the family tree. Vengeance was meted out when Malcolm was killed on November 25, 1034. Details about the assassination are difficult to untangle, but they suggest that he died in battle at the hands of Gruoch's family. The contemporary *Prophecy of Berchán* says that Malcolm died in the battle of Moin or the moor. A more informative version of events comes from John of Fordun.[35] He admits that Malcolm had murdered members of Kenneth's family but had done so lawfully. Nevertheless, the survivors plotted his death and waited in ambush all night for the king near his residence at Glamis. As the king emerged in the morning to attend his affairs, the plotters attacked. The place of his death was believed to be marked by a stone pillar, apparently the symbol stone now known as Glamis 2 that has a carving of two men fighting with axes.[36]

Duncan the King

Malcolm's calculations, nevertheless, worked perfectly. Five days after his grandfather's death, Duncan, the son of the abbot of Dunkeld, was made king. Malcolm's preparations for Duncan's accession went beyond eliminating rivals. He had given Duncan lordship over Strathclyde—the north British kingdom that had been annexed fifteen years earlier and continued as a training ground for future Scottish monarchs.[37] Duncan was not the venerable ancient in real life that he became in later stories, and the *Annals of Tigernach* claim that he was "at a youthful age" when he died. A legend told by Andrew of Wyntoun remembers him as a man of passion.[38] One day Duncan went hunting in the forest near Forteviot. He stayed out later than he should, and when night came, he had to seek shelter from the local miller. The miller had a daughter who spent the night in Duncan's arms. From that casual liaison came a child who would later be known as Malcolm Canmore. Is this story true or merely fiction? Andrew certainly thought it was correct and gives a long discourse on how, in his mind, the greatest of the early Scots kings came from humble

Macbeth Emerges

origins. Nevertheless, the only information about Duncan's wife is that she was Anglo-Danish, a kinswoman of the Northumbrian Earl Siward according to the historian John of Fordun, while the fourteenth-century king-list known as "I" claims that her name was Suthen, similar to Gaelic Suithcern.[39]

Whatever his romantic escapades, more worrying to his subjects were Duncan's failings as king. The first test of his reign came in 1039, when the Britons of Strathclyde were attacked by the English of Northumbria.[40] The assault called for retaliation. Rather than assail the perpetrators in their lair, in this instance the fortress of Bamburgh on the eastern coast, Duncan aimed for a richer target, and in the following year, the Scots once again attacked the cathedral at Durham. The timing might reflect events in England. After the death of Cnut in November 1035, rule had effectively been taken by his son Harold, even though his half-brother Hardacnut appears to have been the intended heir to his father's domain. Harold died on the feast of St. Patrick (March 17) in 1040, and Hardacnut arrived in England in June. The assault on Durham may have been during the transition. The attack was a repeat of the tactics that had been tried by Duncan's grandfather thirty-five years earlier when the community's defensive works were newer and probably hastily erected. A generation was sufficient time for a relieved community to reinforce its defenses. What had not changed was the rapidly narrowing rock face, which meant that any assault on the church still meant a fight uphill on a steep incline with little room for maneuver.

Macbeth appears to have been involved in this expedition, possibly with the dubious honor of leading the Scottish force. The contemporary Irish chronicler Marianus Scotus describes him as Duncan's general.[41] This seems to indicate that Macbeth had acknowledged the political supremacy of Duncan. Unlike Irish or English armies that used only foot soldiers, the Scots employed both cavalry and infantry. While the Scots had a mobile element to their attack, any element of surprise by the horsemen was eliminated by the slowness of the foot soldiers. There are no details about this assault on Durham beyond the prosaic announcement of the battle. Some idea of how the Scots attack unfolded can be gleaned from reports of other battles. Well into the twelfth century, the Scottish infantry fought wearing only light clothing, which led their opponents to claim that they were unclothed. At the Battle of the Standard, fought in Yorkshire on August 22, 1138, between the Scottish and English armies, the "bare" infantry of King David astonished the heavily armored cavalry opposing them. Few clothes were, however, a sensible uniform on marshy soil that required fast movement for victory. The weight of English armor doomed Edward II's troops at the battle of Bannockburn in the fourteenth century, when Robert the Bruce's lightly armored Scots infantry slaughtered their heavier opponents as they attempted to extract themselves from the marshes round the Bannock "burn" or stream. An eleventh-century Irish account in the *Fragmentary Annals* about a tenth-century Scots battle, probably relying on knowledge of current fighting tactics, describes an army of Scots advancing with their battle standard, the previously mentioned crosier of St. Columba called *Cathbuaid* (Battle Triumph).[42] They might even have used dogs in the initial charge as they did in the Battle of the Standard in 1138.

From their citadel, the defenders of Durham had plenty of warning of impending danger, both from the reports of frantic farmers fleeing for safety behind the walls as well as their view over the countryside. They had time to make their plans. Once again the raid was a fiasco for the Scots, with the army unable to breech the walls. Then the defenders became the attackers and used their geographical advantage of fighting downhill. According to the "History of the Church of Durham" (*Historia Dunelmensis Ecclesiastiae*), the cavalry managed to escape, but the infantry was slaughtered. The heads of the slain were carried into the market place and set on stakes.[43]

Duncan had failed in the eyes of his subjects. A good king enriched his people with plunder and enhanced their reputation as fierce fighters. Success was considered a sign that God was pleased with a prince, and the disaster reflected badly upon Duncan. When he returned home, Duncan had to reestablish his authority. The common method was to collect his taxes in person in order to show his ability to collect them. As he was making his rounds, Duncan decided to venture into Macbeth's territory to collect his subject's contribution. This was an unwise strategy, both because of the ancient hostility between the two peoples and also because it made Macbeth's subordinate status that much clearer. On August 16, 1040, a disgusted Macbeth challenged him to a fight. The ensuing battle is almost completely obscure save for a scrap of information that it was fought at a place known only as Bothgavene, somewhere in the vicinity of modern Elgin where, in the thirteenth century, King Alexander II established a mass chaplaincy. Only the outcome of the battle is known for certain: Duncan was slain, and Macbeth took his place as overlord.

Macbeth: Survival and Supremacy

Macbeth's elevation as king of all the Scots was an unlikely achievement. When Finlay son of Rory was slain in 1020, he was merely another unsuccessful prince. The life expectancy for the children (especially male children) of deceased royals was short. Macbeth survived and in less than a decade he succeeded his cousin Malcolm as king. At the beginning of his reign he was forced into political affairs in Scandinavia when Cnut of England and Denmark negotiated with him to side with the Danes as they fought for control of Scandinavia. Immediately this put Macbeth in opposition with his cousin Jarl Thorfinn of the Orkney Isles, who not only was a supporter of Cnut's foe St. Olaf of Norway but was also casting covetous eyes on northern Scotland. The verses of Arnórr Jarls'Poet give the impression of Thorfinn's constant triumphs over Macbeth. Yet it was Macbeth, not Thorfinn, who became the king of the Scots.

Energy and intelligence were necessary for the successful prince, to which can be added a long memory. Did Macbeth organize the death by burning of his cousin Gilla Coemgáin? No surviving source points to him, but the entire episode begs the question: who else could it have been? In the eleventh century, any lord wanted to be feared rather than loved. Public murders reinforced the point. Macbeth shows what could be accomplished with the correct lineage, some energy, and the ability to choose the right friends. Sometimes the choice was clear, such as making terms with Cnut. At other times the choice was less obvious but was important nonetheless, as in his marriage with Gruoch. Less recognized was Macbeth's connection with the Scandinavian world. Becoming "the man" of a powerful monarch such as Cnut was not a casual matter and his foes were your foes. The fight with Jarl Thorfinn of the Orkneys was part of a contest that was being played out throughout the northeast Atlantic. Macbeth was a "winner" in two cultures.

3

King of All the Scots

IN AUGUST OF 1040, Macbeth son of Finlay became the sole king over all the Scots, and he ruled for seventeen years, until August 1057. Macbeth's achievement was significant: for the first time there were no other kings—subordinate or otherwise—among the Scots. His overthrow of Duncan showed the differences between the two men and the dissimilar ways they came to power. Duncan's hands were clean of murder because his grandfather's blood-stained hands did it for him. Macbeth, however, did his own butchery. He slaughtered his way to the kingship as his predecessors had done and as his rivals tried to do. A summary assessment of Macbeth's reign is given in the contemporary *Prophecy of Berchán*:

> [After Duncan's death] the red king [Macbeth] will take sovereignty, the kingship of noble Scotland of hilly aspect; after slaughter of Gaels, after slaughter of Vikings, the generous king of Fortriu will take sovereignty.
>
> The red, tall, golden-haired one, he will be pleasant to me among them; Scotland will be brimful, west and east, during the reign of the furious red one.
>
> Thirty years over Scotland, a high-king ruling; in the middle of Scone he will spew blood on the evening of a night after a duel.[1]

The poet's description of Macbeth as the "red king" (i.e., bloodstained) shows a vigorous man, while the ineffectual Duncan had been dismissed earlier as "a king whose name is the many diseases" or, to phrase it more succinctly, "the hypochondriac."

The verses also give the first description of a Scottish prince's appearance. Only occasionally are there images or descriptions of people in this early period of history, but Macbeth seems to have been unusual looking by the standards of his day. His appearance as "red, tall, and golden-haired" suggests that Macbeth was gangly, blond, and had a ruddy complexion. He was not a handsome man by the standards of eleventh-century Scottish society that expected the ideal warrior to have black hair, a pale complexion, and a muscular figure as suggested by the descriptions of heroes in literature. Macbeth might be unattractive, but he had to be clever if he wanted to live. A wise prince was always on his guard against rivals plotting revenge, and for Macbeth they were the supporters of Duncan's two sons—Malcolm Canmore (MI *ceann mhór,* "big head") and Donald Ban (MI *ban,* "the fair")—who, if the fourteenth-century historian John of Fordun is correct, remained in Scotland for several years after their father's death. Eventually they sought sanctuary outside the kingdom; John claims that Malcolm was about seven years old when he fled to England, while Donald was five.[2]

Their departure might have been connected with an attempted coup d'état by their grandfather Crinán in 1044. The Annals of Tigernach describe it as "a battle among the Scots together" (*cath etir Albancho ar aen rían*), which means that it was a clash between armies rather than a raid or ambush. The result was another disaster for Duncan's family. Crinán was slain together with one hundred eighty of his followers. That might not have been the only attack because the "Durham Annals" (*Annales Dunelmenses*), a late eleventh-/early twelfth-century production, have a unique entry that claims Earl Siward of Northumbria led an army into Scotland in 1046 and expelled Macbeth, who recovered his monarchy after the Northumbrians departed. This seems to be a misplaced notice of Siward's invasion of Scotland in 1054, but the possibility cannot be discounted that it refers to a separate assault.

Macbeth's Scotland: Economy and Culture

Macbeth's reign took place during a period of change in the British Isles and throughout Europe. The warming known as the European Climatic Optimum increased the production of food while, at the same time, commerce generally revived in northern Europe. The arrival of the Vikings in the ninth century had impeded economic activity, but this changed in the tenth century when the raiders turned their warships into trading vessels and carried merchandise as well as warriors. Fortified pirate encampments such as Dublin or Rouen became markets where goods purchased from the local population were sold or traded by the descendants of the earlier pirates. Bulkier cargoes could be carried more cheaply in seagoing ships than in overland transport. Within the

British Isles, northern England and eastern Ireland were becoming wealthy from this commercial activity.[3] The Scots were not. Success against the Vikings had the unexpected result of turning their land into an economic backwater. Even the descendants of the settlers from Scandinavia in the Hebrides and Orkneys carried out only some minor manufacturing, mainly of a rough, weather-resistant cloth called *röggvaldr*. As other kingdoms became wealthy from industry and trade, poverty dogged the agrarian Scots.

Was Macbeth's kingdom the savage wilderness familiar from Shakespeare's play or was it something less of a cliché for barbarism? A few clues survive from a curious poem written about a Welsh bishop named Sulien (medieval Welsh for Solomon) by his son Ieun, who was also his pupil. The verses, written in the last years of the eleventh century, provide an unusual insight into Macbeth's kingdom. Sulien was born about the year 1011, and when he was about thirty years old, c. 1041, he decided to sail to Ireland to study at the famous schools. His voyage across the Irish Sea became more exciting than he had planned when a storm arose and blew his boat off course, or to paraphrase Ieun: "Moved by gusts of wind, he landed in the country which they call by the name of Scotland." Sulien remained there either because he felt that he had been led there by Providence or simply because he decided to make the best of the situation. Once again Ieun remarks: "Remaining there for five years, unwearied he pursued his desire ... persisting diligently (in his studies) by night and day, extracted continuously from the pure stream of the sevenfold fountain [i.e., the seven liberal arts] cupfuls fragrant with mellifluous aroma."[4]

Ieun, in his florid style, makes an interesting claim, namely, that Scotland had an intellectual culture that could interest a scholar from outside the land. Regardless of the circumstances of Sulien's arrival, his sojourn indicates that the Scots were more sophisticated than generally believed. Ireland is a day's sail away from Scotland, and storms do not rage continuously for five years. A ship seeking a safe haven on the western coast would likely have gone through the North Channel and then past the Isle of Bute into the Firth of Clyde. The schools of Scotland that attracted Sulien were well developed. In Gaelophone regions, the head of the school was an official known in Middle Irish as *fer léighinn* whose title means literally "the reading man." An important "reading man" in the home territory of Macbeth was Domongart at the church of Turriff who witnessed one of the charter notes in the *Book of Deer*.[5] The *fer léighinn* oversaw the education of the student, known as a *scollog*. During Macbeth's lifetime, the student was declining in status, and by the end of the Middle Ages the *scollog* was simply a farm-worker. The education of the tenth-century Scottish reformer Catroe was entrusted to a kinsman named Bean. When Catroe's foster parents were robbed and he prepared to pursue the thieves, Bean successfully hindered Catroe by producing the Gospels that he had used to instruct the child and read selected passages to calm his ardor. Subsequently, Catroe wished to be ordained a priest and went to the seminary at Armagh. On his return, he taught in his homeland (where, his hagiographer notes, there were many teachers but few interpreters of Holy Scripture) before moving to the continent. The scholarly exchange continued for centuries. Macbeth's contemporary Dubtach "the Scotsman" died at Armagh in 1065. Perhaps Sulien went to the ancient church and school founded by St. Kentigern at what is now Glasgow, in the heart of what had been the ancient British kingdom of Strathclyde. There is the question of what sort of dialect was spoken in the region, but a Welsh speaker such as Sulien might have found it familiar. Another possibility is that Sulien traveled to the eastern coast and pursued his studies at St. Andrews, where the scholars of the church would gather to greet the bishop-elect Eadmer in 1120.

Sulien was also interested in art, and he might have a connection with two Psalters, one in Scotland and another in Wales. Early in the eleventh century—probably some time between 1020 and 1030—a service book now known as the *Edinburgh Psalter* was produced.[6] Precisely where it was made is unknown, but it seems to have been in Edinburgh by the end of the century. Even though it has many features in common with designs from Ireland, particularly those produced at the church of Clonmacnoise, there is no immediate reason not to assign it a Scottish origin. The text is based on St. Jerome's Hebraic version of the psalms, in which the verses are divided into three groups of fifty each, but of more immediate concern is the *Edinburgh Psalter*'s place in the development of floral ornamentation (or foliage motif) in Irish/Scottish illuminations. An occasional flourish by the illustrator was to notch the curve of the marginal interlace in such a way as to resemble a half-palmette together with a knotted black outline of initials. These features appear in another eleventh-century manuscript, the famous *Psalter of Ricemarch*, illustrated by Sulien's son Ieun.[7] This psalter, too, follows the Hebraic version of the Psalms, and it has the half-palmette similar to that in the Edinburgh manuscript. Did Sulien see the *Edinburgh Psalter* during his stay in Scotland and make a copy of it? Was it the model followed by his son for his own manuscript?

Surrounded by the Extraordinary

Culture molded Macbeth and made his legend. Northern Britain is unusually rich in art, especially sculpture. Technical competence, however, could vary widely. The images in the *Book of Deer*, for example, are not the glorious images found in the magnificent earlier Book of Kells but human figures that are little more than stylistic representations using geometric ornamentation.[8] Nonetheless, they reveal some of the ideals of Macbeth's society. The warrior ethos is reflected by the illustration introducing the first section of the *Book of Deer*, the Gospel of St. Matthew, which shows a seated figure holding a sword. This is a rare, although correct, depiction of St. Matthew. The evangelists Mark and Luke are carrying objects that appear to be books with ornamented covers. The sword and the book are useful symbols for understanding the violent and literate society that produced Macbeth.

As Macbeth traveled through the countryside, he would have been reminded constantly of earlier inhabitants. The past was never far away. Prehistoric tombs and graves are scattered throughout the landscape in addition to the so-called Pictish symbol stones, reminders of the great North British artistic culture.[9] There must have been many more in Macbeth's day before time, farming, and the scavenging of the stones for building materials had taken their toll. Pictish symbol stones have displays of fantastic images: what seem to be mirrors and combs; crescents bisected with lines in the form of a "V"; circles connected with parallel lines; and lines in the form of a "Z" with decorated ends. Equally captivating are the animals: bulls, birds, fish, snakes, and a creature known only as the "Pictish water beast." Their meanings have yet to be deciphered to general scholarly satisfaction. Explanations include boundary markers, memorials of marriages, monuments to fallen nobles, and general signposts. Some simply defy easy explanation. About twenty-five miles north of Lumphanan stands the *Maiden Stone*, a pillar of pink granite. On one side is a crucifix surmounted by a man flanked by two large fish beings and on the other side are four panels containing, in descending order, a centaur, geometric objects, a "water beast," and a mirror and comb.

The symbols stones also give an insight into the aristocratic world through which Macbeth moved. Hunting was the sport of nobles in Scotland as elsewhere, and a stylized version was carved on stones, with the aristocrats in the center, the huntsmen with dogs and horns following the fleeing stags, seen in a hunting scene on the Aberlemno symbol stone number 1.

Stones did not have to have carvings to be significant. One of the boundaries in a charter note in the *Book of Deer* is a field is marked by a

FIG. 3.1 Midmar Church Recumbent Stone. Photograph by Robert Hudson.

"pillar stone." They might have had a spiritual significance. There is an especially interesting stone circle within the churchyard at Midmar, ten miles from Macbeth's fortress of Lumphanan, where a recumbent stone or "Druid's Altar" is a part of the assembly.

Christianity made its contribution to legends. There was a popular belief in angelic intrusion in human affairs. Macbeth's contemporary, the poet who wrote the *Prophecy of Berchán*, probably Dubtach "the Scotsman," prophesized that angels would carry him from Scotland to Ireland.[10] A genre that combined monsters and marvels with piety was voyage literature such as the *Voyage of St. Brendan* (*Navigatio sancti Brendani*). The saint and his companions sailed into exile for the love of God where they saw wonders on the deep and celebrated mass on Easter Sunday atop a whale. Among the Scots he was known as Brandan and, he is mentioned in an eleventh-century litany used at the Scottish church at Rome; the later medieval historian John of Fordun cites a now lost story of Brandan in his chronicle.[11]

Fascination with the fantastic had another manifestation. Macbeth was born into a society that believed it was witnessing the Last Days, a period when the world would be destroyed and then reappear as the New Jerusalem.[12] Beginning in the mid-tenth century, a number of tracts were written on the Second Coming of Christ and the Day of Judgment or Doomsday. Apocalyptic stories give an indication of the worries and preoccupations of Macbeth's society. Stories circulating during Macbeth's lifetime are preserved in the previously mentioned Irish miscellany called *The Book of the Dun Cow* (*Lebor na Huidre*), which was compiled at the monastery of Clonmacnoise no later than the beginning of the twelfth century. A major patron of the church was the tenth-century Irish high king Flann "of the Shannon" who was married to the Scottish princess Máel Muire the daughter of Kenneth I. Two particular themes are the signs heralding the approaching End of Time and the events of the dread day. These texts have titles such as "Tidings of Doomsday" (*Scéla Lái Brátha*), "Two Sorrows of the Kingdom of Heaven" (*Dá Brón Flatha Nime*), and the "Vision of Adomnán" (*Fís Adomnán*). "Day of Judgment" describes the conditions that await the souls destined for damnation.[13] Their torments are hunger, cold, stifling smoke, and great thirst. The lost soul sees devilish faces and terrible monsters in a burning sea. Particularly vulnerable to damnation are proud clergy, lying brehons (the interpreters of native law), satirists, and impious leaders. "Tidings of Doomsday" explains the division of souls at the Last Judgment. Doomsday itself lasts a thousand years, and the damned soul falls for thirty years before reaching the bottom of the pit of hell. Less horrific is the "Two Sorrows of the Kingdom of Heaven" who are the prophets Enoch and Elias, waiting for the End of Time in order to die.

As noted earlier, churches preserved and passed on information. The material varied according to the interests of the local clergy or their visitors. Historians visited various churches to gather information, which could be compiled into a narrative written hundreds of miles away. The Irish chronicler Marianus Scotus (1029—c. 1083) was an exact contemporary of Macbeth, and in the year 1056 he journeyed from Ireland to Cologne, where he arrived at the monastery of St. Martin in August. As a member of the clergy, Marianus would have moved from one religious house to another and would have been able to inspect their archives. Within his chronicle are specific dates for the reigns of Malcolm II, Duncan, Macbeth, and Lulach. He wrote that "Duncan, king of Scotland was slain in the autumn by his general Macbeth son of Finlay who succeeded to the kingship for seventeen years."[14] Information could be brought up-to-date. There is a note on the margin of Marianus's chronicle, probably supplied to him by his amanuensis, also named Marianus, who traveled across Scotland to the monastery of St. Martin of Mainz in 1072: "Duncan reigned five years, that is from the Mass of St. Andrews to the same and beyond to the nativity of Mary. Then the son of Finlay reigned seventeen years to the same Mass of St. Mary"; among the Gaels, the *nativitas* of Mary was celebrated on August 16.[15]

The clergy did not have a monopoly on remembrance of the past, and far more important for the aristocracy than monkish chronicles were the historical performance pieces at the royal and noble courts. Ferocious consumption of intoxicating drinks was accompanied by recitation of works recalling the glories of the past. An eighth-century list of ales, which had associations with sovereignty, claims that the warriors of Dál Riata "performed great feats for the sake of the drinking," while the Picts had "ales red like wine."[16] Occasionally, ale was a medium for prophecy. The *vita* of the Irish St. Berach claims that druids at the court of Duncan's ancestor Áedán mac Gabráin were able to see across space and identify the saint after drinking new beer and then sleeping on wooden frames made from the rowan tree.[17]

Courtly entertainment was not a casual matter. Irish and Welsh texts composed during Macbeth's time mention the formal arrangement of the hall, which was the social and governmental heart of the kingdom. One description (complete with a diagram) comes from Ireland in a tract on the Banqueting Hall (MI *Tech Midchúarda*) at Tara in the *Book of Leinster*.[18] The literal and symbolic center of the hall was the hearth beside which was the lord's seat and above it was the cauldron (MI *davoch*) where the meal was cooked. The closer one sat to the fire, the higher was one's status. Admission to the hall was an honor as is made clear in the famous Welsh tale "How Culwuch won Olwen" (Medieval Welsh *Culhwch ac Olwen*). Culwuch arrived at the hall of his kinsman King Arthur after the doors had been closed and was told that "knife has gone into meat and drink into horn and there is a thronging in Arthur's hall."[19] The "throng" included the important people of the kingdom. The list of officials given in the tale is confirmed by historical tracts, such as the laws of the tenth-century King Hywel Dda ("the Good"). There was the steward, who oversaw the king's personal affairs. The judge sat opposite the king and upheld the royal authority in legal matters. Beyond these great magnates were the more specialized officials such as the masters of the hawks, hounds, and horses as well as the historians.

Returning to Scotland, among the historical materials possibly performed by the seanachies was a poem that seems to have been composed specifically for Macbeth's court, the previously mentioned "Coming of the Cruthne [Picts] from Thrace to Ireland and their coming from Ireland to Britain" (*Tochomlod Cruithnech a Tracia co hÉrind ocus a Thochomlod ó hÉrind co Albain*).[20] "Coming of the Cruthne" recounts their adventures when they left Scythia, which was believed to be their homeland, and settled in northern

Britain. The general story is that a king of Thrace wanted to marry a certain woman but was unwilling to pay her bride price. She had six brothers who, to avoid the shame, fled by ship to Poitiers. They sailed thence to southeast Ireland, to what is now Wexford Harbour (MI Inber Slaine) and won the battle of Forth Mountain (MI Ard Lemnacht). The victory was won despite the magic used by the druids of their opponents who cured poisoned wounds with fresh milk. Cruithne's success aroused the hostility of the Irish who, according to some versions, gave them wives and agreed to support an incursion into northern Britain, but only if the succession to the kingship would be through the mother rather than the father.

"Coming of the Cruthne" brings together various episodes found in other writings, such as the Venerable Bede in his *Ecclesiastical History*.[21] Depending on the manuscript, the story ends with a list of the kings: first, of the Picts; and then the Scots concluding with what seems to be a reference to Macbeth. In this genre of literature, the last prince is normally the dedicatee at whose court the piece was performed. The pertinent text from the *Book of Ballymote*, copied c. 1400, concludes: "Fifty kings, a marauding sequence, together from the seed of Eochaid; from Fergus, it was true, to the mighty *mac Bret*[n]*ach* ('British youth')."[22] That passage becomes comprehensible when going back a couple of verses where the triumph of the Scots over the Picts, in the person of Kenneth I, is noted. So who is the British youth? Depending how one counts, the fiftieth king from Fergus was Macbeth. Furthermore, if the -r- in *Bretach* is a superfluous addition, then the name is *Macbetach*, a garbled, but comprehensible spelling of Macbeth's name.[23]

Relations with the Church

The successful Christian prince needed good relations with the Church, and Macbeth was no different. Faced with powerful and influential rivals— Malcolm Canmore at the court of his southern neighbor King Edward of England and Jarl Thorfinn of the Orkneys to his north—Macbeth knew that the clergy were invaluable allies. The support of the clergy included remembrance of favored princes, such as Giric in the "Dunkeld Litany" and sermons that reminded the faithful of divinely mandated obedience to earthly rulers. More materially, the clergy controlled vast tracts of land that supplied men and materials. Bishops had their own armies, and a twelfth-century charter had among its witnesses two generals of the army of the bishop of St. Andrews.[24]

During Macbeth's reign, churches in Scotland, as throughout Europe, were recovering from the ravages of the Vikings, and that included their wealth, which was used for refurbishing and repair. There were also new structures such as the round towers, which were built from the tenth to twelfth centuries. Surviving Scottish round towers at Brechin and Abernethy were built in the eleventh century and consciously imitated the great church towers found on the continent, which were symbols of prosperity as well as guideposts for travelers.

The eleventh century was also a time of religious controversy among the Gaels as it was throughout Europe. In common with the more fervent denunciations of simony (the buying and selling of church offices) found elsewhere, a particular goal of the reformers among the Irish and Scots was the desire for the physical as well as religious management of church affairs by the bishop. Bishops were primarily spiritual leaders rather than administrators, and the actual head of the church was the saint's *comarbae* (heir), which is occasionally and erroneously called "abbot" in Latin texts. An example is Duncan's father Crinán, who was the head of the church of Dunkeld. Many *comarbae* were not in holy orders but were members of the powerful local families. The bitter fight between innovators and reactionaries is visible in a work composed in the generation after Macbeth's death called "The Second Vision of Adomnán," which claimed that saints refused to visit churches overseen by men who were not in holy orders. The earlier "First Vision of Adomnán" places the wicked clergy who are not in holy orders into the swamps of perdition.[25] The matter was settled in the twelfth century as reforming synods in Ireland acknowledged episcopal authority.

The Church provided a useful avenue for international relations. Communication was eased by the lack of a language barrier since all clergy spoke Latin. One sign of his good relations with the clergy is the pilgrimage Macbeth made to Rome during the pontificate of Pope Leo IX 1050, possibly in connection with the Easter synod in that year. There has been the suggestion that he stayed at the English School (Schola Anglorum or Schola Saxonum) on Vatican Hill.[26] Since the opening of the routes from Britain to Rome by the English and Danish King Cnut in 1027, many individuals—lay and cleric—had made the journey to the Eternal City. Macbeth may have been inspired by accounts of Cnut's pilgrimage during their meeting of 1031. A pilgrimage to Rome was both an act of piety and a holiday, a mark of wealth and sophistication. Cnut's pilgrimage had benefited him very much, taking him from the ranks of barbarian chiefs to inclusion among the foremost Christian princes. Perhaps Macbeth hoped to enjoy similar acclaim.

A pilgrimage was also a sign of security. No king even vaguely uncertain of his subjects' loyalty would allow his enemies the luxury of an open field

68   MACBETH BEFORE SHAKESPEARE

for rebellion. Macbeth's journey was not undertaken at the end of life, but in the midst of a vigorous career. Not wishing to appear as an impoverished bumpkin, Macbeth cultivated the image of the generous prince while at Rome. Contemporaries were impressed by his lavish gifts and, according to Marianus Scotus, he "scattered silver as though it were seed to the poor." Marianus's remark deserves comment because it was more than just a pleasantry. This suggests a man of generous spirit. Monarchs were expected to enrich churches, but the distribution of cash directly to the poor was so unusual that it excited comment. The customary method was to give a gift to a particular church as alms, where it would be distributed as seen fit by the local clerics. Had Macbeth been making a calculated show of piety, the money would have been better spent on gifts to influential individuals or some worthy (and noticeable) building project such as the repair of one of the many churches in Rome. The poor would profit him nothing in this life.

Leo IX's pontificate was an unusual one for a pilgrimage by a king.[27] Disliked by many monarchs, such as the king of France, Leo was even less fondly considered after the events of the previous year. Following his election as pontiff, as part of the farewell tour of his home region in 1049, Leo went to Reims to assist in the consecration of a new church for the monastery of St. Remigius, the same place where he would hold an ecclesiastical council. The ceremonies included the transfer of Remigius's bones to the high altar. In honor of the occasion, many bishops and abbots had been summoned by Pope Leo but only a few actually arrived. They were the unlucky ones. When the moment came for depositing the bones, Pope Leo ordered them to remain on the high altar and the following day, at the beginning of the council, he commanded all present to declare that they had not bought their office. In other words, he was accusing the company of simony and giving them the opportunity to deny it. In the presence of a saintly witness many could not, and stern justice was dispensed. At the end of the week, the shattered gathering staggered home, aware that the new pontiff was serious about breaking the control of the aristocracy in church affairs.

Pope Leo could take such arbitrary action because he was a kinsman of the powerful princes of the Holy Roman Empire and his father was a cousin of Emperor Conrad II. The emperor's prestige, if not actual power, extended as far as the Gaelic-speaking clergy who migrated to churches in the Empire, whence they sent the occasional notices of the emperors that are found in the Irish annals. Emperor Otto II, for example, is mentioned in the verses of *Saltair na Rann*.[28] The Irish *Annals of Ulster* and the so-called Annals of Tigernach mention the coronation of Emperor Conrad, called "king of the world," and include his victory over Count Eudes of Champagne in 1037.

More than previous popes, Leo had an interest in northern Europe and was instrumental in establishing the archbishopric of Hamburg/Bremen as the metropolitan of Scandinavia, Iceland, Greenland, and, eventually, Vinland. Leo also had a connection with the Gaelic-speaking world. He had attended the school at the monastery of Toul, where a community of clergy from the Gaelic lands had been established in the mid-tenth century by Bishop Gérard (reigned 963 to 994). Not only did Gérard feed and shelter them at his own expense, but he also allowed them separate chapels for worship. His biographer Widric, writing between 1027 and 1049, claims that on the day Gérard died, one of his Irish dependents roamed through the streets at dawn bewailing his approaching end.[29] Widric wrote during Leo's tenure as bishop of Toul, which had an atmosphere steeped with goodwill toward the Gaels. Toul is beside the Moselle River and not far upriver from Metz, where Catroe was abbot of the monastery of St. Clements c. 953 to 978. A sign of Leo's good relations with the Gaelic clergy is that they attended his synod at Reims in 1049. The pontiff returned the compliment when he oversaw the foundation of the Church of the Holy Trinity of the Scots (Sanctae Trinitatis Scottorum) on the Coelian Hill at Rome.[30] Since "Scot" could still refer to either Irish or Scot, the dedication simply referred to anyone from the Gaelic-speaking lands. The liturgy from that church still survives where, conspicuous among the saints, is Brandan or Brendan the Navigator.[31] Macbeth's pilgrimage might have been in connection with the founding of the church. That Macbeth did make a pilgrimage to Rome but probably did not attend the council of Rheims is suggested by conflict in the Holy Roman Empire. In 1049, Count Baldwin of Flanders was being pursued by the Holy Roman emperor Henry III. The emperor asked neighboring princes, including King Edward of England, to prevent Baldwin's escape. The year 1050 provided an entirely different situation. Threat of an invasion into Scotland lessened in 1050 when Edward the Confessor reduced his fleet from twelve ships to five and cashiered his household troops.[32]

A clue that Macbeth was a sincere supporter of Leo's reforming aims, and not just another royal tourist, comes from two gifts he gave to the Céli Dé who served the church of St. Serf at Loch Leven in Fife. Records of the grants survive in the late medieval *Register of the Priory of St. Andrews*, where they were copied because the originals were disintegrating.[33] Macbeth made the first donation jointly with Lady Macbeth, which suggests that these were her family lands. The first grant was Kirkness (promontory of the church) situated in the southeast of the parish of Portmoak about a mile southeast of Loch Leven and the village of Portmoak (MS *Pethmokanne*, the farm/field of

Mochan) from St. Serf's church. In addition to the land donation, the royal couple released the Céli Dé from the payment of certain taxes, a significant benefit. An interesting aspect of Macbeth's grant is that the exemptions are spelled out: freedom from all taxes owed to the king, his son, nobles, and anyone else; freedom from the obligation to repair bridges; and freedom from the obligation to provide provisions for the army. At some point in its subsequent recopying, a story was added to the charter concerning some badly behaved Irishmen who gave the name to a local landmark called the Stone of the Irishmen. The entire grant, as it is now preserved reads:

> Macbeth the son of Finlay and Gruoch the daughter of Boete, the king and queen of the Scots, gave Kirkness with its boundaries and limits to all-powerful God and the Céli Dé of the island of Loch Leven for the sake of their prayers. These are the boundaries and limits of Kirkness and the little village of Portmoak: from the place of *Moneloccodhan* [? a marsh from which flowed the Louchty] beyond the river that is called Leven, and the same [distance] in breadth. The same [distance] to the public street that leads to Inverkeithing, beyond to the Stone of the Irishmen, and the same in length.
>
> And [it] is called the Stone of the Irishmen, since King Malcolm son of Duncan gave it, which in Scots was called *Connane*.[34] The Irishmen went to Kirkness to the house of that same man named Mochan, who was absent and the women were alone in the house who the Irishmen violently oppressed. The matter came to the ears of Mochan that Irishmen had come to and infested his own house with his mother. Urging constantly his mother to be sensible and go outside, which she did not want to do, but the Irishmen wanted friendship and to make peace with them who had known the savagery and sacrilege, in the midst of flames of fire that the mother energetically ignited. And from this cause that place was called the stone of the Irishmen.
>
> To the village of Kirkness to all-powerful God and the Céli Déi, with all freedom from all gifts, burdens and taxes of the king and son of the king, the nobles and others, and without the restoration of bridges, without [supplying] soldiers and traversing, but pious contemplation and intercessory prayers to be gathered for God.

The second grant, made only in Macbeth's name, gave land to the Céli Dé that had belonged to Bolgyn the son of Thorfinn. The name Bolgyn is a compound of OI *bolg* (leather sack) and the diminutive "little"; together the

King of All the Scots

name elements mean "little sack." His father had the ON name Thorfinnr. The land was later known as Bolgyn and today is Bolgie, located in the parish of Abbotshall, a little over ten miles southeast of Portmoak:

> With greatest veneration and devotion, King Macbeth gave to God and to St. Serf of Loch Leven and to the hermits there, to the servants of God [i.e., Céli Déi], [the land of] Bolgyne the son of Torfyny with all freedom and without the burden of the army of the king and his son or vicecomes and without tax of other things but charity and intercessory prayers.[35]

Once again there is the release from payments of various taxes to king, his son, and nobles. In this grant the reasons for the exemptions are so that the community can practice charity and devote themselves to prayer. Copies of medieval charters from before the twelfth century present some difficulties because copyists could make mistakes or translate words into modern forms. The latter happened in the grant of Bolgyne's land, where the term *vicecomes* (sheriff) refers to an office that dates after the eleventh century.

These two charters gave significant benefits to the monks. Gifts of lands provided food, fuel, and some rents in the form of foodstuffs or services. They were generous gifts, especially since the king and queen were losing a valuable source of income. The exemptions freed the monks from helping to build bridges and to provide men for the royal army. There was also the guarantee that their lands would not be hunted by the king or his family or subjects. All this was done so that the monks could devote themselves to religious exercises.

These brief and not entirely clear records of land transfer reveal some significant information about Macbeth's personal relationships. The first grant suggests the type of marriage enjoyed by Macbeth and Gruoch. There were various kinds of union, but this seems to be what was known among the Gaels as "Union with joint property" (OI *lánamnus comthinchuir*). Husband and wife contributed equally land, livestock, and household goods. The wife had the same status, "of equal lordship" (OI *be cuitehernsa*), as her husband so her consent was needed for any disposal of jointly held property.[36] Unique among Scottish charters is provision for the king's son. Many grants include children, either generally or specifically, in their notices, but none proscribe the behavior of a son of the prince. Curiously, a contemporary document that does address the king's son is a tract known as *Leges inter Brettos et Scottos*.[37] Almost nothing is known of this document other than its existence during the English occupation of Scotland in the early fourteenth century, when one of the ordinances of Edward I mentions it. The name of the tract suggests that it dates from the amalgamation of the Scottish and Strathclyde kingdoms in the eleventh century. This is a list of wergilds (*cró*) for various grades of status beginning with the king and continuing down the social scale to the freemen. Among them is the information that the *cró* for the king's son is the same as that for an earl.

Was this genuine piety or merely ostentatious gift giving? Pious charity was expected of Scottish queens and Gruoch would be in charge of the family's charitable acts. Malcolm Canmore's queen Margaret was famous for her bequests to churches and, in the next century her daughter-in-law Queen Sibyl, the wife of King Alexander I, gave the land of Beeth to the church of Dunfermline, which was valuable because it had a coal seam that supplied the abbey.[38] There was no need for Macbeth to make these grants and they were expensive. While any statement involving numbers is suspect for this era, there is a point worth noting. These are the only grants known to have been made by Macbeth. This is also the same number of grants that has survived for Malcolm Canmore, who is famed as the friend of the church.

The few surviving scraps of information about Macbeth's relations with the church suggest a man torn by conflicting interests. His patronage of the

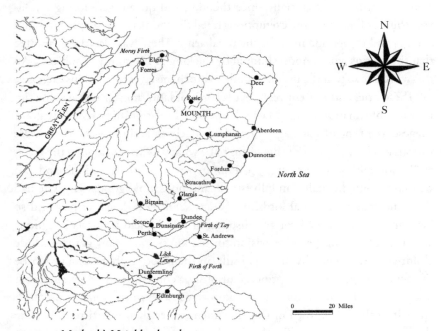

FIG. 3.2 Macbeth's Neighborhood.

Céli Dé of Loch Leven shows loyalty to a religious ideal. Even his Christian name was one that members of the order used to address one another. And yet he made a pilgrimage to Rome during the pontificate of a man avowedly a reformer and opponent of the antique vested interests represented by communities such as the Céli Dé. The new order of Pope Leo might explain Macbeth's generosity in relinquishing such a sweeping array of dues to the type of religious community of which the pontiff was critical. Macbeth threw away the dearest thing princes owned, tax revenues, as though they were careless trifles.

Lady Macbeth

Macbeth's wife Gruoch (Lady Macbeth as she is now known) was introduced in the previous chapter. She remains an intriguing individual whose modern fame overshadows what is known of the historical individual. The literary figure emerged only in the fifteenth century when she made an appearance as Macbeth's love interest in the history written by Andrew of Wyntoun. Gruoch is a phonetic spelling of Middle Irish Grúacach and pronounced Grūac due to internal lenition, in much the same way that Macbeth is a contracted form of Mac bethad.[39] *Grúacach* means "tresses" or "long haired"; later it acquired the meaning of "enchanter." The children of aristocratic parents were often fostered, usually until their fourteenth to seventeenth birthdays, as a means of making alliances among families. Gruoch probably had the customary education for a future noblewoman. According to the Old Irish legal tract "The Law of the Fosterage Fee" (OI *Cáin Íarrait*), the daughter of a king or a noble must be taught sewing, cloth-cutting, and embroidery.[40]

The charter concerning Kirkness gives some clues to Gruoch's ancestry. First, as was pointed out, that she is mentioned as donor suggests that her marriage was of the type known as "Union with joint property" (OI *lánamnus comthinchuir*) according to the Old Irish law tract "Law of Couples" (*Cáin Lánamna*).[41] Husband and wife contributed equally land, livestock, and household goods. The wife had the same status or "of equal lordship" (*be cuitehernsa*) as her husband so her consent was needed for any disposal of jointly held property.[42] The location of the donation offers a clue about her extended lineage. Kirkness (promontory of the church) is situated in the southeast of the parish of Portmoak about a mile southeast of Loch Leven and the village of Portmoak (MS *Pethmokanne*, the farm/field of Mochan). Since Macbeth came from farther north, the land probably belonged to Gruoch's family and she disposed of it as a "female heir" (OI *banchomarbae*). Women inherited family land only when their clan was in danger of extinction, that is, the male members were all dead. The death of her nephew on the orders of Malcolm II in 1033 is worth remembering in this context. The announcement of that death in the Annals of Ulster suggests that it was no commonplace murder; the Irish annals were obsessed with royalty.

Where did a queen's loyalties lie? Marriage did not replace a woman's allegiance to her family. Her immediate commitment was to her husband and children, but she had no obligations to any member of her husband's family, only her "birth" kindred. Discussion of loyalties leads to the question of whether Gruoch had a husband and child before Macbeth; the question of children with Macbeth is examined in Appendix 1. As is known from the pedigree in the afore-mentioned Bodleian manuscript Rawlinson B. 502, Macbeth's successor Lulach was the son of his cousin Gilla Coemgáin, and the fourteenth-century historian John of Fordun is the only medieval commentator to make a link between the two men when he calls them cousins.[43] What is less certain is whether Gruoch was married to Gilla Coemgáin and Lulach was her son, even though this is now accepted by scholars. The only evidence connecting them comes from the fourteenth-century Poppleton Manuscript (Paris BN,

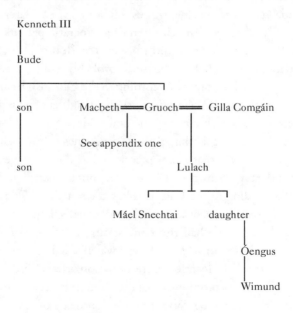

FIG. 3.3 Lady Macbeth's Family.

MS latin 4126, folio 30r.a) where Lulach is described as the nephew of the son of Buide (*Lulac nepos filii Boide*).[44] Buide, it will be remembered was the grandfather of a victim of Malcolm II in 1033. Since Gruoch was the daughter of Buide, her son would be her brother's nephew.

Ireland

The story of the badly behaved Irishmen inserted into the notice of Macbeth and Gruoch's donation of Kirkness and the other properties to the Céli Dé is a reminder that Macbeth's cultural world was oriented toward the west, to Ireland. His power and importance also appear to have extended among the O'Neill confederation. A hint comes from a poem written by the Irish poet and historian Fland (known as Flann Mainistrech) of the monastery of Monasterboice in County Louth, Ireland, who died on November 25, 1056, about nine months before Macbeth.[45] Among his poems on the important kings of Ireland was "Their deeds, their death-dealings, their devastations were manly" (*A ngluind a néchta a n-orgni batar infir*). There, Fland states that the mother of the fifth-century Irish king Muirchertach, son of Erc of the northern O'Neill clan of Cenél nEógáin, was popularly called Erc, but her true name was Erca and her father was Macbeth's ancestor Loarn: "By charm of his courtship [Muirchertach's father] won to wife Erc daughter of Loarn" (*dia beirt bindgil tuc Eirc ingin Loairn*).[46] This is incorrect. First, Muirchertach's fame meant that his genealogy was well known and that his father was Erc. Second, Erc was a man's name to which had been appended a feminine termination, -*a*-. Fland's novel interpretation persisted and is found in later works, such as the twelfth-century story "Violent death of Muirchertach son of Erca" (*Aided Muirchertaig meic Erca*).[47] Why did the northern O'Neill of Cenél nEógáin want to invent a family link with Macbeth's ancestors? A possible reason to make a connection, no matter how transparently fabricated, was to gain a powerful dynastic relationship and deter potential aggressors. All the O'Neill clans were in a period of obscurity during the eleventh century. Part of the reason was the meteoric rise to prominence of the southern Irish dynasty of O'Brien in the person of the famous Brian *bóruma* (Brian "of the cattle taxes"). Another reason was economic stagnation. With their capital in the Inishowen Peninsula in northwest Ireland, their success against the Vikings had condemned them to poverty. Continuing to rely on income from agriculture and the occasional purloining of the neighbors' cattle, the northernmost O'Neill families could only dream of the revenues flowing into the coffers of their rivals, such as Diarmait son of Donnchada Máel na mbó ("Servant of the cows," that is, cattle thief, d. 1072) of Leinster who controlled prosperous Viking towns on the eastern Irish coast. The O'Neill families might have desired to imitate their rivals and establish commercial ties with their neighbors to the east. Other reasons could be offered, but the appearance of Erca suggests that Macbeth's influence was not limited to northern Britain, but extended to Ireland.

Fabricated lineages were not limited to one dynasty, and a similar experiment appears to have been attempted with Duncan's family. During the eleventh century there appears a story called the "Birth of Brandub son of Eochu and Áedan son of Gabrán" (*Gein Branduib maic Echach ocus Áedáin maic Gabráin*) that claims ancestors of Duncan and those of the previously mentioned Diarmait were related.[48] The motif is twins switched at birth. Eochu and his wife Fedelmid are forced to flee into exile in Dál Riata to the king Gabrán and his wife, who is unnamed. The women deliver their children at the same time, but Fedelmid has twin boys while Gabran's wife has twin girls. Desperate for a son, Gabrán's wife urges an exchange of a boy for a girl with Fedelmid, who agrees. Before handing over her child, Fedelmid takes a piece of gold from the stem of her writing stylus and inserts it under the left shoulder blade of the child. When the children become adults, Gabrán's supposed son Áedan is king of Dál Riata while his brother, named Brandub, is king of Leinster. Áedan invades Leinster but is convinced to withdraw when the aged Fedelmid tells him his true parentage and extracts the piece of gold, which fits perfectly into her stylus. Composition of this story in Ireland rather than Britain is suggested by the author's knowing Fedelmid's name, but not the name of Gabrán's wife. Brandub was a dynast of Uí Cheinnselaig of southeast Leinster, the kingdom ruled by the aforementioned Diarmait.

Beginning of the End

For the final half dozen years of his reign, Macbeth became involved in complex English political affairs. The fourteenth-century writer John of Fordun was the first to claim that Duncan's son Malcolm Canmore fled from Scotland to England for fear of Macbeth. Later, he claims that Malcolm was living in England where he was found by Macduff, where the two men had their conversation on the morality of a king and then sought King Edward the Confessor to request troops. To understand this period, it is necessary to rehearse some history of the Scots' southern neighbor. The ruler of England since 1042, the year that Duncan's sons supposedly fled Scotland, was Edward "the Confessor" the son of AEthelred "the Unready." Edward had lived in exile in Normandy for a quarter century until 1041 when his half-brother Hardacnut, king of England and Denmark, the grandson of his father's conqueror, recalled him from exile. The death of Hardacnut in 1042 led to the restoration of the Old English royal family. Edward succeeded to the throne as a middle-aged man who was French to all appearances. He learned that succession to the kingship came at a price, an alliance with the family of Godwin of Wessex. Godwin's background is a mystery, and information about his origins was probably suppressed by his own family; there is the possibility that his father was a pirate named Wulfnoth. There is less obscurity about his career because Godwin owed everything to Cnut and was a tireless promoter of Danish interests. After the death of Cnut's last son Hardacnut, he was determined to keep the new king of the English under his control. He forced Edward to marry his daughter Edith, ensuring that his sons occupied the highest offices in the land.

Edward preferred the company of people from Normandy, and they came into the kingdom where they occupied various official posts. Edward's relations with his wife's family were formal rather than friendly as became apparent in the year 1051 when Edward's brother-in-law Eustace of Boulogne (the second husband of his sister Godgifu) traveled to England to visit him. When he and his entourage returned home by way of the port of Dover they stayed overnight in the town and demanded lodgings from the inhabitants. A fight broke out when a citizen of Dover refused to cooperate. At the end, about twenty men on either side had been killed. Eustace promptly returned to Edward and gave his account. Edward wanted to exercise rough justice and ordered Godwin to ravage the town. Godwin, however, refused to obey the king's wishes and his family was banished from the kingdom; the queen was sent to a convent. Godwin's son Harold fled to Ireland to the court of the afore-mentioned Diarmait of Leinster.

Resentment among the English against the Normans grew, and it was adroitly exploited by the supporters of Godwin and his sons, who posed as champions of "Englishness." Their tactics worked. The English aristocracy refused to fight on Edward's behalf when Godwin and his sons reappeared in the summer of 1052 and the king was forced to restore them to their former high positions. Among those arguing against the restoration of Godwin and his family were Edward's Norman friends. He had been appointing them to offices and lordships of various regions. One district was in the west where the earl of Hereford from 1050 to 1057 was Edward's nephew Raoul (anglicized as Ralph), the son of the king's sister Godgifu and her first husband Dreux, comte de Mantes. The castle of Raoul's soldier Osbern Pentecoste became a refuge for the Normans after the restoration of Godwin.[49] Osbern, together with his ally Hugh, had been stationed in the west to guard the Welsh border. With the return of Godwin, and bowing to public sentiment, they surrendered their castles and applied to Earl Leofric of Mercia for permission to travel through his lands to Macbeth's kingdom.[50] The Welsh border became even more unsteady after the exit of Osbern, Hugh, and their followers; English border guards were slain at Westbury the following year.

The reception of the Normans is an unexpected discovery in Macbeth's diplomatic relations. Edward's role in the emigration of Osbern is both obscure and interesting, especially since they were valuable troops. Their departure was orderly relocation, not frenzied flight, and there must have been an invitation from Macbeth. Macbeth needed those warriors because Duncan's sons were becoming old enough to challenge him for the kingship. Returning to John of Fordun's calculations, if Malcolm Canmore had been seven years old in 1042, then he was seventeen years old in 1052 and his brother Donald Ban would have been fifteen years old. Malcolm certainly had reached adulthood and Donald was not far behind.

Once again, Macbeth stands out from his peers in the Gaelic-speaking world. He was not the only warrior from the British Isles who traveled to Rome, but he seems to have been the only one to understand the change in warfare. His journey across the continent on the way to Rome took him through lands where cavalry was supplanting infantry. While in Rome he met a pope who was unsuccessfully fighting Norman knights, and Macbeth was too good a soldier not to see that warfare was changing. For a prince with modest resources, Macbeth saw the Normans as a way to redress the balance. As the attack on Durham in 1040 shows, he was familiar with cavalry. Scotland was famous for its horses and they were exported to Ireland where, according to the lists preserved in the *Book of Rights* (*Lebor na Ceart*), they were used in the diplomatic gift exchange between lords and subjects.[51]

Osbern, Hugh, and their friends remained in Scotland for a couple of years before they were given the opportunity to repay Macbeth's hospitality in 1054 when Earl Siward of Northumbria led an army into Scotland. Almost all the records agree that the aim of the incursion was to reinstate Malcolm into the kingdom. The Irish accounts remark on the carnage; the *Annals of Tigernach* claim the casualties were many while the *Annals of Ulster* claim that the Scots lost 3,000 men and the Anglo-Saxons had 1,500 dead including a warrior named Dolfin, son of Finntur. The earliest English accounts of this expedition come from two eleventh-century versions of the *Anglo-Saxon Chronicle* (versions C and D) that announce the invasion by land and sea as

King of All the Scots 79

a victory for Siward; version D gives the additional information of Macbeth's name together with Siward's son Osbern and nephew Siward as well as several of the king's bodyguard, the victor's seizure of a massive plunder, and that the battle was fought on the feast of the Seven Sleepers (July 27).[52] Less than a century later, the command for the battle is said by John of Worcester to have come from King Edward who sent Siward to attack in order to place Duncan's son Malcolm in the kingship of the Scots; among the slain were the Normans who had fled to Macbeth.[53] There are two variations on the account of the Anglo-Saxon Chronicle. One is David Powel's sixteenth-century *The historie of Cambria now called Wales* where he claims that King Edward personally led the troops, which can be set aside.[54] The second is found in the twelfth-century Anglo-Norman verse chronicle composed by Geoffrey Gaimar and known as *L'estoire des Engleis*.[55] Geoffrey claims that Siward and Macbeth had a peace treaty that the latter violated, and the expedition was retaliation for Scots raids into Northumbria. He continues with the claim that Siward divided his force into naval and land contingents, defeated Macbeth, and took plunder in the form of gold, silver, harnesses, and swords. The brusque narrative of the earliest accounts leaves open the possibility that Geoffrey Gaimair's connection of Siward's attack with cross-border raiding is accurate. Powel's claim of personal command by King Edward is unlikely and might be just a reworking of history in light of the Macbeth legend. John of Worcester might have been influenced by more recent history. By the twelfth century, Malcolm Canmore and his sons had become clients of the English kings. One of the duties of an overlord was to protect his vassals' interests. So writers such as John of Worcester were projecting the circumstances of their own day into the past.

This leads to another question: did Siward reestablish Malcolm in the Scots kingdom? The answer seems to be that Malcolm probably was in Scotland after the summer of 1054, if one follows the English records. As will be seen, the Scottish records agree that he attacked Macbeth at Lumphanan in Aberdeenshire in August 1057. If he led an army from the Scottish-English border, it would have been a distance of 183 miles and it is hardly likely that Macbeth would have tarried until his enemies were at the gates of his home. Had Malcolm been reinstated in his family's lands west of Stonehaven, he would have had to travel about twenty-seven miles from the fortress of Dunnottar. For the next three years a peace was maintained. Wariness at being trapped outside his main area of support could explain why the later Scottish king lists insist that Macbeth made his base of operations at Lumphanan on the edge of the Highlands. His fears were realized on August 14, 1057, when

Malcolm led an army to attack Lumphanan. If the object was murder of the king, the raid failed. Macbeth was wounded, according to the *Prophecy of Berchán*. He returned to Scone to prevent his rival from taking the ceremonial site and proclaiming himself king. While tradition claims that Macbeth traveled via the land route over the famed Cairn O' Mount, it is equally possibly that he took a water route on the river Dee to the North Sea, sailing along the coast to the Firth of Tay and then upriver to Scone. A water route would have been quicker than a land route, even though the distance would have been greater. But the king had suffered a fatal wound. A hurried journey back to Scone only made matters worse and the following day, according to the *Prophecy of Berchán*, Macbeth bled to death. His grave is unknown. Late medieval lists of Scottish kings claim that he was interred in Iona, but that is claimed for most princes up to Malcolm Canmore.[56]

Aftermath

The interpretation of the historical Mac bethad's reign depends on a few scraps of information, some from the chronicles and others from saga. Total reliance on either is unwise. Irish annals, for example, wrongly place the date of Macbeth's death among the events of the year 1058 and following the death of his stepson Lulach. Without the guidance of the chronicle of Marianus Scottus, there might be numerous learned essays suggesting that Macbeth killed Lulach as part of his villainous persona.

Macbeth was neither a terrible tyrant nor a slandered saint. His actions were fairly typical of his time and place. Unafraid to strike hard when the situation allowed, such as Crinán's rebellion, his marriage to Gruoch shows that he was capable of peaceful diplomacy. His piety was the kind expected from kings, as illustrated by the donations to the church of St. Serf's at Loch Leven. Even though Macbeth had many traits in common with his fellow princes, he was also original. He is the first known Scottish king to make a pilgrimage to Rome. His journey during the pontificate of a man who had personal connections with the Gaels suggests an element of deliberate timing. Macbeth was also the first to use mercenaries other than the peoples of the British Isles. His Normans were, of course, exiles from the court of Edward the Confessor, but Macbeth must have been in contact with them in order to secure their services. The absence of a subordinate king to rule either Cenél Loairn or Cenél nGabráin shows a political mind. Macbeth seems to have been aware of the successful accumulation of power by the kings of Wessex as they became the kings of all the English.

The most striking testament to Macbeth's reign was its quiet. The two texts that emphasize the tranquility of his reign—the *Prophecy of Berchán* and the *Verse Chronicle*—both show that calm for other princes was a scarce commodity. During his seventeen-year reign over all the Scots, Macbeth had two major incidents: the rebellion of Abbot Crinán and the invasion by Earl Siward in support of Malcolm Canmore. Since Siward was the kinsman of Malcolm, both were the type of clan feud found in Scots history. Only the second succeeded, and it was a partial victory with Malcolm still not king, the avowed goal of the exercise.

How did his subjects remember Macbeth immediately after his death? A rough, but informative, way of judging is by a name. Fashions in names changed throughout the Middle Ages. They were chosen from among saints or royalty, sometimes even the heroes of legend. The numerous Scots princes called Malcolm reflected admiration of the several Scots kings with that name. The opposite was also true and certain names were avoided because of unfortunate associations with unpopular persons. Moving several centuries into the future, the real name of the fourteenth-century King Robert III of Scotland was John. He changed it on his elevation to the throne because it had been the name of the despised King John Balliol who was remembered as a pawn of the English and later known as Toom Tabard ("Empty Shirt").

As noted earlier, the name Macbeth was not common, although not unknown, in Ireland, and King Macbeth is the first person known to have had that name in Scotland. In the generation after his death, however, the name Macbeth achieved a brief popularity. There were Bishop Macbeth of Rosemarkie, Macbeth of Liberton, Macbeth the thane of Falleland, Macbeth the son of Thorfinn (no relation to the jarl of the Orkney Islands), and Macbeth the son of Ided whose generosity to the church was recorded in the *Book of Deer*. There survive very few records from early Scotland, of course, and fewer than half a dozen examples is hardly a naming frenzy. Nonetheless, these were all important individuals whose families were extremely careful about details such as names. By comparison, in the great collections of Irish annals and genealogies that span from prehistory to the middle of the twelfth century, there is about the same number of men named Macbeth as there are for just the generation after his death in Scotland.

Why did Macbeth become a figure of legend? The question will be asked again, but for the historical period the answer is simple. Legend was one of the ways in which his culture remembered the past. Those tales were considered to be as valid as the monastic chronicles, sometimes even more so. Macbeth was judged by extremes. To his rivals he was the success that they wished to become. To his subjects, he was the prince who gave them the stability that was so valuable. Macbeth had fought to gain his kingdom, and he had to fight to keep it. How did he pass into legend? The following chapters offer some suggestions.

4

Fame and Defamation

BATTLEFIELDS ARE NOT the only places where conflicts are fought. The cliché that history is written by the winners underlines the combat that takes place in literature. Those skirmishes were fought in historical tracts or in folklore and from them emerged the legends connected with Macbeth, Duncan, and Malcolm Canmore. Once again the descendants of Malcolm Canmore were successful. In the literary works fashioned by their allies, the historical Macbeth was replaced by a literary character who suited their political agenda. Literary success, however, depended on historical circumstances. Malcolm Canmore and his descendants were fortunate to rule during a time that was later seen as a golden age of freedom and prosperity for the Scots. The warming period in the northern hemisphere was bringing increases in food production and population. Some foodstuffs were grown farther north than they had been for centuries and standards of living rose. Malcolm and his clan depended on English support, and (generally) good relations flourished between the Scots and English. Not so well remembered, except in the occasional chronicle entry, were the less attractive moments. Severity of conquest and a lack of compassion became hallmarks of Malcolm Canmore and his descendants.[1] To be fair, they would not have survived otherwise. Among the casualties were Macbeth's clan and his reputation.

Macbeth's prompt return to Scone after his battle with Malcolm allowed his stepson Lulach to succeed him. Lulach was a mature warrior who was at least twenty-five years old when Macbeth died in August 1057. He was married with children, and his son Máel Snechtai was king of Cenél Loairn nineteen years after his death; there was also a daughter whose name is not known.[2] Setting aside the casual disdain with which he is treated in the later medieval records, Lulach was an important individual both in his own day and for the next several generations. The genealogy of the Cenél Loairn

84 MACBETH BEFORE SHAKESPEARE

kings in the late twelfth-century *Book of Leinster*, composed about three generations after his death, is called the "Genealogy of Clan of Lulach" (*Genelach Clainde Lulaig*).

The political decline of Lady Macbeth's family accelerated during this period as they became Malcolm's prey. Lulach's reign was brief, little more than seven months, and he was slain on St. Patrick's Day (March 17) 1058 in a battle with Malcolm Canmore at Essie (west of Rhynie in Strathbogie). According to legend, a son of Macbeth's named Luath was buried about ten miles from the place of Lulach's death to the east of the town of Alford in Aberdeenshire.[3] Luath might be a collapsed form of Lulach, which leads to the possibility that the name of Macbeth's legendary son is actually a shortened form of the name of Macbeth's stepson. Despite armed conflicts that continued for decades, the cause of Macbeth's clan was lost on that St. Patrick's Day. Malcolm was a savage opponent whose ferocity was passed to his descendants. But this was not a complete victory, because the separatist nature of the Scots took hold and the northern Scots refused to accept him as king. When their next king is mentioned, he is Lulach's son Máel Snechtai. Máel Snechtai's reign over Cenél Loairn was a clear danger to Malcolm, who had to be on his guard against another invasion from the north. Like his step-grandfather, Máel Snechtai was a patron of the church and he gave Maldub's farm (Pett Malduib) to the church at Deer.[4] Religious piety did not protect him from attack, and in 1078 Malcolm led his forces north in a raid on Máel Snechtai's home.[5] The damage was impressive as Máel Snechtai's mother was captured as well as some of his men, his treasures, and cattle. Máel Snechtai escaped and, according to the Annals of Ulster, died in possession of his kingship when he happily ended his life in 1085. Nonetheless, Macbeth's clan was diminishing and even the Irish annals show scant interest in them.

Malcolm Canmore and his descendants became masters at destroying their rivals. Their labors bore fruit with the reunion of all the Scots during the reign of Malcolm's son David, but this harvest was bitter. The Canmore dynasty was engaged in almost constant warfare throughout northern Britain for the next two centuries. Military power was only one of their tactics. They also began a program of commercial enterprise that brought their kingdom into the northern European economy. A final stratagem was the manipulation of the historical records by their supporters. By the fourteenth century the hero, so to speak, of the Macbeth legend was his nemesis Malcolm Canmore; as the fortunes of Clan "Canmore" prospered, those of Macbeth's family fell.

Fame and Defamation 85

Malcolm the Conqueror

While much attention has been directed toward Macbeth, very little has been given to his foe Malcolm Canmore (correctly Máel Coluim mac Donnchada). Setting aside the character found in literature, who was the historical person?[6] A hint comes from an episode early in his career, not long after the battle with Lulach. Malcolm's best friend, described in the contemporary records as his "sworn brother," was Tostig the earl of Northumbria, a son of Earl Godwin of Wessex. They had met when Malcolm was an exile, possibly at the court of Edward the Confessor, the brother-in-law of Tostig (and the only member of his wife's family whom he liked). When Earl Siward of Northumbria died in 1055, a year after his invasion of Scotland, Tostig was given lordship over the earldom. Their close relationship notwithstanding, when Tostig made a pilgrimage to Rome in 1060, Malcolm devastated his lands. Despite this betrayal, there were no hard feelings. Tostig journeyed to Scotland in the summer of 1066 to meet with the Norwegian King Harald "Hardrada" and plan an assault.[7]

Malcolm's opportunistic behavior was not unusual amid the petty warfare and border raiding of the day. What is surprising is how little he repaid the generosity he received from his supporters. Not only had the English sheltered him, but troops from Northumbria had fought on his behalf against Macbeth. Even his personal relations meant little to him. Nothing changed after William of Normandy's conquest of England. Malcolm was considered to have so few scruples that the Normans believed the only way to limit his aggression was through taking hostages. One of these guarantees for Malcolm's good behavior was his son Duncan, who was in captivity for sixteen years and released after the death of William the Conqueror in 1087. Nevertheless, Malcolm raided Northumbria several more times.[8] Anecdotes from those campaigns reveal a vicious and devious captain. His raid in 1070, for example, caught Malcolm's victims off guard when he began in the west at Carlisle and followed the ancient Roman military road that served Hadrian's Wall rather than the usual northern route. News traveled quickly, however, and the natives hid. In order to lure his intended victims, Malcolm sent part of his army home so the inhabitants would think that he had departed and they could come out of hiding. When they did so, he pounced on them with the remainder of his force. A more illuminating episode comes during another incursion south of Hadrian's Wall in 1079. This was a slave and plundering expedition, pure and simple, whose targets were the wealthy church and community at Hexham. His attack was so relentless that when heavy fog briefly halted the devastation one morning, the weather conditions were thought to be divinely sent. Lest this anecdote be dismissed as character assassination by the English enemy, the story was told by Ailred of Rievaulx, the friend of Malcolm's son King David I and his former butler.[9]

Malcolm's relations with women display the same type of ruthlessness. His first wife was Ingibjorg daughter of Finn, also known as Ingibjorg "Earls' Mother." From Austråttborgen in Norway, Ingibjorg had a distinguished background.[10] Her father Finn was the military administrator (ON *Lendmann*) of the district and her mother Bergljót was the niece of St. Olaf. She had been married previously to Jarl Thorfinn of the Orkneys, with whom she had the future jarls named Paul and Erlend. She must have married Malcolm shortly after Thorfinn's death c. 1065 and presumably died before 1070; they had one son, Duncan.

Malcolm's second wife was Margaret, the great-niece of his patron Edward the Confessor. She had arrived in England from Hungary with her father, sister, and brother in 1057 and fled to Scotland as a refugee with her brother Edgar c. 1070 in the aftermath of the savage suppression of an Anglo-Saxon revolt by William the Conqueror.[11] There might have been a hint of compulsion behind Malcolm's offer of marriage, and the writer of this chronicle entry explains that it was accepted because "[Margaret's] brother could scarcely do other than grant the king's wish, for they were in his power."[12]

Malcolm employed an equally high-handed attitude in relations with his daughters Edith and Mary. The last time he saw them was in August 1093 when he traveled to England to confer with the English king William II Rufus. His daughters were at the convent at Romsey under the care of their Aunt Christine. Although Edith and Mary were not novices, they had been dressed in religious garb to discourage the amorous attentions of the wild soldiers of the neighborhood.[13] This did not please the king at all, for his daughters' main value was their future marriages as a part of the complex diplomatic bargaining of the day. Upon seeing Edith and Mary in the habits of nuns, Malcolm erupted in a fury. He ripped the veils from their heads and stamped them into the floor. A stormy interview with his sister-in-law concluded the visit. Malcolm, who had had about the same success with the English king, rode north with a mind full of dark thoughts. His first act on reaching Scotland was to summon his troops for yet another raid on Northumbria. This time the result was a disaster for the Scots as Malcolm fell in an ambush set by Robert de Mowbray at the river Alne where he was slain by Robert's steward Morel of Bamborough on November 13, 1093.[14]

Fame and Defamation 87

A glimpse into the personalities of Malcolm and Margaret is provided by the biography of Margaret that was commissioned by their daughter Edith after she had become the English queen and had changed her name to Matilda (which sounded more French).[15] She knew little about her mother and so asked someone identified only as T (believed to be Turgot, Margaret's confessor and later bishop of St. Andrews) to gather the bits of information that survived.[16] In addition to giving the expected expressions of Margaret's sanctity and wisdom, the text allows for a glimpse inside the Scottish court. The king and queen complemented each other with their talents. Malcolm was illiterate, but fluent in several languages. He had learned English during his years as an exile in England and probably French at the same time. So the king acted as translator for his wife and her non-Gaelic speaking visitors. Margaret was literate, and after reading sacred texts, discussed them with learned men. She was also a collector of manuscripts. Her biographer had been her agent in procuring volumes and building up a royal library. One of those volumes became a sign of her sanctity. Once when the queen was fording a river, a book that she was carrying fell into the water. The current carried it away, and the tome was given up for lost. Later, however, the book was discovered without any sign of damage from water. Unusually, the object of this miracle survives, and the story in Margaret's biography is confirmed by an inscription in the volume, which is known today as St. Margaret's Gospel.[17] Margaret's literary interest might explain why several historical pieces written during Malcolm's reign were designed to show him as the heir of the kings of both the Scots and Picts.

Malcolm and Margaret complemented one another, but their marriage had its unsteady moments. One source of friction was the family budget. Although he was illiterate, Malcolm could count and he spent very sparingly. Margaret, on the other hand, had a more lavish hand. She was also famous for being generous toward anyone in need. With her husband keeping a close eye on the household finances, the queen was forced to take valuable family objects in order to give alms to the poor. Malcolm soon discovered what Margaret was doing so he would set traps for her, and when she was caught in the act, he laughed at her pious thefts. Margaret also changed the physical appearance and personnel of the royal court. She had seen palaces that dazzled visitors with their splendor. So her first efforts were to transform a Celtic fortress into something that resembled the royal palaces she remembered from her youth. Introduced were silken cloths decorating the halls as well as new silverware and table settings together with plate made of gold and silver.

Malcolm was persuaded to turn his entourage of hired swords into something that resembled a palace guard.

New palace furnishings and charitable deeds required capital. One of the unsung aspects of Malcolm's reign was economic progress. He encouraged refugees from the Anglo-Saxon nobility to come to Scotland after the disaster of the battle of Hastings in 1066 and the subsequent failed rebellions of 1068 and 1069. Their familiarity with improved farming techniques and the commerce of village life was welcomed by a prince who depended on their output for some of his revenues. Margaret's biographer reflected her concerns about Scotland's economic difficulties by claiming that the queen encouraged commerce in her new home. She enticed merchants from diverse lands, who brought new items, such as cloths of various hues. Her son David was praised for continuing these innovations by his friend Ailred of Rievaulx who claimed that he made his subjects exchange their shaggy cloaks for fine clothes.[18]

Historical Writings: Motivations and Methods

The generations after the death of Macbeth saw a revival of interest in history. Part of this was due to the new families flooding into the island in the wake of the Norman Conquest. They were curious about their new home, and while satisfying their curiosity, they made history fashionable, in what has been called in another context "the cult of the antique by the masters of the land."[19] An example of their interest comes from a collection of materials gathered some time after the mid-twelfth century, but surviving in the fourteenth-century text known as the Poppleton manuscript.[20] There are lists of kings, extracts about northern Britain and its inhabitants from ancient authorities such as Isidore of Seville, the brief chronicle for the period c. 858 to 973 known as the "Scottish Chronicle," a tract on early political organization known as *De Situ Albanie*, and legends connected with the church of St. Andrews. Modern scholars owe a debt to this interest in the past because later transcriptions such as the Poppleton Manuscript preserve many ancient political, diplomatic, religious, and administrative records. A similar process is visible for ecclesiastical works, where fantasy and fact mingled. Materials about ancient saintly patrons were sought out and reworked to enhance the reputation of churches whose clergy were attempting to reform them. Ailred of Rievaulx wrote a new *vita* of Ninian of Whithorn, and the church at Glasgow employed a professional hagiographer named Jocelyn of Furness in the late twelfth century to write a new vita of its founder St. Kentigern that would be less liable to charges of heresy than its predecessor.[21]

Not all preservation was disinterested. Charters are an example of documents that, although used as historical texts, were originally utilitarian memoranda for transfer or confirmation of changes in ownership or use. Wars, deaths, and differing memories about the actual terms of land transfers meant that the courts were flooded with disputes over ownership. Charters were collected by landowners trying to keep their property or those who felt that the land belonged to them. Sometimes charters were gathered in anticipation of challenges, as was seen in the *Book of Deer* where information about Macbeth's family can be gleaned from the records of their land donations to the church of Deer.

Information about Macbeth and his rivals is found in performance pieces that are preserved in two texts surviving in Irish manuscripts. Since they describe Malcolm Canmore in terms that imply he was still alive, both items must have been intended to be recited at his court and completed prior to his death in 1093. They give an indication of Macbeth's reputation in the years immediately following his death. The first is a catalogue of kings with the uninspired modern name of "King List B" that is found in a mid-fifteenth-century Irish manuscript.[22] The piece begins with a list of Pictish kings followed by (without a break) the Scottish monarchs descending from Kenneth I. The recitation of princes is interrupted by the occasional aside, such as King Nechtan's donation of the church at Abernethy to St. Brigit or St. Columba's baptism of King Brude. Macbeth is the third name from the end and given the slightly abbreviated reign length of sixteen years.

The second work is a verse list called "The Scottish Poem" (*Duan Albanach*), surviving only in a seventeenth-century Irish transcription. Unlike the mere listing of names found in "King List B," "The Scottish Poem" is a counting poem extending from prehistory to the eleventh century. The first six quatrains are a brief synopsis of rulers in Scotland, beginning with the legendary figures Albanus and Brutus. There are references to the learned tales on the coming of the Gaels to Ireland, with mention of Conaing's Tower, and the arrival of the Picts. At the seventh quatrain starts the list of historical princes, first in Dál Riata and then the southern Scots kings of Cenél Loairn. Surprisingly, since the verses were intended to be recited to King Malcolm and his guests, the respect given to Macbeth is impressive:

> *Pure, wise Duncan reigned for six years,*
> *The son of Finlay [i.e., Macbeth] ruled for seventeen years.*
> *After famous Macbeth,*
> *There were seven months in the reign of Lulach.*

> *Malcolm is now the king,*
> *The handsome and lively son of Duncan;*
> *How long he will reign no one knows,*
> *Except the Learned One who is Learned [i.e., God].*[23]

Unsurprisingly, the poet reserved his choicest flattery for the still living Malcolm, whom he calls handsome and lively. Malcolm's father Duncan is given an equally generous appraisal as pure and wise. Macbeth is described as "the famous" (MI *co mblaidh*), while Lulach is included with his seven-month reign. A noteworthy feature of "The Scottish Poem" is its popularity in Ireland, and there is an explanatory stanza attached to the poem, giving an introduction to the verses for the enlightenment of an Irish audience. The poem might have been sent to Ireland along with the camel sent c. 1105 by the Scottish king (assumed to be Malcolm's son Edgar) to the Irish king Muirchertach Ua Briain.[24]

Lists of kings such as "The Scottish Poem" had a different purpose from the historical tales. The text is an administrative document in which the patron was set among the previous monarchs to show that he was their true heir and had a right to enjoy the kingship. Omitted or slandered are those men whose appearance might give a basis to competing families' claims on the kingship. An example is Lulach. The earliest lists such as "King List B" or the "Scottish Poem" simply give his name and reign length. When they were revised in the following centuries, his reputation suffered and, as will be seen, the king lists of the later Middle Ages call him Lulach *fatuus*, "Lulach the fool." The appearance of Macbeth and Lulach in "King List B" and "The Scottish Poem" is not necessarily a sign of Malcolm's generosity toward his rivals. Their reigns had occurred too recently to be ignored without comment, and many of the nobles associated with Macbeth had transferred their allegiance to Malcolm. In eleventh-century Scotland, as elsewhere, loyalty could be a matter of convenience rather than conviction.

Beginnings of the Legend of Malcolm Canmore

For two centuries after the death of Macbeth, his rivals in the family of Malcolm Canmore are popularly believed to have gone from strength to strength. Such a view depends on a selective reading of the surviving records. The reality was less tidy. For a year following Malcolm's death, his clan was in turmoil. First the kingship was seized by his brother Donald Ban. But there was another claimant, Malcolm's son Duncan by his first wife Ingibjorg.

Fame and Defamation 91

Duncan, it will be remembered, had been a hostage at the court of William the Conqueror as a surety for the good behavior of his father and he was released by King William II "Rufus" in 1087. Apparently, he so enjoyed his life at the English court that he remained. The succession of his Uncle Donald in 1093, prompted Duncan to ask for and receive military aid in the form of knights from the English king. In a quick campaign he fought his way into Scotland and seized the kingship.[25] His new subjects were less than happy to have him as king and they especially did not want Duncan's foreign troops. First they set an ambush for the king, which he barely survived. Then they agreed to accept him as king, but only if he would dismiss his alien knights. That was a disastrous decision. Once his supporters were gone, Duncan was killed and Donald Ban took the throne again. Donald ruled for several years and not very well. Stanzas in the *Prophecy of Berchán*, at that time being written by a third poet, specifically name him and claim that he abandoned Scotland to Vikings. More threatening were his nephews. In 1097 Edgar, another son of Malcolm, this time by his second wife Margaret, led a band of warriors (once again supplied by William Rufus) to Scotland. Donald was defeated again and permanently deposed. Now, thanks to the support of the English king, for almost two centuries, beginning with his sons—Edgar, Alexander I, and David—rule passed through the male line of the descendants of Malcolm Canmore.

The legend of Malcolm Canmore began to take form during the reigns of his sons. His English neighbors remembered Malcolm as a blood-thirsty maniac and their version of his career was not favorable. Two twelfth-century northern English works—the *History of the Kings* (*Historia Regum*) attributed to a monk of Durham named Symeon, and a chronicle compiled by Roger of Howden—have an unpleasant story concerning his death.[26] Roger includes more details, but they both say essentially that Malcolm's death in an ambush was a just judgment of God, who struck him down as vengeance for his career of butchery. Symeon and Roger made much of the fact that his reign was marked by raids into the north of England, of which there were five major invasions during the reigns of three kings of England. Their conclusion was that God had dealt with Malcolm exactly the same way Malcolm had dealt with his neighbors.

Malcolm's children, not surprisingly, promoted another interpretation, which became the basis for later histories. The historical revision began with Ailred of Rievaulx. Among his writings is "Letter on the Genealogy of the English Kings," a treatise on the lineage of the (soon-to-be) English king Henry II, in which he stressed the prince's Scottish antecedents (Henry was the great-grandson of Malcolm). In the "Letter" he tells a story about Malcolm Canmore.[27] Malcolm was at a banquet when he learned of an assassination plot by one of his nobles. Determined not to fall into an ambush, Malcolm invited the traitor to a hunting party. The king set the hunters to their various stations and insisted that the traitor remain with him. When the two men were alone, Malcolm produced swords and challenged the villain to a duel so that they could decide the matter like brave men. At this the wretched man fell to the ground and begged for clemency, overwhelmed by the king's courage. Malcolm showed mercy and forgave him. He was not entirely sure that the repentance would last, so the king insisted that hostages be sent to the royal castle to ensure good behavior. Ailred says that he was told the story by his friend King David, who seems to have been told the story as a very young boy by his father.

This anecdote illustrates the importance of the oral literary tradition. In common with the Irish "Learned Tales," these stories circulated at the highest levels of society. They also were shared among the lesser folk as their usual form of entertainment and in public performance at the *óenach*, a regional assembly of which a modern equivalent is the Highland Games.[28] There are only scattered references to oral literature in Scotland during this time. One of them concerns the visit to the court of Malcolm's son David by his friend Malachy the famous Irish bishop upon whom have been fathered a series of prophecies concerning the popes. Malachy entertained the king with stories about famous saints having an association with Scotland. One of these, according to Malachy, was the famous Anglo-Saxon St. Cuthbert, founder of the church at Lindisfarne, who he claimed had been born in Ireland.[29]

Rewriting History

Echoes of this revision carried to a land where Malcolm's children were influential: England. Around the year 1136, a teacher in the schools at Oxford named Geoffrey of Monmouth claimed to have translated into Latin an old book written in Welsh that had been given to him by his friend Walter the Archdeacon. The book was called *History of the Kings of Britain* (*Historia Regum Britanniae*) and became one of the most influential works of its day. A fictional account of the kings of Britain from a mythical figure called Brutus up to the settlement of the Anglo-Saxons, this is the volume that began the popularity of legends about King Arthur and his court.

Efforts to destroy the historical reputation of Macbeth's homeland are visible in the *History of the Kings of Britain*. There is, for example, an episode in

Fame and Defamation 93

which the Scots and Picts besiege Arthur's nephew Hoel in the city of Alclud (modern Dumbarton Rock northwest of Glasgow). Arthur leads his army to raise the siege. The attackers are defeated and flee north to Moray, described as a wild and barbarous region, where they take refuge in Loch Lomond. As Arthur gathers boats for a siege, the Picts and Scots are unexpectedly relieved by a fleet led by Gilmaurius (MI *Gille Maire*, "Servant of [the Virgin] Mary"), the king of Ireland. Arthur defeats the Irish and they sail home, after which begins the extermination of the Scots and Picts. The slaughter ends when the bishops and clergy of Moray confront the king with their most precious holy relics and petition him to stop the bloodshed. Arthur pardons the survivors and returns home. In a ceremony at York, he gives the kingdom of the Scots to Auguselus, the rule of Moray to his brother Urian, and the dukedom of Lothian to Loth.[30] This political division in a work of literature suggests how the family of Malcolm Canmore wanted the past to be remembered. There could not be a denial of two kingdoms among the Scots; that fact was too recent. So there had to be a slight reordering of the political geography. The kingship of Scotland was reserved for King David's family, while the "other" kingship was confined to a savage wilderness called Moray, Macbeth's home.

The horror of Geoffrey's "Moray Massacre" is relieved by a digression on the miraculous nature of Loch Lomond; it is claimed that the lake has sixty islands with sixty streams feeding it and sixty crags with sixty eagles' nests. Like Duncan's horses in Shakespeare's drama, the eagles were prophets. Geoffrey claims that they screamed in concert before any momentous event. When Hoel remarks on the curiosity of the lake, Arthur tells him that a nearby pool was four hundred feet square with four different types of fish dwelling in each of the four corners. These observations on local curiosities belong to the genre of "wonder" stories in which supernatural aspects are credited to geographical features. Stories about marvels were a literary fashion when Geoffrey was writing, and they appeared in sober histories in the British Isles and beyond. A generation earlier, Bishop Patrick of Dublin (died 1084) had written a brief treatise called "The Wonders of Ireland" that was filled with (so to say) miraculous pools and strangely behaving animals.[31] Geoffrey's harsh critic Gerald of Wales repeated many of those stories in his *History and Topography of Ireland* a generation later.[32] Geoffrey, for his part, had borrowed the Loch Lomond episode from the ninth-century *History of the Britons* by Nennius, where the lake is Loch Leven, in Fife, with a single river and eagles' nests on every rock, but there is no mention of the birds screaming.[33] Geoffrey merely relocated the action closer to Dumbarton, probably because he mistranslated the original. The pool with the clannish fish might also owe something of its origin to

Nennius, who claims that Lough Lein in Ireland is surrounded by four circles made of four different metals: tin, lead, iron, and copper.

Arthur's slaughter of the Picts and Scots reflects Geoffrey's dislike of both groups. This aversion probably was intellectual rather than personal because Geoffrey is unlikely to have known any Scots beyond a few aristocrats who were part of the francophone elite. Certainly he would have known no Picts. This disdain probably traces back to the sixth-century Gildas's *Ruin of Britain* that mentions invasions of the Britons by combined forces of Pictish and Scottish raiders.[34] If so, Geoffrey understood only half of his source since Gildas meant "Irish" when he used the Latin term Scoti. By Geoffrey's day the term was limited to the Gaelic speakers living in Britain, while the inhabitants of Ireland were Hibernenses. Geoffrey's literary malice reveals only the vaguest idea of anything connected with Scotland or the Scots, as seen by placing Loch Lomond near the Moray Firth when it is actually just north of the Firth of Clyde. He knows only a few other Scottish places—Lothian, Caithness, Calidon (for Caledonia, the Latin name for Scotland), Calatria (the Carse of Falkirk), and the Maidens' Castle (the old name for Edinburgh Castle)—all current during Geoffrey's life.[35] Lothian and Caledonia were well-known names, while Caithness was the name of a recently established bishopric; the road from Totnes to Caithness ran the length of Britain according to Geoffrey's contemporary Henry of Huntingdon. Calatria appears several times in twelfth-century Scottish charters, and the Maidens' Castle is mentioned in the biography of Malcolm Canmore's Queen Margaret. But there is no doubt that so far as Geoffrey was concerned, the wicked Picts and Scots came from Moray.

Where did Geoffrey get his information? If the "old book" of Walter the archdeacon was not his sole source of information, then another possibility is the family of Macbeth's enemy Malcolm Canmore. Malcolm's daughter Matilda had been the queen of England and raised her younger brothers Alexander and David after the deaths of their parents. Matilda's daughter, the Empress Matilda (so-called because of her marriage to the Holy Roman Emperor Henry V), was the half-sister of King Henry's illegitimate son Robert of Gloucester, the patron of Geoffrey of Monmouth. Geoffrey was well placed to be acquainted with these men, for he was an individual with good connections to powerful individuals, which helped him to become bishop of St. Asaph's (in North Wales).

Among these aristocrats, the defamation of one's opponents was a standard tactic. In addition to the gossip circulating around the noble courts, there was the practice of slandering an enemy before a battle. A selective historical

Fame and Defamation 95

memory and a flexible interpretation of truth were useful on such occasions. An illustration of this comes from another individual accustomed to moving among exalted company: the historian Henry of Huntingdon. He claims that when Robert of Gloucester was preparing to attack the forces of King Stephen at Lincoln in 1141, he listed his adversaries by name and rallied the troops with an account of their wickedness.[36] Henry was not present at the battle, so he must have learned the details some time later, but he would not have strayed too far from the truth since his audience would include men who had been at that battle.

Returning to the question of Geoffrey's source of information, most of his northern British material probably came from King David of Scotland and his entourage. Warriors traveled widely during the twelfth century and their knowledge of the world stretched from Jerusalem to Iceland. David was also a major landowner in England after marrying a wealthy widow named Matilda of Northampton and Huntingdon. Apart from his brother-in-law King Henry, he was probably the wealthiest individual in Britain.[37] He was often resident in his southern estates, where contemporaries sought him out for his skills as a lawyer. When the army of Moray invaded as far south as Strathcathro in 1130, David was in England, so his nobles mounted the defense. As relatives and supporters of the Empress Matilda, King David and Earl Robert were frequently in contact.

King David was also an avid antiquarian who loved old stories. According to William of Newburgh, he purchased a cup that purportedly had been the property of a mysterious green man who had emerged from a burial mound.[38] Antiquarianism occasionally had other uses. When David was the lord of Strathclyde during the reign of his brother Alexander, he had gathered together information about the ancient bounds of the diocese of Glasgow founded by the early medieval St. Kentigern, which was presented to his nobles at an *inquistio* or an official inquiry. This information was used to determine the current boundaries of the see of Glasgow and to ensure that the bishop did not attempt to claim jurisdiction outside his diocese.[39] There is a connection with Geoffrey of Monmouth's *History of the Kings of Britain* in that all the place names he mentions had some connection with King David. Caledonia is obvious. The Castle of the Maidens (Edinburgh Castle) was David's childhood home, the place where his mother had died, and the site of his beloved private garden. Calatria was the home of an aristocrat named Dufoter (probably for MI Dub Ottir or "dark Ohthere") who was a member of the royal entourage and a witness when David gave his estate of Perdyc to Glasgow Cathedral.[40] The earliest known bishop of Caithness, Andrew, was a frequent visitor to the royal court and one of the informants for the geographical tract *De Situ Albanie*.[41] Finally, Loch Lomond was part of the ancient kingdom of Strathclyde, while the prophetic value of the eagles' cry is something that would interest a royal antiquarian such as King David.

Moray had a special place in David's nightmares because it was the home of his family's ancient rivals. Not only had a prince from Moray killed his grandfather King Duncan I, but its army invaded his lands in 1130 and a bishop of the Isles named Wimund (see below) justified his attacks on David's lands by claiming to be a descendant of Lady Macbeth's great-grandson. Geoffrey's story, then, can be one example of how Moray was the target of vilification by the dynasty of Malcolm Canmore. The inhabitants of Moray are shown as savages who attack the weak and flee from the strong. The place names included in this section of the *History*, together with the unique bits of folklore, point to someone native to Scotland but someone unusually well-traveled with an antiquarian interest. Was that someone King David of Scotland or a member of his entourage? The Moray episode is another instance of history written by the winners.

The Old Order Fades Away

Geoffrey of Monmouth's *History of the Kings of Britain* is one of several indications that the collapse of Macbeth's family coincided with a major cultural change among the Scots. By the twelfth century the world of Macbeth and Malcolm Canmore was seen as backward and old-fashioned. Nobles with Gaelic names such as Rory (Ruaidrí) of Mar continued to be important, but King David's personal friends all had French names. This brought its own snobbery. Because his elder brother Alexander spoke French with an accent, the francophone aristocracy dismissed him as a semi-savage. David, on the other hand, spoke perfect French and was considered one of them by the lords and ladies who dominated England and were moving into Scotland under his patronage.[42]

Churches were not exempt from change. Modernization was done by individuals who had been trained in the aftermath of the reforms begun by Pope Leo IX, although they are called the Gregorian reforms after his successor Pope Gregory VII. One reform was replacement and reorientation of the hereditary Celtic clergy that Macbeth had supported. In Ireland, the "heir" of St. Patrick took a new title in the twelfth century when he was called the bishop of Armagh. New and innovative reformed religious orders began to replace the traditional *familia* (family) of a saint. Malcolm and Margaret are credited with establishing monks of the Benedictine Order at Dunfermline, while their son Alexander (reigned 1107–1124) founded a house of canons regular (priests living under monastic discipline) of the Order of St. Augustine at the royal inaugural center of Scone. The old ascetic order of the Céli Dé at St. Andrews battled (unsuccessfully) to maintain its place in the church. Macbeth's patronage of the Céli Dé at Loch Leven, in Fife, did not help the community, and they were summarily expelled c. 1150, while their library of liturgical texts was catalogued and given to the community of Augustinian canons at St. Andrews. When the clergy of the church of Deer petitioned King David for permission to keep their lands around 1130, they brought to him the church's Bible with the land grants written in Gaelic and arranged in the older form of notes. David, however, had his confirmation charter written in Latin in the new diplomatic style.

The change of orientation for the churches within Scotland was made within a generation. When the so-called *Chronicle of Holyrood* (probably composed at Coupar Angus) was being written in the late twelfth or early thirteenth century by a monk of the newly introduced Cistercian Order, the chronicler began Scottish history with the death of King Alexander I in 1124. A contemporary chronicle called the *Chronicle of Melrose*, maintained at the monastery of that name in Lothian, follows an exemplar similar to the northern English record known as Symeon of Durham's *History of the Kings*, and its first unique item of Scottish information is the death in 1130 of Angus of Moray in the battle of Stracathro. For these newcomers, the history of Scotland started with the family of Malcolm Canmore.

Fashion extended to warfare. As Macbeth demonstrated with his hospitality to the Normans expelled from England, cavalry had become the preferred method of fighting, and infantry was reserved for peasants or savages. Macbeth's kindred of Cenél Loairn continued to maintain a contingent of mounted warriors and, c. 1116, a raiding party made an unsuccessful attempt to capture Malcolm Canmore's son King Alexander I. The attack was so incompetently executed that Alexander chased his enemies back into their own land. Finally, in 1130, Cenél Loairn tried one last time to overthrow their southern rivals. Led by Lulach's grandson Angus, the invading force marched south to Stracathro. The old-style Celtic raid in which a band of intrepid warriors attacks deep into the heart of their rivals' territory was revealed as obsolete when the army was confronted by a group of Norman warriors that David I had introduced into Scotland; they completely destroyed Angus's army. The victory was even more impressive because David was not even in the kingdom at the time.

David began the pacification of his rivals' lands when he returned to Scotland. Those who wished to survive needed to accommodate the new master of the land. Among them were the clerics of the church of Deer, whose representatives met the king at Aberdeen. The clergy wanted to keep their lands and privileges, and to do that they needed the blessing of the new power. King David was happy to oblige. The victory at Stracathro already had made the point that his army was to be feared. But he had no wish to fight an expensive war of attrition far from his center of power around the Firth of Forth. So (he might have thought) let the monks keep their fields, farms, and privileges. They could show their appreciation with sermons on the theme of complying with God's plan in His choice of earthly rulers, and the choice of the moment was David. The last charter in the *Book of Deer* shows a conqueror who could afford to be generous: "King David of the Scots to all his true men, greetings. Let all of you know that the clerics of Deer are quit and free from all secular officials and payments, as is written in their book." The old order was gone, and the church of Deer had bowed to the new regime.[43]

As the army from Moray learned at Stracathro in 1130, the Celtic warrior was becoming an antiquarian curiosity rather than an effective fighter. In a direct confrontation on level ground, the lightly armed warrior was no match for the heavily shielded cavalry. The contrast was clearly made at the Battle of the Standard, fought in 1138.[44] David invaded England in support of his niece Matilda's claim to the English throne against her cousin, and David's nephew, King Stephen. The Scottish army was devastated as its mix of a few knights and many more archaic native soldiers confronted the modern cavalry directed by Archbishop Thurstan of York. An account of the battle particularly mentions David's soldiers from Galloway, fighting with little protection and unsuccessfully against the armored knights.

When David died on May 24, 1153, full of years and honors, the kingship of all the Scots was inherited by his young grandson Malcolm IV, better known as Malcolm "the Maiden" because of his reputed lifelong virginity; his lieutenant was a younger brother who would become known as William the Lion. The break with the past was accelerating. Malcolm had the family name "Servant of Columba," yet his brother had the French name William (Guillaume). The boys wanted to be knights. When they finally persuaded their distant cousin King Henry II of England (who had been knighted by their grandfather) to perform the ceremony, he agreed only after divesting the young Scots of the northern English counties that had been surrendered to King David. Despite the fury of their nobles at the poor bargain, the imitation of all things foreign continued briskly, but not uniformly. Administration,

Fame and Defamation   99

buildings, and even clothing all imitated the styles found to the east of the Scots, rather than the west. This proved to be a boon for the historian, because among the new fashions was the keeping of records in greater abundance.

The clan of Macbeth and Lady Macbeth, such as it had been, was broken, but not entirely eliminated. For the rest of the twelfth century various individuals appeared who claimed to be their heirs, such as "Fair" Donald MacWilliam who led rebellions throughout the north into the thirteenth century. Pretenders appeared in unlikely places, and one of the most colorful was a bishop of the diocese of Sodor (the Isle of Man and the Hebrides) named Wimund.[45] Originally he had been a monk of the newly founded Abbey of Furness in what is now Cumbria, a house at that time part of the Congregation of Savigny, one of the new reformed monastic orders. Sometime in the second quarter of the century, King Olaf "Little Bit" (ON *bitling*) Godredsson of the Isles asked for monks from Furness to establish a daughter house on the Isle of Man. He also wanted them to provide a bishop for the diocese of Sodor from their ranks. Wimund was among the monks sent to the Isle of Man to assist in setting up a new church. There, his eloquence so impressed the Manx that they chose him to be their bishop. Wimund agreed, but after his consecration he began to behave less like a bishop and more like a pirate king. He returned to Britain and gathered a warrior band, "not as a shepherd guarding his flock, but as a wolf seeking his prey," in the words of the chronicler William of Newburgh, who was acquainted with him.[46] Wimund justified his actions with the claim that he was a freedom fighter, not a brigand, and a descendant of Lady Macbeth through her great-grandson Angus. His military career ended when he was captured, blinded, and castrated. Although the punishment sounds horrific (and it was), this was the gentle treatment meted out to members of a royal family. Commoners were simply killed. The old reprobate was sent to live out his days at the monastery of Byland where he fascinated the young William of Newburgh. William thought his claims of royal ancestry were fiction (he maintained that Wimund was really English), but he was fond of the old rascal and recorded Wimund's final boast: "Had I the eye of a sparrow, my enemies would have no reason to rejoice!"

The last act in the destruction of Macbeth's kingdom was played out early one morning in the year 1230, when a man carried an infant girl into the middle of the market in the town of Forfar. Standing before the market cross he made a public proclamation. Treason had been attempted against the king, and the penalty for that crime was death. This unnamed infant was guilty of the crime of having as her father "Fair" Donald MacWilliam, who rebelled against the current king, Malcolm Canmore's great-great-grandson,

Alexander II. Rumors that Donald had the blood of Lady Macbeth's son Lulach flowing through his veins enticed people to support him in rebellion, but it failed and the victors took a bloody revenge. The child was seized by the legs and her head smashed against the column of the cross.[47] Another threat to the dynasty of Malcolm Canmore had been eliminated. From the killing of Lulach until their own male line became extinct at the end of the thirteenth century, the House of Canmore left a bloodstained trail behind them while bringing the north of Britain under their control.

Political Union and Historical Revisionism

The Canmore dynasty prospered because its members were successful at the politics of their day. Malcolm Canmore's descendants unified Scots into one kingdom by an adroit mixture of diplomacy, intimidation, and military might; they justified their actions through a selective reading of history. The twelfth century was the most productive of all times for the aggrandizement of the Canmore clan. Galloway, Caithness, Sutherland, Moray, and, at one time or another, northern England from Penrith to the river Tyne were of their domain. The price for such expansion was conflict, which did not end until the last years of Alexander III. There were setbacks, and among the losses were the lands of northern England and, more important, the Hebrides. That island chain had been ceded to the Norse King Magnus "Barefoot" (Magnús III Óláfsson) in 1098; he was mainly responsible for assembling the Norwegian colonial empire that extended from the Shetland Islands in the north as far south as the Isle of Man.

Image and public opinion were equally important in the Middle Ages as in the modern world, and the consequences of an unfavorable assessment were more severe. To take a non-Scottish example, the successful portrayal at the papal court of the Irish clergy as incompetent led to the issue of the bull *Laudabiliter* by Pope Adrian IV and the justification for the subsequent English invasion of the island. Fashion in princes had changed in the twelfth century, and a king needed to demonstrate those qualities considered especially Christian: kindness to the weak, mercy to those who asked for it, and piety toward the Church. The representation of Malcolm and his sons as tough fighters—better warriors and more clever than their enemies—had to be balanced. This led Malcolm's descendants to revise his public image. They did not want to ignore the battle victories or savage destruction of his foes, which were useful in giving potential adversaries reason to pause before attacking. But the old king needed to be shown to the world as more than a killer. So

Fame and Defamation

Malcolm's transition into an acceptable type of monarch came at the expense of Macbeth's homeland, which was portrayed as a wilderness populated by barbarians. This marked the beginning of the famous "Highland/Lowland" divide that would split Scottish society for centuries.

Crucial to the successful princely family was a favorable representation in stories. Ailred's anecdote about Malcolm and the traitor, passed on from King David, emphasizes how popular entertainment was an important avenue for historical memory. While it is fortunate for later scholars that he preserved the story in writing, it is important to remember that he heard it directly from the first man of the kingdom. Was the episode true? Apparently Ailred was satisfied as to its verity and so was his audience. A more conclusive example on the importance of literature in the creation of history comes from the late thirteenth century, when Edward I of England was asked by the Scots to judge among the more than a dozen candidates for the kingship. Edward I was unsure of his legal status and sent a famous summons to the monasteries for information about relations between the Scots and the English. In their replies, the single most frequently cited "historical" text was Geoffrey of Monmouth's *History of the Kings of Britain*.

5

Not the Beginning of the Legend

BY THE LATE Middle Ages, the eleventh to thirteenth centuries were seen as a golden age of freedom and prosperity for the Scots. This coincided with the supremacy of the House of Canmore, which shared in the reflected glow. Forgotten were the raids by Malcolm Canmore and his sons for captives, loot, and the elimination their rivals. Conversely, those centuries had been disastrous for Macbeth's clan of Cenél Loairn. Despite rebellions that continued for decades, their cause was lost, and they came under the command of their southern rivals. As was seen with Geoffrey of Monmouth's *History of the Kings of Britain*, literature reflected the political situation. For those who knew the north only through Geoffrey's writings, Macbeth's territory around the Moray Firth was a savage wilderness, and its inhabitants were howling barbarians. That perception of savagery eventually led to a new assessment of Macbeth.

Fergus of Galloway

Blending history with fantasy was not unique to the legend of Macbeth, and a brief examination of an earlier historical/fantasy biography is instructive. A work now known as the *Romance of Fergus of Galloway* uses the characters of Arthurian legend in a story with a Scottish setting.[1] In common with the legend of Macbeth, the hero Fergus is based on a historical person. Little is known of the career of the real Fergus of Galloway. The romance (and modern scholarship) places his home at an earthen-work fortress near modern Cruggleton in Wigtownshire. There is only speculation about Fergus's parentage or even the name of his wife, but he had three important children.[2] His daughter Affrica was the wife of Olaf "Little Bit" (ON *bitling*), king of the Isle of Man and the Isles while Fergus's sons Uhtred and Gilbert succeeded

Not the Beginning of the Legend

him in Galloway. Affrica's son Godred was later king of the Isles (reigned 1152–1158 and 1164–1187). A royal connection did not spare Fergus from attacks. In either 1152 or 1153 there was an unsuccessful invasion of Galloway from the Isle of Man. In retaliation for their defeat, the Manx either killed or expelled all the Galwegians on their island. When King Malcolm IV traveled to Toulouse to be knighted by his cousin, the English king Henry II, and gave Cumberland and Westmorland as the fee, Fergus was among those outraged. On the king's return, Fergus and five other lords besieged Malcolm at Perth in 1160. Malcolm retaliated with three invasions of Galloway, and Fergus left his domain to enter religious retirement in Holyrood Abbey, which was probably the price he paid to prevent the forfeiture of his lordship. His spiritual awakening need not have been feigned. He is associated with the foundation of two religious houses. One is the Premonstratensian Abbey of Soulseat, in Wigtownshire, which might be the *Viridium Stagnum* (Green Loch) founded by St. Malachy in 1148. Whether or not he was actively involved in the foundation of the Cistercian abbey at Dundrennan in 1142, which usually is credited to King David I, his cooperation would have been necessary. Fergus died on May 12, 1161.

Fergus's family continued to hold power in Galloway for several generations and the *Romance of Fergus* might have been composed for his great-grandson Alan sometime after the year 1200. The story was written by someone who either was a native of or had lived in Scotland; there are too many specific place names and topographical details to suggest authorship by anyone unfamiliar with the kingdom. The surviving story is written in medieval French and at its conclusion the author calls himself "Guillaime." One candidate for authorship is William Malvoisine, the chancellor of King William the Lion. He was French and traveled round the kingdom as a royal official.[3] William was elected bishop of Glasgow in the fall of 1199, consecrated at Lyon by Bishop Reginald de Forez of Lyons, and translated to the bishopric St. Andrews in 1202; he died on July 9, 1238. Glasgow cathedral is just seventy miles north of Fergus's fortress. This speculation, however, must remain as such; there was more than one "Guillaime" in Scotland and there is no other indication that William Malvoisine was an author.

As part of the Arthurian canon, the *Romance of Fergus* has similarities with the legend of Percival. Fergus lives in a ramshackle castle with towers made of turf on the coast of the Irish Sea. One day he sees Arthur's court on a hunt and desires to join the knights. Taking his antique weapons (a knotted scourge, smoke-blackened spear, old shield, six short spears, and an axe) he goes to Arthur's encampment. Fergus is mocked when his disheveled appearance is compared with that of the stately knights. To prove himself worthy, Fergus goes on an adventure. He drinks from a spring close by a chapel guarded by a dwarf who foretells his future and then goes to Dunnottar Castle to seize a shield that is guarded by a hag. Afterward he boards a ship for Lothian, where he discovers that his true love Galiere is held captive in her castle by the giant of Melrose Mountain. All this time, Arthur has had his court hunting for Fergus.

As we shall see, there are incidental parallels between the *Romance of Fergus* and the legend of Macbeth. Both men were portrayed as coming from primitive regions and both are doughty warriors. Their actions are influenced by fantastic beings. The hag/witch in *Fergus* is a guardian while Macbeth's witches/hags/weird sisters are prophetesses. *Fergus*, too, has a prophet of sorts in the dwarf at the chapel. In either tale, the historical figure is submerged in the fantasy element. Perhaps the most significant feature of *Fergus* is the rapidity of its appearance. There was little more than a generation between the death of the historical Fergus in 1161 and the writing of the romance c. 1200. There is possibly one other similarity: longevity in drama. A later medieval play known as "The Funeral of the Virgin Mary," part of the medieval York Corpus Christi play cycle, has a character called Fergus whose hand remains attached to the Virgin's coffin. The name is otherwise unknown in pageant literature, and the model might have been based on Fergus of Galloway.[4]

The Verse Chronicle

By the thirteenth century, the world of Macbeth had become a matter of interest only to those few eccentrics who delighted in studying the past, and Macbeth was only one name among many. This is clearly seen in a long poem in Latin elegiac couplets now called the *Verse Chronicle* that is a catalogue of Scottish kings from the ninth-century Kenneth I to (in the longest version) the thirteenth-century Alexander III. The *Verse Chronicle* survives in four medieval texts that show how selective was the preservation of information. The earliest version is in the thirteenth-century manuscript of the Chronicle of Melrose (BL Cotton MS Faustina B. ix) where the verses are written in the margins beside the entry for the relevant king up to the death of King William in 1214. The second text is Oxford, Bodleian Library Bodley MS 302 (f. 138ff), which has the only text of the poem as a single piece and concludes with the beginning of the reign of Alexander III. Andrew of Wyntoun's early fifteenth-century *Original Chronicle* uses the chronicle as far as the reign of Lulach, while Walter Bower's later fifteenth-century *Scotichronicon* incorporates a version that went as far as the beginning of the reign of Alexander II.

The *Verse Chronicle* notes that Macbeth's reign was distinguished by an abundance of food and his demise is described as a "cruel death":

> From [Bethoc] was born Duncan by name,
> An elderly king of Scotland.
> Macbeth, from Finlay born, struck him;
> The king died at Elgin from a lethal wound.
> Macbeth was king of Scotland for seventeen years,
> His reign was a bountiful time.
> Then he was cruelly beheaded at Lumphanan,
> By the child of Duncan named Malcolm.
> Unhappy Lulach was king for three months,
> By weapons the same Malcolm killed him.
> The fated man was in Strathbogie, in Essie,
> Alas, the careless, wretched king was killed.[5]

Macbeth is given a generous interpretation and he is presented as a good king. Even his stepson Lulach receives a polite mention in the *Verse Chronicle*, and his fatal affray with Malcolm Canmore is described as incautious. The connection of Macbeth with abundant food is an aspect of sympathetic magic that evaluates a king's reign by its prosperity. Mention has been made of the excerpt from the *Prophecy of Berchán* that seems to be from the Scottish king-making ceremony of the tenth century when the reign of King Constantine II (reigned 900–943) is described as "with plenty of milk and corn." In Irish literature the prosperity of a king's reign was crucial to his reputation. The prosperity of the reign of Conaire, the hero/anti-hero of the early medieval Irish classic *The Destruction of Da Derga's Hostel* (Togail Bruidne Dá Derga) is noted by the seven ships that arrived every summer at *Inver Culptha* (mouth of the river Boyne at Drogheda) together with plentiful food.[6] The wisdom tract associated with the legendary Irish king Cormac mac Airt claims that the reign of a good king had plentiful food together with the arrival of trade goods.[7] The seventh-century Irish tract known as the *Testament of Morann* (Audacht Moraind) states that there was an abundance of grain and the land was fertile during the reign of a good ruler, while the contemporary *Twelve Abuses of the Ages* (De Duodecim Abusivis Saeculi) explains at length that the king's justice is the fertility of the land and the same idea is found in the legal tract *Collection of Irish Church Law* (Collectio Canonum Hibernensis).[8]

As versions of the *Verse Chronicle* were being written, there was also the composition of lists of monarchs known as king lists. The monarchs appear in the order of succession with the length of their reigns and occasionally a historical item. Some important ones for the study of Macbeth have been discussed earlier, such as the *Prophecy of Berchán*, "King List B," and the "Scottish Poem"; all of these are from the eleventh century. One school of thought proposes that the king lists from the twelfth century onward were based on one of two earlier tracts.[9] The first was composed c. 1166 while a second list was composed c. 1214 and it expanded on the information of the earlier catalogue. Like the "Scottish Poem" or the *Prophecy of Berchán*, the later Scots king lists might have been intended in some way as performance pieces. The list of works performed at the *oóenach* or Fair of Carman included recitations of royal pedigrees (MI *réim ríg*). A description of just such a performance among the Scots survives from John of Fordun's chronicle telling of the inauguration ceremony for King Alexander III when a senachie (*senchaid*) stepped from the crowd to recite the king's lineage.[10]

Information about Macbeth in those king lists can be summarized briefly using a fourteenth-century king list designated I as an example. This list begins with the Pictish princes, which are followed by a list of the kings of Dál Riata.[11] A third section begins after the death of Alpin, the father of Kenneth I, with the note "And then the kingship of the Scots was moved to the land of the Picts" (*Et tunc translatum est regnum Scotorum ad terram Pictorum*) and a chronological summary (three hundred seven years and three months from Fergus to Alpin). Kenneth heads the third section, which concludes with the death of Alexander III and another chronological note. Macbeth is named twice: once as the slayer of Duncan and the second time for his reign. The synopsis of his reign mentions that he ruled seventeen years, was killed at Lumphanan by Duncan's son Malcolm, and was buried in Iona. He is followed by Lulach, called "the fool" (*fatuus*).

In addition to the *Verse Chronicle* and the king lists, a poem on Malcolm Canmore containing some elements of the Macbeth legend might have been circulating at that time.[12] Such a poem could explain why King Alexander II (called "the Little Red Fox" by his father-in-law King John of England) endowed a mass-chaplaincy at Elgin on April 21, 1235, in honor of the soul of Duncan I.[13] Perhaps an echo of such a legend is behind the tract "The Kings of Scotland descended from Malcolm son of Duncan, otherwise Canmore, and St. Margaret the Queen" that is appended to "King List D."[14] Another possible work from this period is a history that might have been composed by a man who is called Veremond in sixteenth-century texts. In 1267 a Ricardus Veyrement [*sic*] was a witness to two charters that were preserved in the *Chartulary of St. Andrews*.[15] He is probably the same man described as a Spaniard and archdeacon of St. Andrews by the historian Hector Boece. Boece cites Veremond's work in his *Scottish History* (*Scotorum Historiae a Prima Gentis Origine*) and claims that it was a history, written in Latin, of Scottish history from the coming of the Scots to Britain to the reign of Malcolm Canmore. Veremond is copied from Boece by another sixteenth-century historian, David Chambers of Ormond, in his *Brief History of all the kings of France, England, and Scotland* (Histoire abrégée de tous les roys de France, Angleterre et Escosse).

Two Deaths and a Search

On the morning of March 19, 1286, the body of Malcolm Canmore's descendant King Alexander III was found at the foot of a cliff at Kinghorn in Fife. The king had slipped away from his companions the previous evening to spend the night with his second wife Yolande de Dreux to whom he had been married only six months. Apparently losing his way in the darkness while riding atop the cliffs, King Alexander plunged over the precipice. His successor was a three-year-old granddaughter named Margaret (1283–1290), later known as the Maid of Norway, who resided in Norway with her father King Eirík II Magnússon (1268–1299). Her great-uncle King Edward I (1239–1307) of England promptly made plans to unite the English and Scottish crowns by marrying Margaret to her two-year-old cousin Edward, the future king Edward II of England. Mortality put an end to all the plans when, four years later, the young girl went to the grave on September 26, 1290.

A brief overview of Scottish history in the aftermath of Alexander's death is necessary to understand the remembrance of Macbeth in later works beginning with the chronicle of John of Fordun. A council of nobles called the Guardians had ruled Scotland during the reign of the Maid of Norway, but they had a problem after her death. The senior branch of the House of Canmore was extinct and a new monarch had to be found among the cadet branches of the royal house. Although fifteen candidates came forward, the two strongest claims were presented by John Balliol and Robert Bruce, the grandfather of the future king Robert I. The Scots nobles needed a commanding lord to adjudicate among these powerful and influential men.

Among the unhappy miscalculations of history was the invitation from the nobles to King Edward I of England to adjudicate. Regardless of any assurances Edward might have given to the Scots nobles, he saw the invitation as acknowledgment of his lordship over them. To be fair to Edward, their request was worded so vaguely that almost any interpretation could be put on it.[16] Edward, however, was one of the most legalistically minded monarchs of his day. Whatever his private views on the relationship of the English and Scots princes, he wanted to be sure of his lawful position. So he sent an enquiry to the religious houses of England, asking them to search their archives and send to him all the materials they possessed on the history of the relations between the English and Scottish kings.[17] The unstated purpose, because everyone was aware of it, was to find written evidence that the Scots kings were the subordinates of the English monarchs. The surviving replies were collected in the nineteenth century by Sir Frances Palgrave in *Documents and Records Illustrating the History of Scotland and the Transactions between the Crowns of Scotland and England (21 Henry III–35 Edward I)*. The documents provide an insight into the way history was understood during the Middle Ages, especially the distinction between historical texts and pseudo-historical materials. One response began its reply by citing Geoffrey of Monmouth's *History of the Kings of Britain*.[18] At other times, historical memory was very shallow and another respondent believed that the Scots and English had discovered each other only in the twelfth century with the Treaty of Falaise made between Henry II of England and William the Lion of Scotland.[19]

A reply that merits special mention came from the church of St. Mary's, Huntingdon.[20] Huntingdon had been connected with the Scottish crown since the twelfth century when it came into the possession of King David I through his marriage to Matilda of Huntingdon, and passed first to his son Henry of Huntingdon and then to Henry's son, David of Huntingdon. The church's contribution contains some interesting items on Scottish history, including the earliest claim of kinship between Macbeth and the family of Duncan, as the church's chronicle claims that Macbeth was the grandson of Malcolm. Somewhat similar information comes from a contemporary work that was not part of the materials requested by Edward: the chronicle of Peter Langtoft. Peter Langtoft (d. 1305) was a canon of the Augustinian priory at Bridlington and wrote his chronicle in Anglo-Norman verse beginning with the legendary history of Britain (courtesy of Geoffrey of Monmouth) and concluding in the year 1307. He was an enthusiast for the union of Scotland with England and gives two pieces of information about Macbeth.[21] The first is that Macbeth was the brother of Malcolm II whose homage for Scotland was accepted by King Cnut in anticipation of his eventual succession. The second item is that the expedition of Earl Siward of Northumbria into Scotland in 1054 was in response to Macbeth's rebellion against King Edward the Confessor. The Huntingdon chronicle includes Siward's invasion but merely notes that Macbeth fled and Malcolm Canmore was set up as king. Interestingly, the Huntingdon chronicle completely omits Lulach's reign.

Not the Beginning of the Legend 109

The Political Background to the Appearance of Macbeth in Legend

King Edward chose John Balliol to be the king of Scots. But the question of Anglo-Scots royal relations soon was reopened. There were rumors that Balliol had made extravagant promises to Edward in return for his selection. Edward did not help matters with his high-handed attitude to the Scots (which he extended to everybody). The precarious nature of King John's reign became visible in 1293 when he was summoned to Edward's court to answer charges brought by his subject Macduff of Fife. Balliol refused to attend, since that would have been open acceptance of the English prince's lordship. Edward used this as an excuse for an invasion. When the English armies marched into Scotland in 1296, they were faced by an outnumbered and poorly equipped Scottish force. Within weeks Balliol was forced to abdicate and Scotland was a conquered land. The Scots became Edward's northernmost subjects.

Not everyone was willing to accept the new order. The country divided between pro-English and pro-Scottish factions. Hard pressed, the pro-Scottish element made an alliance with France and became increasingly dependent on the francophone world. The alliance between Scotland and France led to interchanges on various social levels between those two countries. From the literature of late medieval France come two of the images that are often cited in the context of English views of the Scots: poverty and ferocity. French visitors to Scotland were unprepared for a culture different from their own.[22] The thirteenth century romance *Sone de Nausay* has the hero Sone travel to the Scots court where he is scandalized by the bad manners. The king excuses his subjects by claiming that poverty makes them gluttons at the table. The Scots mercenary soldiers who were recruited to fight for the French during the late Middle Ages were famed for their penury as well as their tenacity in battle. Their foreign employment gave rise to the accompanying perception of wanderlust as a result of poverty. By the beginning of the sixteenth century, the idea of poverty had become a standard allusion, despite the fact that the Scots archers in France had been organized into a royal bodyguard in 1425. The "Will of the gentle [i.e., not a commoner] Scot" (Le Testament du gentil Cossois), supposedly the last will of one of these royal Scots archers, has the dying man claim that he stole only on a few occasions to keep himself alive.[23]

In the turmoil of the period, two men came forth whose names would become intertwined with Scottish self-determination. The first was William Wallace, an obscure member of the lowest rank of the nobility. From his family home outside Glasgow, he became one of the leaders of the resistance. Most of what we think we know about him comes from a poem popularly called "The Wallace" written in the fifteenth century by a minstrel named "Blind Hary" (c. 1440–1492).[24] His legend began at the battle of Stirling Bridge in 1297 when he led the Scots to victory over a larger and better equipped English force. Many among the Scottish nobility desired a different outcome, however, and they betrayed Wallace the following year. He was forced into flight, and was ultimately captured and executed in 1305 by the English.

This brought to the fore Robert Bruce (1274–1329), the grandson of John Balliol's competitor. Hurried king-making ceremonies at Scone in March 1306 (there were two and the second was carried out by Isabel, Countess of Buchan, who claimed the right of a Macduff to place the crown on the king's head; see below) made King Robert I the target for English retaliation. After early reverses, he gradually cleared Scotland of English garrisons. This was due not only to Robert's undoubted military talents but also to the death of his opponent Edward I in 1307 when he was leading another army to Scotland, despite being so frail that he had to be held upright in his chair in order to eat. The new king of the English was Edward's incompetent son Edward II (1284–1327), the prospective husband of the Maid of Norway. He had lived in terror of his father, who punctuated their meetings with profane abuse and hair-pulling. In addition to the distance in abilities between the two princes, Edward failed to counter Bruce's maneuvers, in part, because of tensions with the English nobles who found him an easy mark for their resentments once his feared sire was dead. As the English squabbled among themselves, it was the turn of the Scots to direct affairs. One by one the strongholds of the occupiers were captured until, by 1314, the only English garrison north of the Forth was at Stirling castle. In the best chivalric tradition the Scots and English made a bargain. If the castle's garrison had not been relieved by midsummer, the fortress would be surrendered to the Scots and the English troops would be allowed to withdraw to the border. When Edward learned of the agreement he wasted time in prevarication before finally moving to relieve the garrison. Further humiliation awaited him in Scotland as he faced King Robert at the great Battle of Bannockburn. The Scots won a famous victory against an English army several times its size. The earliest detailed account of the battle is a verse romance called *The Brus* (The Bruce) written by the archdeacon of the church of St. Machar in Aberdeen named John Barbour (c. 1320–1395); scholars accept it as generally historically accurate.[25]

Acknowledged as the foremost soldier in Britain, King Robert demonstrated that he also was an able diplomat. His victory at Bannockburn made him a hero to the foes of the English, such as the Irish princes who chafed under the control of an increasingly ineffective English regime based

Not the Beginning of the Legend

at Dublin. In 1315 Robert sent his brother Edward with an army to Ireland.[26] At first it was all too easy. The Irish princes deviated from custom and set aside their incessant quarrels to make common cause against the enemy. Edward Bruce was declared high king and pushed the English armies back into the Pale, the English-controlled area along the eastern coast, through a series of victories mainly in the north of the island. Dominance quickly turned to dispersal, however, when Edward was slain in 1318 and the Scotto-Irish alliance collapsed.

Nonetheless, Robert continued to prove himself to be a master political strategist when, in reaction to English maneuvers at the papal court, the Scots produced the *Declaration of Arbroath* in 1320. The *Declaration* was not original in itself but a litany of complaints known as a remonstrance, in which the subjects (the nobles) complain about the lack of good government. The innovation in the *Declaration of Arbroath* was the insistence that the authority of the king of the Scots derived from his subjects, here expressed as the Community of the Realm. This was an inspired statement of national aspiration and places the *Declaration of Arbroath* together with *Magna Carta* as a milestone in the history of suffrage.

The death of Robert the Bruce in 1329, when he was probably a leper, signaled the end of the brief Scottish ascendancy. Survived by a four-year-old son who became King David II (1324–1371), the Scots faced a more formidable foe than the ineffectual Edward II in his son Edward III. The future hero of the Hundred Years' War against France was more in the mold of his ferocious grandsire. Now it was the turn of the English to direct events. First, they sent north their puppet Edward Balliol, the son of King John, to claim the Scottish kingship; he was crowned on September 24, 1332. Although expelled in December, Edward returned the following year and continued as king until 1336. Twenty years later he formally surrendered his claim to the Scottish crown to Edward III. By then he had served his purpose. Scot was pitted against Scot and the kingdom fractured into warring clans.

Political disunity was matched by military defeat. Without the genius of King Robert to direct them, the Scots armies were rolled back by the English. Military rout led to political disaster when the young King David was captured in 1346. Although he was eventually released, the brief golden age of Robert "the Bruce" had ended. David II died without heir, and the kingship passed to his nephew Robert II who was the first Stewart (later to be spelled Stuart in England) king. Robert was the son of Robert Bruce's daughter Marjorie; his surname reflected his family's original position as royal servants. Only English adventures on the continent against the French, such as the battles of

Crécy (1346) and Poitiers (1356), which absorbed time and treasure, gave the Scots respite.[27]

As the political and military situations deteriorated for the Scots, so, too, did the weather. Europe was in the grip of the early stages of what became known as the "Mini Ice-Age." A series of poor harvests from 1315 to 1321 heralded a period of cooler temperatures that continued until the nineteenth century. Glaciers began to advance in Iceland and in the Alps. The growing season shortened, and food became a status symbol. To add to the misery, in the middle of the century an incurable disease ravaged Europe: the bubonic plague. Against this backdrop of military defeat, inexplicable death, and economic hardship, the Macbeth legend took shape.

John of Fordun and Macbeth

An imaginative Scot in the late fourteenth century could be forgiven for thinking that Scotland had become the stable for the Four Horsemen of the Apocalypse. Hunger, Disease, War, and Death stalked the land. As the climate cooled, even Nature appeared to set her hand against the Scots. The Anglo-Scottish Wars not only introduced new hostilities between formerly friendly neighbors, but they also led to a burst of historical writing. Documentary and literary materials were examined for what they could tell about the past. As one tribulation gave way to another, an obscure priest in Aberdeen named John of Fordun embarked on an ambitious project: to write a history of the Scottish people from the earliest times to his own day. He took the surviving scraps of information on early Scottish history and fashioned them into a narrative that is popularly known in English as the *Chronicle of the Scottish People*. John finished his narrative only up to the middle of the twelfth century and the death of King David I in 1153, but his notes for the remainder of the history were appended to the finished work. That continuation had to wait until the next century when the entire narrative was reedited and new material added by Walter Bower. John of Fordun's chronicle is usually the farthest investigation into the sources for Shakespeare's *Macbeth*, and his basic outline would be repeated during the next two centuries.

Asides in manuscript copies of his work supply almost everything known about John of Fordun. One preface to his chronicle, written about two generations after his death, claims that he was a chantry priest serving the cathedral at Aberdeen.[28] John was writing in the last quarter of the fourteenth century as revealed by his acknowledgment of the loan of a genealogy from Walter, Cardinal Wardlaw. Wardlaw was made cardinal without title by the Anti-Pope

Clement VII on December 23, 1383, and he died probably in September 1387.[29] Prefaces in two medieval copies of his work claim to give Fordun's motivation for writing his *Chronicle of the Scottish People* and the method he used in his work. They state what John made no secret: he felt the histories written by English writers were biased against the Scots. Throughout the narrative he remarks that he was giving the Scottish side of the story.[30]

Fordun's Macbeth Episode

The Macbeth (called Machabeus in the text) episode is in the fourth book of the *Chronicle of the Scottish People*, from chapters 44 to the end, and continuing in the fifth book from the first to eighth chapters.[31] The story opens with clan conflicts in Scotland, which leave the way open for foreign invasion—in this instance, Viking raids. The wretchedness continues when the strong government of the old king, Malcolm II, ends with his death in a battle against Scots rivals, a family who had also killed his father Kenneth. Duncan succeeds his grandfather, but he is too good and gentle for a kingdom that demands a firm ruler. A man more suited to the task is his lieutenant Macbeth, a harsh and competent captain who inspires fear. When Duncan makes a circuit of his kingdom to dispense justice, Macbeth takes the opportunity to seize the crown. He kills the king in battle and usurps the kingship. The true heirs—Duncan's sons Malcolm Canmore and Donald Ban—are forced to flee. As Macbeth crushes all opposition, some of the nobles begin to plot for Malcolm Canmore's return.

Macduff

History, however partisan, is interrupted at this point with the introduction of Macduff of Fife.[32] Macduff is one of the main characters in Shakespeare's drama, and John of Fordun was the first writer to mention him in connection with Macbeth. His flight from Macbeth's realm spells the beginning of the end for the tyrant. Macduff escapes from Scotland after he is denounced as a traitor to Macbeth, who furiously declared that he will yoke him like an ox. Any contemporary reader of this passage would have understood the implied brutality. The yoking of oxen was associated with cruelty during the Middle Ages. The controversy was ancient, and there were differences of opinion about the correct method. In his tract on farming called "Concerning Rural Affairs," the Roman writer Columella condemns the head yoke, which was considered especially painful for the animal and urges the use of a withers yoke as the more humane alternative.[33] The medieval Irish story "Wooing of Étaín" (Tochmarc Étaíne) reveals that in the eleventh century the two methods of yoking oxen were still used in Ireland and Scotland.[34] There is an implication that the "yoking" of adversaries occurred in a real sense when the eulogy in the *Annals of Ulster* for the Irish king Gilla Mochonna of Brega (north of Dublin), who died in 1013, declares that he "yoked Vikings to the plough" (*leis dorata na Gaill fon arathar*).

For the historian, the question of whether there was a real Macduff contemporary with Macbeth remains undecided, despite the valiant efforts by generations of scholars to settle the matter one way or the other. This solution is complicated by several factors. Macduff is an adaptation of Gaelic Mac Duib and the name translates literally as "son of the dark/black-haired one." Dub was a common name, so Mac Duib was a patronymic long before the time of Macbeth. There was, moreover, a Macduff who was a king early in the eleventh century: Lady Macbeth's grandfather King Kenneth III mac Duib (MI Cináed mac Duib). Men whose patronymic is Macduff are found ruling in Fife in the eleventh century and throughout the Middle Ages. The first Macduff associated with Fife was the eleventh-century Constantine Macduff. He was not an earl (a title that appeared in Scotland only later), but a "great steward" (MI *mórmáer*) and was a witness to a charter of Edgar, the son of Malcolm Canmore, when he gave land to the church of Durham sometime around the year 1093, just after the death of Malcolm.[35] His last appearance was around the year 1128 when he was the senior member of a panel of three judges presiding over the adjudication of a dispute concerning land between the Céli Dé of Loch Leven and a knight named Robert of Burgundy. One of his fellow judges was Máel Doun son of Macbeth. By the eleventh century Dub/Duff was being used as a collective name. The early twelfth-century collection of Irish genealogies at Oxford, Bodleian MS Rawlinson B. 502 (f. 152 a 20) refers to the O'Duffs, who lived in Munster. At roughly the same time Macduff makes his appearance in John of Fordun's chronicle.

To return to the narrative, Macduff flees to England to encourage Malcolm to return. Malcolm doubts Macduff's sincerity and wonders if he was sent by Macbeth to trap him. So he tests Macduff with three claims of his unworthiness to be king: he is lecherous; he is rapacious; and he is untruthful. The conversation between Malcolm and Macduff is in the form of a disputation, a favorite literary form for scholars and proponents of courtly love. John of Fordun indulges himself when his characters argue in typical scholastic fashion taking their examples from history. He is alerting his readers to his excellent education while also demonstrating his knowledge of history.

Macduff is able to counter Malcolm's argument for the first two vices of lechery and greed. The third vice–deception–defeats him, however, and he prepares to depart. Malcolm, convinced of his honesty, reveals his test and agrees to lead an army north. He receives license from his host, the English king Edward the Confessor, to recruit among his subjects. Siward, the Danish earl of Northumbria, agrees to join him, and they invade Scotland. Confronting Macbeth at Lumphanan, Malcolm defeats and kills him. Despite his victory, Macbeth's stepson Lulach seizes the kingship. Only after killing Lulach several months later does Malcolm finally ascend to his father's royal office.

The Legend of Malcolm Canmore

The irony of presenting John of Fordun as originator of the Macbeth story is that he was not writing about Macbeth; he was writing the legend of Malcolm Canmore. Except for the chapter in which his father is murdered, Malcolm appears in all following ten chapters that are connected with Macbeth's reign. Macbeth appears in only three of them. Malcolm is a well-developed character, brave and resourceful as well as an accomplished actor who can deceive Macduff about his personality. Macbeth, on the other hand, is a one-dimensional villain who embodies all the worst in John of Fordun's view. He represents a rival family at war with the Scots kings and is naturally predisposed toward evil. No matter how civilized he tries to appear, his true nature cannot be concealed, especially at the end of his life when he retreats from Malcolm's forces into his wilderness home. The only time his character is allowed any expression is a burst of outrage against the disloyalty of Macduff. In John of Fordun's hands, Macbeth is nothing more than a caricature of wickedness.

For the first time, the historical King Mac bethad of the eleventh century is transformed into the literary ogre Macbeth. Other characters also assume familiar forms. The Duncan who is described as a failure and hypochondriac in earlier accounts vanishes. John replaces him with the good and wise man so well known today. The real Malcolm Canmore, whose belligerence and opportunism were famous in his time, becomes a reluctant warrior who has to be sought out and persuaded to fight for his ancestral throne.

Sources and Speculation

This leads to the question, where did John of Fordun find his material? Like many medieval writers, he used a variety of standard works for his moral and historical episodes. Asides in various medieval manuscripts of the *Chronicle* claim that his search for materials took him on a journey to libraries in Britain and Ireland.[36] Sometimes he mentions his sources such as the twelfth-century English historian William of Malmesbury and eleventh-century Irish chronicler Marianus Scotus. John of Fordun was also a historiographer and noted William of Malmesbury's comments on the eccentric dating in Marianus's chronicle, which placed events twenty-two years ahead of the anno domini chronology followed by everyone.[37] So the historical foundation is a mixture. The circumstances of Macbeth's seizure of power are found in various earlier texts while the death of Macbeth during the invasion by Siward of Northumbria is incorrect and comes from William of Malmesbury.[38] So, too, does the date of Macbeth's death, incorrectly placed on December 5, 1056. The fight at Lumphanan with Malcolm, however, is given in the king lists.

The hostilities of the fourteenth century, though, left their imprint even on someone who wished to think of himself as cosmopolitan. While John openly acknowledged his debt to William of Malmesbury, he could not conceal his grudge against the national enemy. When commenting on the role played by Earl Siward of Northumbria against Macbeth, he observes:

> This is how William [of Malmesbury], ascribing no praise for the victory to Malcolm, assigns it all to Siward. The truth is that the victory was entirely belonging to [Malcolm]. Even if King Edward had been there with his men, had Malcolm not been there, then [the Scots in Macbeth's army] would not have fled from the battlefield.[39]

John of Fordun's name suggests that his home was the village of Fordun in the Mearns. The village is about equidistant from Macbeth's fortress at Lumphanan and the city of Aberdeen, on the border between Highland and Lowland Scotland; his contemporary Jean Froissart described Aberdeen as being on the border of wildest Scotland.[40] Unexpectedly for someone whose name suggests that his home was on the edge of the Highlands, John of Fordun feared and disliked Highlanders. The highland/lowland border was not an affectation, and he saw the Scots kingdom divided between the civilized lowlands and the savage highlands; in the next century his editor and continuator Walter Bower used the terms "town" and "country" Scots. The town or lowland Scots were wealthy, steadfast, and worthy of admiration. The country or Highland Scots were poor, treacherous, and the disreputable race of a barbarous land. The Highland Scots spoke Gaelic while the Lowland Scots spoke "Scots" a language similar to the northern dialect of Middle English. The

Not the Beginning of the Legend   117

Highlanders looked toward Ireland as part of their cultural world while the Lowlanders looked toward France. Economy revolved around livestock in the highlands and fishing or trade in the lowlands. The difference even spread to diet. The Lowlanders drank ale, but the Highlanders drank water or buttermilk. Servants ate barley-bread in the lowlands, while their counterparts in the highlands ate oatcakes.[41] That contrast becomes clear in John's chronicle when Malcolm and Siward lead their troops into Scotland. Macbeth flees from the prosperous (lowland) south and hurries to the safety of the thickets and valleys of the (highland) north. Malcolm proves his mettle by pursuing him into the wilderness and confronting him at Lumphanan.

John of Fordun did not know Gaelic, even though he used some Gaelic terms. He explained the title *abthane* [*sic*] borne by Duncan's father Crinán as a compound of *ab* "abbot" and *thane* "thane" to mean both cleric and aristocrat. *Abthane* originally was Gaelic *apdaine* and it meant simply "abbot" with an extended meaning of "mastership." The term was still used in John's day, and his misunderstanding of the word suggests that he was quite aware of the aristocratic domination of many old-style religious houses.[42] He made an intelligent, but wrong, guess at the meaning of the word. Intriguingly, Fordun seems to have been familiar with Gaelic literature, and this brings up the question (not to be investigated here) of translations. In the debate between Macduff and Malcolm, John of Fordun gave the example of the Irish high king Rory O'Connor (MI Ruaidrí Ua Conchobair reigned 1156–1186, died 1198) as a sensualist. This is wildly out of chronological order, for Rory died a century and a half after Macbeth. While it could be evidence that John had traveled in Ireland, possibly this is evidence of Irish materials circulating around Scotland. There might be a connection with the Irish campaigns of Edward Bruce, which would have been an opportune time for materials from Ireland to be taken to Scotland. A transcription of the famous *Remonstrance of the Irish Princes*, which asked for papal intervention in the cause of Irish freedom, is found in the fifteenth-century edition of Fordun's chronicle by Walter Bower.[43]

The misplacement of Rory O'Connor and the mistranslation of *abthane* lead to the question of how much antiquarian information connected with Macbeth is preserved in John of Fordun's account. Did he faithfully follow the information that he found or was he interjecting his own interpretation, possibly even speculation? One item that has been cited as evidence for the authenticity of John of Fordun's source materials is his claim that Macduff landed at Ravenseyr in England during his journey to meet Malcolm Canmore at the court of King Edward. Ravenseyr is Old Norse, which is anglicized Ravensey, and means Raven's Island. According to the thirteenth-century account by the Icelandic historian Snorri Sturluson in *Heimskringla*, the survivors from the army of the Norwegian King Harald Hardrada fled there after their defeat at the battle of Stamford Bridge in September 1066.[44] The famous Raven's Island where the defeated Norse retreated in 1066 was a different place. John of Fordun's site is usually identified as Ravenser's Spur (today known as Spur Head), a sand spit/peninsula in the Holderness region of Yorkshire at the entrance to the river Humber. Is this an instance of his preserving an archaic piece of information? The answer is no, because the port came into being during the thirteenth century; Ravenser's Spur was used as a staging point for the English forces in the invasions of Scotland in the late thirteenth and fourteenth centuries. Rather than an authentic antiquarian item, this information seems to have been Fordun's effort to use current events to explain the past.[45]

A New View of History

John of Fordun was a man on a mission, and he made no secret that his goal was to correct what he considered to be false views of Scottish history. Toward that end he was, by turns, a mixture of genuine storyteller, as in his contrast of Duncan with Macbeth, and pedant in such matters as the debate between Macduff and Malcolm. More to the point, he was a clergyman who subscribed to the interpretation of history known as the Augustinian view of history, credited to St. Augustine of Hippo, the fourth/fifth century church father. In this, God's plan for humanity is made visible to humans—who are limited by time and place—in the hindsight of history. Contemporary turmoil, dislike of Highlanders, and pique at what he considered biased English writers are all reflected in John of Fordun's story of Macbeth. The greatest influence came from recent history. His chronicle reflects that the Viking Age ended late for the Scots. The last so-called Viking raid had been only a century earlier in 1263 by the Norwegian King Håkon Håkonarson. That explains why John of Fordun unconsciously refers to the earlier enemy, the Vikings, by calling them Norwegians, the later enemy.

The divided loyalties among the Scottish nobles of his day shaped John of Fordun's perceptions. Treachery is a prominent theme throughout the chronicle, reflecting the violent difference of opinions among the Scots concerning English lordship. Many Scots wanted a union with England and approved the proposal of Edward I to marry his son to the Maid of Norway. John of Fordun wanted to establish the existence of only one legitimate line of kings over the Scots: the descendants of Malcolm III. Earlier he had used the theme of betrayal in the description of the death of Malcolm II and returned to the topic later with the story of Malcolm Canmore and the traitor, first mentioned by

Ailred of Rievaulx in *Genealogia Regum Angliae*. Even in his long lament on the death of King David I, who died a natural death and throughout his life cultivated very good relations with his English neighbors (often better than with the Scots), John urges his compatriots to "let the trials of the English teach you to be faithful to kings."[46] Not surprisingly, the entire Macbeth episode deals with the issue of disloyalty.

John of Fordun can be excused much, because his Scotland was so very different from the Celtic kingdom. The days when princes did glorious acts had become, in the fourteenth century, a more mundane one of diplomacy and finance. Scone still was the symbolic center of the kingdom, but the real heart of power was in the towns in the "civilized" lowlands; sometimes this information found its way into literature. Kings increasingly looked after urban interests because they needed the revenues from the towns. For example, a popular (and inexpensive) means of distributing royal patronage was to reissue charters of previous kings. Townsmen were willing to pay for these confirmations because they jealously guarded their rights to collect customs duties. The king represented the only power that could enforce those rights. A charter of King Robert "the Bruce" issued at Scone on October 20, 1325, gave land to the burgesses of the town of Dundee so that they could set up a tollbooth.[47] That charter shows John of Fordun was writing in an era when historical research was a profitable activity. In a charter from Perth dated April 10, 1365, King David II demanded that all ships sailing on the river Tay unload their cargoes upstream from Drumlay Sands. In other words, the goods were to be landed at Perth, where the royal customs officials were stationed. This was a reissue of a grant from the early thirteenth-century King William, who was confirming, in turn, a charter of his grandfather King David I. Antiquarianism begat antiquarianism, and the charter of David II was reissued by King Robert III on May 6, 1399.[48]

John of Fordun's narrative shows him attempting to describe an earlier world that he did not completely understand. He was in thrall to the use of tradition as a means of understanding the present: one need only to view history as the working-out of God's plan in order to comprehend the past, a part of the intellectual world of the High Middle Ages. While John's narrative became part of the outline of Shakespeare's version of the Macbeth legend, his real contribution was the introduction of Macbeth the villain. The bad Macbeth versus the gentle King Duncan and the good Malcolm Canmore became the basis of the story even as details were added throughout the next two centuries. When it is realized that John of Fordun was writing a legend of Malcolm Canmore rather than Macbeth, the cliché of a villain is sensible. His history is a product of the medieval schools, with its use of classical examples in scholarly disputation, and this makes clear the theological significance of the Macbeth episode. A bad man temporarily profits from his wickedness but eventually is overthrown by the rightful prince. Fordun's view of the history of the world as symbol for the eternal consequences awaiting all mankind had its own influence on a play that would be written more than two centuries later.

Fordun and Walter Bower

In the middle of the fifteenth century there was a reworking of John of Fordun's *Chronicle* material by Walter Bower who occasionally included additional materials; the finished work was called the *Scotichronicon*. Walter Bower (1385–1449) was a cleric from Haddingdon who had trained for his vocation at the cathedral priory of St Andrews. He was the first university trained interpreter of the Macbeth legend, and apparently received his degree at the new University of St. Andrews, which was founded in 1410. Appointed the abbot of Inchcolm, an island in the Firth of Forth, when in his early thirties, Bower spent the rest of his life as a busy ecclesiastical lord. His historical work was written at the request of a local magnate, Sir David Steward of Rosyth. Bower did not attempt a new work, but edited/expanded Fordun's chronicle, which becomes increasingly valuable as Fordun's work becomes gradually more a series of notes.

Bower contributed almost nothing original to the Macbeth legend, which ends the fourth book (chapter 49) and opens the fifth book (chapters 1–7) of his *Scotichronicon*.[49] The few new items are pieces of moralizing, such as an account of the duty of a king (chapter 50). There is the occasional detail, such as the name of the castle that was home to Macduff. Fordun does not identify it, but Andrew of Wyntoun and Bower both call it Kennoway. This castle is located in central Fife about twenty-four miles from Edinburgh, with a sweeping view of the Firth of Forth. Bower does give a couple of interesting details that either might have been his own invention or reflect his researches. These include the claim that Macbeth murdered Duncan clandestinely and that Malcolm Canmore was being advised by Siward of Northumbria prior to his flight from the kingdom. Finally an important item contributed by a manuscript of Bower's *Scotichronicon* is the first picture connected with the Macbeth legend.[50] This is an illustration of Macduff meeting Malcolm Canmore. The two men are standing in an empty room; one man, apparently Malcolm Canmore, is seated with a head covering while the second man, apparently Macduff, stands to the left of the picture. On the beam above them is the inscription: "*de rege malcolmo kenremor et thano de Fiffe*" (concerning Malcolm Canmore and the thane of Fife).[51]

FIG. 5.1 Thane of Fife and Malcolm Canmore. Corpus Christi College, Cambridge, MS 171, f. 88. Used by permission.

An Approved Scots History

John of Fordun's chronicle shows that Scots history was being edited in the interests of Malcolm Canmore and his descendants. He used the methodology of the king lists that began to appear during Malcolm Canmore's reign. Those lists merge the kingships of the Picts and of the Scots in the mid-ninth century with Kenneth I. From that time, the records become a family history. Selective editing omitted the temporary domination of his kindred in the late ninth century by dynasts of Cenél Loairn—Giric, Eochaid, and Giric's brother Constantine—that are found in some texts using earlier materials. Macbeth's dynasty was being expunged from the records.[52]

John of Fordun was following the policy of the royal Scottish government that, shortly before the beginning of the fourteen century, began actively promoting a particular view of the past. Initially, this view was not subjective; Robert of Logy was paid by the royal treasury in 1292 for masses for the royal family and their ancestors at the monastery of Scone, beside the famous king-making site.[53] By the fourteenth century, the Anglo-Scottish Wars included literary skirmishes. The archdeacon of Aberdeen, John Barbour, was a courtier of King Robert II and received a life pension in 1378 for writing *The Bruce*. Beginning three years after his death, and continuing for a century, the Scottish exchequer paid 20 shillings to the church of Aberdeen on the occasion of the anniversary of Barbour's death.[54] Some members of the royal family were scholars, and in 1364 a poor scholar who was a cousin of King David II received four pounds Scots.[55] Moving ahead a century, Blind Hary, the author of *The Wallace* was at the royal court five times between 1490 and 1491 where he was paid for reciting stories.[56]

Slightly more than three centuries lie between Macbeth's death and John of Fordun's *Chronicle of the Scottish Nation*, and in this time, Macbeth the historical prince made his transition to literary character. He was not the first in Scotland, and the historical Fergus of Galloway had made a similar transition. Fergus went from historical warlord to literary romantic hero. There was a parallel with Macbeth who was presented as a good king in the thirteenth-century *Verse Chronicle*. Yet the Anglo-Scots wars that followed the extinction of Malcolm Canmore's dynasty in the senior line changed historical need. By the time John of Fordun wrote the Macbeth episode for his fourteenth-century chronicle, there were some problems. First, the right of Malcolm to the throne had to be emphasized, so that the cadet branches competing for the kingship could be presented as the rightful heirs. Any challenge to the Canmore dynasty became treason. Another problem was the English, who

Not the Beginning of the Legend   123

were now the enemies of the Scots. Malcolm, however, had been reinstated in Scotland with the aid of an English army. So an explanation was needed. John of Fordun's account of Malcolm Canmore's flight from Scotland and his mistrust of the Scots nobles provided a clarification, up to a point. So John of Fordun directly attacked the account of the half-English William of Malmesbury, in whose chronicle he found the information, and claimed that he failed to state that the Scots would not have fought if Malcolm had not been present.

As John of Fordun's career was ending, that of the next important interpreter of Macbeth was beginning. Macbeth the featureless bully would be expanded into a complicated individual in a history composed in Fife by a cleric named Andrew of Wyntoun. His version of the Macbeth legend would eventually find its way to the attention of William Shakespeare.

6

Weird Sisters and the Prior of Loch Leven

A MODERN READER comes away unsatisfied by the story of Macbeth in John of Fordun's *Chronicle of the Scottish Nation*. The outline is familiar, but many of the details in Shakespeare's tragedy are missing. There is Macbeth, but no Lady Macbeth, and Macduff, but no Lady Macduff. Also absent are Birnam Wood, the fortress on Dunsinane Hill, prophecies uttered by ethereal women, and vengeance performed by a man not born of a woman. All these appear in another chronicle written by a Scots cleric, the *Original Chronicle* of Andrew of Wyntoun, the prior of the community of Augustinian canons serving the church of St. Serf at Loch Leven. While the broad outline is similar to the one used by John of Fordun, Andrew's history differs in more than just new details. An immediate divergence is their audience. John's prose narrative was written in Latin for an educated and clerical audience while Andrew wrote in the Scots vernacular and in verse with octosyllabic metre (verse-lines of eight syllables, linked together by end-rhyme), which guaranteed him a larger audience than a few scholars. John of Fordun devoted much space to arguments with his real and imaginary English adversaries, but Andrew of Wyntoun placed Scottish history within the larger context of world history.

Andrew of Wyntoun was born c. 1350 and became a canon regular (priest who lived under monastic discipline) at the cathedral of St. Andrews.[1] In the last decade of the century (c. 1393) he was elected prior of the church of St. Serf's at Loch Leven, a dependency of St. Andrews whose ancient patrons had included Macbeth and Gruoch. Andrew first appears in documents when he led a group of dignitaries that perambulated the boundary in Kirkness between the priory's lands and those of the barony of Kynnymond on July 6, 1395.[2] After serving for more than a quarter century, Andrew petitioned Pope

Martin V to be released from his duties late in 1422. His request was granted, and a new prior is named in a document of 1423. Andrew probably was at the point of death when he made his request because the latter document refers to him in the past tense.[3]

Andrew wrote *The Original Chronicle of Scotland* at the request of Sir John Wemyss of Leuchars (d. 1429), laird of Kincaldrum and Reres, who wanted a history of Scotland from the earliest times to his own day. The title merely means that the work begins with the earliest history ("original") of Scotland. Andrew produced at least two, and possibly three, versions of his chronicle during the period from 1390 to 1422.[4] The first version ends about the time that he was elected prior of St. Serf's in the last decade of the fourteenth century. The second version was finished about the year 1413, just after Andrew had completed legal research (between the years 1406 and 1411) in the archives at St. Andrews. There might have been another revision completed just before his death, although editorial changes introduced afterward might give the appearance of another version.

For a modern reader, the different versions of the *Original Chronicle* are easy to keep separate because they were published in two editions during the nineteenth and early twentieth centuries. The second version of c. 1413 was edited by the famous textual scholar David Laing.[5] He was a very old man by that time and died shortly after the proof sheets were sent to the printer. This edition is important because Laing was working from Andrew's mature version of the *Original Chronicle*. The first and third versions were edited by a French teacher from Glasgow named F. J. Amours, and he too died before his edition was published.[6]

The different versions of the *Original Chronicle* are significant because, when writing the second version, Andrew changed the focus of the Macbeth episode. The first version introduces the chapter about Macbeth with the title "How Malcolm Canmore came to the crown and took possession of Scotland." In the second version, the chapter title is changed to "When Macbeth-Finlay Rose and Reigned in Scotland." The entire emphasis shifts from a prologue for Malcolm's reign to a study of Macbeth's rule. During the intervening years, Wyntoun found something that made him change his mind about the importance of Macbeth. What was it? One possible answer comes from comparison of the first and second versions. The first version of his chronicle is vague about the names of persons and places connected with the Macbeth episode while the second version gives more details and specific information. To take one example, the first version of Andrew's history does not give Lady Macbeth's Christian name; she is merely described as his uncle's wife. The second version gives her name as Dame Grwok for Lady Gruoch. Is the answer that Andrew found a new source of information?

Duncan and the Miller's Daughter

Andrew occasionally diverged from his main story, and this discussion will begin in the same fashion. One story that is not explicitly part of the Macbeth episode but has a connection is the tale of an irregular union between King Duncan and the daughter of the miller of Forteviot. In the *Original Chronicle*, the young king was hunting in the forest and at nightfall was stranded at the town of Forteviot where the miller, who had a beautiful daughter, offered him lodging. For Duncan and the miller's daughter, it was love at first sight. They spent the night together and nine months later their son, Malcolm Canmore, was born. Andrew was not interested in lewdness, but he was interested in genealogy and origin stories and, so far as is known, was the first to suggest that the royal Scottish line had a tie with commoners.[7] Perhaps it was no coincidence that the reigning monarch, King Robert III (reigned 1390—1406), was also born out of wedlock. His mother Elizabeth Mure had been the mistress of King Robert II, the first monarch of the Stewart dynasty, and the children of that union were not legitimized until their parents' marriage in 1347.

Andrew of Wyntoun's Macbeth

Andrew of Wyntoun begins his story with Macbeth living at the court of Duncan and Gruoch, his uncle and aunt. One night he has a dream in which he is sitting with the king who holds two greyhounds on a leash in the midst of a hunt. Three women, called weird sisters, pass by and address him with titles of increasing status: thane of Cromarty, thane of Moray, and, finally, king. Macbeth duly becomes thane and then desires to be king. So he kills Duncan and marries Gruoch. Duncan's sons flee the kingdom, not because they are suspected of committing the murder, but because they fear Macbeth will serve them as he did their father. At the beginning of his reign, however, Macbeth makes good laws and goes on a pilgrimage to Rome.

At that point, Andrew abruptly introduces a second legend with the phrase "But as we find by some stories, he was conceived wondrously" (*Bot as we fynd be sum storys, Gottyne he wes on ferly wys*); the significance of "stories" is discussed below. Macbeth's mother goes to play in the woods, where she meets a handsome man. He seduces her, and Macbeth is conceived. The handsome man then reveals that he is a devil and gives her a ring that she can use to summon him. He assures her that their son has supernatural protection and that only a man who was not born of woman can slay him. At this point either Andrew or his source becomes confused, and when the child is born, he is given the name Macbeth-Finlay.

Andrew resumes his story with the expulsion of Duncan's sons from the kingdom followed by the confrontation between Macbeth and Macduff during the building of the fortress at Dunsinane. Dunsinane Hill is near the town of Collace and eight miles northeast of Perth in the Sidlaw Hills. The summit is 1012 feet above sea level and on top are the remains of an ancient fort that is 210 feet long and 130 feet wide.[8] Andrew might have seen ruins of the fortress, which he and modern excavators describe as a timber and stone construction. The fort features in Andrew's story when Macbeth compels his subjects to send oxen to pull the stone and timber to the top of the hill. The task was too great for one team of oxen, and when Macbeth asked who owned the team, he was told that it belonged to Macduff of Fife. In a fury the king said he would put Macduff's neck in the yoke and have him pull the load. Macduff then made a plan to escape from the royal court. Just before the evening meal, Macduff took a loaf of bread from the *spenser* (the official in charge of the king's larder) and left without the king's consent. Departure without permission was a serious breach of courtly etiquette and an insult to the king. Macduff fled across to the river Earn to a place called Portnebaryan and the loaf paid for his passage. Macbeth was told of Macduff's flight and prepared to follow him. For the first time, Lady Macduff makes her appearance in the Macbeth tale. Macduff arrived at his castle of Kennoway in Fife and told his wife that the king would soon be at their home. She was to occupy him until she saw the ship that carried Macduff sail away. All was done and Lady Macduff had the pleasure of telling Macbeth that her husband was safely departed; in this version, however, she survived the encounter.

At this point in the narration, Andrew inserted some interesting, but irrelevant, information about sailing regulations on the river Earn, particularly which side of the river craft should occupy according to the direction of travel. He concluded by stating that four pennies were the standard fee for carrying freight. Why did Andrew include this material? Possibly it is an example of a local legend. Or perhaps the rate for haulage of goods was the type of information that the head of a religious house was forced to know, and river regulations were spelled out in contemporary charters. This passage does show, however, that Andrew of Wyntoun did not know the geography of the area. The river Earn is not near Dunsinane, but ten miles away on the

FIG. 6.1 Looking South from Dunsinane Fort. Photograph by Robert Hudson.

opposite shore of the river Tay; they converge north of Abernethy. Macduff would have had a long journey overland and across the Tay to reach the river from Dunsinane and an equally long trek to his home. Andrew returns to his main story with Macduff reaching England and an interview with Malcolm Canmore. Malcolm tests Macduff's sincerity with claims that he was unfit to rule because he was a lecher, a thief, and a liar. After Macduff began to leave, Malcolm called him back and announced that he passed the test, Malcolm's host King Edward agreed to sponsor an invasion led by Earl Siward of Northumbria.

After this, however, Andrew gives two details not related by John of Fordun that would be followed by later interpreters. When Malcolm Canmore's army assembled at Birnam Wood, it was revealed that Macbeth believed he was safe until Birnam Wood came to Dunsinane. The prophecy was fulfilled when Malcolm and Siward camouflaged their troops with branches taken from Birnam Wood's trees for the fifteen-mile march. When standing within the ramparts of Dunsinane, the countryside to Birnam Wood is easily seen. Macbeth fled Dunsinane toward his fortress at Lumphanan. He was overtaken and slain by a knight "not of woman born" fulfilling the prophecy made to his mother.

Weird Sisters 129

Andrew of Wyntoun gives an interesting epilogue not mentioned by John of Fordun but added by his fifteenth-century editor Walter Bower. This is a list of the privileges granted to Macduff and his heirs by Malcolm Canmore in recognition of his service in overthrowing Macbeth. There are three grants. First, a Macduff shall place the king-to-be on the throne for his inauguration. Second, a Macduff has the honor of carrying the king's banner into battle, and his clan is placed in the first row of the army. Finally, any member of Clan Macduff who commits an unpremeditated and involuntary killing can plead "Macduff's Law" whereby the death of a noble is compensated by the payment of twenty-four *merks* while twelve *merks* are the fine for the death of a commoner.[9] Macduff's privileges were real rights enjoyed by Clan Macduff, and a document of 1384 describes the earl of Fife as "the head of the law of Clan Macduff" (*capitalis legis de Clenmcduffe*).[10] The heads of Clan Macduff (now called earls) in their role as the lords of Fife were crucial in the inauguration of a king. The earl of Fife was such an important member of the Scottish court that during the reign of King Robert I "the Bruce" a legal document was drawn up that gave details about the necessity for that position to be maintained.[11] At the coronation of Alexander II, the earl of Fife was the first in a line of nobles who led the king to the king-making site at Scone. A generation later the earl of Fife was one of two nobles who enthroned the king and gave the monarch his sword of state. In addition, the immunity or "Macduff's Law" is mentioned in late medieval Scottish charters. Anyone who was related to Macduff to the ninth degree could escape punishment for unpremeditated murder (involuntary manslaughter) by the payment of nine cows at the cross of Macduff.[12]

As this brief sketch of the Macbeth legend in the *Original Chronicle* of Andrew of Wyntoun shows, his contribution to its development was significant, and many of his features eventually found their way into Shakespeare's *Macbeth*. Even when Andrew uses the same outline as John of Fordun, he gives a different interpretation. To take one example, both John and Andrew make much of Duncan's soft nature, but when comparing Duncan with Macbeth, Andrew states that the latter was the better candidate for king. Macbeth the villain was already a cliché, however, so Andrew quickly qualified this assessment by pointing out that Macbeth's great cruelty, which was visible later, clearly disqualified him from high office. This is a curious example of special pleading because successful princes were expected to be fierce.[13] They could not be unjust or tyrannical, but brutality toward their enemies (real and perceived) was expected, although Christianity demanded that it be tempered with mercy. The favorable assessment of Macbeth as a prince who could keep order in his kingdom might be a comment on a crime wave that seems to have been a problem during Wyntoun's day. There are only a few documents dealing with it, but they are significant. A charter of King Robert III, given under his privy (i.e., private) seal in literally the last month of his life, permits the burgesses of Perth to apprehend any strangers who commit fraud; particular mention is made of merchants from Flanders.[14] Robert III was a famously ineffectual monarch, and the real power was his brother Robert, the duke of Albany, a competent and fearsome individual; Andrew's contrast of Duncan with Macbeth could be applied to the royal family of his day.

Searching for Macbeth: Scholarly

Andrew of Wyntoun presents two additional elements that would be crucial in the evolution of the Macbeth legend: tales/stories and prophecy. Andrew of Wyntoun knew at least two different versions of the Macbeth legend and possibly several more. His attempt to reconcile the several elements was only partly successful. The tales—such as a liaison between Macbeth's mother and a demon—were part of the storytelling tradition that lay outside the formal writing of official records or courtly literature. Sometimes the episodes did not merge well but show where the different tales were incorporated.

The interest of Andrew of Wyntoun in details is one of the ways to trace different versions. He traced routes and places, giving specific names whenever possible: Dunsinane, Birnam, the Mounth, Lumphanan, the Earn, and the Tay. The same specificity appears in his genealogical materials, which are unique. John of Fordun noted that Macbeth belonged to a rival family. Andrew, however, gave more fulsome information, such as Macbeth was Duncan's sister's son and that Duncan was Macbeth's *eme* (uncle) who raised his nephew at his court. As has been shown, ties of kinship between Duncan's family and Macbeth are found in the chronicle of the canons of St. Mary's, Huntingdon, and Pierre de Langtoft's chronicle. Andrew's claim that Macbeth married his Aunt Gruoch after Duncan's death is, however, a novelty. This came from a literary source because Gruoch's husband before Macbeth was his cousin Gilla Coemgain. The adultery/incest motif is not an uncommon feature in later medieval legends, and a similarity with versions of the Arthurian legend can hardly have escaped the notice of Andrew's audience, because the Scots versions of the Arthurian stories emphasize the liaison between Arthur and his sister.

Where did he find his materials? Part of the answer is written materials such as the *Verse Chronicle* from which he copied the appropriate stanzas

Weird Sisters

to conclude the discussion of each reign. The place where some of his material probably was collected was the Archive or Public Armorial (*archivum seu armarium publicum*) of the cathedral of St. Andrews. There he sought materials regarding his church's lands in preparation for appearances in the Court of the Official of the Diocese at St. Andrews. That research had benefits for later historians. For example, the donation of the estate of Bolgyn by Macbeth to St. Serf's is known because Andrew copied it prior to an appearance in court (on February 19, 1406); the original document was too frail to be displayed.[15] Andrew also used a volume called simply *Registrum*, but now known as the "Great Register of the Priory of St. Andrews." He used the *Registrum* in the years between the writing of the first and second versions of his chronicle. The "Great Register" is the mystery manuscript of Scottish history and was last known to have been in the possession of James Nairn, the minister at Holyrood House in 1660. All that survives is a copy of its table of contents, which indicates that the manuscript was a miscellany of copies of charters and historical notes of which one item was called simply *Historia* (folios 58 to 99).[16] Of the many questions connected with the development of the Macbeth legend is what, if any, unique material was in the "Great Register."

There is also the possibility that Andrew discovered material in the volumes from the old Céli Dé library at St. Serf's church of Loch Leven. The earliest surviving inventory for any Scottish library is that at St. Serf's which is listed in a charter of Bishop Robert of St. Andrews, c. 1150.[17] Robert was an Englishman who had left St. Oswald's at Nosthill (near Pontefract in Yorkshire) as one of five canons regular of the Order of St. Augustine to migrate to the new foundation at Scone c. 1115.[18] He had little knowledge of (and no sympathy for) ancient unreformed communities, so it is little wonder that he was the foe of the Céli Dé and wanted to remove them from positions of authority. He gave the church and its goods to men of whom he approved: the Priory of the Canons Regular of the Order of St. Augustine at St. Andrews. Seventeen items from the Céli Dé library are in the charter recording the transfer: a Pastoral, a Gradual, a Missal, the *Origine*, the *Sentences* of the Abbot Bernard of Clairvaux, three quaternions[19] concerning the Sacraments, part of a Bible with a *Leccionarius*, the *Acts of the Apostles*, and the Gospels, *Prosperus*, three books of Solomon, a gloss on the *Song of Songs*, a tract on the interpretation of words, the *Collection of Sentences*, a commentary on *Genesis*, and excerpts from ecclesiastical regulations.[20] This was a fairly standard collection of texts that follows the guide given in the late eighth-century Rule of Bishop Chrodegang of Metz, which has the Missal, Letters (Epistles),

132   MACBETH BEFORE SHAKESPEARE

Gospels, Penitentials, Calendar, and night readings as the texts necessary for
any monastery.[21] How many, if any, of the volumes were actually transferred
to St Andrews is unknown.

Andrew used at least one of the works in the list: *Prosper*, correctly Prosper
of Aquitaine (c. 390–c. 463), a fifth-century supporter of St. Augustine on the
issue of the overarching importance of divine grace. Of his major works, his
Epitoma Chronicon (an expansion of Jerome's continuation of the chronicle of
the fourth-century historian Eusebius) was especially well known in Britain
and Ireland.[22] *Epitoma Chronicon* was important to Scottish historians for
information on the ordination of Palladius in 431 as the first bishop of the
Scoti. A copy of some portion of this book was circulating in Scotland during
the later Middle Ages. John of Fordun quotes it in connection with the disa-
greement between Prosper and Sigibert of Gembloux (d. 1112) concerning the
year in which St. Martin of Tours died.[23] Prosper's information is found only
in the *Epitoma Chronicon*. There is another possible contribution. Andrew
took the greater part of the first book of his chronicle from the *Imago Mundi*
written by Honorius of Autun (c. 1080–c. 1140) for which an alternative
name was the *Origine*. The *Origine* in the catalogue of St. Serf's library might
be referring to that work by Honorius, rather than the *Etymologies* of Bishop
Isidore of Seville, for which it was also an alternative name.[24]

Searching for Macbeth: Popular

Whatever anecdotes he might have found in his scholarly research, Andrew's
statement that there was more than one story about Macbeth gives an indication of the legends circulating among the commonality. Popular stories,
known as "telling tales" in contemporary tracts, were an important part
of entertainment even at the highest levels of society. How much did the
refinements to the Macbeth legend owe to popular traditions? According to
Andrew's account, they were significant and gave almost contradictory views.
Searching for a solution to the problem is not made simpler by the certainty
that many tales, even those for which the title is known, have not survived.[25]
The presentation of history in the form of entertainment or "Learned Tales"
was the role of the *senachie* or historian.[26]

Modern scholars usually have a rigid separation between history from
documents and history from stories. The medieval world was more fluid
in its employment of both types of history. Andrew's *bot as we fynd be sum
storys* reveals that Macbeth was a character in popular literature or tales. They
were well received at the highest level of society, and payment for "telling

tales" comes from the financial records of the royal court in the accounts of the Lord High Treasurer. The surviving records begin two generations after Andrew's death and the first payment to a tale-teller was in the reign of King James IV on April 9, 1491, when a royal courier named Wallace received eighteen shillings.[27] On November 29 he reappeared at the court as a messenger but was identified as a performer: "Wallace who tells the tales to pass with letters for the Lords Grey, Glammis, and Oliphant" (Wallass that tellis the tayllis, to pass with letteres for the Lordis Grey, Glammis and Olyfant), for which he received ten shillings.[28] Another tale-teller was a fowler called *Widderspune* who combined his occupations on December 9, 1496 when six shillings and eight pence were paid to "Widderspoon the fowler who told tales and brought fowls to the king" (Widderspune the foulare that told talis and brocht foules to the king). He returned three days later in the company of "Watschod the tale tellare" and the pair were paid eighteen shillings. When he next appeared at the court, on April 23, 1497, eighteen shillings were paid to "Widderspune the fowlar for fowlis and tales telling."[29] The accounts can be precise about the form of entertainment and even the name of the story. On the same day that Widderspune was paid for his birds and stories, two "fiddlers who sang Graysteil to the King" (fithelaris that sang Graysteil to the King) received nine shillings: "Graysteil" is popularly known today as "Syr Egeir and Syr Gryme." Compared with other performers, the tale-tellers were well paid. Although Duncan Campbell's bard was given five shillings on September 4, 1506, while "ane tale teller" received only three shillings on the same day, "a poor man who told tales to the king" (ane pure man tald tales to the king) was given a reward of six shillings and eight pence while on August 22 of that year a tale-teller of Dunfermline received five shillings.

An indication of the types of tales that Wallace, Widderspoon, and others were telling the king comes from a list found in the sixteenth-century text called the *Complaynt of Scotland*. This tract presents the Scots' point of view during the "Rough Wooing" when King Henry VIII attempted to force a marriage between his son the future king Edward VI and Mary, the daughter of King James V of Scotland, the future Mary, Queen of Scots. A list of stories and songs is given in the sixth chapter, which is known as the "Recreation" because the author suspends his main narrative to describe a period of leisure among some shepherds. Some of the works are well known, such as the *Canterbury Tales* or the tale of *Rauf Coilyear*. More curious is the title of a tale that suggests a parallel with an episode in Andrew of Wyntoun's version of the Macbeth legend, the "tale of the three weird sisters" (tail of the thre veird systers).[30]

MACBETH BEFORE SHAKESPEARE

Finally, there were the performance pieces with music and acting. There are references to minstrels, players, mimes, and musicians in Scotland from the thirteenth century onward. Confining the brief discussion to the royal court, in 1278 Alexander III's court entertainers went on tour in England. His harpist Master Elias, trumpeters, and two minstrels (in addition to four freelancers) performed at Westminster on October 29 and in the same year the minstrels performed at Durham; later, both Robert I and David II had minstrels at their courts.[31] The exchequer accounts provide more detail. David paid sixty-six pounds Scots thirteen shillings and four pence to the minstrels who performed at his wedding in 1329, and nearly the same amount was paid to the minstrels who performed at the Christmas festival the following year.[32] Twenty pounds Scots were paid to the minstrels who performed at his coronation in 1331 with an additional ten pounds given by Queen Joanna.[33] Thomas the Harper received a pension of sixty pounds in 1329 while William the Harper received twenty shillings for a performance in 1360.[34] During the reign of Robert II, the royal minstrel was Thomas Acarsane who received a pension from the treasury.[35] Robert enjoyed performances and in the same year (1377) paid thirteen shillings and six pence to minstrels.

Only occasionally is there an indication of the material presented. At the wedding banquet of Alexander III at Jedburgh Abbey, the singing and dancing of the performers was silenced when a figure dressed as death glided among them.[36] There were less lofty performances among the population of which Robin Hood stories seem to have predominated.

Prophecy

Andrew of Wyntoun is the first to introduce prophecy into the legend of Macbeth. This was both more respectable and more dangerous. The respectability came from biblical endorsement of individuals who were prophets and the process of prophecy as stated in Acts 2: 17 "And it shall come to pass in the last days says God I will pour out of my spirit upon all flesh; and your sons and your daughters shall prophesy, and your young men shall see visions, and your old men shall dream dreams." The danger came from the belief in foretelling of battle victories or royal deaths.

Andrew's use of prophecy, especially in connection with royal succession, was daring. Prediction was becoming increasingly important both in literature and as a crime during the later Middle Ages. Prophecy is a useful term to cover several different types of foreknowledge, and Andrew used two. The first was the theologically acceptable forecast from a dream, such as that in which Macbeth sees the "weird sisters." The other was the unacceptable demonic pronouncement, which by its very nature had an element of deceit, when the demon supposedly reassures Macbeth's mother that her son will be invincible. In Andrew's narrative, prophecy drives the Macbeth legend as expectations from future knowledge give Macbeth the motivation for his actions.

The two prophetic episodes in the account of Andrew of Wyntoun reflect literary forms of the time.[37] The first episode is his dream of the king with two greyhounds and the three weird sisters, announcing Macbeth's rise to the kingship. The use of dreams as the entrance to another reality, one more truthful than this world, is found in different contexts during the fourteenth and fifteenth centuries. Dante's *Divine Comedy* and Langland's *Piers the Ploughman* both use dreams or dreamlike states to begin the story. While Dante has historical people as well as fantastic beings, Langland's vision is populated entirely with allegorical figures. Andrew's episode is more similar to Dante, with a real person (the king) and also fantastic beings (the weird sisters) although in another piece of Scots literature, the contemporary *The King's Quair* attributed to King James I, it was the inability to fall asleep that starts the action. The second prophetic episode, in which Macbeth's mother is assured by her demon lover of the child's invulnerability, is tied more with the idea of the hero as found in Gaelic literary traditions.

In using prophecy, Andrew was working in forms that had an ancient lineage. Prophecies had been a part of the oral and literary culture in the British Isles for centuries. Foreknowledge was a sign of sanctity for Christians, and St. Patrick refers frequently to a divine gift of the knowledge of future events in his *Confessions*, including his escape from twelve (unnamed) dangers.[38] Adomnán, the head of the church on the Isle of Iona, devotes a third of his *Life of Columba* to prophecies, many of which concern contemporary princes. An example is a prince named Áed the Black who killed the Irish King Diarmait, selected by God to be king of all Ireland according to Adomnán. In penance Áed abandoned his rule and was ordained a priest, although Columba claimed that his motives were impure. He prophesied that Áed would return to his kingdom and die when he was pierced through by a spear and would fall from wood to drown in water. The prophecy was fulfilled when the king was killed in a battle fought on a lake where he was hit by a spear and fell from his wooden boat into the water and drowned.[39] By employing the idea of divine inspiration, prophecy also became a method of expounding history throughout the Gaelic sphere from southern Ireland to northern Scotland. The eleventh-century history of Irish and Scots princes known as the *Prophecy of Berchán* justifies its prognostications with the claim that the information came from an angel. Prophecies about the end of time were equally popular, concerning the Day of Judgment and the signs of its imminent arrival. Tracts with modern titles such as "Tidings of Doomsday" or "The Second Vision of Adomnán" purported to forecast either the culmination of biblical time or local calamities.[40]

Prophecy became a popular literary form in the twelfth century thanks largely to Geoffrey of Monmouth's *History of the Kings of Britain*. His legendary retelling of British history has a chapter devoted to the prophecies of Merlin.[41] Merlin was a minor figure in early Welsh literature (where he was called Myrddin) who had been driven mad by the horrors of war and thereafter shunned human company, preferring to live alone in the forest, where he uttered prophecies. Geoffrey transformed him into the child of a union between a woman and a demon, much as Andrew of Wyntoun did for Macbeth. As an internationally famous soothsayer, Merlin had numerous prophecies attributed to him that imitated the form found in the *History of the Kings of Britain*, which used animal and color symbolism that predominated in Irish prophecy in order to cultivate a deliberate obscurity. This murkiness was so successful that even in hindsight not every prophecy can be understood. Men who claimed to be writing objective history used Geoffrey's work as the basis for their narratives and his prophecies as a guide. An example is the Peter of Langtoft, the canon of Bridlington, who based the first part of his chronicle (from Brutus to the Norman Conquest) on the *History of the Kings of Britain* and concluded it with Merlin's prophecies. Even in the final section, which is his own work, there are asides showing that the prophecies were never far from his mind. The phrase "As Merlin said" (*Ut Merlinus ait*) is frequently used to introduce prophetic texts, such as the poem "The Kingdom of Scotland was among other kingdoms" (Regnum Scotorum fuit inter caetera regna), concerning the Anglo-Scottish wars.[42]

Not everyone who heard those prophecies did so in a spirit of scholarly interest and, even as Andrew was writing, prophecy was becoming increasingly worrisome to the royal authorities. They saw it as cover for political subterfuge or even an inducement to violently overthrow the monarch. Predictions of imminent invasions, the death of the prince, and events forthcoming were thought to provide incentive to those who wished for their fulfillment and might see themselves as the instruments. The author of a history of Edward II claims that the Welsh uprising of 1315 was due to the "Prophecies of Merlin," which gave hope to the Welsh for expelling the English from their country.[43] Political expediency was given religious cover with the medieval belief that unclean spirits could foretell the future but in such a way that they deceived the listener. An example of this comes from the fourteenth-century vernacular Scots tract *The Bruce* by John Barbour. He gives the outline of a story about Earl Ferrand of Flanders whose mother was a necromancer. She raised the Evil One and asked for future knowledge of the outcome of fighting between her son and the French king. The answer was that the king would fall but remain unburied while her son would enter Paris in the midst of a great throng. The prophecy was correct, but not in the manner envisioned by the mother. The French king fell from his horse during the battle but was helped to his feet and was victorious, while the Flemish count was captured and taken as a part of a crowd of prisoners to Paris.[44]

By the fifteenth century, any prophecy that sought to establish the beginning of a reign, the end of a reign, the manner in which it would occur, or to encourage the population at large to abandon the monarch was considered as treasonous as actually leading a rebellion. A pertinent example is the *Prophecy of the Six Kings* that seems to have been composed in the fourteenth century, but was revived early in the fifteenth century during the reign of Henry IV, an exact contemporary of Andrew of Wyntoun.[45] His Lancastrian supporters saw him as the final animal (a mole) in the prophecy, while his enemies used the same work to foretell his ending when the mole would be succeeded by a dragon who, in turn, shares the kingdom with a lion and a wolf. This prophecy had a wide circulation and it was believed to be responsible for the rebellion of the Welsh Prince Owain Glendower who joined with Henry Percy and Edmund Mortimer in the Tripartite Indenture of 1405. Little imagination was required to see them in terms of the animal symbolism of the prophecy. Welsh minstrels were denounced by Henry's agents for spreading lies in the form of divination that were believed to be the cause of rebellion.[46] Whether or not they were agents for Owain's rebellion, certainly his uprising with Percy and Mortimer gave added credence to the final part of the *Six Kings* prophecy, as unrest was expected when the dragon shared the kingdom with the lion and the wolf.

Contrasting, and often competing, with the divinely inspired prophet was the demonically influenced soothsayer. Andrew's episode concerning Macbeth's birth has his demon father directly telling Macbeth's mother the future. Those who practiced this type of forecasting were usually identified with classical oracles, but the association with a demon or otherworldly being was not unusual. There were unsavory inferences, such as Procopius's *Secret History*, where it is implied that Emperor Justinian's diabolic nature was apparent as he seemed to appear and disappear at a feast. Other tales had similar episodes. In the story "Birth of Cú Chulainn," the hero's mother, Dechtire, turns herself into a bird, and his father was Lug of the Long-arm, from the Tuatha Dé Danann.[47] The diabolic aspect to Macbeth's father has a parallel with the *Second Battle of Mag Tuired* where the king named Bres had a supernatural father who gave a ring to his mother.[48]

There was also the element of security from certain types of death. Macbeth's belief that he could not be killed under certain conditions has a parallel with an incident from the Cú Chulainn story. As a youth, Cú Chulainn encountered a warrior named Foill mac Nechtain, who claimed that neither edge (of sword) nor point (of spear tip) could harm him.[49] So Cú Chulainn killed him with an iron ball. Then Foill's brother Tuachall could be killed only during the initial impact of a battle, which was when Cú Chulainn took his life. Finally a third brother named Fainnle could not be killed on land, so Cú Chulainn defeated him on water. There is an "otherworldly" aspect to these three combats, but in each instance there is also a sensible way of overcoming the perceived security of the warriors.

Fantasy Women

Andrew of Wyntoun's reworking of the Macbeth legend was indebted to folk tradition from Ireland, Scotland, and Scandinavia. This is especially true for the inspired female. The weird sisters who announce Macbeth's future in his dream are a direct borrowing from Scandinavia, where "weird" is from Old Norse *Urd* (the name is cognate with Old English *wyrd* "destiny"). Urd was one of the three Norns or fates who decided the life paths of individuals; the others were *Verdandi* and *Skuld*. All three names are derived from the tenses of the verb *verba* "to become" and Urd means "became." The Old Norse poem *Völupsa* in the *Codex Regius* describes them as wise maidens living in the lake under Yggdrasil, the world tree, who established laws as well as chose the paths of lives for people.[50]

Dream or fantasy women had become increasingly mentioned throughout Europe since the ninth century. They were often in a band known by several designations of which the most common was "the good ladies," and they were visible to humans only in a dream. Their leader was called by various names: the Roman goddess Diana, the Germanic fertility goddess and patroness of the hearth Holda, and the biblical individual who was Herod's daughter, usually named Herodia. Trios of women are found in pagan Celtic religion, such as the fertility goddesses who were worshiped as the *matres* (mothers). Supernatural women in groupings of three are found in literature throughout the British Isles. The Welsh tale "How Culwch won Olwen" has three witches named Lluched, Neved, and Eisywed.[51] Three supernatural women from Scotland are found in the medieval tale with the modern title "Cormac mac Airt and the Witches from Scotland" preserved in the Irish *Book of Lecan* and exactly contemporary with Andrew.[52] Andrew's "weird sisters" could be transformed into figures in a dream, or sibyls.

The inspired female had a long ancestry from classical times. Whether she is a Cassandra with tidings of woe or the Pythia at the oracle of Apollo, the prophetess is well represented. The female clairvoyant is also found in Ireland and Scandinavia, outside the influence of the classical world. Among the Vikings in Ireland during the ninth century was Tuirges, who led a successful campaign in the Irish midlands during the mid-ninth century that culminated with the temporary seizure of the important monastery of Clonmacnoise. There his wife, Auðr, delivered prophecies from the church's high altar.[53] Supernatural women or Valkyries in the Old Norse poem "The Banner Song" (Darraðljóð), preserved in the epic Icelandic work known as "Burnt Njal's Saga" (Brennu-Njáls Saga), are a postscript to the description of the Battle of Clontarf.[54] In this poem, Valkyries chant at a loom that has human heads as weights and swords as the beaters. The chant describes their journey through a battle in which the warriors' fates are determined by their whim. Like the dream ladies of Wyntoun's account, the Valkyries decide who will prosper, but they do so directly through their own efforts. The equivalents of the Valkyries among the Gaels were three goddesses—Mórrígan, Badbh, and Macha—who haunted battlefields and prophesied carnage.

The Valkyrie can also be compared with the Irish banshee, from *ban síde*, "woman of the fairy mound." The amorous nature of these ladies led men into another world. The tale "The Love Sickness of Cú Chulainn" (Serglige Con Chulainn) has the great warrior incapacitated because of his desire for a lady from the fairy mound.[55] Three of her ladies-in-waiting attack the hero, but he can see them only in a vision or dream. They strike him until he is unable to refuse their request to fight for the king of the *síd*. At the same time the fairy king's daughter falls in love with Cú Chulainn and tries to keep him with her. In another tale, Cú Chulainn's impending death is announced when he meets three crones on his journey to what would become his last battle.[56] They are cooking dog, which is a sign of his demise because his name translates as "Hound of Cooley." Conaire, the hero of the saga *The Destruction of Dá Derga's Hostel* (Togail Bruidne Dá Derga) has his death prophesied by a woman and, as a sign of his doom, he is accompanied to his final battle by three horsemen.[57] The power of these fairy or supernatural women was considered to be so great

140   MACBETH BEFORE SHAKESPEARE

that there is even a prayer against their power called "Patrick's Breastplate:" "[protect us] against the spells of women, smiths, and druids" (fri brichtu ban ocus gobann ocus druad).[58] According to the eleventh-century Irish text *War of the Irish against the Vikings* (*Cocad Gaedel re Gallaib*) the Irish high king Brian Boru knew of his impending death because his banshee told him.[59] A pseudo-prophecy concerning the kings of Ireland called "The Phantom's Frenzy" (Baile in Scáil) was written by Macbeth's contemporary Abbot Dubdá-leithe of Armagh, the leading churchman in Ireland. There a supernatural woman, representing the sovereignty of Ireland pours out a cup of ale for each king she announces.[60] There was no anti-Christian element connected with the fairy women in either story, and Brian was considered to be a model Christian king.

Trees

The journey of Birnam Wood to Dunsinane Hill is another example of folk legend. Just as the forest is on the border between tame (i.e., cultivated) and wild land, so too it was on the border between the natural world and the supernatural world. A brief thirteenth-century geographical tract, attached to some copies of the history of the archbishops of Hamburg/Bremen written by the eleventh-century historian Adam of Bremen, notes that the people who lived round the Moray Firth had a strange burial practice.[61] While commoners and others of humble degree were interred in the earth, nobles were buried inside trees. The prophecy that Macbeth would reign until Birnam Wood came to Dunsinane Hill is one of two prophecies that seem to guarantee his safety, but their fulfillment leads to his eventual death. Birnam Wood was a working concern in the late Middle Ages and is mentioned in several late medieval and early modern documents. Andrew probably knew it because of its connection with St. Andrews, which appears in the records after his death when, in 1457, a Ninian Spot was reimbursed forty Scots shillings (*solidi*) for carrying wood from Birnam to Perth on behalf of the brothers of St. Andrews.[62] On September 12, 1499, King James IV gave the woods of Birnam to Bishop George of Dunkeld for a payment of forty shillings per year. The king confirmed his gift on June 18, 1507, stating more precisely that included were "the lands, forest, and woods of Birnam and Logie together with the mill and *le forestarisetis de Birnam*."[63]

Trees had a pronounced symbolism in Irish and Scots literature. A now-lost Irish legal tract called "Tree Judgments" (Fidbretha) described the penalties for destruction of trees as well as their legal status.[64] Trees also featured in eschatology, the study of last things. A tract originally from the ninth century called "Tenga Bithnua" (Evernew Tongue) has the story of the Apostle Philip whose preaching among heathens led their leaders to cut out his tongue, but it always grew again so that he could continue his proselytizing, during which a tree is delivered by a cloud, one of the four trees that have souls and intelligence.[65] Many churches had groves of trees that were considered sacred. "The Calendar of Angus" (Féilire Óengusso), a ninth-century ecclesiastical calendar of church festivals and saints' days to which were appended notes in the eleventh or twelfth century, has the story of the church of Echdruimm (now Aughrim, county Galway) with its magical oak grove. While the church's sacred tree could be seen at a distance, it could not be found once a person was in the grove.[66]

There was a real military importance to forests, which were either places of ambush or places of refuge. A thick forest lay to the south of the town of Dublin during the Middle Ages and when, in 1170, the Anglo-Norman army was traveling northward in its successful attack on the army of the Irish high king Rory O'Connor, they made a detour to the coast in order to avoid going into the trees, where they feared an ambush. Forests also concealed troops. On the Isle of Man in the late eleventh century, the Manx king Godred Crovan, remembered in legend as King Orry, sailed to the port of Ramsey and hid 300 men among the trees on the slope of Sky Hill. As the battle raged the next day, the concealed troops emerged to attack their foes who fled and Godred won the day.[67] A passage in the "War of the Irish against the Vikings" claims that Donnchad, the son of the slain hero Brian, tied his wounded men to wooden stakes when they were fighting their way home after the battle of Clontarf.[68] He wanted them to be upright and face their enemies. Geoffrey of Monmouth's *History of the Kings of Britain* describes the Saxons sheltering among trees.[69] Occasionally man and tree were merged into a unit as warrior bands are compared with woods. There is the imagery of woodsmen clearing a forest to describe the ferocity of the battle of Clontarf.[70] Slightly later, "Battle of Ross of the Kings" (Cath Ruis na Ríg) compares a depleted warrior band with a forest that has been cleared.[71]

Trees also are associated with supernatural females in Irish legend. The tale "Cú Chulainn in the Valley of the Deaf" has Queen Maeve of Connacht wishing to destroy Cú Chulainn, the greatest warrior among her foes, the men of Ulster. So she sends a troop of creatures who are half women and half goblins to lure Cú Chulainn to his death. These monsters take three magic swords and three magic spears. Then they cast spells and create an army from twigs and leaves to arouse his battle fury. Cú Chulainn's wife Emer realizes what Maeve is trying to accomplish, and she also knows that the goblin women have power for only three days. So Emer takes Cú Chulainn to a secluded place to wait for three days, but the adversaries find them and torment him. Unfortunately, the illusions have their intended effect, and Cú Chulainn goes to fight what would be his last battle.[72]

Andrew of Wyntoun and Macbeth

Andrew of Wyntoun represents the humanistic spirit that was beginning to prevail in the fifteenth century. For him the history of Macbeth is worthy of study for its own sake, not simply as a morality lesson. Unlike John of Fordun, who usually identifies his sources even when he wishes to argue against them, Andrew is less candid, but occasionally no less transparent. Elsewhere he alludes to unnamed stories, and his work is an important collection of popular tales. For the first time since the eleventh century, ladies are mentioned in direct connection with Macbeth. Women not only make their appearance at this time, but they drive the action forward. Gruoch is mentioned by name, and her marriage to Macbeth provides him with political legitimacy. The dream ladies set him on his career of regicide. Macduff's wife taunts Macbeth as he arrives too late to stop the flight of her husband. Finally, in reversal of natural function, the usurper is slain by an opponent whose birth denies the usual role of the mother.

Absent from Andrew of Wyntoun's work is any indication of prejudice against the Highlanders. John of Fordun mocked the fastnesses in the northern mountains, but Andrew simply traces Macbeth's flight across the Mounth (i.e., the Grampians) to the final confrontation in a wood at Lumphanan. The antipathy between the Highland and Lowland communities in Scotland is well known, but if later records are a guide, stories and performance pieces moved across the cultural divide. On June 23, 1501, two Highland bards (*tua Heland bardis*) were paid five shillings for their performance before King James IV.[73] On November 18 in that year, the thane of Caldor's harper played at court and was given eighteen shillings. Also present were the Maidens of Forres (*madinnis of Forres*) who were rewarded with nine shillings. The following year, January 2, thirteen shillings were paid to Canongate (*the bard wif in the Canonegait*).

The *Original Chronicle* of Andrew of Wyntoun is the most important stage in the development of the Macbeth legend, not least because it shows that by the fifteenth century there were circulating around Scotland different legends of Macbeth. In some of those stories, Macbeth is a hero—a generous and pious king who made good laws. In other legends, he is a sinister figure of demonic origin whose actions reveal his nature. Andrew changed Macbeth from a stereotypical and one-dimensional villain into the hero/anti-hero of the story. More so than any previous writer, he provided the names of places, character development, historical details and genealogical information that would be adapted by later interpreters of the Macbeth story. The most important difference, however, was that Wyntoun introduced the supernatural elements—fey women, prophecies, and demons—that became a standard part of the legend. A second element was the introduction of female characters. Now Macbeth has a queen, and in the second version she is given a name: Gruoch. Lady Macduff also appears, and she has the pleasure of baiting the furious Macbeth as her husband sails away. Finally and most important, Andrew of Wyntoun transformed the tale of a mere villain into an exposition on the evil that lies in men's hearts.

7

Macbeth and Renaissance Scotland

IF THERE IS an imaginative divide between the works of John of Fordun and Andrew of Wyntoun, there is an equally important intellectual separation between Andrew and the historians who came after him. The renaissance of historical writing in the British Isles that began in the fifteenth century and continued into the sixteenth reveals a keen interest in what is described as the medieval world. That led to curious contradictions. Wealthy merchants whose grandparents had been peasant farmers coveted knighthoods, coats of arms, and other chivalric devices. At the same time, increasingly impoverished aristocrats guarded ever more closely their ancient privileges and titles while they hunted among the despised affluent bourgeoisie for spouses for their children. This revivalism led to the reinterpretation of stories and legends from the Middle Ages. Authors such as Thomas Malory in his *La Morte d'Arthur* contrasted the glamor and religious devotion found in the Arthurian tales with the decadence of his own day. Unmentioned was that the splendor of King Arthur's court had been as much a fantasy when Geoffrey of Monmouth wrote his *History of the Kings of Britain* in the twelfth century as it was during the fifteenth century.[1]

The Macbeth legend increasingly reflected the concerns of its interpreters. For writers in medieval Scotland, this ranged from contacts with Scandinavia to religious controversy. Looking ahead, Macbeth became a foot soldier in the intellectual warfare of the sixteenth century, as conflicting religious identifications combined with equally conflicting theories on the rights and nature of monarchy. This new age saw significant reinterpretations of Macbeth's legend as he was recast into an innovative kind of prince for a different age. John of Fordun's one-dimensional ogre and Andrew of Wyntoun's devil-sired schizophrenic gave way to an evil sophisticate who was less easy to dismiss simply as a bad man. The medieval warlord/usurper was refined into a political animal with style. The man responsible for creating him was Hector Boece, one of the early leaders of the Scottish Renaissance. His Macbeth was a complicated beast. Part bon vivant, part war hero, but entirely an elusive psychological specimen, this Macbeth was able to command the love and loyalty of many. Equally he was an egotistic, savage tyrant who ruthlessly pursued his own ends. This comes very close to a description of the Renaissance prince, such as King Henry VIII of England. Accompanying Macbeth in his transformation were the supporting characters. Lady Macbeth, in particular, emerges to become the main motivator of the action within three generations of her rescue from oblivion by Andrew of Wyntoun.

Hector Boece

The historical work that was the direct ancestor of William Shakespeare's *Tragedie of Macbeth* began as an occasional pastime for a teacher turned university administrator named Hector Boece. While his career spanned the late Middle Ages to the early modern era, Boece was truly a Renaissance man. He had studied in France, where he had seen many examples of the new kind of aristocrat upon whom he modeled Macbeth. He was responsible for transforming Macbeth from a savage medieval chieftain into a Renaissance anti-hero-prince with fashionable interests in the occult and law. Boece's Macbeth is sophisticated and eloquent, a multi-faceted individual who is far removed from the swaggering despot of the medieval histories.

Compared with any previous author of the Macbeth legend, much more is known about Hector Boece (c. 1465–c. 1536). He was born in the city of Dundee, the port town for ships sailing the Firth of Tay. The "Auld Alliance" between the Scots and French was still strong a century and a half after the beginning of the Anglo-Scottish wars, so Hector went to the University of Paris for advanced study. After receiving his degree, he remained there as a teacher in the College of Montaigu, famous for the severity of its routine and the scholarship of its community. Among Boece's friends was Desiderius Erasmus, one of the fathers of modern humanism. When he was about thirty years old, Boece returned to Scotland, taking up residence in Aberdeen, Dundee's commercial rival. Under the leadership of Bishop William Elphinstone, plans were made to establish a university. The original name was the Collegiate Church of St. Mary of the Nativity, later renamed King's College in honor of the patronage of King James IV of Scotland and then the University of Aberdeen. Hector Boece was selected to be the first principal in addition to teaching theology and medicine.

146 MACBETH BEFORE SHAKESPEARE

Boece's return to his homeland allowed him to indulge his antiquarian interests, and two works secured his place among the influential historians of the sixteenth century: *The Lives of the Bishops of Murthlack and Aberdeen* (*Murthlacensium et Aberdonensium Episcoporum Vitae*), which was published in Paris in 1522, and *Scottorum Historiae a prima gentis origine cum aliarum et rerum et gentium illustratione non vulgari*, better known by the short English title *History of the Scots*, which was published in Paris in 1527. In *History of the Scots*, Boece reworks the Macbeth legend within a narrative that begins with the legendary foundation of Scotland and continues to the death of King James I. Although the tone of the narrative is sober, Boece used little scholarly discretion in his selection of material. He seems to have incorporated any materials available. Obviously fantastic tales appear alongside factually accurate information; the remaining narrative might or might not be true. Sixteenth-century historians called him a fantasist or worse. English antiquarian John Leland claimed that Boece's fabrications were as numerous as the waves and the stars, while Welsh scholar Humphrey Lhuyd dispensed with the imagery and bluntly called him a liar.[2] Modern historians use his books with caution.

Boece relates one interesting piece of historiography indicating where he found his information. In the *Lives of the Bishops* he claims that there was an archive at Iona, but the records were transferred to Restennet (in Angus) during the reign of King Alexander the First (1107–1124) and those materials were incorporated into his work.[3] Boece repeats his claim that he used manuscripts from Iona in the *History of the Scots*, but there he writes that five ancient codices were sent to him from Iona, through the good offices of John Campbell; whether he means from the Isle of Iona or from the Iona materials he claims were at Restennet is unclear.[4] Sir John Campbell of Lunie was treasurer to King James V, to whom the *History of the Scots* was dedicated, and himself a student of history. Boece notes the codices were so old that the vellum was stiff and brittle. Before dismissing Boece's "Iona Manuscripts" as fabrication, it is clear that there had been a collection of books at Iona and that all the manuscripts, in whatever library had been there, were removed at some time before the end of the Middle Ages. Some vellum manuscripts from Iona seem to have been taken to the Isle of Skye where leaves from service books almost certainly used at the Benedictine house on Iona were later found among the medical manuscripts of the Beatons, a famous family of physicians who lived on the island.[5] Among the superstitious, there was a belief that liturgical texts, as "holy writ," had a particular healing power.

Boece names two specific sources in the preface of the *History of the Scots.* They were a tract by Bishop Turgot of St. Andrews and a chronicle composed by Vermundus. Turgot is generally thought to be the "T" who composed the vita of St. Margaret of Scotland, but he also wrote a history of his own times. Boece claimed that Vermundus's chronicle covered affairs up to the reign of Malcolm Canmore, to whom it was dedicated.[6] There are three differing views on Veremundus. The traditional opinion, from the sixteenth century, is that Veremundus was simply a creation of Boece's imagination, invented to give a suitably antique authenticity to the narrative. The second view is that Veremundus was probably the Richard Vairmont who was at St. Andrews in the thirteenth century. Finally, there is the conjecture that the chronicle attributed to Veremundus was composed in the fifteenth century for the intended purpose of providing intellectual justification for the aristocratic rebellion against King James III.[7] Another sixteenth-century historian, David Chambers of Ormond, lists *Veremonde Espagnol* as one of his sources in his *Histoire abbregée* of the French, English, and Scots kings. Yet it is clear from his introduction that Chalmers had not seen this work but that he had found it among the sources given in Boece's preface; also present in Chalmer's list are Turgot, John Campbell, and Boece himself.[8]

Boece's Macbeth

Hector Boece's story of Macbeth is found in the twelfth book of *History of the Scots.* He starts somewhat differently from John of Fordun and Andrew of Wyntoun, although he does maintain the connection of kinship between Macbeth and Duncan. Unlike John of Fordun who does not make any claims of kinship between the two men, or Andrew of Wyntoun, who claims that Duncan was Macbeth's uncle, Boece states that Duncan and Macbeth were cousins, the sons of King Malcolm's daughters (respectively) Bethoc and Doada. In another change, Boece widens the scope of the Macbeth legend by placing it in an international setting as he amplifies a rebellion into a national assault. After Duncan succeeds his grandfather Malcolm, he is confronted by an uprising in the Hebrides led by a noble named Macdonald. The rebellion is crushed by Macbeth. Immediately afterward there follows a Norwegian invasion led by King Swein. Duncan is defeated in battle, but the hero Macbeth saves the day with a cunning assault on his foes after they are put to sleep using an herbal drink. As the victorious Macbeth is returning to the king's camp at Forres with his friend Banquo, who makes his first appearance in the legend and is described as the thane of Lochquhaber, they see three apparitions in

148   MACBETH BEFORE SHAKESPEARE

the form of women (Boece will later describe them as nymphs or devils). The apparitions prophesy three ranks of increasing stature—thane of Glamis, thane of Cawdor, and king of Scotland—for Macbeth, while for Banquo they promise the prosperity of his lineage. Initially neither Macbeth nor Banquo takes the pronouncements seriously; they even have a standing joke between themselves, addressing each other by the title the women gave. The joke ends when Duncan invests his son Malcolm with the title prince of Cumbria, thereby designating him to be next in line for the throne. Macbeth fears that his own hopes for the kingship are ruined. Lady Macbeth stirs her husband into action with accusations of cowardice. Macbeth confronts Duncan near Elgin and kills him (Boece is unclear on the precise location: after originally giving Enuernes he offers the alternative of Bothgofuane).

Macbeth begins his reign with the expulsion of Duncan's sons Malcolm and Donald. Then he rules wisely, if not entirely morally. He bribes the nobles into accepting his rule and they enjoy ten years of good lordship. Macbeth, unlike weak Duncan, directs his severity against malefactors and makes good laws that are listed in the text. This benign era ends when Macbeth prepares an ambush for Banquo and his son Fleance at a banquet, a violation of the obligations of hospitality. Banquo is killed, but Fleance escapes to Wales. Next to feel the wrath of the king is Macduff, who escapes from the royal court; Macbeth murders his wife and children in retaliation. Macbeth is sustained in his increasingly criminal acts by the belief that he is invincible. He was told that his overthrow would be made only by a man not born of woman and only when Birnam Wood marches to Lumphanan.[9] Escaping to England, Macduff urges Malcolm to return to Scotland, which he does in the company of Earl Siward. When Macbeth flees from Fife to Dunsinane, Malcolm follows and orders each man to take a branch from Birnam Wood to use as camouflage. After the attackers seize his fortress at Dunsinane, Macbeth flees to Lumphanan, pursued by Macduff who confronts Macbeth and reveals that his (Macduff's) birth was by caesarean section and he was not by "woman born." Macduff kills the tyrant, an event that Boece dates to 1061. Malcolm is proclaimed king and following his coronation, the privileges of Macduff are listed: participation in the royal coronation; fighting in the vanguard of the army; and the enjoyment of legal dispensation for certain crimes. Macbeth's stepson, Lulach, is not mentioned.

Obvious from this brief summary are the ways that Boece's version conflates the Macbeth legend found in John of Fordun's chronicle with that from Andrew of Wyntoun's work. There is no doubt about Boece's reading of the former because his copy of John of Fordun's chronicle survives.[10] This paper manuscript was made during the episcopate of Bishop James Kennedy of St. Andrews (1440–1465) with shortened chapters of Fordun's *Chronicle*. The section of this manuscript relating to Macbeth is generously annotated, showing that Boece used this work attentively. While there is no comparable direct link with Andrew of Wyntoun, the similarities between Boece's history and Andrew's chronicle are too many and too close to allow for coincidence. Numerous copies of the *Original Chronicle* were in circulation.

This leads to the question of Boece's original contributions. Are they the fruits of his research among documents, some of which no longer exist, or are they the products of his imagination? As it relates to the Macbeth episode, part of the answer seems to be that Hector Boece was a collector of historical items, like Andrew of Wyntoun, but he was also a conscientious scholar according to his lights. To give two examples, he gives an alternative location for Duncan's death and is aware of the material claiming that Siward of Northumbria was a kinsman of Malcolm Canmore. He, in company with Andrew of Wyntoun and others (such as the chronicles of the canons of St. Mary's, Huntingdon, and Peter of Langtoft), makes a direct connection of kinship between Macbeth and Duncan. Since Boece claims that Macbeth was also a grandson of Malcolm II, then he acquired the same right to be king as Duncan. Less obvious is the material unique to Boece's version. He is the first to give a name—Doada—to Macbeth's mother who he claims is the daughter of Malcolm II, although Andrew's account implies a parallel connection.

His legal training and interest explain why Boece expands on the laws of Macbeth's reign. Andrew of Wyntoun merely remarked that good laws were made and enforced, but Hector Boece gives a list of them. There might have been a law code connected with Macbeth's name, but it is more likely that Boece took existing legal principles and reworked them. Throughout his list, the overarching principle was that the king was the final legal arbiter in Scotland. This is visible for the Scots princes since the ninth century. The contemporary *Scottish Chronicle* notes that King Donald I (reigned 858–862) ordered all his subjects—Picts and Scots—in the lands of the Picts to use laws imported from Dál Riata, and his nephew Constantine II continued the cultural reorientation when he ordered the churches to use Irish rather than Pictish laws.[11] More ground for speculation is a tract that survives only in a late medieval copy called "The Laws of Malcolm Mac Kenneth," (i.e., Malcolm II).[12] The connection of prince with law becomes obvious in the twelfth century, when Malcolm Canmore's son David I oversaw the legal organization of the Scots kingdom. David used his reign to issue charters, enforce justice, and strictly collect his customary dues, many of which appear for the first time in written sources.

Ironically as it would later transpire, one of the laws fathered on Macbeth concerns actors and other performers: "Actors, pantomimes, mimes and remaining worthless people, if they were not given the king's specific permission, they must be set to another craft; which if they refuse, if not because of inability by virtue of sickness or they will have been mutilated, by the use of draught animals to a plough or they will be made to pull a wagon."[13] The phrase "draught animals to a plough" is interesting in connection with Macbeth's threat to Macduff during the building of the fortress on Dunsinane Hill. That particular law seems to be a summary of efforts to control performers that had been legislated during the fifteenth century. The Scots parliament passed legislation in 1449 to expel fools, bards, and rhymers if they had no visible means of employment, which the parliament of 1457 slightly altered by giving them the opportunity to appear before the king as an alternative to banishment.[14]

Another area of interest for Boece was prophecy, and he expands every instance of fore-knowledge. One reason might have been to emphasize Macbeth's lack of fitness to be king, because of his belief in the prognostications of fortune tellers, which was a mark of evil with a long pedigree. As a Christian cleric, Hector Boece need only open his Bible to find examples of good kings in opposition to auguries, such as 2 Kings 23:24 where Josiah removed sorcerers and prophets. Insular tracts were no less hostile. The seventh-century Old Irish morality tract *Twelve Abuses of the Ages* (*De duodecim abusivis saeculi*), which was popular throughout medieval Europe, claims that an unjust king gives credence to the pronouncements of magicians, prophets, and sorceresses (*magorum, hariolorum et pythonissarum*) while the near-contemporary Old Irish wisdom tract *Testament of Morann* (*Audacht Morainn*) warns against trusting in auguries.[15] The expansion of the occult becomes more pronounced when Boece has Macbeth consult soothsayers described as *aruspeces* (Latin *haruspex*) who warn him about Macduff. Boece is flaunting his classical education in this instance because the *haruspex* was an Etruscan diviner who foretold events by examining entrails of humans. Earlier, in the confusion about the identity of the women who accosted Macbeth and Banquo, Boece suggests that they were *Parcae*; *Parca* was the Roman goddess of fate, which suggests that Boece was aware of the derivation of Scots *weird*. More puzzling is his suggestion that they were nymphs, for these mythical women originally were associated with water, although by the sixteenth century the name had become a generic for a female association with the supernatural.

Additionally, Boece is important for the transition of the "weird sisters." Andrew of Wyntoun's three weird sisters are dream creatures, but this was too close to medieval superstition for a rational man such as Boece. He gives them a real presence and they become apparitions of ladies who physically greet Macbeth and Banquo. Boece is also the first person to place the meeting in a specific place, at the town of Forres (in modern Morayshire) in the Highlands, that region feared and despised by the lowland Scots. Finally, Boece has the apparitions greet Macbeth in slightly different terms. The weird sisters in Wyntoun's history call Macbeth thane of Cromarty, thane of Moray, and king; in Boece the titles are thane of Glamis, thane of Cawdor, and king. Boece also introduces another prophetess who foretells that Macbeth will be invincible until confronted by a man not born of woman. She is merely mentioned and then the story moves on, but it seems to indicate that Boece was uncomfortable with the demon lover found in Andrew of Wyntoun's version. Nonetheless, prophecy becomes a crucial part of the developing legend.

Curiously missing from any version of the Macbeth legend is the more common Latin term *magus*, "magician" or "learned one," and the Romans borrowed the word from the Persians. The *magus* was a standard villain in Irish and Scots hagiography. The three wise men who took gifts to the infant Christ were *magi*. A female *maga* could also be an enchantress. In medieval literature the *magi* were not considered good, but not actively evil, and they were prophets. The episode of the two dragons in Nennius's *History of the Britons*, in which a boy about to be sacrificed saves himself by predicting the discovery of two warring beasts and the significance of their battle, has the *magi* consistently baffled by challenges to their divining abilities.[16] The medieval Gaelic translation of *magus* was *druí*, "druid," which anciently was a member of the learned class, but in medieval literature the name became limited to magician, wizard, or diviner. They were the usual scoundrels of saints' lives and other religious literature whose defeat at the hands of the Christian missionary was a foregone conclusion. Rejection of magic passed into wisdom literature.

The Origins of Banquo

Perhaps the most important contribution made by Boece to the Macbeth legend is the introduction of Banquo, the one major character of Shakespeare's drama who was still missing, together with his son Fleance, who escapes from the ambush that claims his father's life and flees to Wales. Banquo is a significant addition; his supposed ancestry of King James might have been one of the reasons that William Shakespeare decided to write his drama. Shakespeare's play would expand his significance and make Banquo the audience's voice. He is with Macbeth when they meet the women upon the heath, he is the first bystander to give voice to doubts about Macbeth's version of events, and he is the one whose trust in his friend is brutally betrayed. More important, his death will signal the beginning of events leading to the tyrant's eventual destruction.

What were the origins of Banquo? Hector Boece has little to say about him directly, beyond giving him the title "thane of Lochquhabir." Lochquhabir is modern Lochaber, the region where Invernesshire, Perthshire, and Argyllshire meet. With its spectacular scenery it was celebrated as a wild and romantic area in the nineteenth century; wolves were still hunted there in the seventeenth century. Anciently famous was the confluence there of two prominent rivers with an illustrious loch or lake: the rivers Nevis and Lochy enter Loch Linnhe close together. This was the anciently famous "Pool of the river mouths" (*Stagnum Aporum*) mentioned in Adomnán's *Life of Columba* and known in Gaelic as *an Linne Dhubh*, "the Black Pool."

Did Hector Boece obtain his information about Banquo and Fleance from some historical record or are they the products of his imagination? A clue to the origin of Banquo comes from a reference to a now-lost work by John Barbour. Barbour, it will be remembered, wrote *The Bruce*, the long poem on the career of King Robert I during the reign of King Robert II, the first of the Stewart kings of Scotland. Andrew of Wyntoun praises a verse genealogy composed by John Barbour called "The Stewarts' Origin" (*Stewartis Originall*):

> *The Stewarts' Origin*
> *The Archdeacon [i.e., Barbour] has treated well*
> *In fair metre, more virtuously*
> *Than I can contemplate by my study*
> *By good continuation*
> *In successive generation.*[17]

Andrew's remarks suggest that Barbour's poem was widely known, and its essential information probably is found in the family trees of the Stuarts/ Stewarts that were composed in the sixteenth century. Hector Boece might have seen a copy of the *Stewartis Originall* in Aberdeen (where Barbour had served as a priest) because there seems to be a synopsis of it in the fifth chapter of the twelfth book of his *History of the Scots*.[18] The chapter begins with Macbeth enticing Banquo and his son Fleance to a meal, where the father is slain but the son escapes. Then follows a departure from the subject with an account of Fleance's flight to Wales where he is sheltered by the prince. Disregarding the duties owed to a host, Fleance seduces his protector's daughter. Her father is so outraged by this flaunting of his hospitality that he kills Fleance. When his daughter gives birth to a child, it is a boy who is named Walter. One day Walter is taunted by a playmate for not having a father. He resolves to return to Scotland and there produces a family who become the Stewarts. A shortened version of that story is found in the sixteenth-century history of Wales by David Powel called *The Historie of Cambria* that was published in London in 1584. Powel, the vicar of Ruabon and a fellow of All Souls College, Oxford, was a protégé of William Cecil, Baron Burghley, one of Queen Elizabeth I's most influential advisors, but the *Historie of Cambria* was written for Sir Henry Sidney. Powel merely notes the flight of Fleance to Wales, but he also supplies the additional information that his protector was Gruffudd ap Llywellyn, the eleventh-century prince who was famous as the unifier of Wales; he was also Macbeth's exact contemporary.[19] Whether Powel knew this story from Boece's history or from an independent source is unknown.

The Banquo material can be interpreted in various ways. This might be an example of the wholesale manufacture of family origins by newly powerful members of an élite. The Stewarts came from humble origins and owed their possession of the Scottish throne to marriage with the family of Robert I. Or this might be the type of garbled remembrance that is to be expected in the attempt to discover family origins three centuries earlier. If the goal of the story was to provide a glorious heritage for the Stewarts, it failed. While the death in ambush might be seen as mere bad luck, the abuse of hospitality and a violated maiden are hardly magnificent. The selection of Wales as the haven for Fleance suggests that the story preserved by Boece represents an effort on someone's part at genuine historical research. Prior to their emigration to Scotland, the home of the Stewarts was Brittany and their original name was Fitz Allan. The Latin name for Wales in the eleventh-century was Britannia in the early records, while Brittany in France was Brittania minor (Little Britain). Confusion rather than construction seems to be behind the story of Banquo.

Boece the Historian

Despite being criticized as a fantasist, Boece was actually attempting to give a rational narrative, although he did not ignore some supernatural aspects that had become part of the legend. His story of Macbeth reflects the Renaissance humanism that was replacing medieval mysticism. This is most evident in the episode that begins with Macbeth's desire for the crown culminating with his dispatch of Duncan. Differing from Andrew of Wyntoun, Boece's Macbeth is not precipitated to crime by the prophecy of the weird sisters, which he treats lightly, but by the thwarting of his plans for succession. Boece's version of the story makes clear that a period of time passed before Macbeth's attempt on Duncan's life, as well as Lady Macbeth's impatience with the lengthy delay. When Duncan selects his son Malcolm as the heir-designate, Macbeth coolly calculates his response. He makes his claim to the kingship publicly and justifies it by reference to the law that children cannot govern, so their place must be taken by the nearest adult kinsman. When Macbeth finally decides to confront Duncan, his wife's insistence plays an active role, and he gathers his friends for an attack on the king at Inverness. There is nothing clandestine about the hostility; it is conflict between two opposing factions.

Boece was less bigoted than has been claimed. Unlike Fordun, he is not hostile to the Highlanders and is sympathetic to Gaelic culture. By the standards of his day, and in comparison with his predecessors, he emerges as a competent, if slightly sensationalist, historian. The difference was the area of research. Andrew of Wyntoun's chronicle, for example, reflects the types of materials that he found in the archives at St. Andrews or possibly Loch Leven. Boece appears to be incorporating the materials that were circulating in the Highlands. He probably found some of his source materials during his research into the early history of the diocese of Aberdeen. Perhaps informants provided information as well, for then, as now, the university drew its students from the regions of northern Scotland. Like Andrew of Wyntoun, Hector Boece encountered very different accounts of the Macbeth legend. One version remembered a strong, effective prince, while the other conjured a monster whose crimes were heinous even by the standards of the day. How the two men handled their sources is instructive. Wyntoun did not attempt to reconcile the variations but merely included everything as it came to hand; hence his account stops and restarts in places. Boece was a much more polished writer who knew the demands of a narrative and attempted to accommodate them.

Whatever his shortcomings as a historian, Hector Boece's interpretation of Scottish history became the standard for the sixteenth and seventeenth centuries. Part of his success was royal support and another part was the printing press, which allowed numerous copies of his history to circulate, unlike the works of John of Fordun and Andrew of Wyntoun. An additional part was that his tale could be manipulated to suit almost anyone's political agendum, enabling his work to be put to use in Scotland and in England. For the former, Boece's history was called into the service of political theory masquerading as history. When even ideological rivals like George Buchanan and John Leslie could use Boece's basic story, it is clear that he had achieved an interesting feat. The legend of Macbeth was pertinent to theorists in light of the deposition of Queen Mary Stewart and the succession of her son James VI.

Macbeth and Scottish Political History

Hector Boece the historian was criticized during his lifetime by other scholars as a fabulist, fantasist, and liar. Nonetheless, his book had become the "official" version of Scottish history before he died in 1536. He was not the only one writing Scottish history; another was the principal of the University of Glasgow named John Major or Maer (1467–1550). In common with his contemporary Walter Bower, John Major originally came from Lothian. He was educated at the universities of Cambridge and Paris, and taught at Paris, Glasgow, and St. Andrews; he became principal of the University of Glasgow in 1518. The year before Boece's *Lives of the Bishops* appeared, Major published *Historia majoris Britanniae, tam Angliae quam Scotiae*, a treatise that called for a union of Scotland with England. In the *Historia majoris Britanniae* Major's retelling of the Macbeth legend is little more than an abridgement of Fordun's story. Like Fordun, however, his book was a self-proclaimed effort to present the Scots' version of history with the added intention of showing the benefits of cooperation between the Scots and English. Most of the long debate between Malcolm Canmore and Macduff on kingly morality, for example, is reduced to a few pithy sentences. There is no doubt, however, that Macbeth had become a figure of evil. Major is aware of alternative versions of materials about Macbeth with his comment "This Macabeus or Machabeda, as others say" (*Hic Macabeus siue Machabeda (ut alii loquuntur)*), but this does not prevent him from employing pejorative vocabulary in describing his relations with Duncan.[20] Major's main contribution was the application of logic to history, and he began the process of discarding the fantastic and obviously fictional materials.

Logic was no match for fantasy. Hector Boece's blending of possible fact with probable fiction caught the popular imagination, unlike the more sober recitation of his contemporary John Major. Boece would have been just another obscure historian, however, were it not for the official approval given to his work by the Scottish King James V and his mother Margaret Tudor, who initially were responsible for the popularity and dissemination of his history. Within a couple of years of the original publication of the *History of the Scots* (while Boece was still alive) they ordered translations to be made. Both mother and son came from scholarly backgrounds, although they were not scholars themselves. James was the son of the scholar-prince King James IV, the last of the Scottish monarchs to speak Gaelic and considered one of the most intelligent monarchs of his day. Queen Margaret was the elder daughter of King Henry VII and the older sister of King Henry VIII. Educated by her scholarly grandmother Margaret Beaufort, after whom she was named, the future queen of Scotland was not interested in study, although she loved pomp and pageantry. King James, unlike his erudite father, needed a translation into Scots of the *History of the Scots* because his knowledge of Latin was insufficient to cope with Boece's text. Therefore, two translations from Latin into Scots were commanded by the royal mother and son. One of the translations was to be in verse, the other in prose. These tasks were assigned to two members of the royal court: William Stewart for the verse and John Bellenden for the prose.

There were two William Stewarts active at this time, and they were almost exact contemporaries; both were students at the University of St Andrews. Which one translated Boece's work is not entirely certain. One candidate is William Stewart (c. 1479–1545), the bishop of Aberdeen.[21] The other candidate is an obscure member of the court of King James and distantly related to the Scottish royal house through an illegitimate son of Alexander Stewart, the famous "Wolf of Badenock." Margaret Tudor directed one of the two William Stewarts to translate Boece's Latin prose history into Scots verse as a gift for her son. Stewart gave his work the title *The Buik of the Croniclis of Scotland* and worked on his version between the years 1531 and 1535.[22] This might be the same volume as the "Scottis Chronicle written with hand" that was in the library of James's grandson James VI (James I of England). If so, he had little need of it. Unlike his grandfather, the younger James could read Latin easily and he also owned a copy of Boece's history written in Latin.

On the whole, William Stewart makes a faithful translation from Boece's Latin text, but he does take liberties, as a couple of examples illustrate. Stewart omits the long digression on the laws supposedly promulgated by Macbeth but expands the section where Lady Macbeth harangues her husband into killing Duncan. Stewart's account of the murder of Duncan differs slightly from Boece's telling, and his Macbeth provokes what is essentially a street brawl of his supporters with Duncan and his retainers. Also, as a member of the clergy, Stewart was squeamish about the supernatural element connected with the three weird sisters, so in his version the weird sisters become *wemen*. Nevertheless, it is clear that his source material had weird sisters, because he calls the second and third lady "sister" later in the narrative. Finally, the murder of Banquo is removed from the banquet hall when he and Fleance leave Macbeth's presence only to fall into the hands of murderers who have been hired by the king.

The similarities between Stewart's story and Shakespeare's drama have raised the possibility that the latter had consulted the *Buik of Croniclis* and taken his basic plot from it rather than Holinshed's *Chronicles*. There are some difficulties with that proposition. Unless there were more copies than the surviving manuscript, it is unlikely that a mere "player," even one in the king's employ, would have been allowed to use King James's personal library. An equally significant consideration is that none of Stewart's embellishments are literary originals. They are the sort of elaboration that would have come to the mind of anyone wishing to write a scene that was certain to hold the audience in suspense.

While William Stewart was making his verse translation, King James V was personally responsible for commissioning the second translation of Boece's history when he commanded John Bellenden or Bannatyne (c. 1495–c. 1547) to translate Hector Boece's Latin history into Scots prose. The finished work has the modern title *The Chronicles of Scotland, Compiled by Hector Boece, Translated into Scots by John Bellenden*. The selection of Bellenden to write a prose translation is unexpected because he was famous as a poet. He also had long-standing connections with the Scottish royal family. Bellenden's father Patrick was the steward to Queen Mother Margaret Tudor, and his mother Marion had been the nurse of King James. Educated in the law at St. Andrews and Paris, Bellenden was given royal preferment early in his career by being placed in charge of King James's expenses. He prepared two translations of Hector Boece's history. The first version was completed c. 1531 and was in manuscript, but the second was completed by 1536 when it was printed in Edinburgh.[23] This translation can be said to be the true source of the Scots material in the chronicle of Raphael Holinshed because this version was the basis for the later text. Bellenden began his dedication to King James by quoting Boece's friend Erasmus that "there is nothing that excites more admiration in people than the works of kings." Like Stewart, Bellenden introduces some changes into Boece's text. Not surprisingly, given his interests, he retains the legal material that Stewart had omitted. Less squeamish than

Boece or Stewart, Bellenden was not afraid to handle the occult material and he substitutes "witch" for "weird syster" in his copy for King James.[24]

There was a third, unofficial, translation of Boece's history into Scots now known as the "Mar Lodge" version. The circumstances of this work's composition are more obscure than the translations by either John Bellenden or Walter Stewart, and the surviving manuscript is missing material at the beginning and end. Apparently this was a private translation attempted by a less gifted writer than Bellenden. The "Mar Lodge" translator attempts to be more faithful to Boece's Latin original but fails to match it in narrative movement.[25]

What becomes visible from a comparison among the three translations of Hector Boece's *History of the Scots* is that the legend of Macbeth was reworked by each of the trio. None of the translations follows Boece's text exactly. An illustrative example is to look at how three sources all derived from Hector Boece—the Scots verse translation by Stewart, the prose translation of Boece's Latin text into Scots by Bellenden, and the adaptation of Bellenden's translation by Holinshed—treat the death of Duncan at the hands of Macbeth. Stewart claims that Macbeth, with the support of Banquo, met Duncan at Earnmouth in Perthshire and provoked a fight in which Duncan was slain. A different story is told by Bellenden, who claims that Macbeth led an army to Inverness (two hundred miles north) where he killed Duncan at the instigation of his wife. Somewhat between the two extremes is Holinshed's chronicle, following Boece at this point, where Macbeth kills Duncan in battle at Enuerns (?) or Botsgovane (near Elgin) and Banquo is one of Macbeth's allies. This comparison of three works that all derive ultimately from Boece shows that in a crucial episode they have three different versions. In some instances one text is set against the other two, such as Bellenden's use of imperial terminology. When Duncan is gathering his troops to face King Sweno, Bellenden notes that the people came from throughout his empire, which is absent from similar passages in Boece or Stewart.[26] The greatest difference is between Bellenden and Stewart, writing two works that were commissioned deliberately to translate Boece. In short, artistic license is used by these writers.

Hector Boece's Followers

Hector Boece's *History of the Scots* had become the official version of Scots history within a half dozen years of its publication. Later Scots historians followed his general outline and, like Boece's translators Bellenden and Stewart, introduced their own interpretations. This led to a divergence in the use of the Macbeth legend. Among those writers of popular works intended for a mass audience, mainly in England, the more fantastic elements of the Macbeth story appeared as in the chronicles of Raphael Holinshed. In those tales the weird sisters set the tone of the episode and the remaining story follows the supernatural element. Remaining in Scotland, on the other hand, there was a different employment of the Macbeth legend. He became a foot soldier in the Scottish intellectual battles of the sixteenth century, especially in the works of George Buchanan and John Leslie, contemporaries and opponents in the religious strife that engulfed Scotland.[27]

George Buchanan (1506–1582) was possibly the most famous of sixteenth-century intellectuals.[28] He came from Stirlingshire and was probably a Gaelic-speaker; by trade he was a schoolmaster. His uncle James Heriot sent Buchanan to study at the University of Paris, but he was forced to return to Scotland after his uncle's death due to poverty and ill health. When he recovered, Buchanan joined the French mercenaries brought into Scotland for the November 1523 attack on the castle at Wark on Tweed, which guarded one of the main crossings on the river Tweed, part of the border between England and Scotland. Later he entered St. Andrews University and studied with John Major. Even though his opinion of Major was mixed (describing him as "Major in name alone") he followed him to Paris where he renewed his studies and began his career as a teacher. Returning to Scotland, Buchanan became a tutor for King James's son James Stewart. The king failed to protect him during a persecution of Protestants in 1539 and Buchanan fled first to England and then to France. Eventually moving south, he was appointed professor of Latin in the College of Guienne at Bordeaux; among his pupils was the future essayist Michel de Montaigne. Following periods teaching in Paris and Lisbon, where he was tried and imprisoned by the Inquisition, Buchanan returned to Scotland in 1562 and became a tutor to Queen Mary Stewart. He prospered during her reign and was rewarded generously. Nonetheless, his Protestant sympathies became public during the time he was in service to the queen. In 1570, Buchanan was appointed tutor to Mary's son (and the man for whom Shakespeare's *Tragedie of Macbeth* might have been first performed), the future King James VI of Scotland and I of England.

His royal student's attitude to Buchanan was ambivalent and not eased by his former tutor's political views. Buchanan's political theory on kingship was simple in essence: the right to rule flowed from the people and they had the right to remove princes who failed to rule justly. That was not a new idea and basically it was an adaptation of the medieval argument presented by Marsilius of Padua's *Defender of the Peace* (Defensor Pacis, 1324) in which

160 MACBETH BEFORE SHAKESPEARE

both the church and state were agencies for the convenience of "the people." In his *Law of Kingship among the Scots* (*De iure regni apud Scotos dialogus*) of 1579, Buchanan argued for a constitutional monarchy; he employed the later part of his tract in an exposition on tyranny and the right of the people to remove a tyrant. Those political theories were used to direct the narrative of his *History of Scottish Affairs* (*Rerum Scoticarum historia*) that was published in 1582, the year of his death, although it had been completed several years earlier. Buchanan told his friend Thomas Randolph, the English ambassador to Scotland, that the work was intended to correct "English lies and Scottish vanity," although his historical narrative largely follows the outline given by Hector Boece.[29]

Buchanan's version of the Macbeth legend portrays Duncan as a slothful and unenergetic king whose behavior opens up the kingdom to attack. His kinsman Macbeth, in contrast, is energetic, his bravery and cunning saving the kingdom from the rebellion of a noble named Macdonald and conquest by the Norwegian King Swein.[30] One night in a dream, Macbeth sees three beautiful women who predict three offices of increasing power: thane of Angus, thane of Moray, and finally the kingship. When Duncan arbitrarily makes his son Malcolm the thane of Cumbria, the office held by the heir-designate to the kingship, Macbeth feels he must do something or risk obscurity. He and Banquo with their followers ambush Duncan outside Inverness. Duncan's children flee the kingdom: Malcolm goes to Cumbria, and his younger brother Donald escapes to the Hebrides.

Macbeth begins his reign by reconciling with the nobles and instituting peace in the kingdom. To scourge the criminals who had plundered during the leniency of Duncan's reign he sends agents provocateurs among them so that they eliminate themselves through private battles. Macbeth ruthlessly deals with rebellious nobles, forcing them to cease disturbing the realm. He institutes good laws and rules Scotland well for ten years. With the kingdom quiet Macbeth, after years of good governance, begins to behave capriciously and rules like a tyrant. He has Banquo and his son ambushed because of a prophecy that the kingship would flow from them. Then he confiscated goods and used the wealth to pay for the excesses of his personal followers. The nation begins to hate him and Macbeth orders the building of a fortress on the hill of Dunsinane, forcing everyone to contribute. His particular enmity is for Macduff, the thane of Fife, burdening him with extra work and persecuting his friends. In the meantime, Malcolm has fled to the protection of his grandfather Siward of Northumbria and is residing with King Edward of the English where Macduff finds him when escapes first to Lothian and

Macbeth and Renaissance Scotland

then to England. Macduff justifies his flight from the kingdom as the result of Macbeth's tyrannical behavior and asks Malcolm to return to Scotland. In the interview between Macduff and Malcolm, the latter tests the offer by declaring that he is lustful, greedy, and false. After Macduff quails at the last vice, Malcolm reveals his test. For the invasion of Scotland Malcolm essentially borrows ten thousand men from Edward, and they are led by his grandfather Siward. Macbeth retreats to Dunsinane and is forced to hire mercenaries from the Hebrides and Ireland, but to no avail. Malcolm's army put tree branches on their helmets as signs of victory.

George Buchanan's version of the Macbeth legend is clearly edited in light of his political theories.[31] He had little time for the ineffectual Duncan, even giving him the wrong name—Donald—at the beginning of his section. He stresses that Macbeth became king with popular support, but Buchanan is no democratic populist. His "people" is a narrowly defined concept limited to the wealthy and powerful; Buchanan's definition of populism was oligarchy. This point is reinforced when the nobles decide to displace Macbeth and send Macduff to England to offer the crown to Malcolm Canmore. Unlike earlier stories, Buchanan stresses that Macduff was a representative of the entire nation rather than one man acting on his own. The request of the people convinced Malcolm to return to Scotland. The support of the people, however, does not win Malcolm's kingdom; when he and Macduff fight they use an English army, although Buchanan mentions that diverse people fled to him. Macbeth is deserted by the Scots so that only his Irish mercenaries remain with him. Buchanan offers the interesting observation that of Macbeth's seventeen-year reign, the first ten years were happy and set the king among the best kings, but the last seven were cruel and tyrannical.

The concluding comment on Macbeth shows clearly how George Buchanan used his tale. While his work is often presented as the rational counterpart to Boece's fables, he used such of them as suited his purposes. More important, he did not work without an agendum. Certainly his ideas on government and power were different from the usual treatment of history as the preserve of those few who were preordained to rule, which is clearly visible in his narration of the Macbeth legend. Hereditary right was secondary to popular, or at least aristocratic, consent, and Macbeth becomes a representative of the tyrant in the classical Greek sense of a "strong, one-man rule." As an illustration of his concept of government in action, the Macbeth story is perfect. The rise of Macbeth at the expense of Duncan is overshadowed by the main story of how a good ruler turns bad and what should be done about it.

162   MACBETH BEFORE SHAKESPEARE

George Buchanan's *History of Scottish Affairs* did not please many people, including his former pupil King James VI who, in *Basilikon Doron*, expressed himself in no uncertain terms when encouraging his son to study history: "I meane not of such infamous invectives, as *Buchanan's* or *Knoxe's* Chronicles: and if any of these infamous Libels remaine untill your daies, use the Law upon the keepers thereof."[32] More congenial to the king were the political ideas of Buchanan's contemporary John Leslie, whose name became a byword for scheming during his lifetime. Yet he never wavered in his devotion to the one woman who also had been served by George Buchanan. That two men with such different political outlooks should have both been in the service of Queen Mary of Scotland is curious, but John Leslie (1527–1596) remained loyal to her, although he was prepared to deal treacherously with everyone else.[33] A graduate of King's College, Aberdeen, Leslie went to France for further study and then returned to Aberdeen, destined for an academic career. His fortunes changed when, in April 1561, he brought to Mary, then the dowager queen of France, the assurance of the Earl of Huntly that she would be welcomed by Scotland's Catholics if she returned to her native land. Leslie was invited to join Mary's entourage, beginning his rapid ascent to honors and positions of influence. From a professorship at King's College, Aberdeen, he progressed to membership of the Privy Council, then to abbot of the Tironian community at Lindores, before his election to the bishopric of Ross in 1566.[34] His fall from fortune coincided with that of his royal patroness. As Queen Mary's misfortunes multiplied, Leslie never wavered in his dedication to her, and for the last years of his life he was an exile. During his hours of leisure, he wrote *Concerning the customs and deeds of the Scots in ten books* (*De origine moribus, et rebus gestis Scotorum librie decem*) also known by the anglicized short title *Historie of Scotland*, which was finally published in Rome in 1578. As with Buchanan, Leslie's work had a purpose, but it was religious and demonstrated the fidelity of the Scots to the Roman Catholic Church.

Leslie's tale of Macbeth is much briefer than Buchanan's episode and, not surprisingly, emphasizes the concept of loyalty.[35] Perhaps Leslie was thinking of Queen Mary's unsuccessful attempts to rally support among the Scots nobles and people. Macbeth appears first as an avenger against Macdonald of the Isles who had robbed and wounded Banquo while he was attempting to collect the royal taxes. Then Macbeth kills Duncan at the urging of his wife. There is no recourse to weird sisters or strange prophecies, but pure murder for gain. Duncan is described as "most saintly" to heighten the magnitude of Macbeth's crime. Macbeth tries to secure the loyalty of his nobles through gifts and that of the people through humanity and good laws. But he is uneasy because of his deeds and turns into a tyrant. The people send Macduff to ask Malcolm to return; he returns at the head of an English army with ten thousand men. Macbeth retreats to his fortress at Lumphanan, where he is slain.

The point of Leslie's Macbeth story is that allegiance to a monarch whom Divine Providence has placed over a people must be maintained. Equally important is the need of a monarch for the support of his subjects. But, as with Buchanan, this was not a call for democracy. Macbeth overturned the natural order, in Leslie's view, and therefore could not flourish. The people are distressed by how this led to his tyranny, and Malcolm is encouraged to return in order to retake his heritage. The omissions of weird sisters, a moving forest, and an avenger in the person of a man not born of woman were not accidental. Lesley had even more need than Buchanan to give a rational expression to this historical episode. Protestant reformers accused the Roman Catholic Church of superstition and fantasy, so there was no room for any other-worldly beings.

The last historian to be discussed here who used Macbeth as a foil for his political theories was David Chambers, known in some scholarly works as David Chalmers of Ormond (c. 1533–1592). A native of Strichen in Aberdeenshire, he was widely educated, having studied at Paris, Louvain, and Bologna, probably beginning his career at the University of Aberdeen. He was trained as a lawyer, and his earliest patron was James Hepburn, the earl of Bothwell. He remained a supporter of Queen Mary throughout her life and presented his *Dictionary of Scottish Law* to her in 1566.[36] By 1570, Chambers was acting as an envoy for Queen Mary's supporters to France and the Spanish Netherlands; possibly in that year or 1571, he was living at the French court as an advisor. There, in 1572, he wrote his *Histoire abbregée* of the French, English, and Scottish kings; the second edition added the list of popes. His work emphasized the ancient alliance between the French and the Scots while at the same time placing Scotland in a European context. His few facts are embedded in a narrative that was largely fantasy and dependent on Boece's work. The work was not independent scholarship but an effort to recruit history in his efforts to further Mary's cause in a land where she was a dowager queen.

The employment of Macbeth in the intellectual warfare of Scotland's historians in the sixteenth century shows how the legend—even in its more fantastic forms—was called into the service of political theory. Outside Scotland, however, Macbeth was being called into service of a different sort. If the pen is mightier than the sword, then popular entertainment is mightier than historical research, no matter how well presented. In concluding his section on Macbeth, George Buchanan noted, "Some of our writers to here record many fables which are like Milesian tales and fitter for the stage than a history, and therefore I omit them."[37] He could not know how prescient he was.

8

The Literary Scot in Tudor England

THE FIRST OF July in the year 1578 was a busy day for literary London as an unusual number of books were registered for publication (an ancestor of the modern copyright) with the Worshipful Company of Stationers. For those readers with a classical interest, there was Appian of Alexandria's *Romaine Civill warres*. The more theologically minded could choose John Bradford's *Godly meditations upon the lordes prayer, the belief and the Ten commaundementes with other comfortable meditations, praiers and exercises whereunto is annexed a defence of GODs eternall eleccon and predestination.* Less serious readers could divert themselves with *A courtly Controuersie of CUPIDS Cautels.* And then, for those with a taste for popular history, there was *Raphael Hollingeshedes Cronycle*, the book better known today as Holinshed's *Chronicles*.[1] Within the trade, its immediate claim to fame was the twenty shillings that the publishers had been charged, the largest registration fee for a new book up to that time. The *Cronycle* was published in two massive volumes with illustrations, covering the history of England, Ireland, Scotland, and Wales.

Holinshed's *Chronicles* is often the earliest limit of inquiry for those interested in the sources of Shakespeare's Macbeth story. While the debate continues on what other sources or influences are to be found in his *Tragedie of Macbeth*, there is no doubt that the basic story comes from the *Chronicles*. Their success and authority show how popular interest in the past created a demand for semi-scholarly/semi-popular history. This fashionable interest in history was mined, in turn, by playwrights for the Elizabethan/Stuart theater.

The credit for authorship given to Holinshed belongs initially to a London printer named Reyne Wolfe. His ambition was to become wealthy by writing and publishing a history of the world. The project was too vast for one busy man, so sometime around the year 1548 he hired a Cambridge

University graduate named Raphael Holinshed to prepare the section on the British Isles. When Wolfe died in 1573, three other printers—his son-in-law John Harrison, George Bishop, and Luke Harrison—purchased the rights to the work. By this time it was obvious that the original project of a world history needed to be limited in scope, so they decided on Holinshed's section on the British Isles. This was fairly advanced toward a publishable form because two of the three sections were mainly reprints. Holinshed had based his Scottish section on John Bellenden's translation of Hector Boece's history of the Scots, while the Irish section followed a history written by Edmund Campion. To hasten completion of the project, two men were engaged as Holinshed's assistants: William Harrison worked on the English and Scottish sections, while Richard Stanyhurst worked on the Irish section.

The two volumes of *Raphael Hollingeshedes Cronycle* appeared five years after Wolfe's death. From the beginning it was clear that this was a piece of historical narrative deliberately crafted for public consumption. To burnish its scholarly credentials, the work was dedicated to William Cecil, Baron Burghley, the *éminence grise* of Queen Elizabeth's court and one of the most powerful men in the kingdom. More particularly, the selection of Cecil reflects his fame as an antiquary, collector of manuscripts, and patron of historians. He was also an ideal choice for a work that wanted to find its audience among the prosperous and ambitious middle class. Cecil's origins were in the lower aristocracy, and his family prospered during the reign of the queen's father Henry VIII. Holinshed's *Chronicles* were directed toward those who, like Cecil, had risen to a position of eminence largely through their own abilities.

Holinshed's *Chronicles* were an immediate success. Two weeks after publication, a license to print was sold to Thomas Woodcock, a sign that the publishers could not keep up with demand. Raphael Holinshed lived just long enough to see the initial success of the book, and he died in 1580. Among the members of the reading public who purchased the book was King James VI of Scotland, the future King James I of England. His copy was purchased from Jhon Provend and is described as a *Historie of Ingland, Scotland, and Ireland in tua faire volumes* in the library list compiled by his tutor Peter Young.[2]

The chronicle's favorable reception led to the decision to produce a second edition. The new editor was a West Country historian from the city of Exeter named John Hooker (c. 1527–1601). He had studied at Oxford, been elected to both the Irish and English parliaments, and was a formidable scholar. Hooker hired a fresh group of assistants, of whom the most important was John Stow (1525–1605). A tailor by profession, Stow was famous for his research made possible by a remarkable skill at discovering ancient records.

When he was hired to work on the new edition of Holinshed's *Chronicle*, Stow was one of the leading historians in England, famous as the author of the *Survey of London*.

When the new edition of *Holinshed's Chronicles* appeared in 1587, it became even more widely popular than the first. This is unexpected because the editing was uneven. While much of the English section was reworked, less was done on the Scottish part. For the casual page turner, the most immediate difference in the new edition was the absence of illustrations.

Holinshed's Macbeth

Holinshed follows Hector Boece's story of Macbeth, although there are some original details.[3] The Macbeth episode begins with Banquo, now a royal tax collector, set upon by rebels as he is going through the country. An insurgent named Macdonald seizes the opportunity provided by the attack to lead a rebellion with the aid of soldiers from the Western Isles as well as mercenary kernes and gallowglasses from Ireland. When a captain named Malcolm leads the royal forces into Lochquhaber he is defeated and beheaded. King Duncan calls a council to deal with the rebels at which Macbeth claims that if he and Banquo were allowed to lead a force, the rebellion would be ended. Macdonald gives them battle and is defeated. Afterward he kills his wife and children before committing suicide.

There follows an invasion of Scotland by the Norwegian King Sueno. Duncan is his customary ineffectual self, but he assembles an army and divides the command into three under himself, Macbeth, and Banquo. In the first battle, against another commander named Malcolm, Sueno is victorious. Duncan retreats to a castle where he is besieged by Sueno. He sends food and drink laced with sleep-inducing berries to the Danish army. Macbeth leads his troops against the sleeping invaders and slaughters them. Then Cnut of England and Denmark attacks the Scots and, once again, Macbeth and Banquo are victorious. The survivors ask permission to bury their dead in Inch Colum Chille, an island in the Firth of Forth, which Macbeth allows. As Macbeth and Banquo ride toward the king's camp at Forres, they encounter three women in strange and *ferly* (i.e., wondrous) clothes. The women individually salute Macbeth, first as thane of Glamis, then as thane of Cawdor, and finally as king of Scotland. When Banquo complains that he has no prophecy, the women reply that he will be the ancestor of kings, but Macbeth will not. Subsequently, as the meeting becomes common knowledge, the usual opinion is that the ladies are weird sisters, the goddesses of destiny, having the form of nymphs or fairies. The opinions of Macbeth and Banquo begin to change when Macbeth, already the thane of Glamis, shortly afterward becomes thane of Cawdor. Banquo remarks that Macbeth had gained two of the offices promised by the weird sisters, and Macbeth considers how to gain the third, but decides to wait.

Duncan declares his son Malcolm, by his wife the daughter of Siward, earl of Northumbria, to be his heir, and Macbeth decides that he has been unjustly denied the throne. Urged by his wife and taking an army of followers that includes Banquo, he slays Duncan at Enuernes. Then Macbeth travels to Scone for his king-making ceremony. Duncan's sons Malcolm and Donald Bane flee to Cumberland for fear that Macbeth will destroy them. At the beginning of his reign, Macbeth rules wisely and justly, ending the wave of crime that had engulfed the kingdom during the feeble rule of Duncan. He decrees new laws, which are introduced by the claim "according as I find them in Hector Boethius."

Soon, however, his conscience causes Macbeth to fear being served in the same way he did Duncan. He arranges the murder of Banquo and his son Fleance by criminals outside his castle. Banquo is slain, but Fleance escapes to Wales. (Here the *Chronicles* has a brief excursus on the adventures of Fleance and his descendants beginning with his son Walter and continuing with the kings of the Steward/Stuart dynasty.) After Banquo's death, nothing prospers with Macbeth because of a general dread of him. He begins to kill the nobles, both out of fear of them and as a way to enrich his coffers, placing spies in castles to bring him information. Finally, because of his increasing paranoia, Macbeth orders the construction of a castle at Dunsinane. The work is forced on the aristocrats, but while Macduff of Fife sends his men, he refuses to appear in person. Macbeth sees his absence as a sign of treachery and he plots to destroy Macduff. His rash behavior is encouraged by the prophecy of a witch who had said he would not be slain by a man born of woman and would not be defeated until the wood of Berne (i.e., Birnam Wood) came to Dunsinane. When Macduff flees, Macbeth rushes to his castle and kills Macduff's family.

Macduff goes to England and finds Malcolm Canmore. After explaining the wretched state of Scotland, he asks Malcolm to return. Malcolm prevaricates by declaring himself unworthy for three reasons: he is a sensualist; he is greedy; and he is a liar. After the third objection, when Macduff prepares to depart, Malcolm reveals his test. Then Macduff and Malcolm collect an invading force. Macduff writes letters to the nobles of Scotland while Malcolm receives troops from the English king Edward, who gives Malcolm's grandfather Siward permission to lead a force into Scotland. Macbeth rallies his forces at Dunsinane Castle while Malcolm camps at Birnam Wood and orders his men to use branches as camouflage. On the day of the battle, Macbeth leads his men to the battlefield, but then flees toward Lumphanan with Macduff in pursuit. As the two men prepare to duel, Macduff announces that he was not born of woman, but (from is now called) a caesarian section, and kills Macbeth. Macbeth's death leads to the coronation of Malcolm Canmore, which is dated to April 1057.

Pictures of the Macbeth Legend

Among the pictures in the 1578 edition of Holinshed's chronicle are images illustrating the Macbeth legend. The first is an image of Macbeth discovering the bodies of the rebel Macdonald and his family (240). Next is the famous picture of Macbeth and Banquo meeting the three women, the weird sisters, who foretell their futures (242). The third image is a portrait of Macbeth at his coronation (244), while the fourth depicts criminals being brought to justice (245) and one of the background figures is probably intended for Macbeth. Finally there is the construction of a fortress on Dunsinane Hill (249). Illustrations were expensive to make, so the same picture often served for several scenes. The picture of Macbeth's fortifications on Dunsinane Hill, for example, is also used as an illustration of St. Andrews Cathedral while the depiction of the coronation of Macbeth is the same one as the coronation of Malcolm Canmore.

Sometimes the text and the image do not entirely complement each other. For example, in the narrative, a reader is offered several choices for the nature of the women who prophesize to Macbeth and Banquo. They are called variously "weird sisters," "goddesses of destiny," "nymphs," and "fairies." Within the story, there is the implication that they foretold the future through necromancy (conjuring up the dead). A difference between the illustration and the narrative is that the latter claims that the women were dressed in strange and wild clothes while the former shows them in normal, if unusually decorated, attire. The description in the text, however, makes clear that Holinshed's ladies were sibyls. Sibyls were the prophetesses of the ancient world, recognized by their wild and unkempt appearance, who also lived to a great age. The Cumaean sibyl, made famous by the Roman poet Virgil, supposedly lived for a thousand years.

The choice of the three women for illustration reflects the continuation of interest since the fifteenth century in groupings of three individuals in verbal or pictorial statements of sovereignty in both Scotland and England. Andrew of Wyntoun's three *weird systers* who appeared in Macbeth's dream to make their statements of his future greatness were part of a general European tradition that, in Scotland, can also be seen in the slightly later *Kings Quair*, believed to have been written by King James I of Scotland, that includes three ladies representing virtues.[4] Moving into the sixteenth century, a trio of supernatural women appears in the recreation of the "Judgment of Paris" performed at Edinburgh for the entrance of Margaret Tudor to Scotland in 1503; this was also the theme of the painting *Elizabeth and the Three Goddesses* (1569) formerly attributed to Hans Eworth, but now believed to be the work of Joris Hoefnagel (1542–1601).[5] In the latter painting, Queen Elizabeth I awards a golden apple to herself as Juno's hand gestures toward the sky to indicate that it is divinely ordained while Minerva and Venus watch approvingly. The picture was a favorite of the queen who had it on view in the palace at Whitehall. If anyone had doubts about its interpretation, Latin verses on the frame made the meaning clear. Minerva was a favorite among royalty; when the author of the *King's Quair* is transported to the heavens, one of the beings he meets is Minerva. When King James VI and I visited Oxford, he was greeted by three actors who announced his titles of King of England, King of Ireland, and King of Scotland. The title of the printed version of their salutation claims that they are "sibyls," but they refer to themselves as "prophetic sisters" and "muses" in the text. As a side note, William Shakespeare used groups of three ladies who call themselves sisters for his *A Midsummer's Night Dream*, *Merchant of Venice*, *Henry the Fourth Part Two*, and *King Lear*.

Women representing or announcing sovereignty are the cultural daughters of the goddess who represents the "spirit" of the land—a standard feature of medieval Gaelic literature. The inaugural ceremony for a king in Ireland or Gaelic Scotland was the *banais* (bridal feast), but this goes even further back to the Indo-European idea of the right to rule through a symbolic marriage between the monarch and the land. The idea of a rightful possessor marrying his land is ancient and mentioned in the Bible in Isaiah 62:4–5: "And thy land shall be married. For as a young man marrieth a virgin, so shall thy sons marry thee." In pre-Christian northern Europe, a marriage ceremony was completed when a man and woman sat together on the same seat. The "Stone of Destiny," originally at Scone but now in Edinburgh Castle, was one of these seats where a monarch married the spirit of sovereignty of his kingdom. The connection of sovereignty with a supernatural woman comes from the Irish text "The Phantom's Frenzy" (Baile in Scáil), an eleventh-century pseudo-prophecy very similar to the *Prophecy of Berchán*. The Irish king Conn of the Hundred Battles is told the succession of kings by the sovereignty of Ireland, in the form of a woman who prefaces each name with the rhetorical question, "For whom shall I pour a drink of [the ceremonial] ale?"[6]

Coyness in the definition of the women in Holinshed's *Chronicles* is not limited to artistic license, but it reflects the fact that the employment of prophecy was even more dangerous in the sixteenth century than it had been in the fifteenth. Fear of prophecies as forerunners of rebellion meant that royal paranoia about them had become greater since the late Middle Ages. Hector Boece's otherworldly women, for example, make only the briefest of appearances to Macbeth and they are immediately given the possibility of different identifications. Even the prophecy of Macbeth's invulnerability from any save one not of woman born is tacked on mainly to explain the circumstances of his death. Nevertheless, prophecies continued to be a forbidden obsession.

An example of the popularity of prophecies and how dangerous they were in the eyes of the authorities is evident from the career of a wandering prophet named Richard Lynam during the reign of King Henry VIII. His arrest and imprisonment in the Tower of London was noted in the minutes of the Privy Council on June 7, 1546. Details emerge in a subsequent note on the deliberation of the Privy Council when a fellow prophet and lute player named William Weston gave testimony against Lynam.[7] He claimed to have met Lynam about eighteen years earlier, when he recited the "Cock of the North" prophecy to Weston. For the previous half dozen years before 1546, however, Richard Lynam traveled through the countryside and recited a version of the "Six Kings" prophecy, which foretold anarchy after the death of the last English king. In this case, the last king was to be Henry VIII, who would be torn with the feet of a mole and afterward the Pope would take control of England. The authority for this information was "Malyn" or Merlin. These prophecies were not folk memory, circulating among unlettered people, but contained in manuscripts read by the literate. Lynam's testimony made it clear that the prophecies were written in books and passed among interested parties. He acknowledges knowing another medieval prophecy, "When Rome comes into England," a transcription of which is contained in the minutes. The royal officials were worried by events in the Holy Roman Empire where the followers of Martin Luther were using the clergy to encourage rebellion against the emperor.

One did not even have to be actively involved in prophecy; the mere possession of a prophetic text could be dangerous. Many of the so-called prophecies were couched in such obtuse language that almost any interpretation could be placed on innocent or nonsensical passages. To give one example of how dangerous the royal government considered prophecies to be, among the evidence that convicted the duke of Norfolk on a charge of treason in 1571 was a prophecy in his possession claiming that Elizabeth would be usurped by Queen Mary of Scotland and her children (which came to pass with the succession of Mary's son James VI of Scotland as James I of England).[8] Despite his protestation that the document had been given to him and he had publicly derided it as nonsense, mere possession was a sufficient excuse to prove his guilt. Prophecies were perceived as even more dangerous when a visual element was added. In his testimony concerning Bigod's Rebellion of January 1537, William Todde, the prior of Malton Abbey in Ryedale, recalled seeing about fifteen years earlier a prophecy written on parchment with various images including a waxing moon with the number of years of increase, as well as images of children with weapons.[9]

Popular History

The fame of Holinshed's *Chronicles* brought its own perils. One of these was the whiff of popularity that led many people to dismiss it as historical fluff for the mob. The poet John Donne (1572–1631) was among them, and his opinion is given in *Satyre* (IV, 97–98), a satire on the royal court; in a conversation with one of the courtiers:

> *And askes, what newes? I tell him of new playes*
> *He takes my hand, and as a still, which staies*
> *A Sembriefe, 'twixt each drop, he nigardly,*
> *As loth to enrich mee, so tells many'a lie,*
> *More then ten Hollensheads or Halls or Stowes*
> *Of triviall household trash he knows; he knows*
> *When the Queene frown'd, or smil'd, and he knows what*
> *A subtle Statesman may gather of that.*[10]

Donne's feelings were shared by his contemporary, Norfolk courtier and parliamentarian Philip Gawdy (1562–1617), who kept his elder brother Bassingborne informed with his observations on the contemporary London scene. His letter of June 13, 1601 notes the hearing of a dispute between a Mr. Fowler and his wife concerning her loose living:

The Literary Scot in Tudor England 173

> There was a most notable case handled that day, which [was] held from 8 of the clock till 5, I think it better to be put in Hollingshed's cronycle than any conduyte or Lord Mayor's Henchmen.[11]

Perhaps one reason for the dismissive attitude of Donne and Gawdy is that Holinshed's *Chronicles* were among the historical works used by writers for the stage. A list in the *Nine Days Wonder*, written by Shakespeare's sometime colleague Will Kemp, gives what seems to be the standard historical works consulted by playwrights. They are, in his spelling: *Stow, Hollinshead, Grafton, Hal, and ffroysart*. Three of them—Stow[e], Holinshe(a)d, and Hal[l]—were included in the verses by John Donne. John Stow has been introduced, and Kemp was probably familiar with his *Chronicles of England*, which began with the mythological period of Brutus and continued to his own day (1580). Grafton is Richard Grafton (c. 1513–1573), who might have been known to Kemp in a professional capacity. In 1559, Grafton was one of the organizers of the pageant for Queen Elizabeth's entry into London. Among his historical works was a continuation of the English chronicle of John Hardyng (d. 1465) to the year 1543. Hardyng had surveyed Scotland for King Henry V, who wanted to know the relations between the two kingdoms while holding the Scots King James I as prisoner. The inclusion of Grafton and Stow in the same list conceals their celebrated rivalry; they had been notorious enemies ever since Stow had publicized the errors in Grafton's *Abridgement of the Chronicles of England* (written in 1563). Their quarrel became so infamous that it forced the Stationers' Company to take them to task. Kemp's "Hal," was Edward Hall (c. 1496–1547) a Londoner and a university graduate who was active in the service of King Henry VIII. His historical writings had a dramatic quality about them as demonstrated by some of the titles of the chapters in his *Chronicles*: "the vnquiet tyme of kyng Henry the Fowerth" and "the tragicall doynges of kyng Richard iii." The last person named was Jean Froissart (c. 1337–c. 1404)—"ffroysart" as Kemp styles him—who was the earliest of the group. Froissart lived at the end of the fourteenth/beginning of the fifteenth century, occasionally in residence at the English court of the Black Prince. He gives a view of the last decades of the chivalry that the romantics of the sixteenth century so craved. His accounts of the first stages of the Hundred Years' War have remained the popularly accepted versions although they rely on the work of others.

Authors and Immigrants

Holinshed's *Chronicles* reflect the increasing interest in a combined history of the kingdoms of Britain and Ireland; the legend of Macbeth fit into that narrative. Since the reign of King Edward I in the late thirteenth/early fourteenth century there had been a long-standing desire on the part of aristocratic English society to have a single (English) government ruling all the British Isles. This broadened historical horizon was not limited to writers in England. A "British Isles" view in English works has a parallel in an "Eastern Atlantic" view in Scottish works by the second half of the sixteenth century. A nationalist writer such as Andrew of Wyntoun included foreign princes in his Scottish history, but this is far removed from the history written by a fellow Scot, theologian, and occasional historian John Major, whose *History of Greater Britain as well England as Scotland* (*Historia majoris Britanniae tam Angliae quam Scotiae*) advocated the union of Scotland with England and used the Macbeth legend for support.

Interest in a union of the kingdoms found enthusiasts on the other side of the border, among them William Camden (1551–1623). Camden was the author of *Britannia*, a topographical history of Britain and Ireland that contained a survey of antiquities together with pertinent historical notes; it has been considered the great achievement of Tudor and Stuart antiquarianism. He was especially interested in the Roman era, which was used to connect the individual sections on England, Scotland, and Wales. The first edition appeared in 1586 and five more editions were published during his lifetime. Not surprising, the bulk of the material is concerned with England; in the first edition, Scotland is covered in fewer than a dozen pages.

William Camden was among the many ambitious men of the Tudor era who went from humble origins to prominence based on their own abilities. The son of a London painter, he attended the University of Oxford before becoming a teacher at Westminster School, where his pupils included the future dramatist Ben Jonson. Camden's stipend was supplemented with the prebendary (i.e., receiving the tithes) of the church at Ilfracombe; the two salaries allowed him the leisure to study antiquities. Unlike claims made against Holinshed's *Chronicles*, no one could accuse Camden of writing historical fluff for the mob; *Britannia* was written in Latin and intended for a scholarly readership. In common with Holinshed, however, Camden dedicated his *Britannia* to William Cecil. The British Isles theme of Camden's work was not a new idea, but his conception of a geo-political unity reflects a perception that was recognized internationally. Camden was initially encouraged in his enterprise by Dutch cartographer Abraham Ortelius and subsequently by French scholar Jacques-Auguste de Thou. Unfortunately, William Camden did not know much about Scotland. The first edition had eight and a half pages on Scotland, and there was no division of the Scots material into regions; by comparison, forty-three pages were devoted to Wales and thirty-six pages to Ireland, with both lands divided into regions.

The success of *Britannia* led to Camden's appointment as Clarencaux King of Arms in the College of Heralds in 1597, after which he was able to devote himself completely to scholarly research. With the ascension of King James to the English throne, Camden added more Scottish material when he reworked *Britannia* for the sixth edition of 1607. Like the previous five editions of *Britannia*, published during Elizabeth's lifetime, the sixth edition was written in Latin, but it was translated into English in 1610 by Philemon Holland.[12] For the sixth edition, however, the Scots section expanded by six times its original length to almost fifty pages, with all regions clearly separated and an expanded historical commentary. This was Camden's final edition, his last word on the subject. Via Holland's translation, it was also the one that brought his work to the attention of the general population. Camden's additional material included parts of the Macbeth legend. Among the materials for Fife, the rights of Clan Macduff are outlined, similar to John of Fordun's account. A unique addition is a pillar inscribed with "barbarous verses" on the boundary between Fife and Strathearn known as "Macduff's Pillar" where the law was administered.[13] A second item is in the section "Lochquobher" and it tells how a thane named Banquo was cruelly murdered by Macbeth because some women had prophesied that Banquo's descendants would prosper and fill the kingship, while Macbeth's line would end with him.[14] There then follows the story of Fleance's flight to Wales and the beginning of the Stewart dynasty.

Enthusiasm for political union in the British Isles was tied to another pan-Britannic phenomenon that can be traced from the end of the Middle Ages: immigration. Records that give a general estimate of immigrants begin to appear in the fifteenth century, such as the 1440 levy on aliens in England.[15] There are many uncertainties associated with these records—in the levy on aliens, for example, the criteria for inclusion are obscure and many people listed in them have no identifiable nationality. Nonetheless, they give a very general picture of immigration and settlement. The Scots were a significant proportion of the immigrant population in England; they were about 10 percent overall while the percentage was much greater in the north. Of the 744 identifiable aliens in Northumberland, for example, 741 were Scots. Scots made up roughly 12.5 percent of the identifiable alien population in Yorkshire; in London they were about 10 percent of the total population of aliens and were especially concentrated in the vicinity of Cripplegate.[16] Immigration between the English and the Scots was helped by royal intermarriage. The Scottish king James I married Joan Beaufort, the niece of the English king Henry IV, in 1424 shortly after he had been a prisoner at the English court. Their great-grandson James IV married Margaret Tudor, the sister of King Henry VIII, in August 1503. James's and Margaret's great-grandson was James VI of Scotland, the future James I of England. Both his mother, Mary Queen of Scots, and father, Henry, Lord Darnley, were the great-grandchildren of the English king Henry VII.

Connections at the highest level of society made movement between the Scottish and English kingdoms easier, especially for authors. Richard Holland, the author of the fifteenth-century *Book of the Owl* (Buke of the Howlet), a satire on the social divisions in Scots society, died in exile in England. Holland, probably a native of the Orkney Islands, was employed in Macbeth's home region and had been a member of the earl of Moray's household.[17] In the next generation, King Henry VIII made two payments to a *rymer* (poet) *of Scotlant*. This *rymer* might have been the important Scottish poet William Dunbar who was the author of [*To the City of*] *London*. Books by Scots were also published in England, bringing their work broader exposure. Possibly the first book of Middle Scots verse to be printed was the *Contemplacioun of Synnaris* by William of Touris, which was published at Westminster in 1499, while Robert Henryson's *Testament of Cresseid* was published as part of an edition of Chaucer's works in 1532. Sir William Lindsay's *Testament and Complaynt* was published in England by John Byddell in 1538, and William Copland published Gavin Douglas's *Eneados* and *Palice of Honour*.[18]

One of the problems for modern scholars is trying to understand what "Englishness" was supposed to be at any particular time, and if bigotry was necessarily united with nationalism.[19] This was not true for the one place where it is most expected, in the border country. These were the isolated and lawless lands on either side of the Scottish and English border. The border provided freedom from interception when theft was widespread and atrocities on either side were common. The border ballads popular today are full of outbursts of national pride and challenges hurled at the foreign oppressor, but this antipathy between Scot and English was due largely to Sir Walter Scott and the border ballads that he made popular in the nineteenth century. Nationalism, however, is curiously absent from the original ballads of the sixteenth and seventeenth centuries. Clan rivalries, family feuds, and personal animosities are

The topics of the sixteenth-century border ballads, not nationalist expressions of Scot versus English or vice versa. The earliest border ballads have no conscious national rivalry, and the bold Scot or the vengeful English are absent. The inhabitants of the borders were ruffians, not xenophobes.[20]

Changing English Perception of the Scots

The success of Holinshed's *Chronicles* reveals an increasing interest by the ordinary English about their northern neighbors. The customary interpretation is one of constant hostility toward the Scots by the English, and the usual example is the statement made in 1607 by Sir Christopher Piggott shortly after the date when most scholars think Shakespeare's *Macbeth* was first performed—and it is possible that the performance might have contributed to the outburst. Sir Christopher rose in Parliament and claimed that "[The Scots] are treacherous and murderous; scarcely two of their kings have died in their beds, but have been killed by their fellows."[21] This diatribe sent Sir Christopher to prison, but he also gained historical immortality. Taken together with satires on the Scots, beginning with the reign of King James I, as well as material taken from the diaries or correspondence of various notables, the usual conclusion is one of unrelieved hostility on the part of the English toward the Scots. However, there is evidence that popular feeling toward the Scots was more mixed than is sometimes imagined.[22]

After King Henry VIII's *Act of Supremacy* (1534), Protestantism was perhaps the single most important factor in Anglo-Scottish relations. English Protestants felt threatened in what was a predominantly Catholic Europe. Since Catholic France was Scotland's main ally, popular fears found expression in the theater. The former Carmelite monk John Bale's play *Kynge Johan* (c. 1538) includes a scene in which Papal Legate Pandulphus threatens to lead an army with the French, Spanish, Danish, Norwegian, and Scots kings against the English.[23] The original version of Robert Wilson's *The Three Lords of London* (1581) has an evil character named Fraud, whose origins are not named. When the play was revived in 1588 as *The Three Lords and Three Ladies of London*, Fraud declares that he is "halfe French and halfe Scottish," possibly a reflection of English fears about Scottish Catholics rising up in support of the Spanish invasion.[24]

English religious fervor surmounted nationalistic bias as can be gauged from a pamphlet published in 1593 with the uncompromising title *A discoverye of the unnaturall and trayterous conspiracie of Scottish papists against GOD his churche, their native contrey, the kinges maiesties person and his estate.*

This probably refers to the rumors swirling round Scotland from 1579 to 1582 that there was a conspiracy among Catholic lords led by Esmé Stewart, Lord d'Aubigny (later created Lord Lennox), to capture King James. To prevent his seizure, James was taken by a group of Protestant nobles who kept the prince's person in their power for ten months (August 1582 to June 1583). Even after James regained his freedom, the plotting continued. While it is difficult to know which of the many plots were real and which were imagined, they were taken seriously at the English court, and Queen Elizabeth sent a letter urging caution to her cousin.

Nevertheless, Scotland remained an exotic land to the English and a suitable location in which writers of fictions could place their stories. *A newe Scottishe song* was published in 1579, and several months later a ballad appeared titled *The Lord of Lorne and the false steward*.[25] Scandal seekers were not forgotten, and they were accommodated with the Tudor equivalent of tabloid journalism when Thomas Millington published in 1596 *A wofull ballad of a knightes daughter in Scotland who was murderd by her husband, beinge likewise the husband of another wyfe, and how it was revealed, by his first wyfe and her sonne*. The sensational was balanced by the sensible. Thomas Dekker's *Old Fortunatus* (1599) has a Scot called Morton and a Frenchman named Longaville who are tricked into buying apples of vice, after which they collaborate on a murderous spree in which an innocent man is slain as well as a guilty one. But Dekker refuses to descend into mere chauvinism and deliberately makes the point that evil is a universal phenomenon by linking the Scot and Frenchman with an English woman who was also tricked.[26]

Old habits continued, however, and the competition between the Scots and English found literary expression as the theme of Anthony Munday's *John à Kent and John à Cumber*, written around 1590 and performed at the Rose Theatre in 1594. Anthony Munday (1560–1633) was a Londoner and son of a printer who initially followed his father's profession before becoming a playwright, actor, and, in later life, historian. In addition to his drama, Munday is interesting because, unlike many of his contemporaries, he traveled abroad, and at least one Scot, John Leslie, believed that he was a spy.[27] Although Munday is usually considered to be a zealous Protestant, there has been the suggestion that he was actually a covert Catholic and that *John à Kent and John à Cumber* reveals his recusant (i.e., secret support of Catholicism) sympathies.[28] William Shakespeare seems to have been among Munday's various collaborators. He is generally thought to be the "Hand D" that contributed a speech on loyalty to Munday's *Sir Thomas More*, produced probably in 1593.[29]

John à Kent and John à Cumber could be an example of the type of drama that was performed privately at the homes of the provincial gentry, using the talents of local amateur actors. The unique manuscript was found among the papers of the Mostyn family of North Wales. With little character development and a simple plot, the surviving script does not suggest much depth of composition, although there have been efforts to see it as a call for a return to "Merrie Olde England."[30] In the story, the two daughters of the earl of Chester are affianced respectively to a Welsh nobleman and to a Scots nobleman. Their true loves, however, are two Welsh gentlemen who arrive at the same time as the prospective bridegrooms. On their way to the castle of Chester, the Welsh gentlemen—Griffud and Powess—meet a magician called John à Kent who promises to help them. When the slighted noblemen learn of this, the Scot, Lord Morton, sends to his native Scotland for a magician called John à Cumber. The remainder of the play is a contest between the two magicians to deceive the rival suitors. The result is not in doubt from the outset as John à Kent and his assistant Shrimp show their superiority over John à Cumber. The inevitable conclusion is reached when the ladies marry their true loves.

The ambiguous occult of *John à Kent and John à Cumber* as a choice of subtext was popular. If the works registered with the Stationers' Company give an accurate indication, the other-worldly was a favorite among the public. In one fifteen-year period, from 1579 to 1593, no fewer than thirty publications registered with the Stationers' Company dealt with supernatural beings, prophecy, and marvels. These works had titles such as *The Book of Witches*, *Trigos Dreame or Vision*, and *The Monstrous Child*. There were also works that caution the unwary away from such topics, such as *A warning against the superstition of Wytches and the madnes of magicians* or *A most strange example of the Judgement of God executed uppon Symon Pembrok Coniurer by his sodaune death*.

As was true for the stage-Irishman and Welshman, the stage-Scot was sometimes presented in a manner that set him apart from the English characters and sometimes not. Unlike the first two, however, the Scot came from a completely independent country. This explains why fewer plays had Scottish characters than Irish or Welsh. Scottish characters might have been played on English stages since the Middle Ages. Equally interesting is that those Scottish characters were rarely marked by linguistic eccentricities (to English ears), in contrast with their neighbors to the south and west whose dialects had become almost cliché. That can be a problem in deciding whether a play has a Scots character. An example, from a work clearly intended to be played, but for which there is no evidence that it was, is Nathaniel Woodes's *Conflict of Conscience* (c. 1570). Woodes was a minister at Norwich, yet he appears to have written his drama while still a student at Cambridge University. His narrative is essentially a morality play against Catholicism in which the priest named Caconos is presented as abusing his office for his own profit. Caconos may or may not be Scots, and there is some doubt about whether his dialect is Scots or northern English, a problem also found in Robert Greene's *History of King James the Fourth* (see below). *Conflict of Conscience* is violently anti-Catholic, but the linguistic location was probably of little consequence to Woodes's audience, who would be expected to address their attention to the clerical abuses rather than the geographical origin of the character.

Returning to *John à Kent and John à Cumber*, the play shows that regardless of religious sympathies, the general English mistrust of foreigners extended to the Scots. Suspicion easily became condescension as seen in the title of Thomas Churchyard's *The misere of Flanders, the calamitie of ffrance, misfortune of Portugale, unquietness of Ireland, troubles of Scotland, and the blessed state of England* (1579). Churchyard fantasizes a murderous and blood-stained climate of fear among the Scots, noting, "When murder might, serve time or turn for need:/ and nuzzled thus, they were godwot in blood,/ in rage they would, not spare, neither high nor low . . ." (When murther might, serve tyme or turne for neede:/ and nousled thus, thei were Godwot in Blood,/ In rage thei would, not spare, ne hye nor lowe. . .). The perceived "blood-stained" events among the Scots continued to attract English interest. The deaths of two cousins of Queen Elizabeth were popularly celebrated. The first was Henry Stewart, Lord Darnley, husband of Mary Stewart (Mary Queen of Scots). His death on February 10, 1567 was remembered in *A Dittie of the lord Darley [sic] somtyme kinge of Scottes*. The house where he had been staying, Kirk O'Field, was destroyed in an explosion, and Darnley's body was found dead (by strangulation) in a nearby garden. The culprit was widely believed to have been Mary's lover and soon-to-be third husband, James Hepburn, earl of Bothwell. Mary, in turn, received even rougher treatment. She was disliked by the English for being Catholic, dowager queen of France, and someone who was believed to be plotting against the English queen. After her execution on February 8, 1587, an account of her trial and execution was published in a pamphlet titled *An excellent dyttye made as a general reioycinge for the cutting of the Scottishe queene* (An excellent song made as a general rejoicing for the beheading of the Scottish queen).

Scottish Kings and the English Stage

After his appearance in *Holinshead's Chronicle*, Macbeth's legend continued its development in England within the context of religious change and national bigotry. At this point it is interesting to look, briefly, at representations of the Scots kings in plays performed in England during the last decades of the Tudor Age and the first years of the Stuart period. Plays that include a king of the Scots had been played at the royal court since the mid-sixteenth century. In 1567, the Children of the Chapel Royal performed the *Tragedie of the king of Scottes*, a story probably written by their master William Hunnis. The "Children" were boy choristers who served the royal chapel and traveled with the court on its perambulations among the various palaces. Companies of boy actors had performed since the Middle Ages and assisted with the splendid entertainments at the royal court, especially during the winter season from late November until early February, together with jugglers, musicians, and professional (adult) actors. While plays occasionally had been presented at court by the Children of the Chapel Royal, since the early decades of the sixteenth century they had become regular visitors in the reign of Elizabeth.[31]

Little is known of the *Tragedie of the king of Scottes* beyond a reference to it in the account of the Master of the Revels, the official charged with providing entertainment for the royal court. On June 9, 1568, Sir Thomas Benger was authorized to receive funds to pay for plays that were performed at court.[32] The last item was *The sevoenthe of Orestes and a Tragedie of the kinge of Scottes, to ye whiche belonged diuers howse, for the setting forthe of the same as Stratoes howse, Gobbyns howse, Orestioes howse Rome, the Pallace of prosperitie Scotlande and a gret Castell on thothere side*. This is an example of two plays being grouped together, using the same scenery and actors. *Orestes* is the story of a prince of Mycenae who returns to his kingdom to discover that his mother and her lover had killed his father. In revenge, he kills his mother and then is pursued by the Furies. The houses (sing. *howse*) were booths made of canvas and wood. Precisely what was the *palace of prosperitie* is unknown, and *a gret Castell* is so general that it could be almost anywhere.

If William Hunnis (d. 1597) did write the *Tragedie of the king of Scottes*, then he is a useful indicator of English interest in the Scots monarchs at both the high and low levels of society. The *Tragedie of the king of Scottes* was performed a year after the death of Henry, Lord Darnley, the husband of Queen Mary of Scots. While the drama might be about him, he had been denied the crown matrimonial by Mary. If William Hunnis were the author of the play, Darnley's inclinations toward Protestantism might have led to some literary license. Hunnis came from obscure origins and had been a musician of the Chapel Royal during the reign of King Edward VI. He was also a staunch partisan of the Princess Elizabeth, to such an extent that he confessed to being a conspirator in a plot to kill Queen Mary and her husband Phillip of Spain in 1556 and place Elizabeth on the throne. After imprisonment in the Tower of London, he was released on Elizabeth's accession to the throne in 1558. He became Master of the Children of the Chapel in 1566, and directed plays they presented at court from 1568 to 1575 and again from 1581 to 1584. He is known to have written devotional works and music; so it is widely assumed that he was the author of some of the pieces the Children of the Chapel performed at court.

In consideration of the Macbeth legend it is instructive to look at five plays in which there are characters who are Scots kings. They were written between 1592 (when Shakespeare is definitely known to have been in London) and 1600 (date of the earliest reference other than Holinshed to a work about Macbeth). They are, in chronological order (so far as it can be determined) *The Scottish Historie of James the fourth slayne at Flodden* by Robert Greene (1592), the anonymously authored *George a Greene, the Pinner of Wakefield* (1593), George Peel's *Edward I* (1593), the anonymously authored *Raigne of Edward III* (1596), and Robart the second written by Thomas Dekker, Henry Chettle, John Marston, and Ben Johnson (1599). The surviving texts of two of the five plays—*George a Greene* and *Edward I*—were thought to be memory reconstructions of the original plays, but that view has been disputed.[33]

The play with the most similarity to *Macbeth,* and that is only incidental, is Robert Greene's *The Scottish Historie of James the fourth slayne at Flodden, entermixed with a pleasant Comedie, presented by Oboram King of Fayeries.*[34] *The Scottish Historie* was registered with the Stationers' Company on May 14, 1594 (two years after its author's death) but survives only in an edition of 1598, which may have been its first appearance in print. Unusually among these five plays, the setting for the action is Scotland, with a Scottish king and his wife as the main characters. The king is a bad man but redeemed at the end, and he is surrounded by equally villainous or unattractive subjects. The heroine is his wife Queen Dorothea (apparently also the name of Greene's wife) who is the daughter of the king of England.

The Scottish Historie of King James the fourth is based on an episode from *De gli Hecatommithi* by G. B. Giraldi (1504–1573), popularly known as Cinthio.[35] In the original story the princes are a king of Ireland and king of Scots, but there is no connection with any historic monarch. Greene's version has nothing that can be connected with the reign of King James IV other than the fact that the historical monarch was Scots and married to the daughter of the King of England. James's name appears only on the title page and nowhere else in the play. The plot is simple. The king of Scotland is married to the daughter of the king of England, but he falls in love with another woman,

Ida, the daughter of the countess of Arran. So the prince schemes to have his wife murdered in order to remarry. When the queen learns of the plan, she flees from the court disguised as a young man. In the meantime, Ida marries another man, her true love. Now the murder plot rebounds on the king of Scotland. News of the queen's presumed death reaches the English court, and her father leads an army north to avenge his daughter. Just before the Scots and English monarchs join battle, the queen reappears. She urges reconciliation between her father and husband, thus ending the war between the two countries.

This is the most violently anti-Scottish play of the group discussed here, but Greene was a broad-minded bigot. The villainous king is assisted by the equally criminal French captain Jacques who speaks a patois of Franglais and wounds the queen during an attempted assassination. Greene obviously had his doubts about that plot holding the attention of his audience, so a *"pleasant comedie presented by Oboram king of fayeries"* was blended into the story to provide some light relief. Greene's *Historie of King James the Fourth* is also the only contemporary play that purports to have much Scottish dialogue. Analysis of the language reveals that he knew little Scots and apparently neither did his audience. Almost all the supposed dialect words are in act I and spoken mainly by the comic foil Bohun and Sir Bartram the Scottish lord. Bohn is described as a Scot, but his home is located at Redesdale, which is on the English, not Scottish, side of the border. Many of the so-called Scots words and phrases were also current in northern England. Some of the vocabulary is actually a Yorkshire dialect—such as *guid* for *good*. More than a few words—such *sale* (soul), *sayd* (side), *lovely* (friendly), *nene* (none), and *wemb* (belly)—were not found among the Scots.[36] Greene's confusion is understandable as he came from Norwich and lived most of his adult life in London. There is no evidence that he ever visited Scotland or even traveled outside England, although he claimed to have been to Italy and Spain. Where Greene acquired the dialect words for his dialogue is difficult to say, but there was a long history of unintelligibility between northern and southern English speakers. As far back as the twelfth century, historian William of Malmesbury complained that someone from southern England could not understand a Yorkshire accent.[37]

Robert Greene (1558–1592) was a Cambridge University graduate and one of the so-called University Wits, notorious for his scandals and literary quarrels. Among the targets for Greene's poison pen were contemporaries such as Christopher Marlowe and Gabriel Harvey. Nonetheless, he was one of the outstanding authors of his day, penning plays such as *Friar Bacon and*

184   MACBETH BEFORE SHAKESPEARE

Friar Bungay, Orlando Furioso, and *A Looking Glass for London and England*. Those plays were performed, posthumously so far as can be discovered, by the leading companies of the day: the Queen's Men, Lord Strange's Men, and the Admiral's Men. Greene lived up to his reputation as a troublemaker with *The Scottish Historie of King James the fourth*. He deliberately reworked the original play to turn it into a confrontation between England and Scotland. The accusation that the reigning Scottish monarch's great-grandfather was a murderous adulterer would have been scandalous for an audience that had been taught to respect its social superiors. Despite the claim on the title page that *The Scottish Historie* had been acted many times, there is so much material that could have landed Greene in prison (or worse) that the work might not have been played during his lifetime.

His poisonous reputation explains why Greene is best remembered for the veiled attack on William Shakespeare in *Greenes Groatsworth of Wit* (1592):

> [A]n upstart crow, beautified with our feathers, that with his Tygers heart wrapt in a Players hide, supposes that he is as well able to bombast out a blank verse as the best of you; an being an absolute *Iohannes fac totum* is in his owne conceit the onley Shake-scene in a country.

The phrase "Tygers heart wrapt in a Players hide" echoes a line from *Henry VI Part 3* (act I, scene 4) when Queen Margaret is said to have a "Tygers heart wrapt in a womans hide." For a long time *Groatsworth of Wit* was believed to have been written as Greene lay dying in his lodgings at Dowgate and reflects the anger at what he felt was the lack of appreciation from his profession. More recently the probability has shifted to its authorship by a printer named Henry Chettle who fathered it on the lately departed Greene.[38]

Whether or not Greene was actually responsible for his famous jibe, it shows the hostility between the university-trained writers and their less formally educated rivals on the bruising London literary scene. Insults traveled in both directions and the lightly schooled yokels could give as good as they got. An anonymous work known as *The Return from Parnassus or the Scourge of Simony* (1602) has a line in which Will Kemp says to Richard Burbage (the principal actor of the Chamberlain's Men and his former business partner):

> Few of the university men pen plays well. They smell too much of that writer Ovid and that writer Metamorphosis, and talk too much of Proserpina and Jupiter. Why here's our fellow Shakespeare puts them all down; aye, and Ben Jonson too.[39]

There might or might not be a connection between Robert Greene and *A Pleasant Conceited Comedy of George a Greene, the Pinner of Wakefield* that was acted several times during December 1593 and January 1594 by the Earl of Sussex's Men, the Lord Admiral's Men, and by the Lord Chamberlain's Men. There are two stories in this play. The first concerns an invasion of England by a Scots army led by a King James. The English King Edward moves his troops to intercept the invaders, and the two forces meet outside the town of Wakefield. Prior to the battle, the Scots nobles enter Wakefield, where they stable their horses in violation of the town's ordinance and King James attempts to seduce one of the virtuous townswomen. Both actions are stopped by George a Greene, the *pinner* (an official who impounds stray animals) of the town. Although the Scots king is the villain of his section, he is rehabilitated after his capture. When the Scots are defeated by King Edward, the second story is introduced. Robin Hood and his band, having heard of the prowess of George a Greene, seek him out in order to challenge him to a fight, which George wins. Unusually among these plays, there is no pretense at historical accuracy in *George a Greene*. Setting aside the obvious fiction of the Robin Hood episode, a king named Edward never ruled the English at the same time that a king named James reigned over the Scots.

George a Greene was entered into the Stationers' Register on April 1, 1595, but the only surviving copies were published in 1599 by Simon Stafford.[40] William Shakespeare is connected with this play in certainly one and possibly two ways. In a copy held by the Folger Shakespeare Library, a note in the hand of George Buc (Master of the Revels from 1610 to 1622), who had purchased the rights to *George a Greene*, describes his efforts to learn the name of the author.[41] He consulted two men whose companies had played the piece: William Shakespeare for the Lord Chamberlain's Men and Edward Juby who was a member of the Lord Admiral's Men. According to Buc's annotation, Juby gave the credit for authorship of the work to Robert Greene; Shakespeare said merely that the actor was also the playwright.

More developed is the work of another Londoner; George Peele's *Edward I*. Peel (1556–1596) was another of the so-called University Wits, a graduate of the University of Oxford. His *Edward I* is an idealized and semi-fictitious account of the career of the medieval English king, who, to a sixteenth-century English audience, was a model prince. This might be the same play as *Longshanks*, Edward's nickname, which was performed more than a dozen times between August 1595 and July 1596. *Edward I* catered to the Tudor era's fascination with the Middle Ages, with pronounced nationalist overtones; the Scots appear in only two episodes. The first is Edward's adjudication of the Scottish kingship and the second episode is the conflict with the successful claimant, John Balliol. Other than the fact of the events, everything else is complete fantasy. To take two examples: in the play the adjudication takes place at Edward's palace, when in reality it took place on the border between Scotland and England at Norham; and there are nine Scottish claimants in the play, but fifteen in reality. John Balliol is portrayed as the enthusiastic supporter of Edward's claim to be the overlord of the Scots when he is seeking the Scottish kingship, but he callously breaks his word after his coronation and leads the Scots in rebellion. The depth of his corruption is revealed when the Scots treacherously invade England (in fact it was the English who invaded Scotland) and his emissary, called Verses, gives Balliol's challenge to Edward. Edward rewards his bravery by presenting him with a valuable necklace. When Verses tells Balliol about his good fortune, the king condemns him. Balliol is eventually defeated and brought to Edward for justice. Even in chains the Scot is made to turn once again and grovel before Edward, who commutes his sentence of death to banishment to his own estates. Here is the same dichotomy seen in the Macbeth legend: the good Scot and the bad Scot. In this play, the character of John Balliol is a thoroughly bad man, who is prepared to commit any crime or suffer any humiliation in order to further his own ends. In contrast, his servant Verses is a brave and faithful man. His loyalty is so great that even an adversary can recognize and reward it.

A play whose theme is the reign of the grandson of Edward I, is the popular *Raigne of Edward III* (1596), one of most intriguing of these plays. The Scots characters are King David II and Lord Douglas together with their messengers. King David and Lord Douglas appear in the second scene of the first act when the Scots besiege Roxborough Castle as part of their raid on the north of England. So confident are they of taking the castle that the king and his vassal argue over who has the right to marry the countess sheltering within its walls. When the king claims his superior right, his lieutenant tries to claim the lady's jewels, which the king insists comes with her. This conversation ends suddenly when one of the Scots outriders hurriedly informs the king that the English army is approaching:

The Sunne, reflecting on the armour, shewed/ A field of plate, a wood of picks (?pikes) advanced.

King David and Lord Douglas leave quickly. David reappears briefly in act 5 scene 1 once he is captured and brought before Edward.

Only his title gives any indication of David's nationality. Not even his behavior can be seen as particularly anti-Scots. Edward is guilty of far worse designs. He makes advances toward the Countess that are stopped when she shows him two daggers; one will be used to kill the queen and the other will be used by the countess to commit suicide. At one point King David uses the word "bonny" to describe his troops, and when the countess of Salisbury speaks to King Edward about the Scots, he claims that she *spoke broad with epithites and accents of the Scots*, although he does not give any example. Audience members are forced to use their imagination.

William Shakespeare might have had at least some part in writing the *Raigne of Edward III*.[42] Whoever wrote the play used Holinshed's *Chronicles* and Jean Froissart's *Chronicles*. Without wishing to make too much of isolated lines, two examples have similarities with Shakespeare's *Tragedie of Macbeth*. There is a moving forest, the "wood of picks" advancing on the fortress, which reads like the journey of Birnam Wood to Macbeth's fortress. When the countess of Salisbury flourishes her two daggers, there might be echoes with Lady Macbeth and her daggers for a similarly bloody cause.

Finally, there is a play for which the text has not been discovered, although it is mentioned in several places, *Robart the second, Kinge of Scottes Tragedie* (The Tragedy of Robert II, King of Scots) written by Thomas Dekker, Henry Chettle, John Marston, and Ben Johnson. In September 1599, Philip Henslowe made four payments for the *boocke* (script) of this play for the Admiral's Men.[43] No trace of the play's contents has been discovered so far and there is no evidence that it was even played. The choice of the medieval King Robert for the playhouse is not obvious. Of course, like Greene's *James IV* there might have been no connection with the historical figure beyond the name and a few coincidental details. Any historical content probably depended on Robert's place as the first of the Stewart kings in Scotland. His other claim to fame was the production of offspring; he had more than twenty-five children with various mothers, not all of whom he married. Again, the most convenient source of information for the play's writers would have been Holinshed's *Chronicles*.

As this brief survey shows, during the decade prior to the accension of King James VI of Scotland as King James I of England, there were plays in which a Scots king features, either as an important supporting character or as the main one. Among the four plays for which information survives, the Scots king is always presented as a villain, although that could take various guises. In addition, there is the strong possibility that William Shakespeare contributed a substantial amount to *Edward III*, a play that has a number of features in common with his own *Tragedie of Macbeth*.

English Theater and the Scots

A brief survey of a handful of plays produced during a decade is hardly conclusive. Bearing in mind these limits, however, the English attitude toward the Scots is complex. There are bad Scots and good Scots in about the same proportions as there are good English and bad English. More plays with Scottish scenes or characters were produced or scripted that have not survived, but unless they were intended for publication, the work would not have been registered with the Register of the Stationers' Company of London.

The records of the late Elizabethan and early Stuart theater are neither as complete nor as informative as we would wish. Nevertheless, several points do emerge. The first is that an English audience was interested mainly in Scottish aristocrats rather than the ordinary Scot. Second, for the popular theater there was little attempt to give the Scots ethnic characteristics, other than an occasional phrase. Finally, the Scots are treated with an even hand. The villain of Woode's *Conflict of Conscience* may have been either northern English or Scots, but there is no mistaking that he is a thoroughly bad character and a hypocrite. In *Edward I* John Balliol is duplicitous and a faith-breaker. He is willing to swear undying loyalty one moment and then rise in rebellion when it suits his purpose. In *John à Kent and John à Cumber*, however, Lord Morton calls on the assistance of John à Cumber only after learning that the magician John à Kent is working against him. Morton is neither good nor bad; he is simply not the choice of his fiancée. Even though the behavior of King David and Lord Douglas in *Edward III* is ungracious, bartering for the countess of Salisbury as though she were simply one of the livestock, they do not go beyond bad manners. They are not the only ones exhibiting poor behavior, and King Edward himself initially behaves no better than his Scots counterpart toward the countess. Only in *The Historie of James the Fourth* is there actual animosity toward the Scots, but the bad Scots are the king and his henchmen; the great Scottish lords are horrified by his actions.

Finally there is the question of how realistic were the Scots in plays produced in England? If the illustrations in the first edition of Holinshed's *Chronicles* are an indication, there was nothing in the costume to suggest their origins. This leads to the language. In most of the plays there is little or no dialect beyond the names of people and/or places. One certain exception is Robert Greene's *Scottish Historie of James the fourth*, which uses some words that supposedly represent the Scots language, but these are almost all in the first act for the misanthropist Bohun and Sir Bartram. Bohun's connection with Redesdale, on the English side of the border, explains why that the passages containing words from a northern dialect have more from the vernacular of northern English than purely Scots vocabulary.

Perception of the Scots, Scottish history, and the story of Macbeth among the English in the latter part of the sixteenth and early years of the seventeenth century was multi-faceted rather than unremittingly bigoted and hostile, even though those aspects have received the majority of scholarly attention. To be sure, there were those English who saw the Scots in generally hostile terms, but there were many who had a more benign attitude. In northern England, a neighbor might be Scots or of Scottish origin, in London a supplier or customer might be a Scot. The interest in the Scots was providing material for the ambitious writer, especially as the reign of Queen Elizabeth came to an end and her cousin James Stewart edged closer to the English throne.[44]

9

Macbeth before Shakespeare

ENGLISH LITERARY INTEREST in the Scots increased for more than a decade before Shakespeare is believed to have written the *Tragedie of Macbeth*. As a wedding for Queen Elizabeth became ever more unlikely, eliminating the possibility that she would produce children, speculation increased concerning her heir. Regardless of whatever machinations there were at diplomatic levels, when Elizabeth celebrated her fiftieth birthday in 1583, the most likely successor in the public mind was her cousin James Stewart, King James VI of Scotland. With Wales and Ireland already owing allegiance to the English monarch, amalgamation with Scotland would complete the "United Kingdom," which had been promoted since the fourteenth century.

Increasing popular interest in the Scottish royal family is visible as the succession of the Scottish king to the English throne became more probable. Then, as now, a royal wedding was a theme for comment and, once again, the Register of the Stationers' Company of London gives examples. James married Anne of Denmark in August 1589, and he brought her to Scotland on 1 May 1590. A few weeks later in June, the London printer William Wright published *An excellent Dyttye made upon the arryvall of the Kinge of Scottes with his ladye from Denmarke upon Maye daye laste with her coronacon* (An excellent song composed on the arrival of the King of Scots with his lady from Denmark on May Day, together with her coronation). After their son Henry was born in February 1594, his baptism was the subject of a work published shortly thereafter by Joanne Butter, one of the few women stationers, as *A true report of the Baptisme of the prince of Scotland*. This appears to have been a bestseller because the subject was revisited the following year with a more elaborate title: *The Triumphant and princelie newe ballad declaringe the royaltie and magnificence performed at the Baptisinge of the prince of Scotland*. Certainly by 1600 there was enthusiasm at the highest levels of English society for King

James of Scotland to be the successor of Queen Elizabeth. Sir Robert Cecil, one of Elizabeth's most trusted advisors and son of William Cecil, the patron of Holinshed's *Chronicle* and Camden's *Britannia*, was working actively for James' succession.

The atmosphere of anticipation and speculation left its traces in literature, and Jacques-August de Thou was not the only one who observed that politics could drive popular taste in literature. Enthusiasm for a united Britain, either genuinely felt or assumed, trickled down to the common people. Just about the time Shakespeare is believed to have begun writing *Macbeth*, Anthony Munday produced a play for the inauguration of the Lord Mayor of London on October 29, 1605. His work, *The Triumph of Re-United Britannia*, spoke of the benefits that would accrue from the joining of the English and Scottish crowns. Munday was an opportunist, and as a writer, he seems to be well tuned to popular tastes, so his selection of topic is a useful guide to the public mood in the early years of James's reign in England.

The death of Queen Elizabeth and the arrival of a new king dominated the London publishing world in 1603. From March 3 to April 18, only three of the seventeen works entered into the Register of the Stationers' Company were not concerned with King James. In addition to the expected works of praise, there were treatises on slightly dated events. One pamphlet was *A trewe relacon of the treacherous practise attempted by one Mowbray against the person of our highe and mighte prynce and soverneign lord kinge James*. This probably refers to the alleged complicity of the Earl of Moray in the lawless activities of Francis Stewart, earl of Bothwell, who was slain in 1592. Not neglected was the benefit of the union of monarchies to religious harmony as illustrated by *A panegiricall congratulacon for the concord of the realms of great Brittayne in unitie of religion and one royalty*. Future prospects together with a search for history (or pseudo-history) to foretell them explain the appearance in June 1603 of two pamphlets: *Happie union of the kingdoms of England and Scotland* and *The noble actes nowe newly found of Arthure of the Round Table*.

Royal Patronage

The danger of a story with Scots characters or location became clear even before James began his reign as king of England. He enjoyed plays and kept abreast of English works as well as those in Scotland. Foreign observers at the royal court considered the theater to provide a valuable insight into the thoughts of the monarch. George Nicolson, the English agent at the Scottish court, gave Robert Cecil, his father's successor in political affairs, a list of the plays being performed.[1] King James was aware of the political implications of plays and, even before ascending the English throne, revealed a prickly attitude to perceived slights or insults. A message from Nicolson to Lord Burghley (April 15, 1598) pleads with his lordship, "It is regretted that the comedians of London should scorn [King James] and the people of [Scotland] in their play; and it is wished that the matter be speedily amended lest the King and the country be stirred to anger."[2] A reason for James's sensitivity was not limited to an interest in artistic content; he also used the theater as a tool in the contest for power with the kirk (i.e., the church) and the towns. A year after Nicolson sent his letter to Baron Burghley, he wrote (on November 12, 1599) to the latter's son Robert Cecil, the secretary of state and leading minister after the death of his father in August 1598, that the ministers of the kirk were forbidding their parishioners to attend theatrical performances. In addition, the bellows-blowers (blacksmiths' assistants) were claiming that performances by two English actors called Fletcher and Martin were the acts of English agents who had been sent to sow discord between the king and the kirk. The matter was resolved when King James directly ordered the Edinburgh council and kirk to reverse their bans and allow people to attend performances.[3]

Shortly after King James VI of Scotland became King James I of England (March 24, 1603), he extended his patronage to the English theater and, in a royal patent of May 19, 1603, became the patron of the Lord Chamberlain's men, whose name was changed to the King's Men.[4] The first name on the patent for the actors was Lawrence Fletcher (d. 1608), apparently the same Fletcher who is mentioned in George Nicolson's letter of November 1599. The very next name is William Shakespeare.

His Majesty might be their patron, but the King's Men discovered that plays referring to Scottish events did not always meet with their master's approval. There is the example of a play called the *Tragedie of Gowry* that was twice performed in August 1604 by the company. The *Tragedie of Gowry* had as its subject an incident now known as the "Gowrie Conspiracy," which was a supposed attempt on the king's life in August 1600. When hunting near Falkirk, the king was approached by Alexander Ruthven, the brother of the earl of Gowrie, who said that a man with a pot of gold coins was at his residence called Gowrie House. James rode to the house and afterward claimed that the doors were locked after he was led inside. He came to a room in a turret where there was an armed man. The king dashed to a window where he shouted "Treason." His entourage broke into the house and killed both the earl of Gowrie and his brother.

Macbeth before Shakespeare

Many people did not believe the king's version of events because neither the assassin nor the man with the pot of gold coins was found. The most generous interpretation of the king's report is a description of a confused attempt to assassinate James by Alexander Ruthven who wanted revenge for the execution of his father that had been carried out on the orders of James's regency council. Skepticism about the events might explain why the king's version of the story was rushed into publication, and a pamphlet with the title *Earle of Gowrie's conspiracie against the King's maiestie* was printed late in 1600. Controversy about the incident might be behind the cold reception the King's Men received for their performance. A letter of December 18, 1604 from the prolific letter writer John Chamberlaine (1553–1628) to his friend the diplomat Sir Ralph Winwood (c. 1563–1617) notes:

> The Tragedy of Gowry, with all the Action and Actors hath been twice represented by the King's Players, with exceeding Concourse of all sorts of People. But whether the matter or manner be not well handled, or that it be thought unfit that Princes should be played on the Stage in their Life-time, I hear that some great Councellors [*sic*] are much displeased with it, and so 'tis thought shall be forbidden.[5]

The King's Men were not alone in facing royal displeasure. Possibly the most infamous play involving the Scots was performed just months before the time when *Macbeth* is thought to have been played for the first time. This is *Eastward Ho*, a collaboration of George Chapman with John Marston, and Shakespeare's rival Ben Jonson. The entire enterprise was fraught with peril, beginning with the performers, the Children of the Queen's Revels. Despite their name, when they performed the play at court in the fall of 1605 their status is not entirely clear. Formerly called the Children of the Chapel Royal, they had been awarded royal patronage in February 1604 when the king issued a patent whereby they became the "Children of the Queen's Revels." King James quickly learned that patronage did not necessarily lead to respect. Just before playing *Eastward Ho*, the Children had performed a play at Blackfriars mocking the sovereign and his court. They had so antagonized His Majesty that King James withdrew his choirboys. Satire was no less dangerous at the palace, as the Children were to discover.

While it is clear that the offense came from the dialogue, unusually we have no real idea why *Eastward Ho* provoked such a strong reaction, although it nearly cost the playwrights their ears and noses. The surviving version of the play is a comedy about urban life and a get-rich-quick scheme in the colony of Virginia. One technical issue is that *Eastward Ho* seems to have been played without approval of the manuscript by the Lord Chamberlain, who had authority over the theaters.

There are several passages that might have caused offense, such as act I, 2, where Gertrude is talking with the other women and says:

> Does he come? *"And ever and anon she doubled in her song."* Now Lady's my comfort, what a profane ape's here! Tailor, Poldavis, prithee fit it, fit it, is this a right Scot? Does it clip close and bear up round?[6]

In "fit it, is this a right Scot?" the "it" appears to be a farthingale, a hoop skirt popular in England from the mid-sixteenth to mid-seventeenth century. The implication in the line is that the tailor used too little material, so that the skirt was very tight. The parsimony is denounced by the phrase "a right Scot," which is believed to be a comment on Scottish miserliness. The "profane ape" is believed to have preceded a passage of about nine lines slandering the Scots that was removed from the original script. The tone of the surviving lines is certainly suspect. The "ape" might be a reference to King James. He had weak legs that caused him to walk with an awkward gait, together with a deformity of the mouth that gave him a drooling tongue. His physical characteristics made him a figure of amusement to the English courtiers at his court, and he was sensitive about it. In addition, he would not have appreciated any implications of Scottish poverty, another cause for amusement among the English, especially in connection with the Scottish courtiers who followed James to England.

Whatever the reason, the reaction was brutal. Immediately after its performance, the "Children" disappeared from the royal court for almost a year, and two of the three authors—Chapman and Jonson—were thrown into prison. According to a recollection by his friend William Drummond of Hawthorne, Ben Jonson claimed that he voluntarily joined his fellow author in jail.[7] For twenty weeks, Chapman wrote frantically to any influential person in an attempt to secure their freedom. He claimed that offending lines had been improvised by the actors and were not part of the script. Chapman's protestations eventually were believed, and the writers emerged wiser, although not entirely safer, men. Returning to Jonson's story, he claimed that at a feast given in honor of the playwrights' release, one of the serving maids said that a man had asked for her help to put poison in the wine.

Two Macbeth Texts before Shakespeare

When did works about Macbeth, as distinct from works in which he is part of a narrative on Scottish history, first appear? Did William Shakespeare write the first play about Macbeth? Or to phrase it differently, is the *Tragedie of Macbeth* as found in the *First Folio* the only version of an independent piece about Macbeth? Early in the seventeenth century, when it was becoming increasingly likely that James VI of Scotland would follow Elizabeth Tudor on the English throne, there is evidence for two texts that contain at least part of the legend of Macbeth. Both are now lost, but one is described in some detail that shows parallels with points of the Macbeth episode found in Holinshed's *Chronicle*. The first of the pieces was a ballad and the other was a play.

Evidence for the first of these texts comes in connection with one of the many perils awaiting Elizabethan playwrights: plagiarism. Occasionally this took the form of a pre-emptive publication of a work before the original author could publish it. The illicit work would be rushed into production before an authorized version appeared—a misfortune that befell Shakespeare's fellow player and sometime business partner Will Kemp. In his complaint, he makes reference to a ballad about Macbeth that was circulating in London.

Will Kemp (c. 1560–c. 1603) had been one of Shakespeare's colleagues in the Lord Chamberlain's Men.[8] He was celebrated for his solo performances as a clown and, on joining the troupe, Kemp quickly became the star as a comedian and dancer, famous for his witty repartee and physical routines. Slapstick comedy complemented his favored type of dance, the so-called traditional English jig with its bawdy posturing and ribald humor. The performance was physically demanding, and Kemp's large size made his presentation noteworthy. The comedy, however, disguised a keen mind. While Kemp became famous playing fools, he was not one himself. On stage he cultivated the persona of the blunt-speaking and unsophisticated English "everyman," but in reality he was cosmopolitan with important and influential friends. Kemp traveled around the Continent both professionally and privately; twice he was entrusted with diplomatic missions by aristocratic patrons. He was also a businessman and briefly one of Shakespeare's partners in the lease of the Globe Theater. Sometime around 1599, however, he abruptly departed from the Lord Chamberlain's Men and ended his financial connections with them. No definite reason is known. Perhaps he was piqued because Richard Burbage was becoming the star of the troupe or perhaps there had been a quarrel with some other member of the company or possibly he saw a better business opportunity.

196 MACBETH BEFORE SHAKESPEARE

Shortly after leaving, Kemp performed his (self-proclaimed) greatest triumph that he called the "Nine Days Wonder." The "Wonder" was a Morris Dance that Kemp performed along the 130 miles from London to Norwich. He left London on February 11, 1600, and actually took sixteen days to reach Norwich because he had to wait almost a week at Bury St. Edmunds when he was overtaken by a snowstorm. The exploit was theoretically a profitable one, largely because of the wagers Kemp won for the completion of his dance, but in fact he was able to collect only a few of his winnings. Another effort to profit from his performance was the publication of an account of his triumph as *Kemps nine daies wonder* (Kemp's Nine Days Wonder), to which he appended a curious letter.[9] In the letter, an angry Kemp complained that ballads containing fictitious details about his exploits had appeared before his own account, to the detriment of sales. Addressing his letter to "My notable Shakerags," he complains about the elaborations of an "impudent generation of ballad makers" who misrepresented his adventures.[10] Continuing with the tale of his search for the author of ballads about him, he writes:

Still the search continuing, I met a proper upright youth, only for a little stooping in the shoulders; all hart to the heel, a penny poet" [whose first work was] "the miserable stolen story of Macdoel or Macdobeth, or Macsomewhat" ("*the miserable stolne story of Macdoel or Macdobeth, or Macsomewhat*") for I am sure a Mac it was, though I never had the maw to see it. He told me there was a fat filthy ballad maker that should have once been his journeyman to the trade; who lived about the town; and ten to one but he had thus terribly abused me and my taberer; that he was able to do such a thing in print. . . . [Kemp then tells of an interview with one suspect and the eventual discovery of the culprit]. "Well, God forgive thee honest fellow, I see thou has grace in thee; I pray thee do so no more, leave writing these beastly ballads, make not good wenches Prophetesses, for little or no profit, nor for a six-penny matter, revive not a poor fellow's fault that is hanged for his offence; it may be thy own destiny one day, pray thee be good to them.

Kemp's letter has four interesting pieces of information in connection with the Macbeth legend. First, the name "Shakerags" brings to mind the "Shake-scene," who most scholars are convinced is William Shakespeare, berated in *Greenes Groatsworth of Wit*. Kemp's *Shakerags* might be a similar, but more kindly meant, address to his former colleagues in general and more

Macbeth before Shakespeare

particularly to the man who had been both his associate and business partner. Second, there is *Macdobeth*, a work that was popular enough to be familiar to Kemp and his audience, and also worth someone's illicitly printing it. Kemp's *Macdoel or Macdobeth or Macsomewhat* has usually been brushed aside by scholars as mere verbiage, a nonsense name. *Macdobeth*, however, is a recognizable variation of the name Macbeth, and a similar form of the name is found in William Stewart's *Buik of the Croniclis of Scotland* where Macbeth is called *Makcobey*. Both the forms *Macdobeth* and *Makcobey* represent attempts to render the Latin form *Machabeus* (employed in the Latin chronicles of John of Fordun and his continuator Walter Bower) into the vernacular. Furthermore, the name is rare, and Shakespeare's Macbeth is the only major figure with that name. Equally interesting is that Kemp clearly is using the "mac" as a patronymic. Third, the "penny poet" was a guild master, since he claims that his former journeyman, turned literary thief, was the likely author of the abuse of Kemp. Finally, there is the curious statement at the end of the letter concerning "good wenches" who are turned into prophetesses and "a poor fellow . . . hanged for his offence." This might be coincidence, but the parallels with the Macbeth legend are striking. The good wenches/prophetesses seem very like the weird sisters saluting Macbeth who had been part of the legend since the chronicle of Andrew of Wyntoun; the prophetic salutation is, of course, one of the best-known episodes in *The Tragedie of Macbeth*. The "poor fellow . . . hanged for his offence" has similarities with the executed rebel Macdonwald in the play.

Kemp's letter has been used in the argument that a work connected with the Macbeth legend was circulating at least before 1600 when Kemp undertook his dance to Norwich.[11] If the prophetesses and execution were part of that production, then the similarity with the Macbeth episode in Holinshed's chronicle becomes even more pronounced. Kemp's remark at the end of *Kemps nine daies wonder* leads to an interesting problem. The Register of the Stationers' Company has an entry for August 27, 1596, that records how a stationer named Thomas Millington was fined two shillings and sixpence for printing "*a ballad contrarye to order, which he also presently paid. M[emoran]d[um].—the ballad entituled the "Taminge of a shewe"; also one other ballad of "Macdobeth"*("A ballad contrary to order, which he also presently paid. Memorandum—the ballad entitled the 'Taming of a Shrew'; also one other ballad of 'Macdobeth'); a line is struck through the titles."[12] Thomas Millington (fl. 1583–1603) had his shop at the sign of the gun by the little door of St. Paul's Cathedral and has been mentioned previously in connection with the *Wofull ballad of a knightes daughter in Scotland*, which he published in the same year.[13] Described as one of the "quill-driving parasites" who profited from Shakespeare's work, he produced *Henry VI, part 2*, an early alternative text of Shakespeare's play, in 1594, and *Henry V*, one of the bad quartos of Shakespeare's play.[14] The former was printed by Thomas Creede (fl. 1593–1617), a dubious character who printed several works that were Shakespeare's plays with different titles. He had the distinction of being fined twice in 1595 for violating the rules of the Stationers' Company. Creede also printed Robert Greene's *The Scottish History of James IV*.

To return to the memorandum, is the entry concerning Millington and *Macdobeth* a genuine record of a fine for an unlawfully printed ballad or is it a forgery? This odd question is connected with the man who first brought the item to the attention of the world: John Payne Collier.[15] A hyperactive scholar not uncommon in the Victorian Age, his career began in poverty, progressed to respectability, and ended with charges of dishonesty. An acknowledged authority on the literature of the Tudor and Stuart Ages, Collier was a keen student of Shakespeare and of the scraps of evidence concerning Macbeth prior to the publication of the *First Folio*. In addition to announcing the supposed Millington entry in the Register of the Stationers' Company, he also announced the description of the performance of *Macbeth* found in the playbook of Simon Forman (see below), and he was associated with the man who discovered the Master of the Revels' account of Hunnison's production of a play on the king of Scots. In every case, Collier's connection has led to accusations of academic dishonesty or outright fraud, although at least with the materials for Forman and Hunnison, Collier was innocent of the charges.

Remembered today primarily by scholars of nineteenth-century antiquarianism, John Payne Collier (1789–1883) was one of the most famous or infamous men of his era. He was either a forger who shamelessly practiced on his gullible contemporaries or he was the victim of the most outrageous slanders.[16] Possibly there is some truth in either claim. Collier came from a privileged childhood that ended in poverty, thanks to the financial miscalculations of his father. So John Collier had to make his own way in the world. Earning his living initially as a writer, he held a variety of posts, but his real love was the literature of the sixteenth and seventeenth centuries. His credentials as a scholar are impressive. Librarian to the duke of Devonshire, for whom he built up one of the important private collections of early English texts, he was also a leader in the intellectual community and was one of the founders of the Camden Society, which remains dedicated to the dissemination of textual editions. Collier's erudition was respected by his friends and associates, who included some of the most important scholars of his day.

Macbeth before Shakespeare 199

In his *History of English Dramatic Poetry*, written when Collier was about forty years old, evidence of suspicious materials first began to be noticed. The possibility of forgery was not immediately touted, but during the next twenty years there was a steady accumulation of texts cited by Collier that other scholars could not find. Additionally, he published dubious readings from genuine texts. By this time John Collier had many important friends and was an influential person in his own right, so the skeptics treaded warily. Matters came to a head, however, in 1852 when Collier announced that he had discovered the Perkin's Folio, a copy of the "Second Folio" of Shakespeare's works that had extensive annotations. Soon the floodgates of criticism swung open and a plethora of scholars gave voice to their long-held misgivings, with one going so far as to level a charge of forgery at Collier. Collier responded vigorously by bringing a suit for libel and declaring that anything he printed was already present in the manuscript when making his transcriptions.

This leads to the *Macdobeth* entry in the Register of the Stationers' Company. The first person to bring this material to the public view was John Payne Collier. Even though many modern scholars consider it to be a forgery, the matter remains obscure because, prior to Collier's announcement, this section of the Register of the Stationers' Company had not been copied in its entirety. While different hands are found through the Register, the script for the *Macdobeth* entry is different from that employed in the surrounding entries especially for the forms of some letters such as –s–. If Collier did forge that item, then the scribal variation is curious, since he had read enough sixteenth-century texts to know what scripts were common in the late Tudor period. A dark line through titles was used in the eleventh-century *Domesday Book* to draw the reader's attention while the twelfth-century English financial guide known as *Dialogue of the Exchequer* notes that a line drawn through the notice of a fine was a sign that the penalty had been paid.[17] This leads to the question, if the goal were forgery, why call attention to it so obviously with archaic signs? For a man accused of passing off a forged copy of the *Second Folio* of Shakespeare's works, however, a note at the bottom of a page would be but the work of a moment. So the question remains: is it a genuine entry or did John Payne Collier write the *Macdobeth* entry in the Register of the Stationers' Company or did someone else add it?

At this point it is informative to leave *Macdobeth* momentarily and examine another missing text, a contemporary play that probably had Macbeth as a character. In the last year of Queen Elizabeth's reign, Philip Henslowe, the manager and financier of the Admiral's Men (a rival of Shakespeare's company), paid five pounds on April 18, 1602, to Charles Massey for the *playe boocke called Malcolm Kynge of Scottes* (script of a play called Malcolm, king of Scots).[18] Charles Massey was an actor, playwright, and part owner of the Admiral's Men. Only a couple of his plays are known, and *Malcolm* does not seem to have been one of his successes. Even the name was not settled until after Henslowe laid down his money; in his journal a blank space had been reserved for the eventual title. Apparently the piece was played because, on April 27, Henslowe lent thirty shillings to Thomas Downton, another member of the Admiral's Men, to purchase *a sueut of motley for the scotchmen for the play called Malcolm Kynge of Scotes*.[19] The "suit of motley" was a costume of various colors that was traditionally worn by a jester or fool. Since the suits were purchased for more than one individual, this leads to the speculation that Massey's production was attempting to portray the characters in traditional Highland dress with an early version of tartans. Both motleys and tartans used variegated colors and, to one unfamiliar with the latter term, could be used interchangeably.

Malcolm Kynge of Scotes is another example of how quickly texts could disappear. Without Henslowe's account there would have been no record of the play, and all that is known of it is the title. The title, however, prompts another question: which Malcolm? Four Scots kings were named Malcolm, but only the third, Malcolm Canmore, appeared in legend. So it was probably a drama about his career, which means that Macbeth would almost certainly have appeared in it, possibly in the same manner as he appeared in John of Fordun's chronicle: the villain in the legend of Malcolm Canmore. In the first recension of Andrew of Wyntoun's *Original Chronicle*, the Macbeth episode was contained within a section "How Malcolm Canmore came to the crown and took possession of Scotland," which was changed in the second recension to "When Macbeth-Finlay Rose and Reigned in Scotland." Massey's *Malcolm Kynge of Scottes* probably had at least a part of the Macbeth legend.

The Tragedie of Macbeth

Over a year later, King James visited the University of Oxford and shortly afterward, sometime during the winter of 1605/1606, many scholars believe that William Shakespeare wrote the *Tragedie of Macbeth* and that it was first performed at Hampton Court in the summer of 1606 during the visit to England of His Majesty's brother-in-law, King Christian of Denmark. William Shakespeare was not the only one adding Macbeth to his repertoire. A popular contemporary poet named William Warner wrote a long compendium of history and fantasy called *Albion's England* in 1586 to which he added

Macbeth before Shakespeare

material periodically. The version of 1606 contains a synopsis of the Macbeth legend from Holinshed's *Chronicle* that begins:

> *One Macbeth who had traitorously his sometimes sovereign slain,*
> *And like a monster, not a man, usurp in Scotland reign,*
> *Whose guilty conscience did itself so feelingly accuse,*
> *As nothing not applied by him against himself he views,*
> *No whispering but of him, gainst him all weapons he feares he borne*
> *All beings jointly to revenge his murders thinks he sworn,*
> *Wherefore (for such are ever such in self-tormenting mind)*
> *But to proceed in blood he thought no safety to find.*[20]

The verses continue with the remainder of the legend, including the murder of Banquo and subsequent flight of Fleance to Wales.

While speculation about the date of the play's performance continues, the earliest surviving reference to the play is almost five years later. The lapse need not be significant; during the period from January 1608 to December 1610, the theaters were closed for twenty-eight of the thirty-six months. The theater-diary or *Book of Plaies* that belonged to a London physician named Simon Forman has the first description of the drama as one of four Shakespeare plays that he watched.[21] Forman would be expected to have some professional curiosity about *Macbeth* since he was an astrologer as well as a physician and he dabbled in necromancy.[22] Although comfortably well-off at the time of his death, his early years had been hardscrabble, and there were occasions when Forman paid for his education at Oxford by working as a carpenter. He made his fortune as a medical astrologer, casting horoscopes to determine treatments or the most favorable times for procedures. His studies of the occult led to trouble with the authorities, and he had been in court several times; he was imprisoned in Salisbury in 1587 for being in possession of several magic books. Forman's claim that he had cured himself of the plague in 1592 led to his wealth. Prosperity allowed him the leisure for other interests, among which was Scottish history. Forman wrote a treatise that claimed to demonstrate his descent from the noble families of Scotland, beginning in 1028 with the reign of Malcolm II.

According to his playbook, Forman was in the audience for the performance of *The Tragedie of Macbeth* at the Globe on April 20, 1611. His recollection of the play begins with Macbeth and Banquo accosted by three women fairies or nymphs who hail Macbeth as "king of Codon" (i.e., Cawdor), but claim he will be a king, yet beget no kings, while Banquo is warned he will not be king, yet produce kings. Macbeth arrives at Duncan's court, where he is made prince of Northumberland and then the king visits Macbeth's castle, where he is slain by Macbeth at the persuading of Lady Macbeth. There are omens, and the blood on Macbeth and his wife's fingers could not be removed. Duncan's sons flee the kingdom to England and Wales. Macbeth is proclaimed king and causes Banquo to be killed in an ambush. At a banquet the following night, Banquo's ghost appears and Macbeth's reaction produces suspicion in the minds of his guests about the culprit. Macduff flees to England, for which Macbeth kills his family. Macduff has an interview with Duncan's son; they raise an army and kill Macbeth at Dunsinane. The synopsis closes with Lady Macbeth's sleepwalking episode.

Forman's account differs from the earliest printed text, in the *First Folio*, mainly in details, such as saying that the individuals who addressed Macbeth and Banquo were fairies or nymphs, not witches, and that they said to Macbeth after announcing each title "you shall be a king but shall beget no kings." The *First Folio* text reserves this announcement, slightly rephrased, until Banquo asks why he has been neglected. Forman's recollection has Macbeth made prince of Northumberland, while Malcolm and Donalbain flee from Scotland to England and Wales, respectively, rather than to England and Ireland. There are two significant omissions. First, the supernatural women who are so prominent in the *First Folio* text make only a single appearance in Forman's recollection. Second, and equally conspicuous by its absence, is the battle scene at the beginning of the play, when Macbeth proves his prowess in combat.

The differences between Simon Forman's account and the play as found in the *First Folio* might be more apparent than real. The note is brief, and Forman obviously wrote down only the parts that struck him as significant. In a crowded and noisy theater some of the dialogue could have been difficult to hear. Finally, he simply may have forgotten or misremembered parts of the play. Nonetheless, the memoir indicates that the *Macbeth* Forman watched was not identical with the work that was printed in the *First Folio* collection of Shakespeare's works.

Most scholars believe that Forman's recollections are genuine. For the few who are not convinced, the problem is once again John Payne Collier.[23] Forman's manuscript was discovered at Oxford in 1832 by Henry Black who was cataloguing the Ashmole manuscripts in the Bodleian Library. Black sent Collier a transcription and the latter published details from it in his *New Particulars Regarding the Works of Shakespeare* (1836). At the time, and for decades later, the entry about Forman's attendance at a performance of

Macbeth was accepted as genuine. Doubt about the authenticity of the *Book of Plaies* appeared, however, in the twentieth century when Samuel Tannenbaum, a New York psychiatrist turned literary sleuth, published a series of essays in which he claimed to have discovered more forgeries made by Collier.[24] While some of his work had merit, much of it was pure speculation. Among the "new" forgeries, Tannenbaum claimed that Forman's *Book of Plaies* was actually the work of Collier. Even though his accusations on that point were eventually disproved, the taint of imposture continues to cling to Forman's recollections.

The Various Guises of Macbeth

There was an increased interest in the Scots in general and Macbeth in particular during the reign of Elizabeth I. The ambiguities of who would be her successor combined with religious parallelism to provide the ground in which the Scots became more fascinating to the English. By the time King James VI of Scotland added England to his domain, there was an audience for Scottish themes. The literary character of Macbeth was clearly becoming more prominent, undoubtedly due to the popularity of Holinshed's *Chronicle*. When William Shakespeare wrote his *Tragedie of Macbeth*, the peripheral characters had already been tested, from the sibyls praising King James on his entrance to Oxford to the alliance of England and Scotland. Macbeth was also a dangerous subject. King James had more than the usual royal fear of assassination while his mistrust of English intentions was well known. Nonetheless, Macbeth became one of the plays that defined his era.

An indication of the *Tragedie of Macbeth*'s popularity and how far it traveled is the printing of two works in Scotland: the *Wallace* by the minstrel Blind Hary, about the fourteenth-century leader William Wallace; and John Barbour's *The Bruce*, the history of the events leading up to and during the battle of Bannockburn in 1314, which defined the career of the Scottish king Robert Bruce.[25] Both works had been published in Scotland in the sixteenth century, but they were reprinted in quick succession in less than a decade after Simon Forman had watched the production of *Macbeth* in 1611. In 1616, *The Actes and Life of the Most Victorious Conqueror Robert Bruce* was printed by the Edinburgh publisher Andro Hart. He followed this two years later with the publication of *The Life and Acts of the Most Famous & Valiant Champion, Syr William Wallace, Knight of Ellerslie; Maintainer of the Libertie of Scotland*. Both books were reprinted in 1620. This might have been coincidence, but that the publications were a reaction to the *Tragedie of*

Macbeth is suggested by the fact that the *Bruce* would not be reprinted again until 1648 and then by a university printer. There is something ironic about the possibility that a drama about a Scots king written by an English playwright might have encouraged a Scottish printer to revisit biographies of his own countrymen. There remains much that is unknown about Macbeth the person and Macbeth the literary character.

Conclusion

THIS STUDY HAS come back to the point where it began, in late 1605/early 1606 when William Shakespeare might have begun writing the play known as *The Tragedie of Macbeth*. The search for Macbeth has spanned centuries, from Irish immigrants into Britain to a drama of medieval Scotland played on the English stage. The historical king came from a culture of immigrant warriors, who had won their lands at the point of a sword and held it by the same manner. Scots fought their neighbors and each other as they built what would become the Scottish kingdom. The legends of larger-than-life warriors mingled with folk memories of monsters, demons, and fertility goddesses. The Scots' conversion to Christianity added another element to the story. Medieval Scottish culture lent itself to the collection of interesting and bizarre facts about important individuals. Macbeth's family history was firmly within this apparent confusion.

Enough hints are found in the historical records to suggest that the historic Macbeth was more powerful and influential than suggested by the gathering of chronicle crumbs about his career. Poets circulated legends that connected his ancestors with powerful Irish families, such as the O'Neill dynasties of the north. Scandinavia also had a connection as Macbeth and his father are remembered in the Old Norse tract called *Orkneyinga Saga* as the opponents of the Orkney jarls. The history of Macbeth is connected with Scandinavia and England. As an ally of the Danes, his battles with the Norse become comprehensible as more than just raids. Macbeth's ties with the English king Edward the Confessor are more obscure and more complex than suggested by later writers. When he allowed Norman refugees into his kingdom, he was admitting the followers of Edward's nephew. His fame might explain why the Irish chroniclers gave so much attention to Macbeth and his family for more than a century, from 1020 to 1130. He was famous because he was powerful, and to gain such authority, Macbeth had to be willing to kill anyone, even members of his family, if it suited his purposes. There was, however, more to supremacy than brutishness. Macbeth was capable of less horrific behavior, such as giving lands to churches or patronizing scholarship. He was neither as great a sinner as later works attempted to portray him nor was he the saint that his modern supporters would prefer. A creature of his times, Macbeth had all the virtues and vices of the age in which he lived. When cold-blooded murder suited his ends, he could kill with a steady hand and no apparent remorse. When compassion was a useful emotion, he could adopt his murdered rival's son.

Macbeth was different from preceding and subsequent Scots princes. He is the only medieval Scots king known to have gone to Rome and, until the later twelfth century, the only one to have traveled beyond the British Isles. His pilgrimage was more than the "luxury" holiday of the time; in common with other contemporary princes on the margins of Europe, it showed a man determined to take his place among the foremost Christian princes. Travel also provided the opportunity for observation. Macbeth was attentive enough to invite Norman mercenaries, the new fighting machine of the age, into his kingdom. Rituals and display of Christianity were changing as well; again, some of these appear to have been transported to the Scots kingdom. The surviving notice of Macbeth's largesse to the church is also curious for someone whose piety is regularly called into question. No other royal grant to a church so thoroughly frees a religious house from secular interference. Later kings might give more lands, buildings, or monies, but they were careful to reserve something for themselves. Macbeth was demonstrating behavior encouraged by one of the great reforming pontiffs of the age: Leo IX.

After his death, the transition to Shakespeare's literary character was a process that took generations. Many aspects of Macbeth's culture helped to shape his subsequent story. During his lifetime, a taste for the fantastic and the supernatural meant that tales about the Day of Judgment circulated together with hero tales. Angels, fairies, and demons were all believed to be in contact with humans. There was also the praise of a winner. An intensely competitive society was not always scrupulous in observing niceties. So long as he won, a clever scoundrel was valued above a dull saint. Finally, there is the adage that "History is written by the winner." His dynasty lost to the family of Malcolm Canmore and that loss was a significant element in the formation of his legend.

For the first two centuries after his death, Macbeth was remembered as a good king. The prosperity of his reign was celebrated into the thirteenth

Conclusion 207

century. Even a poem composed in the generation after his death at the court of his successor Malcolm Canmore speaks well of him. The image of Macbeth in the first century after his death was unremarkable if noted for its extremes; this he shared with many other princes both within and without Scotland. The fruitfulness of his reign was remembered, always an important consideration in a farming community. So, too, was his role in the death of Duncan.

A change began in the twelfth century. Popular literature, such as Geoffrey of Monmouth's *History of the Kings of Britain*, describes his homeland of Moray as a barbaric and savage place. Slandering one's rivals was a common tactic and is seen often in contemporary histories; the losers, of course, were not given the opportunity to reply. A turning point in the Macbeth legend might have been in connection with the endowment of a mass chaplaincy for the soul of Duncan by his descendant King Alexander II. The youthful, impulsive lover was replaced with a good and gentle Duncan. Such a substitution required the villainy of his murderer, and it is easy to imagine how this contributed to the formation of the wicked Macbeth. Whether or not a poem in praise of Malcolm Canmore as the restorer of his family's fortunes was composed at the same time, the contrast between the Macbeth of the twelfth century and the Macbeth of the fourteenth century is startling.

How did stories about Macbeth become well known and gain wide circulation? Popular literature as distinct from scholarly records was one method. There were folklore, minstrel songs, plays, and recitations. Andrew of Wyntoun comments on the variety when he refers to the alternative versions of the Macbeth legend. Another answer may be that Macbeth first appears as a villain in someone else's legend—Malcolm Canmore—rather than his own. The patronage of Malcolm's heirs for their version of eleventh-century history is behind the Macbeth legends told by John of Fordun and Andrew of Wyntoun. How successfully the Canmore dynasty version would be received depended on a larger-than-life scoundrel in opposition to the hero. Villains can be more interesting than heroes, and the more Macbeth was slandered, the more interesting he became and gradually overshadowed his nemesis.

The story continued to be retold for centuries, apparently with details added and subtracted. Changes in society added to the encrustation of fictional elaboration on the development of the Macbeth legend. Scotland's culture altered during the reign of Malcolm Canmore's sons as a francophone aristocracy settled in the kingdom. These immigrants were warriors and, although Malcolm's descendants were the eventual victors in the competition for supremacy among the Scots, they had a long fight for it. Two and a half centuries after the death of Macbeth, the family of Malcolm Canmore faced their own crisis with the extinction of the direct male line. The ensuing confusion and uncertainty opened the way for their southern neighbor, the English king Edward I, to attempt to annex the kingdom. During that time of tribulation, the Scots looked for heroes and found one in the person of Robert Bruce, the earl of Carrick, later to be King Robert I. Propagandists for both the English and the Scots labored to advance their cause in this confused political landscape. Edward sent a request to the English religious houses asking for proof that the Scots kings had been vassals of an English overlord. Two generations later, a priest from Aberdeen named John Barbour wrote his verse epic *The Bruce* celebrating the victory of King Robert I over Edward's son King Edward II at the battle of Bannockburn in 1314. In its essentials, *The Bruce* is a story of an oppressor who is unjustly seizing power until he is overcome by a prince who is divinely ordained to rule.

While John Barbour was composing his poem, another clergyman from Aberdeen named John of Fordun was collecting materials for his great chronicle of the Scots. John of Fordun had a different point of view, and after two generations of literary warfare, he wanted to refute the English histories with what he described as their biased accounts. More than historical research, there was the need to write a morality drama for his age. A time of troubles had descended on the Scots because of their quarrels among themselves. In part this was due to their unwillingness to unite behind the line of true kings, represented by Malcolm Canmore and his family. Macbeth was the object of that chaos and only when he was defeated by the prince and harmony was restored, would the Scots reap the benefits of peace.

John of Fordun is often the earliest writer in source collections for the story of Macbeth, but he is actually at the end of one period in the development of the story. In pursuit of the chimera that was believed to be a golden age of Malcolm Canmore, John of Fordun's *Chronicle of the Scottish Nation* presents a wicked Macbeth for Malcolm to overthrow. His outline of the legend became the foundation for subsequent writers. Macbeth is a thoroughly evil man who usurps the kingship and then presides over crime and misery. He is a tyrant who is cast down by Malcolm Canmore, the restorer of the true line of kings. John's Macbeth is simply a pastiche of a villain, with nothing more than savagery. The few details that are supplied, such as Macduff's disembarkation at Ravenspur Point, reflect the circumstances and interpretations of his own day. Even the character of Macduff seems to be based on contemporary events rather than legend from the eleventh century. The similarity between Macbeth and Malcolm together with the more recent historical individuals, Edward of England and Robert "the Bruce," are clear.

Conclusion 209

John of Fordun's story includes the earliest appearance of the famous debate between Malcolm Canmore and Macduff with its emphasis on the good rule of a rightful prince. This typically medieval episode is the centerpiece of his narrative and it becomes a fossilized incident for the ensuing centuries.

If John of Fordun were a propagandist, the interpreter of the next generation, Andrew of Wyntoun, was a collector. While quite happy to follow the lead of his predecessor, he has little of the bile that infects his predecessor's work. Andrew was also more willing to accommodate new information, as the changes to his *Original Chronicle* show. Like all good historians, he was searching for the detail that might illuminate an obscure corner of the historical scene. Fortunately for his readers, he was less of an artist than researcher. It is easy to see where he is trying to insert new items or a completely different incident. Andrew of Wyntoun introduces the occult into the story with weird sisters who appear in dreams and claims that Macbeth was the offspring from his mother's liaison with a devil. Not only was Macbeth demonized, but the conflict between Highland (Gaelic) culture and Lowland (Anglophone) culture also played its part, as ideas (prophecy) and characters (the product of unnatural birth) from Celtic literature were used to emphasize the gullibility and guilt of Macbeth. Andrew of Wyntoun supplied material that Hector Boece used for his reworking of the Macbeth legend that, in turn, found its way into William Shakespeare's play. This poses the now unanswerable question: how much of that material was known to Fordun or to Fordun's editor/reviser Walter Bower?

Vital contributions from the fantasy literature of Celtic Britain complement the Macbeth legend beginning with Andrew of Wyntoun and continuing to Hector Boece. From the meeting with the three women on the blasted heath to the march of Birnam Wood, there is a link going back to the great boasting contests of the ancient Celts mentioned by classical writers. The literary tradition presents the larger than life exploits of warriors such as Fergus son of Erc and the Irish champion Cú Chulainn before culminating with the memoirs of the Viking wars of the High Middle Ages. The Macbeth legend accumulated characters and incidents. Unnatural birth, prophetic women, omens of future events, and shifting landscape are all found in popular literature. Miraculous and mundane exist together in situations that might or might not be extraordinary. The changes were not all additions. Macbeth's diabolical parentage and magic ring are found in Andrew of Wyntoun's account and omitted in later versions.

John of Fordun the propagandist and Andrew of Wyntoun the collector were complemented by Hector Boece the stylist. The final reshaping of the

Macbeth legend took place at a university. Boece, the first principal of the University of Aberdeen, used his training at Paris in the service of his interest in Scottish history. In his hands, Macbeth became an urbane and suave Renaissance prince, a far cry from the brutal beast of John of Fordun or the superstitious sovereign from Andrew of Wyntoun. Examples of this new type of king, debonair and deadly, could be found in many of the royal courts of Europe. The "Renaissance" Macbeth could laugh at the pronouncements of apparitions of women, and then remember their prophecy when he wanted an excuse for his tyranny. Equally important was the introduction of a new main character named Banquo, who was both a foil to the tyrant and also flattered Boece's patrons, the Stewart royal family. He joined Macduff as an important supporting character. Shakespeare followed Boece's Macbeth story at third hand, because the *Chronicles* of Raphael Holinshed state that Holinshed used the translation made by John Bellenden.

Several trends in the sixteenth century benefited the story. The first was the growth of theater with its immense popularity. Audiences wanted new plays with new characters. Then there was also the growth of interest in the supernatural, as can be seen from even a casual glance at the records of new pieces licensed in the Register of the Stationers' Company. Added to this was the dissemination of Boece's work, admittedly at third hand, first in the translation of Bellenden (and possibly also the verse of William Stewart) then in its amalgamation into the chronicle of Raphael Holinshed. When the tale of Macbeth was incorporated into the *Chronicles* of Raphael Holinshed, the story had expanded far beyond the history of an eleventh-century prince. History, morality, and the supernatural combined in a legend that was fascinating. English interest in matters Scottish had increased by the last decades of the sixteenth century as the childless state of Queen Elizabeth I made it more likely that she would be succeeded by the Scots king James VI.

A reference in the year 1600 to a work called *Macdobeth* by Will Kemp is hardly conclusive, but it does suggest that some form of the story of Macbeth was circulating around London even before the death of Queen Elizabeth in 1603. Who was the author? William Kemp's postscript to his "Nine Days Wonder," addressed to "Shakerags," tells of his adventure in discovering the author of a stolen story of "Mac something." Was Shakespeare the "Shakerags" to whom Will Kemp addressed his letter concerning his adventures with the author of the "miserable stolen ballad"? Whenever the premier of *The Tragedie of Macbeth*—in August of 1606 as some authorities believe—the original play was probably different from the one of the *First Folio* if the summary of its performance in 1611 is accurate. This is not surprising, for additions, deletions, and rearrangements are to be expected of works that were accommodating their audiences' tastes. Modern scholars enjoying the luxury of well-stocked libraries and well-paid time for research might forget that the aim of theater companies was to make money. The competition was fierce. To be successful,

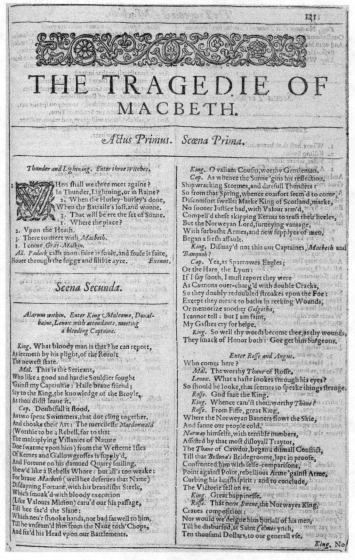

FIG. C.1 First Folio of William Shakespeare's *The Tragedie of Macbeth* (1623). STC 22273 Fo.1 no.68. Used by permission of the Folger Shakespeare Library.

they had to gauge the reaction of their audience, be it a noble court or the groundlings at the Globe Theater.

William Shakespeare's *Tragedie of Macbeth* is one of his shortest dramas, but the legend on which it was based developed over half a millennium. The character of the prince who gave it his name underwent many changes in the years between the lifetime of the historical figure and the creation of the character performed in the theater of the Stuart Age. Many questions have been asked about Macbeth, king and character, and answers will continue to be sought.

APPENDIX I

The Children of Macbeth?

Among the most vocal of those who criticize William Shakespeare's *Tragedie of Macbeth* are individuals who believe that Macbeth is their ancestor. Their usual distinguishing feature is that they have the surname Macbeth somewhere in their background. Claims of descent from Macbeth fly in the face of general scholarly disbelief. If there is any general agreement about any part of the historical Macbeth's life, it is that he had no children.[1] The argument has worked to a consistent theme. If Macbeth and Gruoch had children, at least some mention of them would have survived, and a biological son, rather than a stepson, would have succeeded Macbeth. The succession of Lulach, Gruoch's son from her first marriage, is considered definitive proof of a barren union.[2] There are, however, several records that imply a less tidy scenario.[3] First, there is a genealogy for Clan MacQuarrie claiming that Macbeth did have children. Then there is the bequest to the church of St. Serf's where a king's son is mentioned in connection with Macbeth's donation. Finally, there are several charters from the late eleventh and early twelfth centuries in which appear two men who were sons of a man named Macbeth and of the correct generation to be his children. Furthermore their careers were in the regions connected with Macbeth and Gruoch, where they had contacts with noble, even royal, courts.

The Clan MacQuarrie genealogy is the weakest argument for Macbeth's children. This tract is found in a collection of pedigrees for Highland clans formerly known as Killbride MS 1467, but now National Library of Scotland Advocates MS 72.1.1; the composition of this genealogy has been dated *circa* 1400.[4] Genealogies were revised at various times, and this one shows signs of imperfect survival at best and deliberate fabrication at worse. According to this pedigree Macbeth son of Findláech had a son named Ferchach *og* (Ferchach the Young). Prior to Macbeth is a *lacuna* of about 10 generations back to the seventh-century king Ferchar the Tall while following Ferchach is another

214   *Appendix 1*

lacuna of about the same number of generations necessary to carry the lineage to the mid-sixteenth century.

The second record is the reference to the king's son in Macbeth's charter granting the lands of Bolgyn to the Céli Dé community serving the church of St. Serf at Loch Leven. When Macbeth and Gruoch released the Céli Dé from the payment of certain taxes, among them were the dues owed to the son of the king. That provision was unknown among the Scots in the later Middle Ages when the grant was copied in the surviving note, so it is unlikely to be a later insertion. Medieval Scots law gave no special tax privilege to the son of a king simply because of his parentage; he had to hold an office that justified this concession. A special consideration for a king's son is found, however, in a law code, probably from Strathclyde, known as "The Laws between the Scots and Britons" (*Leges inter Scotos et Brittos* in Edinburgh, National Archives of Scotland MS PA5/1), the purpose of which seems to have been to regularize the laws of the two peoples. Of course, if, as seems likely, the grant was of Gruoch's personal estate, then the emphasis is that the grant was being made in perpetuity rather than for the lifetime of the queen, and the inclusion of the "king's son" was specifically added in order to emphasize the point. The provision in the charters could refer to Lulach, whom Macbeth had adopted or it could refer to a natural son.

So far the evidence for natural children of Macbeth and Gruoch has been slight and not convincing. This leads to the third reason for questioning the conventional wisdom that Macbeth and Gruoch were childless and the evidence comes from charters preserved in two volumes: the afore-mentioned *Book of Deer* and the cartulary of the priory of St. Andrews (*Liber Cartarum Prioratus Sancti Andree*), where they survive in a late copy. Among the witnesses to charters covering a forty year span from the late eleventh-century to the early twelfth-century (roughly 1091 to 1131) are two men named Cormac and Máel Doun who were the sons of a man named Macbeth. Their names suggest parents who were both learned and pious. Cormac, for example, was a name associated with wisdom, particularly with the legendary King Cormac mac Airt, whose insight and clever sayings were proverbial. More historical, but almost as legendary, was Cormac mac Cuilennáin the bishop/ king of Munster whose death in battle (at Ballagmoone, co. Kildare) in 908 is recorded in the *Scottish Chronicle*. Cormac was a scholar and among the texts credited to him is *Cormac's Glossary*, an early form of dictionary that gave the meanings of obscure and rare words. The name Máel Doun was less celebrated, but more immediately connected with Macbeth and Scotland as it was the name of the bishop of St. Andrews who died in 1055. Bishop Máel Doun also gave land—the church of Markinch—to the Céli Dé of the church of St. Serf's at Loch Leven.

Cormac son of Macbeth was a witness to one surviving charter. About the year 1093 a noble named AEthelred gave the estate of Auchmore (east of Loch Leven) to the community of Céli Dé at St. Serf's.[5] AEthelred was the abbot of Dunkeld and had been the earl (*comes*) of Fife. More importantly he was the son of Malcolm Canmore. Cormac is described as a priest. As Crinán of Dunkeld and AEthelred illustrate, this was no

Appendix 1 215

barrier to secular prominence. Nor did it preclude a family, as clerical celibacy was not a requirement for the priesthood at this time, although the idea was becoming more popular among church reformers such as Pope Leo IX.

Cormac might make another, oblique, appearance in a charter. A man named Gilla Crist ("Servant of Christ") son of Cormac is included among the witnesses in a charter preserved in the *Book of Deer*. The donation was made about the year 1131 and it was a generous gift of land called *Pett Meic Gobraig* ("field/farm of the son of Gobrach"). This was the same farm whose taxes were given to the church by King Malcolm II. It should be noted, however, that Cormac was a popular name in this area at that time. Abbot Cormac of Turriff was a witness to two charters in the *Book of Deer*, while a Cormac mac Kennedy (MI *mac Cennédig*) gave Skillymarno (MI *Scáli Merlec* "den of thieves"), located about 3 miles north of Old Deer, to the church of Deer.

Turning to the other man, Máel Doun son of Macbeth circulated among the highest levels of society. He appears in several documents from the early twelfth century.[6] He was an *iudex* ("judge") who is described as "good and discerning." Máel Doun was among the witnesses to two charters to the church of Dunfermline, the burial place of Malcolm Canmore and Margaret, and practically a royal chapel. The first charter was issued in 1126 when King David I gave three serfs—Ragewin, Gille Patrick, and Ulchil—to the church of Dunfermline. Two years later (1128) Máel Doun was a witness to charter in which King David confirmed the gifts given to the church of Dunfermline by his family. What is clear from a reading of the endorsers—the queen, the king's son Henry, four bishops and five counts—is that the charter was issued during an important gathering. Also among the other dignitaries was a man with a suggestive patronymic named Gille Michel mac Duff. The surviving copy of the charter contains an interesting variation on Máel Doun's patronymic: *Macocbeth*. Reading it as *Mac-oc-beth*, the name means "the younger son of life," but the *–oc–* might have been an explanatory gloss that was absorbed into the name through tmesis (in which one word is inserted into the middle of another word). That explanation would be necessary only if Máel Doun had a prominent elder brother. At this point it should be noted that those charters were issued more than seventy years after the death of Macbeth.

The most interesting appearance of Máel Doun is as a member of the judicial tribunal that heard a case involving a Norman knight named Robert of Burgundy ("the fire and furnace of iniquity" according to the overwrought record of the trial).[7] Once again the Céli Dé of St. Serf's were involved, this time as the plaintiffs. This is the earliest record of any non-royal legal proceeding in Scotland. The issue in dispute was Robert's claim to a fourth part of Kirkness, the land that had been granted to the Céli Dé by Macbeth and Gruoch. For the first time, the Céli Dé emerged from the shadows as individuals. They were Duftah (correctly Dubthach) the priest and abbot, Sarran the son of Sodelne, Eogan the monk, Donald the grandson of Leod, Morrehat an old man who was Irish, and Old Cathan. One of the other judges sitting with Máel Doun was Constantine mac Duff, the earl or *comes* of Fife, who also was a witness to AEthelred's grant of Auchmore together with Cormac the son of Macbeth. Constantine possibly

Appendix 1

was the brother of Gille Michel mac Duff, one of the witnesses to the Dunfermline confirmation of 1128. All that survives of the proceedings is the decision of the court, which gave a verdict in favor of the clergy.

Máel Doun the son of Macbeth might also be mentioned in a charter of circa 1131, the charter that also has Gille Crist mac Cormaic as a witness. There is some uncertainty because the spelling of the name is garbled. The manuscript reads *Maledoni* with a sign of suspension above the letter *-o-* normally representing *-m-* but possibly standing for *-n-*. Once again, the date might seem to exclude any child of Macbeth, but if Máel Doun were born *circa* 1055, he would have been about 75 years old in 1130, a very old man for the time, but not impossibly so. The tenth-century King Constantine I was at least in his mid-seventies when he died in 952, and might have been substantially older, for he is called 'middle aged' by the Berchán poet upon his ascension to the kinship in 900. Malcolm Canmore's son King David I was almost 70 years old when he died in 1153, and his grandson King William 'the Lion' was about 72 years old when he died in 1214.

This leads back to the question: were Cormac and Máel Doun the sons of Macbeth and Gruoch? A definitive answer is not possible at the moment. All that remains is the weighing of possibilities. The two men had a father named Macbeth before the name became popular throughout the kingdom. In the case of Máel Doun, his first name is sufficiently uncommon to make remote the possibility that there were many other men with that Christian name and that patronymic in the kingdom. Cormac and Máel Doun are active in the very same areas as Macbeth and Gruoch. They were men of importance in Fife, a place where Gruoch apparently owned property. Cormac and Máel Doun had associations with the Céli Dé at Loch Leven and might have had connections with the church of Deer. This divergence is important, because the nobles who witness the St. Serf documents and those of the Deer charter-notes form quite distinct groups. Finally, they were men of influence within the kingdom, even occasionally attending the royal court. In an age that worshiped lineage, there had to be some reason for Cormac or Máel Doun to circulate among the great and the good.

If Cormac and Máel Doun were the sons of Macbeth and Gruoch, then why is it not said? The answer is simple; there was no need since they were not monarchs. A plethora of information in modern times obscures the scarcity of it for earlier eras. To take one example, while Cluniac historian Ralf Glauber mentions that Malcolm II had a son, this is his only memorial and not even his name survives. The records from Scotland during this period are few even for the royal family, and they are much fewer for anyone else.

Why, if Macbeth had children, did they not succeed him in the kingship or attempt to seize it? If the children of Macbeth and Gruoch were too young to succeed in 1057, then Lulach would have been the obvious choice. This leads to another area of speculation about Macbeth's pilgrimage to Rome; it might have had a connection with children. People went to Rome for many reasons, and Macbeth undoubtedly had a sound political or diplomatic motivation for such a journey. Pilgrimages were also made to ask

Appendix 1 217

for divine blessings, such as children. Did a childless Macbeth go to Rome as a pious act in connection with a prayer for children? If Macbeth and Gruoch had produced children after his pilgrimage, they could not have been more than seven years old when Macbeth died in 1057, far too young to succeed to the kingship.

The speculation that Cormac and Máel Doun were the children of Macbeth and Gruoch must remain as speculation. Nonetheless, there are so many areas of overlap between their careers and the regions or entities associated with the king and queen, that possibilities are very nearly probabilities. The question of why Macbeth's legend/history was preserved might be less obscure if his children had a part to play. Religious houses where records were kept would welcome family members eager to pay for remembrances of an ancestor who had held the kingship.

APPENDIX 2

Andrew of Wyntoun's Macbeth Episode: A Translation

This translation from medieval Scots into modern English of the Macbeth episode in *The Original Chronicle* by Andrew of Wyntoun follows the second recension of the text. Since the ultimate goal is to remain as close as possible to the Scots original with a comprehensible English version, this has led to the editorial decision to abandon some of the meaningless words and phrases the Andrew used to fill the metre or make a rhyme. The line numbers are on the right of the text.

WHEN MACBETH-FINLEY WAS RAISED AND REIGNED IN SCOTLAND

In this time, as you heard me tell,	1845
Treason that in England befell,	
In Scotland nearly the like cause	
By Macbeth-Finlay practiced was,	
When he murdered his own eme [*uncle*]	
Because of hope that he had in a dream,	1850
That he saw when he was adolescence,	
In a house dwelling with the prince,	
Who treated him well and fair,	
In everything gave him a share;	
For he was his sister's son,	
Anything he wished was soon done.	

One night he thought, in his dreaming,
That he beside the King was sitting,

At a seat in hunting so,
On a leash had greyhounds two.   1860
He thought while he was thus sitting
He saw three women passing,
And those women that thought he
Three Weird Sisters most likely to be.
The first he heard say going by,
'Lo, yonder the Thane of Cromarty!'
The other woman said again,
'Of Moray, yonder I see the Thane.'
The third then said, 'I see the King.'
All this he heard in his dreaming;   1870
Soon after that, in his young age,
Of those thanedoms he thane was made,
Since next he thought to be the king,
Thus Duncan's days had one of two endings.

The fantasy thus of his dream
Moved him most to slay his *eme*,
As did all forth in deed,
As before you heard me read,
And Dame Gruoch, his uncle's wife
He took and lived with her his life,   1880
And held her both wise and queen,
As before she had been,
While his uncle was living
When he was king with crown reigning.
Then little in honour held he
The relationship of affinity.
All thus when his uncle was dead,
He succeeded in his stead
And seventeen winters full reign
As king in Scotland he was then.   1890
During this time was great plenty,
Abounding both in land and sea.
He was in justice right lawful
And all his laws inspiring awe.
When Leo the Tenth was Pope of Rome,
A pilgrim to the curia he had come
And in alms he scattered money
To poor folk that needed succour
And all time practiced he to work

Appendix 2

Profitably for Holy Church.   1900
But, as we find in some stories,
Begotten he was in a marvellous way.

His mother to the woods often repaired
For the delight of wholesome air.
As she passed upon a day
To a wood, there to play.
She met on occasion with a fair man,
Never any so fair, as she thought, than
Before had she seen with sight.
Of beauty pleasant, and of height   1910
Proportioned well in all measure,
Of limb and life a fair figure.
In that as that befell,
That shortly thereof for to tell,
Where in their game and play
By that person the woman lay
And that time a son she begat
This Macbeth; who after that
Grew to his estate and this height,
To this great power and this might,   1920
As before you have heard me say.
From this person [who] with her played,
And the journey with her done,
[So] that he had gotten on her a son,
And he [was] the devil that him begat,
And told her not afraid to be of that.
But said that her son should be
A man of great state and generosity
And no man should be born of wife
Had power to take from him his life   1930
And of that deed undertaking,
He gave his *lemman* [i.e. lover] there a ring,
And told her that she should keep that well,
And hold for her love that jewel.
After that often practiced he
To come to her in privacy,
And taught her many things that would befall
But truthfully they should not have been all.

At her time she was delivered

And that son the he gave she bore,   1940
Macbeth-Finlay was called his name,
He grew, as you heard, to great fame.
This was Macbeth's offspring
That after him [was] made our king.
As of that some stories say,
Although of his children befell other ways
[And] to be gotten kindly,
As other men are generally,
And when first his rise began,
His uncle's sons two lawful then   1950
For doubt out of the kingdom fled.
Malcolm not begotten of lawful bed,
The third past off the land also,
As banished with his brothers two,
To St. Edward in England,
Who at that time as king there reigned.
He them received thankfully,
And treated them right courteously.

And in Scotland then as king,
This Macbeth made great striving   1960
And set him then in his power
A great citadel to construct there
Upon the height of Dunsinane.
Timber there-till to draw and stone
Of Fife and of Angus he
Ordered many oxen collected be.
So on a day in their travail
Macbeth saw a yoke of oxen fail,
Then spoke Macbeth when espying
The yoke that fail into the drawing.   1970
They answered to Macbeth again
And said, 'Macduff of Fife the Thane
That same yoke of oxen possessing
That he saw fail in the drawing.'
Then spoke Macbeth disparagingly
And to the thane said angrily,
Like all writhing in his skin,
His own neck he should put in
The yoke, and make him draw a drawing.
No doubting all his kin's respect.   1980

Appendix 2 223

For the thane heard Macbeth speak
That he would put in yoke his neck,
Of all his thought he made no song,
But privately out of the throng
With cunning he departed, and the Spenser
Gave a loaf to him for his supper
And as soon as he might see
His time and opportunity
Out of the court he passed and ran,
And that loaf took with him then   1990
To the water of Erne. That bread
He gave the boatward him to ship,
And on the south half him to set,
Without delay or any let (*i.e. hindrance*).
That passage was called after then
[A] long time Portnebaryan,
The Haven of Bread it should be
If it were named properly.
Over the water than he set
Without danger or without any let.   2000
At Dunsinane Macbeth that night.
As soon as his supper was right,
And his marshals him to the hall
Fetched, than among them all
Away the Thane of Fife was missed,
And no man where he was then *wist* [knew].
Yet a knight at that supper,
That to Macbeth was sitting near,
Say to him it was his part
For to with quickly towards what place   2010
The Thane of Fife that time past,
For a wise man was he oft cast,
And in his day was right wily.
To Macbeth he said, for that reason,
For no cost that he could spare
Soon to know where Macduff were.

This greatly moved Macbeth indeed
Against Macduff then to proceed.
Yet Macduff nevertheless
Set southwards on the water was   2020
From Erne then past on in Fife

To Kennoway, where then his wife
Dwelt in a house made of defence
And bade her with great diligence
Keep that house and give the prince
When he comes to make residence,
There only felony to do.
He gave her bidding then that she
Should hold Macbeth in fair entreaty
A bit, while she should sailing see,   2030
From north to the south passing
And when she saw that boat sailing,
Then tell Macbeth the Thane was there
Of Fife, and to Dunsinane to fare
To bide Macbeth, for the Thane
Of Fife thought that he come again
To Kennoway then for to bring
Home with him a lawful king.
To Kennoway Macbeth came soon,
And felony great there would have done,   2040
But this lady, with fair entreaty,
His purpose hindering it done to be
And soon she saw the sail erect
Than to Macbeth, with little respect,
She said, 'Macbeth, look up and see,
Under yon sail forsooth is he,
The thane of Fife, that you have sought;
Believe you well and doubt rightly naught
If ever you shall him see again
He shall you set into great pain,   2050
Since you would have put his neck
Into the yoke. Now will I speak
With you no more, fare on your way
Either well or ill as happen may be.'
That passage since was commonly
In Scotland called the Earl's Ferry.

Of that ferry for to know
Both the statute and the law,
A boat should be on the same side
For to wait and take the tide,   2060
To make them freighted, that would be
From land to land beyond that sea.

Appendix 2

That from the south boats were seen
The lands under sail between
From the south as then sailing
Toward the north the path holding,
The north [a] boat should be ready made
Toward the south to hold the path:
And there should none pay more a share
Than four pennies for their fare, 2070
Wherever his freight would be,
For the sake of freighting over that sea.

This Macduff then as fast
In England upon [safe-] conduct pass,
There Duncan's sons three he found,
Who were banished from Scotland
When Macbeth-Finley their father slew,
And all the kingdom to him drew.
Saint Edward King of England then,
That was of life a holy man, 2080
He treated those children honestly,
Received Macduff right courteously,
When he came into his presence,
And made him honour and reverence,
As pertained to the King,
He told the cause of his coming.
The king then heard him mildly,
And answered him all goodly,
And said, his will and his delight
Was to see for the profit 2090
Of the children; and his will
Was their honour to fulfil.
He counselled this Macduff for that reason
To treat the children courteously.
And which of them would with him depart,
He should make them in everything protect,
As they would them ready make
For their father's death to take
Revenge or would their heritage,
That to them fell be right lineage, 2100
He would help them in all their right
With great support, force, and might.

226 *Appendix 2*

Shortly to say, the lawful two
Brothers forsaken with him to go
For [doubt] that they suffered that peril,
That their father suffered while.
Malcolm the third to say shortly,
Macduff counselled right keenly,
But he was not of lawful bed,
As in this book you have heard read: 2110
Macduff him treated nevertheless
To be stout of heart and boldness,
And manfully to take on hand
To bear the crown then of Scotland:
And bade him there to have no dread,
For king he should be made instead:
And that traitor he to death do,
Who banished him and his brothers two.

Malcolm said he had a viciousness
That would prove his unworthiness 2120
Of Scotland to take the crown.
When he knew his condition.
Forsooth, he said, there was none then
As lecherous a living man,
As he was; and for that thing
He doubted to be made a king.
A king's life, he said, should be
Always led in [great] honesty
For that reason he cowith evilly be a king,
He said that practised such living. 2130

Macduff then said to him again,
That that excuse was in vain:
For give he practised that in deed,
Of women he should have no need;
For of his own land should he
Fair women [have] in great plenty.
Give he had conscience of that plight,
Mend to God, who has the might.

Then Malcolm said, 'There is more,
That prevents me with you to tour: 2140
That is, that I am so burning

Appendix 2   227

In covetousness, that all Scotland
Over little is to my person:
I put nothing thereby a button.'

Macduff said, 'Come on with me;
In riches you shall abundant be.
Truly well the kingdom of Scotland
Is in riches abundant.'

Yet more Malcolm said again
To Macduff of Fife the thane,   2150
'The third vice yet makes for me let [*hindrance*]
My purpose on this thing to set:
I am so false, that no man may
Trust a word that ever I say.'

'Ha, ha! Friend, I leave you there',Macduff said, 'I will no more.
I will not longer converse with you,
Nor of this matter have dialogue;
Since you can nothing hold or say,
In steadfast truth or good faith.   2160
There is no man, of such a breed Hie
Coming but from the Devil's seed,
That can do nothing or say
That along to truth and [to] good faith.
God said of the devil in [a] while
As I have heard read [in] the Evangel [*Gospels*]
[He] is, he said, a liar false:
Such is of him the father of all.   2170
Here now my leave I take of you,
And give up wholly all entreaty.
I care not of the other two
Depravities the value of a straw;
But his treasure he has sold completely,
 When depravity holds [it] in submission.'

To Macduff of Fife the thane
This Malcolm answered then again,
I will, I will, (he said) with you
Pass, and prove how all will be.   2180
I shall be loyal and steadfast aye,
And hold to same man good faith.

And no less in you in truth.
Because my purpose for you is well
For my father's death to take
Revenge and that traitor slay,
That before has my father slain;
Or I shall die of the pain.'

To the king then also fast

To take his leave then Malcolm pass   2190
Macduff with him hand in hand.
This King Edward of England
Gave him his love and his good will,
And great support promised them till,
And help to win his heritage.

On this they took then their expedition
And then this king of England
Ordered the lord of Northumberland,
Sir Siward, to rise with all his might
To help Malcolm win his right.   2200

Then with them from Northumberland
This Malcolm entered into Scotland,
And past our Forth, went straight to Tay,

Up that water the whole way
To Birnam Wood together well.

There they stayed and took counsel.
Since they heard, that Macbeth

In ghostly prophecy had great faith,
And truth had in such fantasy,
By that he believed steadfastly,   2210
Never discomforted to be,
Until with his eyes he could see
The wood brought from Birnam
To the hill of Dunsinane.

From that wood those same men
Each in his hand took a bush then:
Of all his host was no man free,

Appendix 2 229

Than in his hand a bush carried he:
And to Dunsinane all so fast
Against this Macbeth they passed, 2220
For they thought with such a wile
This Macbeth for to beguile,
As for to come in privily
On him or he should warned be.
Off this when he had seen that sight,
He was right away and too the flight:
The flight would they call ay
That [for] a long time after that day.
And over the Mount they chased him then
To the wood of Lumphanan. 2230
This Macduff was there most pitiless,
And on that chase then most ruthless.
But a knight, that in that chase
To this Macbeth then nearest was,
Macbeth turned him again,
And said, 'Villain, you thrust in vain,
For you may not be he, I believe,
That shall slay me dead now.
The man is not born of wife
Of power to rob me of my life.' 2240

The knight said, 'I never was born;
But from my mother's womb was shorn.
Now shall your treason here take end;
For to your father I shall you send.'

Thus slew they Macbeth then
In to the wood of Lumphanan:
And his head they struck off there;
And it with them from there they bare
To Kincarden where the king,
Until their return, made his awaiting. 2250
Of that slaughter is this verse
Written in Latin to rehearse;

'*Macbeth was king of Scotland seventeen years*
In his reign the days were fertile;
He was beheaded, a cruel death, in Lumphanan 2255
By one named Malcolm, born of Duncan'.

Notes

INTRODUCTION

1. The materials in connection with King James's visit were collected by the antiquarian Thomas Hearne and published in his edition of John Leland's "Collections"; see *Lelandi Antiquarii de rebus Britannicis Collecteana*, ii. 626–647.

2. Stringer's account is published by Nichols, *Progresses, Processions and Magnificent Festivities of King James the First*, i. 529–562.

CHAPTER I

1. Herodian, *History of the Empire*, ed. Whittaker, i. 358; Dio, *Roman History*, ed. Cary, ix. 262; Nixon and Rodgers, *In Praise of the Later Roman Emperors*, 226–227.

2. Bede, *Historia Ecclesiastica* in *Opera Omnia*, ed. Plummer, book 3. chapter 4, 133–134.

3. Nennius, *British History and the Welsh Annals*, ed. Morris, 76: *Septimum fuit bellum in silva Celidonis, id est Cat Coit Celidon.*

4. "Life of Margaret" in ES ii. 77.

5. Adomnán, *Life of Columba*, ed. Anderson, f. 74b, 133.

6. Anderson, *Scottish Annals*, 107.

7. Symeonis Monachi, *Historia Regum* in *Opera*, ed. Arnold, ii. 190–192.

8. Symeonis Monachi, *Historia de sancto Cuthberto* in *Opera*, ed. Arnold, i. 212.

9. Symeonis Monachi, *Historia Regum* in *Opera*, ed. Arnold, ii. 211.

10. Earle and Plummer, eds., *Two of the Saxon Chronicles Parallel*, i. 185.

11. Earle and Plummer, eds., *Two of the Saxon Chronicles Parallel*, i. 208.

12. Symeonis Monachi, *Historia Dunelmensis* in *Opera*, ed. Arnold, i. 84; Symeon of Durham, *Historia Regum* in *Opera*, ed. Arnold, ii. 155–156.

232 *Notes to pages 13–18*

13. *Bethu Phátraic: The Tripartite Life of Patrick*, ed. Mulchrone, 30. For an opinion on the date and authorship of this tract, see Mac Donncha, "Dáta Vita Tripartita Sancti Patricii," *Éigse* 18, no. 1 (1980) 125–142, and *Éigse* 19, no. 2 (1983) 354–372.

14. Joseph was an important man in tenth-century Irish and Scottish society: see Lawlor and Best, "Ancient List of the Coarbs of Patrick," 316–362. A study of the tract's language is by Bronner, "Codeswitching in Medieval Ireland," 1–12.

15. For a selection of views on the early history of the Scots in Britain, see Hudson, *Kings of Celtic Scotland*, 1–8; Crawford and Clancy, "Formation of the Scottish Kingdom," 28–95; Nieke and Duncan, "Dalriada," 6–21; Sharpe, "Thriving of Dalriada," 47–61.

16. The question is investigated by Lacy, *Cenél Conaill and the Donegal Kingdoms*; Ó Cróinín, "Ireland, 400–800," 182–234; and Moisl and Hamann, "A Frankish Aristocrat at the Battle of Mag Roth," 36–47.

17. "How the Kingdom of Scotland Was Given to Fiachna" (*Baei sechtaine diumsach oc rig Alban*) is preserved in the late fourteenth-early fifteenth-century *Yellow Book of Lecan* (*Leabhar Buidhe Lecain*), now Trinity College, Dublin, MS 1318, ff. 212 b 35–213 a 37.

18. Nennius, *British History*, ed. Morris, 62.

19. Bannerman, "Dál Riata and Northern Ireland in the Sixth and Seventh Centuries," 1–11; Foster, "Before Alba," 1–31; and Hudson, *Kings of Celtic Scotland*, 17–23.

20. Rennie, "A Possible Boundary between Dal Riata and Pictland," 17–22, and Hudson, *Picts*, 59–60.

21. Ó Cróinín, *Early Medieval Ireland*, 18–19, and Stancliffe, "Christianity amongst the Britons, Dalriadan Irish and Picts," 426–461.

22. The seminal study of the "Learned Tales" is by Mac Cana, *Learned Tales of Medieval Ireland*. One place where these tales were recited was the great O'Neill gathering at Óenach Tailteann "Fair of Teltown" (county Meath) mentioned in the poem "O nobles of the land of Fair Conn" (*"A choému críche Cuind cáin"*) by Cúan Ua Lochlainn, preserved in the *Book of Leinster*, iv. 947–954.

23. John of Fordun, *Johannis de Fordun Chronica Gentis Scotorum*, ed. Skene, i, 87–90 (book 1, chapters 1–4). For a discussion, see Drexler, "Fluid Prejudice," 60–76.

24. Claudius, *De Consulatu Stilichonis liber secundus* in *Carmina*, ed. Hall, 215. For discussions with varying interpretations, see Birley, *The Fasti of Roman Britain*, 374–375; Hudson, *Picts*, 24–35; Kulikowski, "Barbarians in Gaul, Usurpers in Britain," 325–345; and Scharf, "Die Kanzleireform des Stilichs und das römische Britannien," 461–474.

25. The Old Irish legal tract *Críth Gablach*, ed. Binchy, 18–19, gives a succinct and informative description of the levels of kingship and it should be read together with Kelly, *Early Irish Law*, 17–26.

26. See Charles-Edwards, *Early Irish and Welsh Kinship*, 138–140; and Hudson, *Kings of Celtic Scotland*, 5–8.

Notes to pages 18–22   233

27. *Prophecy of Berchán*, ed. Hudson, 87 (stanza 152): *Go mes for cráobhaibh caola, go cuirm, go ceol, go caomhna, go n-ith, go mbliocht, go mbúar mbras, co n-úaill, co n-ádh, co n-erbhas.* The prophecy was begun in the ninth century and finished in the eleventh.

28. Cox and Lathe, "The Question of the Etymology of Dunadd," 21–36.

29. For a discussion of the boar, see Sheehan, "Giants, Boar-Hunts, and Barbering," 3–25. On the foot, see Rees, *Celtic Heritage*, 146.

30. The text was edited and translated by Bannerman in *Studies in the History of Dalriada*, 41–47 (text) and 47–49 (translation) and a good discussion of it is by Ó Muraíle, "Irish Genealogical Collections," 251–264.

31. For the text, see LL f. 248 a 48; Fráech sailed from Dunollie to Ard hua nEchtach (near Iveagh, county Down) in Ireland.

32. Doherty, "Warrior and King in Early Ireland," 88–148; Beougher, "More Savage than the Sword," 185–206; and Charles-Edwards, "Irish Warfare before 1100," 26–51.

33. "Life of Berach," in *Bethada Náem nÉrenn*, ed. and trans. Plummer, ii. 33.

34. Gildas, *Ruin of Britain*, ed. and trans. Winterbottom, 23; and Wooding, "Cargos in Trade along the Western Seaboard," 67–82.

35. Adomnán, *Life of Columba*, ed. and trans. Anderson, 55.

36. Kelly, *Early Irish Law*, 61–62.

37. *Scéla Carno meic Gartnáin*, ed. Binchy, 1. The tale has been studied by Tomás Ó Cathasaigh in "The Theme of Ainmne in Scéla Cano meic Gartnáin," 78–87, and "The Rhetoric of Scéla Cano Meic Gartmain," 233–250.

38. For general discussions, see Crawford, "St. Joseph in Britain: reconsidering the legends, Part 1," 86–98 and "St. Joseph in Britain: Reconsidering the Legends. Part 2," 51–59; Lagorio, "The Evolving Legend of St. Joseph of Glastonbury," 55–81; and Watkin, "The Glastonbury Legends," 77–91.

39. *Patrologia Latina* 51: 594. For the identification of Palladius, see Ó Cróinín, "Who Was Palladius, 'first bishop of the Irish?,'" 205–237.

40. The pioneer in this field was the Welsh geographer E. G. Bowen who constructed his model in works such as "The Cult of St. Brigit," 33–47, "The Irish Sea in the Age of the Saints," 56–71, and *Saints, Seaways and Settlements in the Celtic Lands*.

41. The former is suggested in *Fragmentary Annals of Ireland*, ed. Radner, 170. *Cathach* is now Royal Irish Academy Manuscript 12 R 33.

42. This vexed topic is discussed by Herbert, *Iona, Kells, and Derry*; Tanaka, "Iona and the Kingship of Dál Riata in Adomnán's *Vita Columbae*," 199–214, and Enright, "Further Reflections on Royal Ordinations in the *Vita Columbae*," 20–35.

43. The episode is placed in context by Borsje, "The Monster in the River Ness in *Vita Sancti Columbae*," 27–34.

44. Hudson, *Picts*, 145–147.

45. O'Loughlin, "The Library of Iona at the Time of Adomnán," 570–579. An argument for Iona's contribution for almost all that is known in Irish records of northern Britain is made by Evans, "Irish Chronicles as Sources for the History of Northern

234   *Notes to pages 22–28*

Britain, A.D. 660–800," 1–48, which expands the argument of Bannerman, *Studies in the History of Dalriada*, 9–26, that an Irish monastery in Northern Britain supplied information to *scriptoria* in Ireland.

46. Adomnán, *Life of Columba*, ed. and trans. Anderson, 176 (f. 101b), and MacDonald, "Iona's Style of Government among the Picts and Scots," 174–186.

47. The manuscript is now Oxford, Bodleian MS Rawlinson B. 514, and a modern edition is by Lacey, *Manus O'Donnell's Life of Colum Cille*. For discussions of this text, see Byrne, "*Senchas*: The Nature of Gaelic Historical Tradition," 137–159; and Rekdal, "*Betha Coluimb Chille*: The Life as a Shrine," 407–414.

48. Oxford, Bodleian MS Rawlinson B. 480. Berchán is in the twelfth-century Book of Leinster, f. 350c (ed. Bergin et al., vi, 1557); this text with variants from other manuscripts is printed by Ó Riain, *Corpus Genealogiarum Sanctorum Hiberniae*, 34. The political uses of these texts are discussed by Murray, "Ticfa didiu rí aili foræ," 111–122.

49. Hudson, *Kings of Celtic Scotland*, 28; Marsden, *Kings, Mormaers, Rebels*, 74; and Shepherd, "The Picts in Moray," 75–90.

50. This vita was copied by John Colgan, *Acta Sanctorum Hiberniae*, 495 (6th of March) and this passage is not easy to follow. The vita of Catroe was composed soon after his death in 978; see Kenney, *Sources for the Early History of Ireland: Ecclesiastical*, 609.

51. Hindmarch and Oram, "Eldbotle," 245–299. One must bear in mind, however, the difficulty of source criticism: see Bell and Ogilvie, "Weather Compilations," 331–348.

52. Lawrie, *Early Scottish Charters*, 4.

53. The descriptions come from Binchy, "Passing of the Old Order," and Wallace-Hadrill. "Vikings in Francia," 220.

54. Dicuil, *Liber de Mensura Orbis Terrae*, 74–77. For comments, see Gautier Dalché, "Principes et modes de la représentation de l'espace géographique durant le haut Moyen Age," 5–30; Gautier Dalché, "Tradition et renouvellement dans la représentation de l'espace géographique au IXe siècle," 121–165; and Lamb, "Knowledge about the Scandinavian North in Ninth-Century England and Francia," 82–93.

55. For the site, see Morrison, "*Orkneyinga saga*, Jarlshof and Viking Sea Routes," 22–26; and Hansen, "Viking Settlement in Shetland. Chronological and Regional Contexts," 87–103. A study of the legend is by Hudson, "Conquest of the Picts," 14.

56. Ní Mhaonaigh, "Friend and Foe: Vikings in Ninth- and Tenth-Century Irish Literature," 381–402.

57. Nicolaisen, *Scottish Place-Names*, 87 and 92.

58. British Library, MS Cotton Domitian A.VII, edited by Rollason and Rollason, *Durham Liber vitae*, f. 12v. a and b, respectively; see also Barrow, "Scots in the Durham *Liber Vitae*," 109–116.

59. Hudson, "Scottish Chronicle," 158, and Hudson, "Scottish Gaze," 29–59. Material in the *Scottish Chronicle* or its source is also found in an account of the origins of

Notes to pages 28–36 235

the Picts and Scots in British Library Cotton MS Vitellius A. 20 (ff. 44rb–45ra), a fourteenth-century manuscript from the Priory of Tynemouth.

60. The "Litany" is preserved in a transcription made by Marianus Brockie for his unpublished *Monasticum Scoticanum* of the mid-eighteenth century and it is now in the University of Aberdeen Library, Scottish Catholic Archives, SK/9 at pages 313–316. The text has been printed by Haddan and Stubbs, *Councils and Ecclesiastical Documents*, iii, 278–285, and Forbes, *Kalendars of Scottish Saints*, lvi–lxv. The relevant passage is "Te rogamus audi nos ut regum nostrum Girich cum exercitu suo ab omnibus inimicorum insidiis tuearis et defendas," based, apparently, on a ninth-century original; see Hudson, *Kings of Celtic Scotland*, 131.

61. Hudson, *Scottish Chronicle*, 149.

62. NASA Eclipse Website 0801–0900 at https://eclipse.gsfc.nasa.gov/SEcat5/SEo 801-0900.html. There are several other martyrs named Ciriacus, but none of their feast days match the criteria of the chronicle.

63. *Prophecy of Berchán*, 45 (stanzas 141 and 142); Skene, *Chronicle of the Picts*, 296–297.

64. Hudson, *Viking Pirates*, 20.

65. On the topic of sword land, see McSparron and Williams, ". . . And They Won Land among the Picts by Friendly Treaty or the Sword," 145–158.

66. NASA Eclipse Web Site 0901 to 1000 at https://eclipse.gsfc.nasa.gov/SEsearch/ SEsearchmap.php?Ecl=09660720. The epicenter was between modern Sweden and Finland.

67. Hudson, *Viking Pirates*, 63–77; Wadden, "Dál Riata c. 1000," 164–181.

68. *Orkneyinga Saga*, ed. Guðmundsson, 24.

69. Sveinsson, ed., *Brennu-Njáls saga*, 451, and, ed. and trans. Magnusson and Pálsson, 348.

CHAPTER 2

1. Humphery-Smith, "The Legend of Macbeth," 368–373, and Cowan, "The Historical MacBeth," 117–141.

2. Ó Corráin, "Creating the Past," 177–208, and Kelleher, "The Pre-Norman Irish Genealogies," 138–153. On a specifically Scots theme, see Kennedy, "The Antiquity of Scottish Civilization," 159–174.

3. Oxford, Bodleian MS Rawlinson B. 502, f. 162 e 21; printed by O'Brien, ed., *Corpus Genealogicarum Hiberniae*, 1. 330.

4. Trinity College, Dublin, MS1339 (shelf number H. 2. 18), f. 336; printed LL vi. 1472; variant readings are printed by O'Brien, ed., *Corpus Genealogicarum Hiberniae*, 1. 330. See the discussion by Ó Muraíle, "The Irish Genealogies as an Onomastic Source," 23–46.

5. The excavation report is by Newton, "Excavations at the Peel of Lumphanan, Aberdeenshire 1975–9," 653–670. Speculation on the meaning of the name has varied. Watson, *History of the Celtic Place-Names of Scotland*, 286, reads *lum-* for

236   *Notes to pages 36–43*

llan "church" plus *Phanan* for *Finan*, yielding the translation "Church of [St.] Finan." An alternative is by Milne, *Celtic Place-Names in Aberdeenshire*, 228, who translates *lum* as a corruption of *lamh* "hill" with *–phanan* as a corruption of *finan* "small" or "the small hill"; he mentions the cairn on page 229.

6. The *Book of Deer* is now Cambridge University Library, MS I.i.6.32 and it was presented to the university in 1715 by King George I as part of the library of Bishop John Moore of Ely.

7. Cameron, "Let Dear Be Its Name from now Onwards," 7.

8. Jackson, *Gaelic Notes in the Book of Deer*, 30–36; Marner, "The Sword of the Spirit, the Word of God and the Book of Deer," 1–28; and Ó Maolalaigh, "Property Records," 119–130.

9. Broun, "Property Records in the Book of Deer as a Source for Early Scottish Society," 313–360. On the structure of lineage, see Charles-Edwards, *Early Irish and Welsh Kinship*, 33–43.

10. Morggán's importance is clear upon discovering his pedigree among the tenth-century royal genealogies attached to some versions of *Senchus Fer nAlban*; see Bannerman, *Studies in the History of Dalriada*, 65–66, where his name is spelled *Mongán*.

11. For an argument against the accuracy of "Scots king," see Woolf, "The 'Moray Question,'" 145–164. For the age of the language of the Annals of Ulster, see Ó Maille, *Language of the Annals of Ulster*.

12. *Orkneyinga Saga*, ed. Guðmundsson, 24–25. The various parts of the saga were probably assembled c. 1190; see Guðmundsson, "On the Writing of *Orkneyinga Saga*," 204–211 and Kristjánsson, "Isländische Handschriften," 218–219. Taylor believes this episode is based "directly on oral tradition," *Orkneyinga Saga*, 51–52; see also Chadwick, "Story of Macbeth," 4–8.

13. Anderson, "Macbeth's Relationship to Malcolm III," 372 and Hudson, *Kings of Celtic Scotland*, 137.

14. F. Palgrave, *Documents and Records*, 100. Grandson is a translation of Latin *nepos*; later the word acquired the more familiar meaning "nephew" and afterward "descendant."

15. *Chronicle of Pierre de Langtoft*, i. 370.

16. Rudolfus Glaber, *Rodulfi Glabri Historiarum libri quinque*, ed. France, 54–56, where it is implied that the duke of Normandy was a peacemaker between the princes. Vague references to children are commonplace throughout the eleventh century even for the kings of the English.

17. *Prophecy of Berchán*, ed. Hudson, stanza 184.

18. *Symeonis Monachi, Historia de sancto Cuthberto* in *Opera Omnia*, ed. Arnold, i. 215–220. For a discussion of this period, see Kappelle, *Norman Conquest of the North*, 17–23; and Meehan, "The Siege of Durham, the Battle of Carham and the Cession of Lothian," 1–19.

Notes to pages 43–54

19. *Symeonis Monachi, Historia Dunelmensis Ecclesiae* in *Opera Omnia* i. 84, notes that a comet appeared for a month before the battle, which is also mentioned in the Annals of Ulster. Alpheus of Metz says the comet appeared after the battle of Vlaardingen, fought July 29, 1018, so the battle of Carham seems to have been fought late in September; see Rij and Abulafia, *Gebeurtenissen van deze tijd*, 76–77, and Nieuwenhuijsen, "De Komeet uit het jaar 1018," 37–41.

20. Owain's presence is noted by Symeon of Durham, *Symeonis Monachi Historia Regum* in *Opera Omnia*, ed. Arnold, ii. 155–156. For an alternative view, see Scott, "Partition of a Kingdom: Strathclyde 1092–1153," 11–40. The legal ramifications are discussed by Wormald, "Anglo-Saxon Law and Scots Law," 192–206 (esp. p. 196).

21. Hudson, "Cnut and the Scottish Kings," 353.

22. See O'Dwyer, *Céli Dé*; and Ó Corráin, "Ireland c. 800: Aspects of Society," in Ó Cróinín, ed., *New History of Ireland*, i. 605–607.

23. For discussion, see Jackson, *Gaelic Notes in the Book of Deer*, 102–107; Hudson, *Kings of Celtic Scotland*, 18–22; and Byrne, "Ireland and Her Neighbours, c.1014–c.1072," 870–872.

24. Jackson, *Gaelic Notes in the Book of Deer*, 30.

25. LL f. 148; *Cert cech ríg co réil*, ed. and trans. O'Donoghue, 258–277; Byrne dates it to the eleventh century, "Ireland and Her Neighbours" 895.

26. Jackson, *Gaelic Notes in the Book of Deer*, 31.

27. Earle and Plummer, ed., *Two Saxon Chronicles Parallel*, i. 157–159; the names of the kings are found in the "E" or Laud version. For identification of the princes, see Hudson, "Cnut and the Scottish Kings," 350–360, and *Viking Pirates and Christian Princes*, 132–135.

28. Hudson, "Cnut and the Scottish Kings," 350–360 and *Viking Pirates and Christian Princes*, 132–135.

29. *Saga Óláfs konungs hins helga*, ed. Johnsen and Helgason, i. 343.

30. The identification of Macbeth with "Karl" was made by Crawford, *Scandinavian Scotland*, 71–72. The Old Norse rendering of Macbeth's name *Magbjóðr* is found in an earlier chapter.

31. *Orkneyinga Saga*, ed. Guðmundsson, 43–52.

32. *Orkneyinga Saga*, ed. Anderson, 362, who also suggests that the reference to Fife is to a sea raid (363). Loch Craignish is in the west of Scotland, on the coast of Argyll between Oban and the Crinan Canal.

33. See *Orkneyinga Saga*, ed. Guðmundsson, 23, for *Magbjóðr*; and *Orkneyinga Saga*, ed. Taylor, 58–62, for the composition of chapter 20.

34. Paris, Bibliothèque nationale de France manuscrit Latin 4126, which is printed in Anderson, *Kings and Kingship*, 254.

35. John of Fordun, *Johannis de Fordun Chronica Gentis Scotorum*, ed. Skene, i. 183–184 and ii. 176–177 (book 4, chapter 41).

36. MacFarlane, *Geographical Collections Relating to Scotland*, ed. Mitchell and Clark, iii. 95.

238   *Notes to pages 54–62*

37. In the account of Siward of Northumbria's invasion of Scotland in 1054 (see chapter 3), Duncan's son Malcolm Canmore is called the son of the king of the Cumbrians (i.e., Strathclyde) by John of Worcester, *Chronicle*, ii. 574.

38. Hudson, "Senchus to Histore," 100–120, and Purdie, "Malcolm, Margaret, Macbeth, and the Miller," 45–63. For a brief biography, see Hudson, "Duncan I," 408.

39. King list I is now Oxford, Bodleian MS Latin Misc. C75. This discussion is based on examination of the manuscript—see Hudson, *Kings of Celtic Scotland*, 123; but a printed edition based on transcriptions is in Anderson, *Kings and Kingship*, 279–285.

40. *Symeonis Monachi, Historia Regum* in *Opera Omnia*, ed. Arnold, ii. 198.

41. The Latin term employed is *dux*. A brief biography is by Hudson, "Marianus Scotus," in *Encyclopedia of Medieval Ireland*, ed. Duffy, 320. For the assault, see Kapelle, *Norman Conquest of the North*, 25; Hudson, *Kings of Celtic Scotland*, 123–124; and Woolf, *From Pictavia to Alba*, 254–255.

42. Radner, *Fragmentary Annals of Ireland*, 429.

43. *Symeonis Monachi*, Historia Dunelmensis Ecclesiae in *Opera Omnia*, ed. Arnold, i. 90–91.

CHAPTER 3

1. *Prophecy of Berchán*, ed. Hudson, 91.

2. John of Fordun, *Chronica Gentis Scotorum*, ed. Skene, i. 188 (book 4, chapter 45).

3. Hudson, "Changing Economy of the Irish Sea Province," 39–66, and "Prologue" in *Studies in the Medieval Atlantic*, 13–18.

4. Lapidge, "Welsh-Latin Poetry of Sulien's Family," 85, and Howlett, "Rhygyfarch Ap Sulien and Ieuan Ap Sulien," 1:701–706; the translations are from Lapidge.

5. Jackson, *Gaelic Notes in the Book of Deer*, 31. For schools generally, see Hudson, "Schools in Early Scotland," 1–27.

6. Henry, *Irish Art during the Viking Invasions*, 106, and McNamara, *Psalter Text and Psalter Study in the Early Irish Church*, 75.

7. Finlayson, *Celtic Psalter*, p. xvii, and note 2 where he compares Psalm 14 with Psalm 83 in Ricemarch's Psalter, see Lawlor, *Psalter and Martyrology of Ricemarch*. For a different opinion, see two essays by Edwards: "11th-century Welsh Illuminated Manuscripts," 147–155, and "The Decoration of the Earliest Welsh Manuscripts," 244–248.

8. Henderson, "Understanding the Figurative Style and Decorative Programme of the Book of Deer," 32–68.

9. A modern catalogue is by Fraser, *Pictish Symbol Stones of Scotland*; there is a discussion by Hudson, *Picts*, 162–181. For different interpretations of their meanings, see Forsyth, "Some Thoughts on Pictish Symbols as a Formal Writing System," 85–98;

Notes to pages 62–69   239

Samson, "Reinterpretation of the Pictish Symbols," 29–65; and Clarke, "Reading the Multiple Lives of Pictish Symbol Stones," 19–39.

10. *Prophecy of Berchán*, ed. Hudson, 40 (§ 113).

11. Salmon, "La composition d'un Libellus precum a l'époque de la réforme grégorienne," 292; Bernier, "Les navires celtiques du Haut Moyen Age," 287–291; and Fordun, *Johannis de Fordun Chronica Gentis Scotorum*, ed. Skene, i. 9.

12. Hudson, "Time Is Short," 113–116, and Mikhailova and Nikolaeva, "The Denotations of Death in Goidelic," 93–115. This was also true for their southern neighbors; see Prideaux-Collins, "Satan's Bonds Are Extremely Loose," 289–310.

13. *Lebor na Huidre*, ed. Best and Bergin, 77–81 (*Scéla Lái Brátha*); 47–49 (*Dá Brón Flatha Nime*); and 67–76 (*Fís Adomnán*). The manuscript is now Dublin, Royal Irish Academy MS 23 E 25.

14. Marianus Scotus, *Chronicon*, ed. Waitz, 557.

15. Marianus Scotus, *Chronicon*, ed. Waitz, 558; Kenney, *Sources*, 615; and *Martyrology of Óengus*, ed. Stokes, 176.

16. *Scéla Cano meic Gartnáin*, ed. Binchy, 17–18.

17. *Bethada Náem nÉrenn*, ed. Plummer, i. 34, and ii. 33 (§57).

18. LL, i. 116 (f. 29a). For the composition of the Irish royal court, see Jaski, "King and Household in Early Medieval Ireland," 89–122.

19. "How Culwuch won Olwen" in *Mabinogion*, ed. Jones and Jones, 97.

20. The surviving copies are attached to an Irish translation of Nennius's *British History*; see *Lebor Bretnach*, ed. Van Hamel, 10–14, for a parallel comparison, and Calisle, *Pictish Sourcebook*, 56–79, for editions and translations of the different manuscripts.

21. Bede, *Historia Ecclesiastica* in *Opera Omnia*, ed. Plummer, i. 11: his account has the emigration from Scythia, the refused settlement in Ireland, and the conditions for the reception of Irish wives.

22. *Book of Ballymote* is now Dublin, Royal Irish Academy MS 23 P 12; transcription in *Lebor Bretnach*, ed. Van Hamel, 14, and Calisle, *Pictish Sourcebook*, 79: *Coeca righ, ceim crechach/ maraen do sil Echdach/ o Feargus rofirad/ co mac mbrigach mBretach.*

23. *Prophecy of Berchán*, ed. Hudson, 226.

24. Lawrie, *Early Scottish Charters*, 67.

25. Stokes, "Second Vision of Adomnan," 420–443, and "Vision of Adomnan," 184–194.

26. Gasquet, *History of the VENERABLE ENGLISH COLLEGE, Rome*, 18.

27. On the "Europeanization" at this time, see Gillingham, "Britain, Ireland, and the South," 202–232.

28. Hudson, "Roll of the Kings in *Saltair na Rann*," 130–131.

29. Kenney, *Sources for the Early History of Ireland*, 611.

30. Wilmart, "La Trinité des Scots à Rome," 218–230.

31. Salmon, "La composition d'un libellus precum," 287.

240   *Notes to pages 69–79*

32. Earle and Plummer, eds., *Two Saxon Chronicles Parallel*: (Baldwin) i. 166; (reduction of the fleet) i.171; and (cashiering of troops) i. 172. For an argument that Macbeth did attend the council, see Woolf, *From Pictavia to Alba*, 259.

33. *Liber Cartarum Prioratus Sancti Andree*, ed. Thomsson, 114. For these place names, see Taylor and Markus, *Place-Names of Fife*, vol. 1, *West Fife between Leven and Forth*, *infra*.

34. This might refer to a now-lost grant by Malcolm, although a reissue by his brother Donald survives; see *Liber Cartarum Prioratus Sanct Andree*, ed. Thomsson, 117.

35. The land was later known as Bolgie or Bogie; it is several miles north by northwest of Kirkcaldy, *Liber Cartarum Prioratus Sanct Andree*, ed. Thomsson, 12: *Cum summa veneratione et devotione Makbeth rex contulit Deo et Sancto Seruano de Loch Leuyn et heremitis ibidem Deo servientibus [terram] Bolgyne filij Torfyny cum omni libertate et sine onere exercitus regis et filij eius vel vicceomitis et sine exacctione alicuius fet caritatis intuitu et oratorum suffragiis.*

36. Kelly, *Early Irish Law*, 70.

37. *Acts of the Parliaments of Scotland*, i. 663–665.

38. *Registrum de Dunfermelyn. Liber cartarum Abbatie Benedictine S.S. Trinitatis et B. Margarete Regine de Dunfermelyn*, ed. Innes, 3.

39. CDIL, G, 166:21.

40. CIH 1760–1761; after Kelly, *Early Irish Law*, 87.

41. CIH 502.29–519.35.

42. Kelly, *Early Irish Law*, 70.

43. John of Fordun, *Chronica Gentis Scotorum*, i. 205 (book 5, chapter 8).

44. Anderson, *Kings and Kingship*, 254. *Nepos* had the dual meanings of "grandson" and "nephew" in Medieval Latin.

45. This follows the argument of Byrne, "Ireland and Her Neighbours," 896–897.

46. LL, iv. 797 (f. 183b), and edited and translated in Flann, "Poems by Flann Mainistrech," ed. Mac Neill, 70 (text) and 75 (translation); the line is two syllables short and the editor suggests the insertion of "fair" (*n-imgil*) before Erc.

47. *Aided Muirchertaig meic Erca*, ed. Níc Dhonnchadha, 28; the reference is convoluted and seems to refer to a tale in which he killed his grandfather Loarn.

48. Meyer, "Gein Branduib maic Echach ocus Aedá," 134–137.

49. Earle and Plummer, eds., *Two Saxon Chronicles Parallel*, i. 181; Osbern's father is identified as Richard, son of Scrob, and the stronghold as "Richard's castle," ii. 240.

50. John of Worcester, *Chronicle*, ed. Darlington et al., ii. 572.

51. *Lebor na Cert*, ed. and trans. Dillon, 97.

52. Earle and Plummer, eds., *Two Saxon Chronicles Parallel*, i. 184–185, *s.a.* 1054.

53. John of Worcester, *Chronicle*, ed. Darlington et al., ii. 574, also claims that Siward attacked on the order of King Edward.

54. David Powel, *The Historie of Cambria Now Called Wales*, 97.

55. Geffroy Gaimar, *Lestorie Des Engles*, ed. Hardy and Martin, ii. 160; Siward's expedition is described at lines 5043–5061.

Notes to pages 80–86 241

56. For an example, see List D in Anderson, *Kings and Kingship*, 268.

CHAPTER 4

1. For a study of the foes of Malcolm and his dynasty, see McDonald, "Soldiers Most Unfortunate," 93–119, and also his *Outlaws of Medieval Scotland*, 17–22.
2. Her son Angus (MI Óengus), called "king of the men of Moray," was killed in the battle of Stracathro in 1130; see *Annals of Ulster, s.a.* 1130.
3. *Statistical Account*, xii, 613.
4. Jackson, *Gaelic Notes*, 31.
5. The only record of this incident is preserved in the eleventh-century manuscript of the *Anglo-Saxon Chronicle* known as "D" or the "Worcester Chronicle"; now London, British Library Cotton MS Tiberius B. iv, f. 85v printed in Earle and Plummer, eds., *Two Saxon Chronicles Parallel*, i. 213. That text might have been intended for the court of Malcolm Canmore.
6. Brief assessments are provided by Duncan, *Scotland*, 117–125; Barrow, *Kingship and Unity*, 27–31; "Malcolm III [Mael Coluim Ceann Mór, Malcolm Canmore] (d. 1093), king of Scots"; and Ritchie, *Normans in Scotland*, 3–83.
7. *Anglo-Saxon Chronicle* E and C versions place the meeting on the Tyne; see Earle and Plummer, eds., *Two Saxon Chronicles Parallel*, i, 197 and 196, respectively. This river is the Tyne in East Lothian which flows into Belhaven harbor.
8. Symeon of Durham lists five major invasions of England by Malcolm, see *Symeonis Dunelmensis Opera Omnia*, ed. Arnold, ii. 221–222.
9. Ailred of Rievaulx, *Saints of Hexham*, in Anderson, *Scottish Annals from English Chroniclers*, 101. For discussions, see Keene, "The Dunfermline vita of St. Margaret of Scotland," 43–61; and Aird, "St. Cuthbert, the Scots and the Normans," 1–20.
10. Ingibjorg's family connections are given in Sturluson, *Heimskringla*, "Saga of Harald Hardrada," chapter 45.
11. Margaret might have been in Scotland in 1068 as John of Worcester, the *Anglo-Saxon Chronicle* version D, and Symeon of Durham agree; for a list of the sources, see Anderson, *Scottish Annals*, 88.
12. *Anglo-Saxon Chronicle* "D" printed in Earle and Plummer, eds., *Two Saxon Chronicles Parallel*, i. 201. See also Tyler, "Crossing Conquests," 171–196. An alternative version is given by the twelfth-century Anglo-Norman historian Orderic Vitalis who claims that Edward the Confessor had negotiated a marriage contract in which Malcolm received Lothian as a part of Margaret's dowry; see *Patrologia Latina* clxxxviii, 619–620 (book 8, chapter 20).
13. Eadmer, *Historia Novella*, 121–126.
14. The E or Peterborough version of the *Anglo-Saxon Chronicle* claims that Malcolm died in an ambush and appears to suggest that he was betrayed by his comrade Morel who was Earl Robert's steward; see Earle and Plummer, eds., *Two Saxon Chronicles Parallel*, i. 228.

242 *Notes to pages 87–92*

15. Orderic Vitalis, *Historica Ecclesiastica*, *Patrologia Latina*, clxxxviii, 619–620 (book 8, chapter 20).
16. A translation is given by Anderson, *Early Sources*, ii. 59–88. See also Dalton," Scottish Influence on Durham 1066–1214," 339–352.
17. Oxford, Bodleian MS Latin Liturg. F. 5.
18. Hudson, *Irish Sea Studies*, 35.
19. Martin, "Foreword," in Mac Niocaill, *Medieval Irish Annals*, 6.
20. Paris, Bibliothèque nationale de France MS lat. 4126, ff 26v–32r; the entire section is printed in Anderson, *Kings and Kingship*, 240–60, and "Poppleton MS," 31–42.
21. The texts were edited by Forbes, *Lives of S. Ninian and S. Kentigern*; Jocelyn's text is at 159–242 (text) and 27–119 (translation). For discussions of Ailred's text on Ninian, see Mayeski, "Clothing Maketh the Saint," 181–190; and MacQueen, "The Literary Sources for the Life of St. Ninian," 17–25. For discussions of Jocelin's work, see Bieler, "Jocelin von Furness als Hagiograph," 410–415; and Breeze, "*Telleyr, Anguen, Gulath*, and the Life of St. Kentigern," 71–79.
22. Oxford, Bodleian MS Laud 610, f. 87ra1–87 rb35. This manuscript is also known as the Psalter of Edmund mac Richard; the section with this king list is known as the Book of Pottlerath; see Byrne, *1,000 Years of Irish Script*, 25–27 and Ó Cuív, *Catalogue of Irish Language Manuscripts in the Bodleian Library at Oxford and Oxford College Libraries*, 62–87; the list is printed in Anderson, *Kings and Kingship*, 261–263 and there is a translation of the Irish text in Skene, *Chronicles of the Picts, Chronicles of the Scots*, 27–30.
23. IE/ UCD/SC/Additional Ms 14; Jackson, "The Poem *A Eolacha Alban Uile*," 104–105 (edition) and "Duan Albanach," 132–133 (translation); and Mac Firbisigh, *Great Book of Irish Genealogies*, edited Ó Muraíle, book 5.
24. *Annals of Inisfallen*, *s.a.* 1105 (262).
25. The chronology is not clear and although the Anglo-Saxon Chronicle version E dates Duncan's entrance into Scotland among the events of 1093, there seems to have been too little time after the death of his father on November 13 for the news to reach the English court and for the gathering of an army; see Earle and Plummer, eds., *Two Saxon Chronicles Parallel*, i. 228 and 230.
26. *Symeonis Monachi Historia Regum* in *Opera Omnia*, ed. Arnold, ii. 221–222, and Roger of Howden *Chronica*, ed. Stubbs, i. 146–147. The minster of Howden is in Yorkshire and there were several Rogers of Howden active at the time; see Gransden, *Historical Writing in England c. 550–c. 1307*, i, 228–230.
27. Ailred of Rievaulx, *Genealogia Regum Anglorum*, cols. 716–717. For a translation with scholarly commentary, see *Aelred of Rievaulx Historical Works*, edited Dutton and translation Freeland; and Anderson, *Scottish Annals from English Chroniclers*, 113–114.
28. The name survives in modern Scotland as *aonach* "fair" and is found in place names such as Aonach[an] west of Spean Bridge. The best-known example is the early medieval Irish "Fair of Carman" (somewhere in the province of Leinster), described

Notes to pages 92–102 243

in an eleventh-century verse *dindshenchus* (place name history) with festivities that
included a public recitation of stories; see Gwynn, *Metrical Dindshenchus*, iii. 20
(lines 237–268).

29. Hudson, "Literary Culture of the Early Scottish Court," 161.
30. Geoffrey of Monmouth, *History of the Kings of Britain*, 221. This episode is discussed
    by Woolf, "Geoffrey of Monmouth and the Picts," 439–450; Hudson, *The Picts*,
    217–218; and Wood, "Where Does Britain End?" 9–23.
31. Patrick, *Writings of Bishop Patrick*, ed. Gwynn, 56–71.
32. Stonehenge is one example: see Gerald of Wales, *History and Topography of Ireland*,
    ed. O'Meara, 100.
33. Nennius, *British History*, ed. Morris, 81.
34. Gildas, *Ruin of Britain*, ed. Winterbottom, 21, 23, 24. A different view is taken by
    Farrell, "History, Prophecy and the Arthur of the Normans," 99–114.
35. Tatlock, *The Legendary History of Britain*, 8–18, gives a useful discussion.
36. Henry of Huntingdon, *History of the English People*, 76–77.
37. For discussions, see Barrow, "The Kings of Scotland and Durham," 311–323; and
    McDonald, "Matrimonial Politics," 227–247.
38. William of Newburgh, *History*, ed. Stevenson, 438.
39. This note on the history and extent of the see of Glasgow is conveniently found in
    Early Scottish Charters, 44–47.
40. Lawrie, *Early Scottish Charters*, 85–86.
41. Anderson, *Kings and Kingship*, 242.
42. See Barrow, "David I of Scotland," 45–65.
43. Oram, "David I and the Scottish Conquest and Colonization of Moray," 1–19.
44. The information scattered among various records is gathered in Anderson, *Scottish
    Annals*, 190–208.
45. McDonald, Andrew, "Wimund (fl. c. 1130–c. 1150)," ODNB.
46. William of Newburgh, *Historia rerum Anglicarum*, i. 73–76.
47. *Chronicon de Lanercost*, ed. Stevenson, 40–41, and McDonald, "Treachery in the
    Remotest Territories of Scotland," 161–192.

CHAPTER 5

1. This discussion follows the latest edition of the text: Guillaume le Clerc, *The
   Romance of Fergus*, ed. Frescoln; and the translation by Owen, "Guillaume le
   Clerc: The Romance of Fergus," 79–183. For other discussions, see Hunt, "The
   Roman de Fergus: Parody or Pastiche?" 55–69; and Hanning, "Inescapable
   History," 55–73 and 264–267.
2. For discussions of Fergus and his career, see McDonald, "Rebels without a Cause?"
   166–186; Stringer, "Reform Monasticism and Celtic Scotland: Galloway, c. 1140–
   c. 1240," 127–165, and "Acts of Lordship: The Records of the Lords of Galloway

Notes to pages 102–109

to 1234," 203–234; Oram, "Fergus, Galloway and the Scots," 117–130; and Brooke, "Fergus of Galloway: Miscellaneous Notes for a Revised Portrait," 47–58.

3. The town of Malvoisine is between Chartres and Orleans. William went to France in 1213 to visit his family; see Bower, *Scotichronicon*, ed. Watt, iv. 472 (book 8, chapter 78).

4. The episode is little more than a name in the surviving texts, but a description is in the *Ordo Paginorum* of 1415; for discussion of the problem, see Beadle, *York Plays*, ii, 424–425; and for the identification of Fergus, see Beckett, ""Pendens super feretrum": Fergus, Aelred, and the York Funeral of the Virgin," 103–125.

5. This translation is based on the unpublished version in the fourteenth-century Oxford, Bodleian MS 302. A facsimile of the *Chronicle of Melrose* is *Chronica de Mailros*, ed. Anderson, Anderson, and Dickens, *Chronicle of Melrose*, and an extensive commentary is *Chronicle of Melrose*, ed. Broun and Harrison.

6. *Togail Bruidne Dá Derga*, ed. Knott, 6 (lines 183–184).

7. Tecosca Cormaic, *The Instructions of King Cormac mac Airt*, ed. and trans., Meyer, 2 (lines 25–27).

8. *Audacht Morainn*, ed. Kelly, lines 17–20; Ps.-Cyprianus, *De xii abusiuis saeculi*, ed. Hellmann, 52–53; and Wasserschleben, ed., *Die irische Kanonensammlung*, 77 (book 25, chapter 3).

9. M. O. Anderson presented this argument in *Kings and Kingship*; see p. 234 for a diagram.

10. John of Fordun, *Johannis de Fordun, Chronica Gentis Scotorum*, ed. Skene, i. 294–295. For discussion, see Bannerman, "King's Poet and the Inauguration of Alexander III," 120–149. For a comment on the role of chroniclers in promoting the antiquity, real or imagined, of Scottish royal lines, see Kennedy, "The Antiquity of Scottish Civilization," 159.

11. King List I is now Oxford, Bodleian MS Latin Misc. C75, ff 53v–54v; previously it was Sir Thomas Phillipps MS 3119.

12. MacDiarmid, "Metrical Chronicles and Non-alliterative Romances," 28.

13. *Registrum Episcopatus Moraviensis*, ed. Innes, 30.

14. NLS, Advocates MS 34.7.3 f. 20v: *Reges Scocie discendenter a Malcomo mak Donchad aliter Canmore et sancta Mergreta Regina*. The manuscript was written c. 1500 and belonged to James Grey of Dunblane; see Anderson, *Kings and Kingship in Early Scotland*, 64–65.

15. Liber cartarum prioratus Sancti Andree in Scotia, ed. Thomson, 312 and 313.

16. Palgrave, *Documents and Records*, 14–21.

17. Stones and Simpson, *Edward I and the Throne of Scotland, 1290–1296*, i. 222.

18. Palgrave, *Documents and Records*, 105.

19. Palgrave, *Documents and Records*, 67–68.

20. Palgrave, *Documents and Records*, 98–104 (at p. 100).

21. Langtoft, *Chronicle of Pierre de Langtoft*, ed. Wright, i. 370 and 388—390.

22. Rickard, *Britain in Medieval French Literature*, 206–220.

Notes to pages 109–118

23. Paris, Bibliothèque nationale MS français 24315. ff 92v–95; see Smith, ed., "Le Testament du Gentil Cossoys," 190–198.

24. *The Actes and Deidis of the Illustre and Vallyeant Campioun Schir William Wallace*, in National Library of Scotland, Advocates MS 19.2.2 written in 1488.

25. Barbour, *The Bruce*, ed. Duncan, 25.

26. Various aspects are discussed in Duffy, ed., *Robert the Bruce's Irish Wars*, especially 45ff.

27. An informative study of Scottish royal finances at this time and the influence on foreign policy is Campbell, "England, Scotland, and the Hundred Years War," 184–216.

28. John of Fordun, *Johannis de Fordun, Chronica Gentis Scotorum*, ed. Skene, i. xvi; the manuscript is now British Library Royal MS 13. E. X also known as the "Black Book of Paisley" written c. 1442.

29. Dowden, *Bishops of Scotland*, 314–316. He might be the same man who, in 1349, was among the masters of the English nation at the University of Paris petitioning for an office in the church of Aberdeen.

30. Webster, "John of Fordun and the Independent Identity of the Scots," 85–102.

31. John of Fordun, *Johannis de Fordun, Chronica Gentis Scotorum*, ed. Skene, i, 187–204. The complexities of historical writing in this period are discussed by Boardman, "Chronicle Propaganda in Fourteenth-Century Scotland," 23–43.

32. On the history of the clan, see Bannerman, "Macduff of Fife," 20–38.

33. *De Re Rustica* [2.2, 22–24].

34. *Tochmarc Étaíne*, ed. Bergin and Best, 178 (§ 7–8).

35. Lawrie, *Early Scottish Charters*, 13, who believes it is spurious, but see Duncan, *Scotland*, 125.

36. For speculation on John's sources, see Anderson, *Kings and Kingship*, 212–215; and John of Fordun, *Johannis de Fordun, Chronica Gentis Scotorum*, ed. Skene, i, xxxiii–xl.

37. John of Fordun, *Johannis de Fordun, Chronica Gentis Scotorum*, ed. Skene, i, 191 (Book 4, chapter 47). The quotation from William of Malmesbury is taken from his *De Gestis Regum Anglorum*, ed. Stubbs, ii. 345; John must have had a copy in front of him because his text follows the original exactly.

38. William of Malmesbury, *De Gestis Regum Anglorum*, ed. Stubbs, i. 237.

39. John of Fordun, *Johannis de Fordun, Chronica Gentis Scotorum*, ed. Skene, i. 204 (book 5, chapter 7).

40. Froissart, *Chronicles*, trans. Bereton, 335.

41. Wilson, *Food and Drink in Britain*, 359 and 220.

42. The *abthane* of Kinghorn received six shillings and eight pence Scots from the exchequer in 1330, *Exchequer Rolls of Scotland*, i. 311.

43. Bower, *Scotichronicon*, gen. ed. Watt, 6. 384–402; Sellar, "Marriage, Divorce, and Concubinage," 467–468, sees this episode as evidence for polygamy.

44. Snorri Sturluson, *Heimskringla*, trans. Hollander, 659.

246   *Notes to pages 118–125*

45. A catalogue of names for Ravenser is in Smith, *Place-Names of the East Riding of Yorkshire*, xiv, 16–17.

46. John of Fordun, *Johannis de Fordun, Chronica Gentis Scotorum*, ed. Skene, i. 245 (book 5, chapter 44).

47. Dundee Municipal Archive, Charter 15 (original document) issued at Scone on October 20, 1325; printed by Duncan, *Acts of Robert I*, 541–542.

48. Perth, City Archives, Charter B.59 23/9 issued at Edinburgh.

49. Bower, *Scotichronicon*, ed. MacQueens, ii. 419–441 and iii. 2–19.

50. Cambridge, Corpus Christi College MS 171, f. 88.

51. Bower, *Scotichronicon*, ed. MacQueens, iii. frontispiece.

52. There are the exception of Eochaid's appearance in the *Scottish Chronicle* and Constantine in the king list now known as L. List L is in British Library, Cotton MS Claudius C vii, f. 6, its last entry is for the year 1334; the king list precedes the *Chronicle of Lanercost*; it is printed in Skene, *Picts and Scots*, 295–297.

53. *Exchequer Rolls*, ed. Stuart and Bennett, iii. 307.

54. The wording of the donation varied, but the most explicit is *Et decano et capitulo ecclesie Aberdonensis, percipientibus annuatim viginti solidos pro anniversario quondam magistri Johannis Barberii pro compilacione libri gestorum Roberti Brus primi regis, de termino compoti, dicto episcopo ex parte dictorum decani et capituli fatente receptum super compotum, X s.* The amount was increased to £2 10 shillings in 1463, *Exchequer Rolls of Scotland*, ed. Stuart and Bennett, vii. 42, 221, 304, 377, 439, 519, and 669.

55. *Exchequer Rolls*, ii. 168.

56. *Accounts of the Lord High Treasurer of Scotland*, i. 133, 174, 176, 181, and 184.

CHAPTER 6

1. This follows the brief biography in Andrew of Wyntoun, *Original Chronicle*, ed. Amours, i, xxx–xxxvii; see also Goldstein, "'I Will My Proces Hald,'" 35–47.

2. *Liber Cartarum Prioratus Sancti Andree in Scotia*, ed. Thomson, 2.

3. Andrew's resignation and death are in documents from the Vatican Library; see Andrew of Wyntoun, *Original Chronicle*, ed. Amours, i. xxxiv–xxxvii.

4. Andrew of Wyntoun, *Original Chronicle*, ed. Amours, i. lxxxvii–xc. Even though Amours divided the text into three variations, he was not entirely certain that Andrew had written three versions and offered the suggestion that there might have been only the original text, its revision, and some copies of the revision with their own features.

5. Andrew of Wyntoun, *Androw of Wyntoun's Orygynale Chronykil of Scotland*, ed. Laing: the Macbeth episode is in volume ii. 127–139 (book 6, chapter 18).

6. The two versions are on facing pages and the complete edition runs to six printed volumes: Andrew of Wyntoun, *Original Chronicle of Andrew of Wyntoun*, ed. Amours; the Macbeth episode is in volume iv. 272–302 (book six).

Notes to pages 126–132

7. Sellar, "Marriage, Divorce and Concubinage," 475; Hudson, "Shenchus to Histoire," 100–120; Purdie, "Malcolm, Margaret, Macbeth, and the Miller," 45–63; and Wingfield, "Qwhen Alexander Our Kynge Was Dede," 27, who sees this episode as the signal that Malcolm Canmore inaugurated a new era.

8. Dunsinane seems to have been crown property until King James III granted it to the Carthusian house at Perth; see *Register of the Great Seal of Scotland*, ed. Thomson, ii. 80 (no. 347) where Dunsinane (spelled *Dusyane* in the document) was transferred on May 12, 1450, in return for an annual payment of forty shillings.

9. A *merk* was a Scots unit of currency that was worth two-thirds of an English pound, i.e., 180 silver pennies rather than 240.

10. *Acts of the Parliaments of Scotland*, vol. 1, ed. Innes and Thomson, 187.

11. This interesting document is in the form of an agreement between Duncan, the earl of Fife, and the king in which Duncan surrenders his earldom to the king and then receives it back, with its privileges; see Duncan, *Regesta Regum Scottorum V*, 354–360.

12. How this worked in practice is described in an account preserved in *Reports of the Royal Commission on Historical Manuscripts*, iii. 417.

13. This is not an isolated example; Wingfield points out in "Qwhen Alexander Our Kynge Was Dede," 24, that the story of Malcolm Canmore granting clemency to a would-be assassin is contrasted with the rapacity of William the Conqueror.

14. Perth, Municipal Archives, MS B.59 23/14, March 5, 1405/6.

15. The lands of Bolgny featured in a lengthy lawsuit in which Andrew claims that William de Berkeley, owner of the estate at that time, failed to deliver to the community the customary eight bolls (the quantity of a boll varied, but generally it was equivalent to six bushels or about 140 pounds) of meal and a pig; see *Liber Cartarum Prioratus Sancti Andree*, ed. Thomas, 6–11. The archive is mentioned at pages 11 and 15.

16. British Library Harleian MS 4628; a transcript is printed in *Liber Cartarum Prioratus Sancti Andree*, ed. Thomson, xxv–xxx.

17. Lawrie, *Early Scottish Charters*, 210.

18. Dowden, *Bishops of Scotland*, 4–6.

19. A quaternion is also known as a quire; it is usually four sheets folded in half to make eight pages or sixteen sides.

20. The catalogue has been printed several times; this list follows Higgitt, *Scottish Libraries*, 222–225.

21. B. Langefeld, *The Old English Version of the Enlarged Rule of Chrodegang* (Frankfurt am Main, 2003); and Jerome Bertram, *The Chrodegang Rules: The Rules for the Common Life of the Secular Clergy from the Eighth and Ninth Centuries. Critical Texts with Translations and Commentary* (Aldershot, 2005).

22. "Prosperi Tironis epitoma chronicon ed. primum a. CCCCXXXIII, continuata ad a. CCCLV," ed. Mommsen, 341–499.

23. John of Fordun, *Chronica Gentis Scotorum*, ed. Skene, i. 81 (book 2, chapter 52).

248 *Notes to pages 132–138*

24. Honorius resided at Canterbury during at least some part of the episcopate of Archbishop Anselm of Bec (1093–1109). At the end of his life, he was possibly a recluse in the Irish monastery at Regensburg.
25. Hudson, "Tracing Medieval Scotland's Lost History," 63–72.
26. The complex interactions of Gaelic Ireland and Scotland are investigated by Eagan, "Playground of the Scots?" 101–121; and see also Chadwick, "Story of Macbeth," 201–211.
27. *Accounts of the Lord High Treasurer of Scotland*, ed. Dickson et al., i.176: "Wallace who tells the stories to the king" (Wallass that tellis the geistis to the king). The surviving accounts begin in 1473 during the reign of King James III.
28. *Accounts of the Lord High Treasurer of Scotland*, ed. Dickson and Paul, i. 183.
29. *Accounts of the Lord High Treasurer of Scotland*, ed. Dickson and Paul, i. 176, 183, 307, and 330.
30. *Complaynt of Scotland*, ed. Stewart, 50.
31. The basic study is Mill, *Mediaeval Plays in Scotland*, 37.
32. *Exchequer Rolls of Scotland*, ed. Stuart and Burnett, i. 141 and 297.
33. *Exchequer Rolls of Scotland*, ed. Stuart and Burnett, i. 398 (s.a. 1331).
34. *Exchequer Rolls of Scotland*, ed. Stuart and Burnett, i. 150 and iv.12.
35. *Exchequer Rolls of Scotland*, ed. Stuart and Burnett, ii. 586 (s.a. 1377).
36. Mill, *Mediaeval Plays in Scotland*, 48.
37. For the context, see Murray, "Dream and Vision in Late-Medieval Scotland," 182, and MacDonald, "Allegorical (Dream-) Vision Poetry in Medieval and Early Modern Scotland," 167–176.
38. Patrick, *His Writings*, ed. Hood, 29.
39. Adomnán, *Life of Columba*, ed. Andersons, 76.
40. A survey with bibliographical references is Hudson, "Time Is Short," 188–191.
41. Geoffrey of Monmouth, *History of the Kings of Britain*, ed. Thorpe, part 5, 170–185.
42. This is found in the "B" manuscript (London, British Library MS Reg. 20 A. ii at f. 139 r); Pierre de Langtoft, *Chronicle*, 448f, and variant texts in Thiolier, *Édition Critique et Commentée de Pierre de Langtoft*, 371–373.
43. *Porro ex dictis Merlini prophetae, sperant adhuc Angliam recuperate. Hinc est quod frequenter insurgunt Walenses, effectum vaticinii implere wolenter; sed qwuia debitum tempus ignorant saepe descipiuntur et in vanum laborant* in *Vita Edwardi Secundi*, ed. Stubbs, ii. 218.
44. Barbour, *The Bruce*, ed. Duncan, 162–165.
45. Minot, *Poems of Laurence Minot*, ed. Hall, 103–111, and, for comment, see Smallwood, "Prophecy of the Six Kings," 571–592.
46. *Rotuli Parliamentorum* 3. 508.
47. Cross and Slover, *Ancient Irish Tales*, 134–136.
48. Cross and Slover, *Ancient Irish Tales*, 28–48. The suggestion has been offered that a redaction of the work is from the fourteenth century; see Breatnach, "Oidheadh Chloinne Tuireann agus Cath Maige Tuired," 35–46.

Notes to pages 138–146

49. Cross and Slover, *Ancient Irish Tales*, 148–149.
50. *Eddadigte*, ed. Helgason, i. 5–6.
51. "How Culwuch Won Olwen," in *The Mabinogion*, ed. Jones and Jones, 120.
52. *Book of Lecan* folio 166 va 17–vb 34.
53. *Cogadh Gaedhel re Gaillaibh*, ed. and trans. Todd, 13.
54. *Njal's Saga*, trans. Magnusson and Pálsson, 349–351.
55. Cross and Slover, *Ancient Irish Tales*, 176–198.
56. Cross and Slover, *Ancient Irish Tales*, 327.
57. Cross and Slover, *Ancient Irish Tales*, 329.
58. Cary, *King of Mysteries*, 133: *fri brichtu ban ocus gobann ocaus druad*.
59. Her name was Aibhell or Aibhinn and she came from Craig Líath (now Carrick Lea) in County Clare; see *Cogadh Gaedhel re Gallaibh*, ed. Todd, 200.
60. *Baile in Scáil*, ed. and trans. Murray, p. 34, paragraph 8: "And the girl who was awaiting them in the house was the sovereignty of Ireland" (*Et ba sin ind ingen boí isin taig ara cind flaith nÉrenn*).
61. Adam of Bremen, *Hamburgische Kirchengeschichte*, ed. Schmeidler, 286.
62. *Exchequer Rolls*, vi. 357.
63. *Register of the Great Seal of Scotland*, ed. Thomson et al., ii. 532 (no. 2502) for 1499 and ii, 662 (no. 3102) for 1507.
64. Kelly, *Early Irish Law*, 223.
65. The version circulating in Macbeth's day was one copied in the twelfth century; see, Nic Énrí and Mac Niocaill, "Second Recension of the Evernew Tongue," 1–60.
66. Stokes, *Martyrology of Oengus the Culdee*, 131.
67. *Chronicle of the Kings of Mann and the Isles*, ed. Broderick and Stowell, 6.
68. *Cogadh Gaedhel re Gallaibh*, ed. and trans. Todd, 277.
69. Geoffrey of Monmouth, *History of the Kings of Britain*, 215.
70. *Cogadh Gaedhel re Gallaibh*, ed. and trans. Todd, 197.
71. *Book of Leinster*, ed. Best et al., iv. 773 (line 23090).
72. Jackson, *Celtic Miscellany*, 46.
73. For this and the following items see the respective entries in *Accounts of the Lord High Treasurer of Scotland*, ed. Dickson and Paul, i. 119, 126, 126, and 132.

CHAPTER 7

1. On the reading of medieval Scots history in the Renaissance, see Mason, "From Chronicle to History," 53–66.
2. Leland, *Epigrammata,* no. 168; Lhuyd, *Commentarioli Britannicae Descriptionis Fragmentum*, calls Boece a liar and fabulist throughout his book with a particularly vituperative passage at f. 38.
3. Boece, *Murthlacensium et Aberdonensium Episcoporum Vitae*, ii. For a discussion of his contribution to historiography, see Farrow, "The Substance and Style of Hector Boece's 'Scotorum Historiae,'" 5–25.

250   *Notes to pages 146–157*

4. Boece, *Scottorum Historiae a prima gentis origine cum aliarum et rerum et gentium illustratione non vulgari*, f. cviii verso.

5. Black, "The Gaelic Manuscripts of Scotland," 161–162.

6. Boece, *Scottorum Historiae a prima gentis origine cum aliarum et rerum et gentium illustratione non vulgari*, f. cxxxviii verso.

7. Black, "Boece Scotorum Historiae," 47–52; and Norbrook, "Macbeth and the Politics of Historiography," 86–87.

8. Chambers, *Histoire Abbregee de Tous Les Roys de France, Angleterre et Escosse*, 13.

9. Boece, *Scottorum Historiae a prima gentis origine cum aliarum et rerum et gentium illustratione non vulgari*, f. ccxlxi *recto*.

10. Trinity College, Cambridge, MS Gale, O. ix. 9; the volume was given by Hector Boece to King's College, Aberdeen, and his generosity is noted in the inscription: "[To] the College of Aberdeen from the gift of Hector Boece its first principal" (*Collegi Aberdon, ex dono Magistri Hectoris Bois primi primarii ejusdem*).

11. Hudson, "Scottish Chronicle," 148 and 150.

12. Printed in *Acts of the Parliaments of Scotland*, i. 709–712.

13. "*Histriones, ludiones, mimi et reliquum ociosorum nebulonun genus, nisi regis peculiari gratia ita permittantur, ad aliquod artificium agendum coguntur; quod si recusent, nisi inepti aegritudine aut mutilatione fuerint, iumentorum more ad aratrum aut plaustrum trahendum adiguntur,*" Boece, *Scottorum Historiae a prima gentis origine cum aliarum et rerum et gentium illustratione non vulgari*, f. cclix *verso*.

14. *Acts of the Parliamenst of Scotland*, 1449, c. 9, ii. 36 and 1457, c. 26, ii. 51, after Mill, *Mediaeval Plays in Scotland*, 295.

15. *Ps.-Cyprianus, De xii abusiuis saeculi*, ed. Hellmann, 51.

16. Nennius, *British History and Welsh Annals*, ed. Morris, 71–72.

17. Andrew of Wyntoun, *Original Chronicle*, book viii, chapter 7: *The Stewartis Orygenalle/ The Archedekyne has tretyd hale,/ In metyre fayre, mare wertwsly/ Than I can think be my study/ Be gud contunuatyown/ In successive generatyown.*

18. Boece, *Scottorum Historiae a prima gentis origine cum aliarum et rerum et gentium illustratione non vulgari*, ff. cclix *verso*—cclx *recto*.

19. Powel, *Historie of Cambria*, 97–98.

20. *Historia majoris Britanniae tam Angliae quam Scotiae*, book 3, ff. xliir–xliiiv, after Farrow, "Historiographical Evolution of the Macbeth Narrative," 5. For a discussion of his work, see Hanna, "A Mass of Incoherencies," 137–155.

21. McDiarmaid, "Metrical Chronicles and Non-alliterative Romances," i. 36. See also McDonald, "William Stewart and the Court Poetry of the Reign of James V," 179–200.

22. The *Buik of Croniclis* now survives in a unique manuscript in the University of Cambridge library (MS K.k.ii. 16). William Stewart, *The Buik of the Croniclis of Scotland*, ed. Turnbull; the Macbeth episode is at ii. 620–657.

23. John Bellenden, *The Chronicles of Scotland*, ed. Chambers, Batho, and Husbands; the Macbeth episode is at ii. 143–162 (book 12, chapters 1–7).

Notes to pages 158–167

251

24. Harikae, "Kingship and Imperial Ideas in the Chronicles," 224.

25. New York, Pierpont Morgan Library MS M. 750; only one volume of the text has been edited; see Watson, ed., *Mar Lodge translation of the History of Scotland*.

26. Harikae, "'Daunting' the Isles, Borders and Highlands," 160–161.

27. Cramsie, "Topography, Ethnogoraphy, and the Catholic Scots in the Religious Culture Wars," 127–151.

28. This paragraph is based on Abbott, "Buchanan, George (1506–1582), poet, historian, and administrator," *Oxford Dictionary of National Biography*, https://doi-org.ezaccess.libraries.psu.edu/10.1093/ref:odnb/3837.

29. Buchanan, *Vernacular Writings of George Buchanan*, ed. Brown, 58; Buchanan's innovative place in Scots thought is suggested in Mason, "Kingship, Tyranny and the Right to Resist in Fifteenth Century Scotland," 125–151.

30. Buchanan, *Rerum Scoticarum historia*; although the section specifically devoted to Macbeth's reign is ff. 61 verso to 62 verso, the prince is introduced and his career begins on f. 60 verso with the rebellion of McDonald (MS *Makdualdus*).

31. Collis, "George Buchanan and the Celts in Britain," 91–107.

32. James VI, *Basilikon Doron* in *Political Writings*, 69.

33. This paragraph is based on Marshall, "Lesley [Leslie], John (1527–1596), bishop of Ross, historian, and conspirator," *Oxford Dictionary of National Biography*, https://doi-org.ezaccess.libraries.psu.edu/10.1093/ref:odnb/16492.

34. The congregation of Tiron was founded by Bernard of Tiron in 1114, when he founded La Sainte-Trinité de Tiron in the diocese of Chartres. Bernard emphasized craftwork and meditation. Lindores Abbey is south of the river Tay and lies on the outskirts of Newburgh in Fife; it was founded c. 1191.

35. Leslie, *De origine moribus, et rebus gestis Scotorum librie decem*: Macbeth first appears during Duncan's reign as his victorious general, ii. 195, while his reign is recounted at ii. 196–197.

36. London, British Library Additional Manuscript 27472.

37. Buchanan, *Rerum Scoticarum historia*, 62: *Multa hic fabulose quidam nostrorum affingunt; sed, quia theatris, aut Milesiis fabulis sunt aptiora, quam historiae ea omitto.*

CHAPTER 8

1. "Receyved of master Harrison and master Bisshop for the licensing of RAPHAELs HOLLINGSHEDEs cronycle . . . xx^s and a copy. *Stationers' Register*, ed. Arber, ii. 329. For essays on specific aspects, see Kewes, Archer, and Heal, eds., *The Oxford Handbook of Holinshed's Chronicles*.

2. Warner, ed., "Library of James VI 1573–1583," xl.

3. For the convenience of readers, references to the Macbeth episode in Holinshed's *Chronicles* are to the early nineteenth-century edition by J. Johnsson, *Holinshed's Chronicle of England, Scotland, and Ireland*, vol. v, 264–277.

Notes to pages 170–179

4. *Kingis Quair* in Bawcutt and Riddy, *Longer Scottish Poems* 1375–1650, i. 27: "At my begynnyng first I clepe and call/ To yow, Cleo, and to yow, Polymye/ With Thesiphone, goddis and sistris all."

5. Mill, *Mediaeval Plays in Scotland*, chart facing page 80; Strong, *Tudor and Stuart Monarchy, Pageantry, Painting, Iconography. II Elizabeth*, 10.

6. *Baile in Scáil*, ed. Murry, 34.

7. These are printed in *Letters and Papers, Foreign and Domestic, Henry VIII*, vol. 21, part 1, January–August 1546, ed. Brewer, Gairdner, and Brodie, 507 (June 7, 1546, number 1013), for Lynam's arrest; 513–514 (June 9, 1546, number 1027) for Weston's testimony; and 514–516 for Lynam's testimony.

8. Taylor, *Political Prophecy*, 106.

9. "Henry VIII: February 1537, 26–28," in *Letters and Papers, Foreign and Domestic, Henry VIII*, vol. 12, part 1, January–May 1537 (1890), 239–254.

10. Donne, *Complete Poetry of John Donne*, ed. Shawcross, 26–34 (lines 97–98).

11. Gawdy, *Letters of Philip Gawdy*, 99: to Bassingborne Gawdy, 13 June 1601.

12. For its construction see Harris, "William Camden, Philomen Holland, and the 1610 Translation of Britannia," 279–303.

13. Camden, *Britannia*, 704.

14. Camden, *Britannia*, 716.

15. The pioneering work was done by Thrupp, "A Survey of the Alien Population of England in 1440," 262–273, and "Aliens in and around London in the Fifteenth Century," 251–272.

16. Ditchburn, *Scotland and Europe*, 255–256.

17. Holland, *Buke of the Howlat*, ed. Hanna, 10–15.

18. Kratzmann, *Anglo-Scottish Literary Relations*, 1–7.

19. Kermode, *Aliens and Englishness in Elizabethan Drama*, 18.

20. Knight, "Borders and Their Ballads," 64.

21. Lockyer, *The Early Stuarts*, 144.

22. The traditional view is given in, for example, Levack, *Formation of the British State*, 193; a different interpretation is found in Hudson, "Auld Inimys?" 3–12.

23. Bale, *Kynge Johan*, 63; for comment, see Hoenselaars, *Images of Englishmen and Foreigners*, 29.

24. Hoenselaars, *Images of Englishmen and Foreigners*, 44.

25. The *Lord of Lorne* might have been in circulation since the reign of Henry VIII of England, which is claimed by Everad Guilpin in the first satire of his *Skialethia*, 31, after Collier, ed., *Miscellaneous Tracts Temp. Eliz. & Jac. I.*

26. Hoenselaars, *Images of Englishmen and Foreigners*, 65–66.

27. Eccles, "Brief Lives: Tudor and Stuart Authors," 99.

28. For a spirited rereading of the play as a piece in the service of Protestant ideology, see Hamilton, *Anthony Munday and the Catholics*, 114–119.

29. Hamilton, *Anthony Munday and the Catholics*, 119.

30. See Johnson, "Spectacle and the Fantasy of Immateriality," 105–126.

Notes to pages 181–198

31. Shapiro, *Children of the Revels*.

32. London, British Library, Harleian MS 146, f.15 r printed in Feuillerat, ed., *Documents relating to the Office of the Revels in the time of Queen Elizabeth*, 119.

33. Maguire, *Shakespearean Suspect Texts*, 243–245 (*Edward I*) and 253–254 (*George a Greene*).

34. Greene, *Scottish History of James the Fourth*, ed. Sanders. A modern edition is at http://elizabethandrama.org/wp-content/uploads/2021/06/James-IV-Annotated.pdf.

35. Giraldi, *De gli Hecatommithi*, f. 136 recto to 140 verso.

36. Another opinion on dialectic differences is Biddulph, "A Romp into Middle Scots—and Can We Learn Anything on the Way?" 1–6.

37. William of Malmesbury, *De Gestis Pontificum Anglorum*, ed. Hamilton, 209.

38. Not all are convinced; see Born, "Why Greene Was Angry at Shakespeare," 133–173, who speculated that Shakespeare had interpolated a work by Greene.

39. *Pilgrimage to Parnassus with the two parts of the return from Parnassus*, ed. Macray, 138.

40. Sykes, "Robert Greene and *George a Greene, the Pinner of Wakefield*," 129–136.

41. Nelson, "George Buc, William Shakespeare, and the Folger George a Greene," 74–83.

42. The argument is the basis of Sams, *Shakespeare's Edward III*.

43. Henslowe, *Diary*, ed. Gregg, 111–112.

44. Hudson, "Auld Inimys," 3.

CHAPTER 9

1. Thorpe, ed., *Calendar of the State Papers relating to Scotland*, ii. 791.

2. Thorpe, ed., *Calendar of the State Papers relating to Scotland*, ii. 749.

3. Thorpe, ed., *Calendar of the State Papers relating to Scotland*, ii. 777, and Roberts, "Business of Playing and Patronage of Players" 84–86.

4. Thomas, *Shakespeare in the Public Records*, 14.

5. Sawyer and Winwood, *Memorials*, ii. 41.

6. Jonson, *Cambridge Edition of the Works of Ben Jonson*, ed. Gossett and Kay, 531–534.

7. *Ben Jonson: The Complete Works*, eds. Herford and Simpson, i. 143.

8. This brief biography follows Martin Butler, "Kemp, William (d. in or after 1610?), actor," *Oxford Dictionary of National Biography*, https://doi-org.ezaccess.libraries.psu.edu/10.1093/ref:odnb/15334.

9. Kemp, *Kemps nine daies vvonder*, 15–17.

10. For the "Shake-rags," see Grote, *Best Actors in the World*, 91–92. On the "Nine Days Wonder," see Wiles, *Shakespeare's Clown*, 24–31.

11. Barrell, "Dr. John Dover's 'New' Macbeth Is a Masterpiece without a Master," 63.

12. Arber, ed., *Transcript of the Registers of the Company of Stationers of London,* Liber B, f. 462r 30–33.

13. Halliday, *A Shakespeare Companion*, 317.

254 *Notes to pages 198–215*

14. Barrell, "Dr. John Dover's 'New' Macbeth Is a Masterpiece without a Master," 63.
15. Freeman and Freeman, *John Payne Collier*, 501–502.
16. Opposing opinions are represented by Freeman and Freeman, *John Payne Collier* (who believe him guilty of forgery) and Ganzel, *Fortune and Men's Eyes* (who believes Collier was the victim of persecution).
17. *De Necessariis Observantiis Scaccarii Dialogus*, book 1, chapter 6 in Stubbs, *Select Charters*, 213: *Debita vero quae solvuntur in integrum et de quibus satisfit, cancellet idem clericus linea ducta per medium.*
18. Henslowe, *Henslowe's Diary*, ed. Foakes, 199.
19. Henslowe, *Henslowe's Diary*, ed. Foakes, 200; Chambers, *Elizabethan Stage*, ii. 143, believed that it was acted the same month.
20. Warner, *A Continuance of Albions England*, 375–376.
21. Oxford, Bodleian Library, MS. Ashmole 208, ff. 207r–207v.
22. The worlds of Shakespeare and Forman overlapped in some interesting ways; for brief biographies, see Kassell, "Forman, Simon," and Cook, *Dr. Simon Forman*.
23. Freeman and Freeman, *John Payne Collier*, ii, 1025.
24. Tannenbaum, *Shakespearian Scraps and Other Elizabethan Fragments*, 23–24.
25. For the following, see Crawford, *Bannockburns*, 52–55.

APPENDIX 1

1. Sigmund Freud argued that this presumed childlessness was the main theme of Shakespeare's *Tragedie of Macbeth*, see: Freud, "Some Character-Types Met with in Psycho-Analytic Work," xiv, 319–322.
2. The question of Macbeth's descendants was debated in the years 1920 and 1921 in a series of brief essays, all with the title "MacBeth or MacHeth," published in the *Scottish Historical Review* by C. Sanford Terry (vol. 17, pp. 155 and 338), James Grey (vol. 17, pp. 338–39), John Macbeth (vol. 18, pp. 153–55), and A. W. Johnston (vol. 18, pp. 155 and 236).
3. See: Hudson, *Kings of Celtic Scotland*, 144–45 for a brief discussion.
4. MacGregor, "Genealogies of the clans," 138; the text is printed in Skene, *Collectanea*, 57 and *Celtic Scotland*, iii, 488.
5. Lawrie, *Early Scottish Charters*, 11.
6. Lawrie, *Early Scottish Charters*, 56, 61–63, and 66–67.
7. Lawrie, Early Scottish Charters, 66–67.

Selected Bibliography

MANUSCRIPTS

Cambridge, Trinity College
   MS O. 9. 9: Boece's copy of Fordun's *Chronicle*
Dublin, Royal Irish Academy
   MS 23 G 4: Prophecy of Berchán
   MS 23 P 2: Book of Lecan
Dublin, Trinity College
   MS 498: Fordun's *Chronicle*
   MS 1282 (H. 1. 8).: Annals of Ulster
Dundee, Municipal Archives
   MS no. 15; 20 October 1325—King Robert I to burgesses of Dundee (Grant of land
      for a tollbooth).
London, Stationers' Hall
   Transcript Liber B, entries of copies 1583–1599 (microfilm).
National Library of Scotland
   Advocates MS 34.7.3: genealogy
Oxford, Bodleian Library
   MS Bodley 302: Verse Chronicle
   MS Bodley C. iv. 3: Verse Chronicle
   MS Laud 610: King List B
   MS Latin misc. C 75: King List I
   MS Rawlinson B. 488: Annals of Tigernach
   MS Rawlinson B. 489: Annals of Ulster
Paris, Bibliothèque nationale de France
   MS latin 4126: Poppleton Manuscript
Perth, Municipal Archives
   MS B 59, 23/2: 10 April 1365—King David II to burgesses of Perth (Ships must not
      unload cargo below Drumlay Sands).

256   *Selected Bibliography*

MS B 59, 23/9: 6 May 1399—King Robert III to burgesses of Perth (When merchant ships sail past Drumlay Sands, they must not unload before they reach Perth).

MS B 59, 23/14: 5 March 1406—King Robert III to burgesses of Perth (Apprehend strangers who commit fraud).

PRIMARY SOURCES

Accounts of the Lord High Treasurer of Scotland: Compota Thesaurariorum Regum Scotorum, ed. Thomas Dickson and Sir James Balfour Paul, 11 vols. (Edinburgh: H. M. General Register House, 1877–1916).

Acts of the Parliaments of Scotland: [1124–1707], ed. Cosmo Innes and Thomas Thomson, vol. 1 (Edinburgh: Record Commission, 1844).

Adam of Bremen, *Hamburgische Kirchengeschichte*, ed. Bernhard Schmeidler (Hannover: Monumenta Germaniae Historica, 3rd ed., 1977).

Adomnán, *Adomnán's Life of Columba*, ed. and trans. A. O. and M. O. Anderson (Oxford: Clarendon Press, 1991).

Aided Muirchertaig meic Erca, ed. Lil Nic Donnchadha, Medieval and Modern Irish Series xix (Dublin: Dublin Institute for Advanced Studies, 1980).

Ailred of Rievaulx, *Genealogia Regum Anglorum* in *Beati Aelredi Rievallis abbatis. Operum pars secunda: Historia*, ed. J.-P. Migne, *Patrologia Latina* (Paris: Garnieri Fratres, 1841–1855) 195: cols. 711–37.

Ailred of Rievaulx, *Historical Works*, ed. Marsha L. Dutton; trans. Jane Patricia Freeland, Cistercian Fathers Series (Kalamazoo: Cistercian Press, 2005).

Ailred of Rievaulx, *Mirror of Charity*, trans. Geoffrey Webb and Adrian Walker (London: A. R. Mowbray, 1962).

Anderson, Alan Orr, *Early Sources of Scottish History, from 550 to 1286*, 2 vols. (Edinburgh, 1922; repr. Stamford: Peter Watkins, 1990).

Anderson, Alan Orr, *Scottish Annals from English Chroniclers, from 550 to 1286* (London: David Nutt, 1908).

Anderson, Margery Ogilvie, *Kings and Kingship in Early Scotland* (Edinburgh: Scottish Academic Press, 1973).

Andrew of Wyntoun, *Androw of Wyntoun's Orygynale Cronykil of Scotland*, ed. David Laing, Historians of Scotland Series 2, 3, and 7, 3 vols. (Edinburgh: Edmonston and Douglas, 1872–78).

Andrew of Wyntoun, *The Original Chronicle of Andrew of Wyntoun*, ed. F. J. Amours, 6 vols., (Edinburgh: Scottish Texts Society, 1903–1914).

Anglo-Saxon Chronicle, trans. G. N. Garmondsway (London: J. M. Dent and Sons, 1972).

Annals of Inisfallen (MS Rawlinson B. 503), ed. Seán Mac Airt (Dublin: Dublin Institute for Advanced Studies, 1951).

Annals of Tigernach, in "Fragmentary Annals of Tigernach," ed. W. Stokes in *Revue Celtique* 17 (1896) 6–33, 116–263, 337–420 (for the annals relevant to this study).

Selected Bibliography 257

Annals of Ulster, ed. S. Mac Airt and G. Mac Niocaill (Dublin: Dublin Institute for Advanced Studies, 1983).

Annals of Ulster, ed. and trans. W. Hennesey and B. Mac Carthy (Dublin: HMSO, 1887–1901).

Arber, Edward, ed., *Transcript of the Registers of the Company of Stationers of London, 1554–1640*, 5 vols. (London: Privately Printed, 1875–1877).

Aubrey, John, *Aubrey's Brief Lives*, edited by Oliver Lawson Dick (Harmondsworth: Penguin, 1978).

Audacht Morainn, ed. and trans. Fergus Kelly (Dublin: Dublin Institute for Advanced Studies, 1976).

Baile in Scáil, The Phantom's Frenzy, ed. Kevin Murray (London: Irish Texts Society, 2004).

Bale, John, *King Johan: A Play in Two Parts*, ed. John Nichol (London: Camden Society, 1838).

Barbour, John, *The Bruce*, ed. A. A. M. Duncan (Edinburgh: Canongate, 1997).

Bawcutt, Priscilla, and Felicity Riddy, *Longer Scottish Poems I: 1375–1650* (Edinburgh: Scottish Academic Press, 1987).

Beadle, Richard, ed., *The York Plays: A Critical Edition of the York Corpus Christi Play as Recorded in British Library Additional MS 35290*, 2 vols. (Oxford: Oxford University Press, 2009–2013).

Bede, *Historia Ecclesiastica*, in *Venerabilis Baedae Opera Historica*, ed. Charles Plummer, 2 vols. (Oxford: Clarendon Press, 1896).

Bellenden, John, *The Chronicles of Scotland, Compiled by Hector Boece, Translated into Scots by John Bellenden*, ed. R. W. Chambers, E. C. Bathos, and H. Winifred Husbands, 2 vols. (Edinburgh: Scottish Text Society, 1938–1941).

Bethada Náem nÉrenn, Lives of Irish Saints, ed. and trans. Charles Plummer, 2 vols. (Oxford: Clarendon Press, 1922).

Bethu Phátraic: The Tripartite Life of Patrick, ed. K. Mulchrone (Dublin: Royal Irish Academy, 1939).

Boece, Hector, *Murthlacensium et Aberdonensium Episcoporum Vita* (Paris, 1522).

Boece, Hector, *Scotorvm historiæ a prima gentis origine, cum aliarum & rerum & gentium illustratione non vulgari: præmissa epistola nu⁻cupatoria, tabellisqz amplissimis, & non pænitenda isagoge quæ ab huius tergo explicabuntur diffusius* (Paris, 1527).

Book of Leinster formerly Lebar na Núachongbála, ed. R. I. Best, O. Bergin, M. A. O'Brien, and A. Sullivan, 6 vols. (Dublin: Dublin Institute for Advanced Studies, 1954–1983).

Bower, Walter, *Scotichronicon*, gen. ed. D. E. R. Watt, 9 vols. (Aberdeen: Aberdeen University Press, 1987–98).

Buchanan, George, *De iure regni apud Scotos dialogus* (Edinburgh: Iohannem Rosseum, 1579).

Buchanan, George, *Rerum Scoticarum historia* (Edinburgh: Alexander Arbuthnot, 1582).

Buchanan, George, *Vernacular Writings of George Buchanan*, ed. P. Hume Brown (Edinburgh: Scottish Text Society, 1892).

Calisle, Joseph, *Pictish Sourcebook* (Westport: Greenwood, 2002).

Camden, William, *Britannia, siue florentissimorum regnorum angliæ, scotiæ, hiberniæ, et insularum adiacentium ex intima antiquitate chorographica descriptio: Nunc postremò recognita, plurimis locis magna accessione adaucta, & chartis chorographicis illustrata. guilielmo camdeno authore* (London: Georgii Bishop and Ioannis Norton, 1607).

Carey, John, *King of Mysteries: Early Irish Religious Writings* (Dublin: Four Courts Press, 2000).

Cert cech ríg co réil, ed. and trans. Tadhg Ó Donoghue, *Miscellany Presented to Kuno Meyer*, ed. Osborn Bergin and Carl Marstrander, 258–277 (Halle A. S.: Max Niemeyer, 1912).

Chambre (Chalmer), David, *Histoire abbregee de tous les roys de France, Angleterre et Escosse, mise en ordre par forme d'harmonie: contenant aussi un brief discours de l'ancienne alliance, & mutuel secours entre la France & l'Escosse: plus, l'epitome de l'histoire romaine des papes & empereurs y est adiousté, & celle d''iceux roys augmentee selon la mesme methode . . . : le tout recueilli & mis en lumiere, auec la recerche tant des singularitez plus remarquables concernant l'estat d'Escosse, que de la succession des femmes aux biens, & gouuernement des empires & royaumes.* (Paris: R. Coulombel, 1579).

Chapman, George, John Marston, and Ben Jonson, *Eastward Ho*, ed. R. W. van Fossen (Manchester: Manchester University Press, 1979).

Chronica Monasterii de Melsa a Fundatione Usque Ad Annum 1396, Auctore Thoma De Burton, Abbate, ed. E. A. Bond, Rolls Series no. 43, 3 vols. (London: HMSO 1866–1868). [Chronicle of Melrose facsimile] *Chronica De Mailros*, ed. A. O. Anderson, M. O. Anderson, and W. C. Dickenson, Studies in Economics and Political Science, No. 100 (London, 1934).

[Chronicle of Peter Langtoft] *Chronicle of Pierre de Langtoft, in French Verse from the earliest period to the death of Edward I*, ed. T. Wright, Rolls Series no. 47, 2 vols. (London: HMSO 1866–1868).

Chronicle of the Kings of Mann and the Isles, ed. and trans. George Broderick and Brian Stowell (Edinburgh: George Broderick, 1973).

Chronicle of Melrose, ed. D. Broun and J. Harrison, Scottish History Society series 6 (Edinburgh, 2007).

Chronicon de Lanercost M.CC.I.–MCCCXLVI: e codice cottoniano nunc primum typis mandatum, ed. Joseph Stevenson (Edinburgh: Bannatyne Club, 1837).

Claudius Claudianus, *Carmina*, ed. John Barrie Hall (Leipzig: Tuebner, 1985).

Cogadh Gaedhel re Gallaibh, War of the Irish against the Foreigners, ed. and trans. J. H. Todd, Rolls Series 48 (London: Longmans, Green, Reader, and Dyer, 1866).

Colgan, John, *Acta Sanctorum Veteris Scotiae seu Hiberniae* (Louvain: Everard de Witt, 1645).

Selected Bibliography 259

[Columella] L. Junius Moderatus Columella, *De Re Rustica*, ed., Karl Löffler, 2 vols. (Tübingen: Gedruckt für den Litterarischen Verein in Stuttgart, 1914).

Collectio Canonum Hibernensis, in Hermann Wasserschleben, ed., *Die irische Kanonensammlung* (Leipzig: Tauchnitz, 2nd ed., 1885).

Complaynt of Scotland, ed. A. M. Stewart (Edinburgh: Scottish Texts Society, 1979).

Collier, J. P., *Miscellaneous Tracts Temp. Eliz. & Jac. I.* (London: Shakespeare Society, 1870).

Corpus Genealogiarum Sanctorum Hiberniae, ed. Pádraig Ó Riain (Dublin: Dublin Institute for Advanced Studies, 1985).

Críth Gablach, ed. D. A. Binchy (Dublin: Dublin Institute for Advanced Studies, 1941, repr. 1979).

Cross, T. P., and Clark Slover, *Ancient Irish Tales* (New York: Henry Holt, 1936).

Dickenson, W. C., G. Donaldson, and I. A. Milne, eds., *Source Book of Scottish History* (Edinburgh: Thomas Nelson, repr. 1963).

Dicuil, *Liber de Mensura Orbis Terrae*, ed., J. J. Tierney (Dublin: Dublin Institute for Advanced Studies, 1967).

Dio, *Roman History*, ed. and trans. Ernest Cary (Cambridge, MA: Harvard University Press, 1914–1927).

Donne, John, *The Complete Poetry of John Donne*, ed. John T. Shawcross (New York: Anchor/Doubleday, 1967).

Dowden, John, *The Bishops of Scotland* (Glasgow: James Maclehose and Sons, 1912).

Duncan, A. M. M., *The Acts of Robert I, Regesta Regum Scottorum V* (Edinburgh: University of Edinburgh Press, 1988).

Duncan, A. M. M., *Regesta Regum Scottorum V: Acts of King Robert I* (Edinburgh: University of Edinburgh Press, 1988).

Eadmer, *Historia Novella in Anglia (c. 960–1122)*, ed. Martin Rule, Rolls Series 81 (London: HMSO, 1884).

Earle, John, and Charles Plummer, eds., *Two Saxon Chronicles Parallel*, 2 vols. (Oxford: Clarendon Press, 1896–1899).

Edward I in *The Works of George Peele*, ed., Alexander Dyce (London: William Pickering, 1829).

Edward III in *The Shakespeare apocrypha: being a collection of fourteen plays which have been ascribed to Shakespeare*, ed., C. F. Tucker Brooke (Oxford: Clarendon Press, 1918).

[*Exchequer Rolls of Scotland*] *Rotuli scaccarii regum scotorum: The Exchequer Rolls of Scotland, 1326–1600*, ed. John Stuart and George Burnett, 23 vols. (Edinburgh: H.M. General Register House, 1878–1908).

Feuillerat, Albert, ed., *Documents relating to the Office of the Revels in the time of Queen Elizabeth* (Louvain: A. Uystpruyst, 1908).

Finlayson, C. P., *Celtic Psalter, Edinburgh University Library MS 56* (Amsterdam: North-Holland Publishing, 1962).

260   *Selected Bibliography*

[Flann Mainistrech] "Poems by Flann Mainistrech on the dynasties of Ailech, Mide, and Brega" ed. Eoin Mac Neill, *Archivium Hibernicum* 3 (1913) 37–102.

Forbes, Alexander Penrose, *Kalendars of Scottish Saints* (Edinburgh: Edmonston and Douglas, 1872).

Forbes, Alexander Penrose, *Lives of S. Ninian and S. Kentigern* (Edinburgh: Edmonston and Douglas, 1874).

Fragmentary Annals of Ireland, ed. Joan Radner (Dublin: Dublin Institute for Advanced Studies, 1978).

Froissart, Jean, *Chronicles*, trans. Geoffrey Brereton (Harmondsworth: Penguin, 1978).

Gawdy, Philip, *Letters of Philip Gawdy of West Harling, Norfolk, and of London to various members of his family, 1579–1616*, ed. Isaac Jeayes (London: J. B. Nichols and Sons, 1906).

Geoffrey of Monmouth, *History of the Kings of Britain*, trans. Lewis Thorpe (Harmondsworth: Penguin, 1966).

[George a Greene] *A pleasant conceyted comedie of George a Greene, the pinner of Vvakefield As it was sundry times acted by the seruants of the right Honourable the Earle of Sussex.* (London: Simon Stafford for Cuthbert Burby, 1599).

[Gerald of Wales] *Giraldi Cambrensis Opera*, ed. J. S. Brewer, J. F. Dimock, and G. F. Warner, Rolls Series no. 21, 8 vols. (London: HMSO, 1861–1891).

Gerald of Wales, *History and Topography of Ireland*, ed. J. J. Ó Meara (London: Penguin, 1982).

Gildas, *The Ruin of Britain and Other Documents*, ed. and trans. Michael Winterbottom (Chichester: Phillimore, 1978).

Giraldi, M. Giovanbattista, "Cinthio," *De gli Hecatommithi Cinthio . . . parte prima (-seconda, nella quale si contengono tre dialoghi della vita civile)* (Mondovi: Leondaro Torrentino, 1565).

Greene, Robert, *Greens Groats-Vvorth of Wit, bought with a million of Repentance. Describing the follie of youth, the falshoode of make-shift flatterers, the miserie of the negligent, and mischiefes of deceiuing Courtezans. Written before his death and published at his dyeing request. Fœlicem fuisse infaustum* (London: Danter, 1592).

Greene, Robert, *The Scottish historie of Iames the fourth, slaine at Flodden Entermixed with a pleasant comedie, presented by Oboram King of Fayeries: as it hath bene sundrie times publikely plaide* (London: Thomas Creede, 1598).

Greene, Robert, *The Scottish History of James the Fourth*, ed., Norman Sanders (London: Metheun, 1970).

Guilpin, Everad, *Skialethia. Or a shadowe of truth, in certaine epigrams and satyres* (London: I[ames] R[oberts] for Nicholas Ling, 1598).

Gwynn, E., *Metrical Dindshenchus*, 5 vols., Todd Lecture Series 8-9-10-11-12 (Dublin: Royal Irish Academy, 1903–1930).

Haddan, Arthur, and William Stubbs, eds., *Councils and Ecclesiastical Documents relating to Great Britain and Ireland* (Oxford: Clarendon Press, 1869–78, repr. 1968).

Selected Bibliography

Henry of Huntingdon, *History of the English People*, ed. and trans. Diana Greenway (Oxford: Oxford University Press, 1996).

Henslowe, Philip, *Henslowe's Diary*, ed. R. A. Foakes (Cambridge: Cambridge University Press, 1961, repr. 2002).

Herodian, *History of the Empire from the time of Marcus Aurelius*, ed. and trans. C. R. Whittaker, 2 vols. (Cambridge: Cambridge University Press, 1969).

Holinshed, Raphael, *Chronicles of England, Scotland and Ireland*, 6 vols. (London: John Harrison, 1578), reissued by J. Johnson *et al.* (Buffalo: William S.Heine & Co.).

Holland, Richard, *The Buke of the Howlat*, ed. Ralph Hanna, Scottish Text Society fifth series no. 12 (Edinburgh, 2014).

Howden, Roger of, *Chronica magistri Rogeri de Houedene*, ed. William Stubbs, Rolls Series 51, 4 vols. (London: HMSO, 1868–1871).

"How Culwuch Won Olwen," in *Mabinogion*, ed. Gwynn Jones and Thomas Jones (London: Everyman, 1974).

Innes, Thomas, *Critical Essay on the Ancient Inhabitants of the Northern Parts of Britain or Scotland* (London: Innys, 1729).

Jackson, K. H., ed., *A Celtic Miscellany* (Harmondsworth: Penguin, repr. 1971).

Jackson, K. H., "Duan Albanach," *Scottish Historical Review* 36 (1957) 125–137.

Jackson, K. H., *Gaelic Notes in the Book of Deer* (Cambridge: Cambridge University Press, 1972).

Jackson, K. H., "The Poem *A Eolacha Alban Uile*," *Celtica* 3 (1955) 149–167.

James VI of Scotland, *Basilikon Doron* (Edinburgh: Robert Waldegrave, 1599).

James VI of Scotland, *The Poems of James VI of Scotland*, ed. James Craigie, Scottish Early Text Society, vols. 22 and 26 (Edinburgh: William Blackwood and Sons, 1955–1958).

James VI of Scotland, *Political Writings*, ed. J. P. Sommerville (Cambridge: Cambridge University Press, 1994).

John of Fordun, *Johannis de Fordun, Chronica Gentis Scotorum*, ed. W. F. Skene and trans. F. J. Skene, 2 vols. (Edinburgh: Edmonston & Douglas, 1871–72).

John of Worcester, *The Chronicle of John of Worcester: The Annals from 1067 to 1140 with The Gloucester Interpolations and The Continuation to 1141*, 3 vols., eds. R. R. Darlington and P. McGurk (Oxford: Clarendon Press, 1995–1998).

[Jonson, Ben], *The Cambridge Edition of the Works of Ben Jonson*, ed. Suzanne Gossett and K. David Kay (Cambridge: Cambridge University Press, 2012).

Jonson, Ben, *Ben Jonson*, eds. Charles Harold Hereford and Percy Simpson, 11 vols. (Oxford: Clarendon Press, 1925–1952).

Kemp, William, *Nine daies wonder* in *Kind-hartes dreame*, ed. G. B. Harrison (London: John Lane, 1923).

Lacey, Brian, ed., *Manus O'Donnell's life of Colum Cille* (Dublin: Four Courts Press, 1998).

Lawlor, Hugh Jackson, *The Psalter and Martyrology of Ricemarch*, Henry Bradshaw Society, vol. 47 (London, 1914).

262 *Selected Bibliography*

Lawrie, Sir Archibald, *Early Scottish Charters prior to 1153* (Glasgow: James MacLehose, 1905).

Lebor Bretnach, ed. A. J. Van Hamel (Dublin: Irish Manuscripts Commission, 1932).

Lebor Gabála Érenn: The book of the taking of Ireland, ed. and trans. R. A. S. Macalister, 5 vols., Irish Texts Society 34–35–39–41–44 (Dublin 1932–1942).

Lebor na Cert: The Book of Rights, ed. and trans. Myles Dillon, Irish Texts Society 46 (Dublin, 1962).

Lebor na Huidre, Book of the Dun Cow, ed. R. I. Best and Osborn Bergin (Dublin: Royal Irish Academy, 1929).

Leland, John, *Epigrammata* (Oxford: John Reynolds, 1589).

Leland, John, *Lelandi Antiquarii de rebus Britannicis collecteana cum Thomas Hearnii praefatione notis et indice ad editionem primam*, ed. Thomas Hearne, 6 vols. (London: White, 1774, repr. 1970).

Leslie, John, *De origine moribus, et rebus gestis Scotorum libri decem* (Rome: AEdibus Populi Romani, 1578).

Letters and Papers, Foreign and Domestic, of the Reign of Henry VIII: Preserved in the Public Record Office, the British Museum, and Elsewhere, ed. J. S. Brewer, James Gairdner, and R. H. Brodie, 21 vols. (London: HMSO, 1864–1920).

Liber Cartarum Prioratus Sancti Andree in Scotia, ed. Thomas Thomson, Bannatyne Club no. 69 (Edinburgh, 1841).

Lhuyd, Humphrey, *Commentarioli Britannicae Descriptionis Fragmentum* (Köln: Ioannem Brickmannus, 1572).

Mabinogion, ed. and trans. Gwyn and Thomas Jones (London: Everyman, revised 1974).

Mac Firbisigh, Dubhaltach, *The Great Book of Irish Genealogies or Leabhar Mór na nGenealach: compiled (1645–66). by Dubhaltach Mac Firbisigh*, ed. with translation and indexes by Nollaig Ó Muraíle (Dublin: Edmund Burke, 2003–4).

Major (Mair), John, *A History of Greater Britain as well England and Scotland*, ed. and trans. Archibald Constable, Scottish History Society, vol. 10 (Edinburgh: T. and A. Constable, 1892).

Mar Lodge Translation of the History of Scotland by Hector Boece, ed. G. Watson, Scottish Text Society 3rd series 17 (Edinburgh, 1943).

Marianus, Scotus, *Mariani Scotti Chronicon*, ed. G. Waitz in *Monumenta Germaniae Historica, Scriptores* 5, 481–562 (Hanover: Impensis Bibliopolii Hanhiani, 1844).

Meyer, Kuno, "Gein Branduib maic Echach ocus Aedáin maic Gabráin inso sís," *Zeitschrift für Celtische Philologie*, 2 (1899) 134–137.

Minot, Laurence, *The Poems of Laurence Minot*, ed. Joseph Hall (Oxford: Clarendon Press, 3rd ed., 1914).

Munday, Anthony, *An edition of Anthony Munday's John a Kent and John a Cumber*, ed. Arthur E. Pennell (New York: Garland, 1980).

Munday, Anthony, *The triumphes of re-vnited Britania Performed at the cost and charges of the Right Worship: Company of the Merchant-Tayulors, in honor of Sir Leonard*

Selected Bibliography

Holliday kni: to solemnize his entrance as Lorde Mayor of the Citty of London, on Tuesday the 29. of October. 1605 (London: W. Jaggard, 1605).

Murphy, Gerard, "The Lament of the Old Woman of Beare," *Proceedings of the Royal Irish Academy* 55 (1952–1953) C: 83–109.

Nennius, *British History and the Welsh Annals*, ed. John Morris (Chichester: Philimore, 1980).

Nic Énrí, U., and G. Mac Niocaill, "The Second Recension of the Evernew Tongue," *Celtica* 9 (1971) 1–60.

Nichols, John, *The Progresses, Processions and Magnificent Festivities of King James the First*, 4 vols. (London: J. B. Nichols, 1829).

Nixon, C. E. V., and Barbara Saylor Rodgers, *In Praise of the Later Roman Emperors* (Berkeley: University of California Press, 1994).

[Njal's Saga] *Brennu-Njáls saga*, ed., Einar Ól. Sveinsson (Reykjavík: Hið Íslenzka Fornritafélag, 1954).

Njal's Saga, ed. and trans. Magnus Magnusson and Hermann Pálsson (Harmondsworth: Penguin, 1972).

O' Brien, M. A., *Corpus Genealogiarum Hiberniae*, vol. 1, ed. John Kelleher (Dublin: Dublin Institute for Advanced Studies, 1976).

Orderic Vitalis, *Historica Ecclesiastica* in *Patrologia . . . Latina*, ed. Migne, 188 (Paris: Garnier, 1841–1855).

Orkneyinga Saga, ed. Joseph Anderson (Edinburgh: Edmonston and Douglas, 1873).

Orkneyinga Saga, ed. Finnbogi Guðmundsson Islenzk fornrit 14 (Reykjavík: Hið Íslenzka Fornritafélag, 1965).

Orkneyinga Saga: A New Translation with Introduction and Notes, ed. Alexander Burt Taylor (London and Edinburgh: Oliver & Boyd, 1938).

Palgrave, Frances, *Documents and Records Illustrating the History of Scotland, and the Transactions Between the Crowns of Scotland and England, Preserved in the Treasury of Her Majesty's Exchequer*, vol. 1 (London: Record Commission, 1837).

Patrick (Bishop of Dublin), *The Writings of Bishop Patrick 1074–1084*, ed. and trans. Aubrey Gwynn (Dublin: Dublin Institute for Advanced Studies, 1955).

Patrick (St.), *His Writings and Muirchu's Life*, ed. A. B. E. Hood (Chichester: Philimore, 1978).

[*Patrologia Latina*] Migne, J.-P., *Patrologiae cursus completus: Series latina*, 221 vols. (Paris: Garnier, 1844–1855).

Patrologiae cursus completus. Series Latina, ed., Jacques-Paul Migne, 221 vols. (Paris: apud Garnier fratres, 1840–1864).

Peele, George, *The famous chronicle of king Edward the first, sirnamed Edward Longshankes with his returne from the holy land. Also the life of Lleuellen rebell in Wales. Lastly, the sinking of Queene Elinor, who sunck at Charingcrosse, and rose againe at Pottershith, now named Queenehith* (London, 1593).

Selected Bibliography

Pierre de Langtoft, *Chronicle of Pierre de Langtoft, in French verse from the earliest period to the death of Edward I*, ed. Thomas Wright, Rolls Series 47, 2 vols. (London 1866–1868).

Pierre de Langtoft, *Édition Critique et Commentée de Pierre de Langtoft, Le Régne D'Edouard Ier*, Jean Claude Thiolier (Crétil: Université de Paris XII, 1989).

Pilgrimage to Parnassus with the two parts of the return from Parnassus. Three comedies performed in St. John's College, Cambridge, A.D. 1597–1601, ed. W. D. Macray (Oxford: Clarendon Press, 1886).

Powel, David, *The Historie of Cambria Now Called Wales* (London: Rafe Newberie and Henrie Denham, 1584).

Prophecy of Berchán, ed. and trans. B. Hudson (Westport: Greenwood, 1996).

Prophecy of the Six Kings in *the Poems of Laurence Minot*, ed. Joseph Hall (Oxford: Clarendon Press, 3rd ed. 1914).

Prosper, "Prosperi Tironis epitoma chronicon ed. primum a. CCCCXXXIII, continuata ad a. CCCLV," ed. Theodor Mommsen in Theodor Mommsen, *Chronica minora saec. IV, V, VI, VII*, vol. 1, Monumenta Germaniae Historica, Scriptores. Auctores antiquissimi 9 (Berlin: Weidmann, 1892) 341–499.

Ps.-Cyprianus. De xii abusiuis saeculi, ed. Siegmund Hellmann, Texte und Untersuchungen zur Geschichte der altchristlichen Literatur 34 (Leipzig, 1909).

(*The*) *Raigne of King Edvvard the third: As it hath bin sundrie times plaied about the Citie of London* (London: Cuthbert Burby, 1596).

Registrum de Dunfermelyn. Liber cartarum Abbatie Benedictine S.S. Trinitatis et B. Margarete Regine de Dunfermelyn, ed. Cosmo Innes, Bannatyne Club no. 74 (Edinburgh: Thomas Constable, 1842).

Registrum Episcopatus Moraviensis, e pluribus codicibus consarcinatum circa A.D. MCCCC. Cum continuatione diplomatum recentiorum usque ad A.D. MDCXXIII, ed. Cosmo Innes, Bannatyne Club no. 58 (Edinburgh, 1837).

Registrum magni sigilli regum Scotorum (The register of the great seal of Scotland), ed. John Maitland Thomson et al., 11 vols. (Edinburgh: Lords Commissioners of H. M. Treasury, 1882–1914).

Reports of the Royal Commission on Historical Manuscripts (London: HMSO, 1870–1961).

[*Romance of Fergus*] Guillaume le Clerc, *The Romance of Fergus*, ed. Wilson Frescoln (Philadelphia: William H. Allen, 1983).

Rotuli Parliamentorum; ut et Petitiones, et Placita in Parliamento, gen. ed. John Strachet (London: House of Lords, 1767–77).

Rudolfus Glaber, *Rodulfi Glabri Historiarum libri quinque*, ed. John France (Oxford: Clarendon Press, 1989).

Saga Óláfs konungs hins helga. Den store saga om Olav den hellige, ed. Oscar Albert Johnsen and Jón Helgason, 2 vols. (Oslo: Norsk Historisk Kjeldeskript-Institutt, 1941).

Selected Bibliography

Sawyer, Edmund, and Ralph Winwood, *Memorials of affairs of state in the reigns of Q. Elizabeth and K. James I* (London: T. Ward, 1725).

Scéla Cano meic Gartnáin, ed. D. A. Binchy (Dublin: Dublin Institute for Advanced Studies, 1975).

"Scottish Chronicle," ed. and trans. B. Hudson, *Scottish Historical Review* 76 (1998) 129–161.

Shakespeare, William, *Mr. VVilliam Shakespeares comedies, histories & tragedies. Published according to the True Original Copies*, compiled by John Heminges and Henry Condell (London: Isaac Issgard, 1623).

Skene, William Forbes, ed. and trans., *Chronicles of the Picts, Chronicles of the Scots and other memorials of early Scottish history* (Edinburgh: HM General Register House, 1867).

Skene, William Forbes, ed. and trans., *Collectanea de rebus Albanicis* (Edinburgh: T. G. Stevenson, 1848).

Smith, David Baird. "Le Testament Du Gentil Cossoys," *Scottish Historical Review* 17 (1920) 190–198.

Stationers' Register: A Transcript of the Register of the Company of Stationers of London 1554–1640 A.D., ed. Edward Arber, 5 vols. (London: P. Smith, repr. 1950).

Statistical Account of Scotland: Drawn up from the communications of the ministers of the different parishes compiled by Sir John Sinclair, 21 vols. (Edinburgh: William Creech, 1791).

Stewart, William, *The Buik of the Croniclis of Scotland*, ed. W. B. Turnbull, 3 vols. (London, Rolls Series 6, 1858).

Stokes, Whitley, *Martyrology of Oengus the Culdee, Félire Óengusso Céli Dé* (London: Henry Bradshaw Society, 1905).

Stokes, Whitley, "Second Vision of Adomnan," *Revue Celtique* 12 (1891) 420–443.

Stokes, Whitley, "Vision of Adomnan," *Fraser's Magazine* (February 1871) 184–194.

Stones, E. L. G., and Grant G. Simpson, *Edward I and the Throne of Scotland, 1290–1296: An edition of the sources for the Great Causei*, 2 vols. (Oxford: Oxford University Press, 1978).

Stuart, John, *Miscellany of the Spalding Club*, vol. 5 (Aberdeen, 1852).

Stubbs, William, *Select Charters and other illustrations of English constitutional history; from the earliest times to the reign of Edward the First* (Oxford: Clarendon Press, 9th ed., 1921).

Sturluson, Snorri, *Heimskringla, History of the Kings of Norway*, trans. Lee Hollander (Austin: University of Texas Press, 1964).

Summerfield, Thea, "The Testimony of Writing: Pierre de Langtoft and the Appeals to History, 1291–1306," in *The Scots and Medieval Arthurian Legend*, ed. Rhiannon Purdie and Nicola Royan, *Arthurian Studies* 61 (2005) 25–41.

Symeon of Durham, *Symeonis Monachi Opera Omnia*, ed. Thomas Arnold, Rolls Series no. 75, 2 vols. (London 1882–1885).

Selected Bibliography

Symeonis Monachi Opera Omnia, ed. Thomas Arnold, 2 vols. (London: Longman and Co., 1882–1885).

Thomas of Erceldonne, *The Romance and Prophecies of Thomas of Erceldonne*, ed. J. A. H. Murry, Early English Text Society 61 (London, 1875).

Thorpe, Markham John, ed., *Calendar of the State Papers relating to Scotland preserved in the State Paper Office of Her Majesty's Public Record Office*, 2 vols. (London: HMSO, 1858).

Thurneysen, R., "Synchronismen der irische Könige," *Zeitschrift für celtische Philologie* 19 (1933) 81–99.

Tecosca Cormaic, *The instructions of King Cormac mac Airt*, ed. and trans. Kuno Meyer, Todd Lecture Series 15 (Dublin, 1909).

Tochmarc Étaíne, ed. R. I. Best and Osborn Bergin, *Ériu* 12 (1934–1938) 137–196.

Togail Bruidne Dá Derga, ed. Eleanor Knott (Dublin: Dublin Institute for Advanced Studies, 1936).

Tristram, Hildegard L. C., "Mac Bethad mac Fin mic Laig. XVII annis regnavit. Macbeth— Verschriftete Wirklichkeit, gelebte Schriftlichkeit, aufgeführte Wirklichkeit," in *Mündlichkeit - Schriftlichkeit - Weltbildwandel: Literarische Kommunikation und Deutungsschemata von Wirklichkeit in der Literatur des Mittelalters und der frühen Neuzeit*, ed. Werner Röcke and Ursula Schaefer, *ScriptOralia* 71 (1996) 196–222.

Vita Edwardi Secundi, in W. Stubbs, ed., *Chronicles of the Reigns of Edward I and Edward II*, Rolls Series 47, 2 vols. (London 1866–1868).

Vitae Sanctorum Hiberniae, ed. Charles Plummer, 2 vols. (Oxford: Clarendon Press, 1910).

Warner, George F., ed., "Library of James VI 1573–1583, from a Manuscript in the hand of Peter Young, his tutor," in *Miscellany of the Scottish History Society 1*, Scottish History Society, vol. 15 (Edinburgh, 1893) xi–lxxv.

Warner, William, *A Continuance of Albions England* (London: Felix Kyngston, 1606).

Wasserschleben, Hermann, ed., *Die irische Kanonensammlung* (Geissen: J. Rickert'sche, 1874).

Watson, George, ed., *The Mar Lodge Translation of the History of Scotland by Hector Boece*, Scottish Texts Society (Edinburgh, 1946).

William of Malmesbury, *De Gestis Pontificum Anglorum*, ed. N. E. S. A. Hamilton, Rolls Series 52 (London, 1870).

William of Malmesbury, *De Gestis Regum Anglorum*, ed. William Stubbs, 2 vols. (London: HMSO, 1887–1889).

William of Newburgh, *The History*, trans. Joseph Stevenson, Church Historians of England 4 (London, 1856).

Woodes, Nathaniel, *The Conflict of Conscience* (London: Richarde Bradocke, 1581).

Selected Bibliography

SECONDARY SOURCES

Aird, William M., "St. Cuthbert, the Scots and the Normans," *Anglo-Norman Studies, XVI: Proceedings of the Battle Conference, 1993*, ed., Marjorie Chibnall 1–20 (Woodbridge, 1994).

Anderson, A. O., "Anglo-Scottish Relations from Constantine II to William," *Scottish Historical Review* 42 (1963) 1–20.

Anderson, A. O., "Macbeth's Relationship to Malcolm II," *Scottish Historical Review* 25 (1928) 372.

Anderson, M. O., "Lothian and the Early Scottish Kings," *Scottish Historical Review* 39 (1960).

Anderson, A. O., "Poppleton Manuscript," *Scottish Historical Review* 28 (1949) 31–42.

Bain, Joseph, *Calendar of Documents Relating to Scotland Preserved in Her Majesty's Public Record Office*, 4 vols. (London: PRO, 1881–1888).

Bannerman, John, "Comarba Coluim Chille," *Innes Review* 44 (1993) 14–47.

Bannerman, John, "The Dál Riata and Northern Ireland in the Sixth and Seventh Centuries," in *Celtic Studies: Essays in Memory of Angus Matheson, 1912–1962*, ed. James Carney and David Greene, 1–11 (London: Routledge and Kegan Paul, 1968).

Bannerman, John, "The King's Poet and the Inauguration of Alexander III," *Scottish Historical Review* 68 (1989) 120–149.

Bannerman, John, "Macduff of Fife," in *Medieval Scotland*, ed. A. Grant and K. Stringer, 20–38 (Edinburgh: Edinburgh University Press, 1993).

Bannerman, John, *Studies in the History of Dalriada* (Edinburgh: Scottish Academic Press, 1974).

Barrell, Charles, "Dr. John Dover's 'New' Macbeth Is a Masterpiece without a Master," *Shakespeare Fellowship Quarterly* (1947–1948) 58–64.

Barrow, G. W. S., "David I of Scotland: The Balance of New and Old," in G. W. S. Barrow, *Scotland and Its Neighbours in the Middle Ages* (London: A and C Black, 1992) 45–65.

Barrow, G. W. S., *Kingship and Unity: Scotland 1000–1306* (Edinburgh: Edinburgh University Press, 1981).

Barrow, G. W. S., "The Kings of Scotland and Durham," in *Anglo-Norman Durham: 1093–1193*, ed. David Rollason, Margaret Harvey, and Michael Prestwich, 311–323 (Woodbridge: Boydell and Brewer, 1994).

Barrow, G. W. S., "Macbeth and Other Mormaers of Moray," in *The Hub of the Highlands: The Book of Inverness and Districts, the Centenary Volume of the Inverness Field Club*, 1875–1975, ed. L. Maclean (Edinburgh: Mercat Press, 1975).

Barrow, G. W. S., "Malcolm III [Mael Coluim Ceann Mór, Malcolm Canmore] (d. 1093) King of Scots," *Oxford Dictionary of National Biography*. https://www-oxforddnb-com.ezaccess.libraries.psu.edu/view/10.1093/ref:odnb/9780198614 128.001.0001/odnb-9780198614128-e-17859.

Barrow, G. W. S., "Scots in the Durham *Liber Vitae*," in *The Durham Liber Vitae and Its Context*, ed. David Rollason, A. J. Piper, Margaret Harvey, and Lynda Rollason, 109–116 (Woodbridge: Boydell, 2004).

Bartley, J. O., *Teague, Shenkin, and Sawney. Being an Historical Study of the Earliest Irish, Welsh, and Scottish Characters in English Plays*. (Cork: Cork University Press, 1954).

Beckett, Jamie, "Pendens super feretrum: Fergus, Aelred, and the York *Funeral of the Virgin*," *Medieval English Theatre* 39 (2017) 103–125.

Bell, W. T., and Astrid E. J. Ogilvie, "Weather Compilations as a Source of Data for the Reconstruction of European Climate during the Medieval Period," *Climatic Change* 1 (1978) 331–348.

Beougher, David, "'More Savage than the Sword': Logistics in the Medieval Atlantic Theater of War," in *Studies in the Medieval Atlantic*, ed. B. Hudson, 185–206 (New York: Routledge, 2012).

Bernier, Gildas, "Les navires celtiques du Haut Moyen Age," *Etudes celtiques* 16 (1979) 287–291.

Biddulph, Joseph, "A Romp into Middle Scots—and Can We Learn Anything on the Way?" *Transactions of the Yorkshire Dialect Society* 23 (2018) 1–6.

Bieler, Ludwig, "Jocelin von Furness als Hagiograph," in *Geschichtsschreibung und geistliches Leben im Mittelalter: Festschrift für Heinz Löwe zum 65. Geburtstag*, ed. Karl Hauck, and Hubert Mordek, 410–415 (Köln: Bohlau Verlag Köln Wien, 1978).

Binchy, D. A., "The Passing of the Old Order," in *The Impact of the Scandinavian Invasions on the Celtic-speaking Peoples c. 800–1100 A.D.*, ed. Brian Ó Cuív, 119–132 (Dublin: Dublin Institute for Advanced Studies, 1975).

Birley, Anthony R., *The Fasti of Roman Britain* (Oxford: Clarendon Press, 1981).

Black, J. B., "Boece Scotorum Historiae," in *University of Aberdeen: Quatercentenary of the Death of Hector Boece*, ed. W. D. Simpson, 30–53 (Aberdeen: Aberdeen University Press, 1932).

Black, Ronald, "The Gaelic Manuscripts of Scotland," in *Gaelic and Scotland Alba agus a" Gàidhlig* ed. William Gilles, 146–174 (Edinburgh: Edinburgh University Press, 1989).

Boardman, Stephen, "Chronicle Propaganda in Fourteenth-Century Scotland: Robert the Stewart, John of Fordun and the Anonymous Chronicle," *Scottish Historical Review* 76 (1997) 23–43.

Born, Hanspeter, "Why Greene Was Angry at Shakespeare," *Medieval and Renaissance Drama in England* 25 (2012) 133–173.

Bowen, E. G., "The Cult of St. Brigit," *Studia Celtica* 8–9 (1974 for 1974) 33–47.

Bowen, E. G., "The Irish Sea in the Age of the Saints," *Studia Celtica* 4 (1969) 56–71.

Bowen, E. G., *Saints, Seaways and Settlements* (Cardiff: University of Wales Press, 1969).

Boyle, A., "Notes on Scottish Saints," *Innes Review* 32 (1981) 59–82.

Breatnach, Caoimhín, "*Oidheadh Chloinne Tuireann* agus *Cath Maige Tuired*: dhá shampla de mhiotas eiseamláireach," *Éigse* 32 (2000) 35–46.

Selected Bibliography

Breeze, Andrew, "*Telleyr, Anguen, Gulath*, and the Life of St. Kentigern," *Scottish Language* 27 (2008) 71–79.

Bronner, Dagmar, "Codeswitching in Medieval Ireland: The Case of the *Vita Tripartita Sancti Patricii*," *Journal of Celtic Linguistics* 9 (2005) 1–12.

Brooke, Daphne, "Fergus of Galloway: Miscellaneous Notes for a Revised Portrait," *Transactions of the Dumfriesshire and Galloway Natural History and Antiquarian Society* 66 (1991) 47–58.

Borsje, Jacqueline, "The Monster in the River Ness in *Vita Sancti Columbae*: A Study of a Miracle," *Peritia* 8 (1994) 27–34.

Broun, D., "Property Records in the Book of Deer as a Source for Early Scottish Society," in *Studies on the Book of Deer*, ed. K. Forsyth, 313–360 (Dublin: Four Courts Press, 2008).

Bullough, Geoffrey, "Macbeth," in *Narrative and Dramatic Sources of Shakespeare* (New York: Columbia University Press, 1973) 423–527.

Butler, Martin, "Kemp, William (d. in or after 1610?) Actor," *Oxford Dictionary of National Biography,* https://doi-org.ezaccess.libraries.psu.edu/10.1093/ref:odnb/15334.

Byrne, F. J., "Ireland and Her Neighbours, c.1014–c.1072," in *A New History of Ireland I: Prehistoric and Early Ireland*, ed. D. Ó Cróinín, 862–898 (Oxford: Oxford University Press, 2005).

Byrne, F. J., *1,000 Years of Irish Script* (Oxford: Bodleian Library, 1979).

Byrne, F. J., "*Senchas*: The Nature of Gaelic Historical Tradition," *Historical Studies* 9 (1974) 137–159.

Cameron, Ali, "Let Dear Be Its Name from Now Onwards: The Search for the Monastery of Deer," *Pictish Arts Society Newsletter*, 90 (2019) 7–8.

Campbell, James, "England, Scotland and the Hundred Years War in the Fourteenth Century," in *Europe in the Late Middle Ages*, ed. J. R. Hale et al., 184–216 (London: Faber, 1965).

Carney, James, "Language and Literature to 1169," in *A New History of Ireland I: Prehistoric and Early Ireland*, ed., Dáibhi Ó Cróinín 451–510 (Oxford: Oxford University Press, 2005)

Cary, John, *King of Mysteries: Early Irish Religious Writings* (Dublin: Four Courts, 2000).

Chadwick, Nora K., "Pictish and Celtic Marriage," *Scottish Gaelic Studies* 8 (1958) 56–115.

Chadwick, Nora K., "The Story of Macbeth: A Study in Gaelic and Norse Tradition," *Scottish Gaelic Studies* 6 (1949) 189–211 and 7 (1951) 1–25.

Chambers, E. K., *The Elizabethan Stage*, 4 vols. (Oxford: Clarendon Press, 1923).

Charles-Edwards, T. M. O., *Early Irish and Welsh Kinship* (Oxford: Clarendon Press, 1993).

Charles-Edwards, T. M. O., "Irish Warfare before 1100," in *A Military History of Ireland*, ed. Thomas Bartlett, and Keith Jeffery, 26–51 (Cambridge: Cambridge University Press, 1996).

Selected Bibliography

Clarke, D. V., "Reading the Multiple Lives of Pictish Symbol Stones," *Medieval Archaeology* 51 (2007) 19–39.

Collis, John, "George Buchanan and the Celts in Britain," in *Celtic Connections: Proceedings of the 10th International Congress of Celtic Studies*, vol. 1: *Language, Literature, History, Culture*, ed. Ronald Black, William Gillies, and Roibeard Ó Maolalaigh, 91–107 (East Linton: Tuckwell, 1999).

Cook, Judith, *Dr. Simon Forman: A Most Notorious Physician* (London: Chatto & Windus, 2001).

Corradini, Richard, *The Construction of Communities in the Early Middle Ages: Texts, Resources and Artefacts* (Leiden: Brill, 2003).

Cowan, E. J., "The Historical Macbeth," in *Moray: Province and People*, ed. W. D. H. Sellar, 117–142 (Edinburgh: Edinburgh University Press, 1993).

Cowan, E. J., "The Scottish Chronicle in the Poppleton Manuscript," *Innes Review* 32 (1981) 3–21.

Cox, Richard A. V., and Richard Lathe, "The Question of the Etymology of *Dunadd*, a Fortress of the Dalriadic Scots," *Journal of Scottish Name Studies* 11 (2017) 21–36.

Craig, Cairns, gen. ed., *The History of Scottish Literature*, 4 vols. (Aberdeen: Aberdeen University Press, 1988).

Cramsie, John, "Topography, Ethnography, and the Catholic Scots in the Religious Culture Wars: From Hector Boece's Scotorum Historiae to John Lesley's Historie of Scotland," in *Scottish Latinitas*, ed. Alessandra Petrina and Ian Johnson, 127–151 (Kalamazoo: University of Eastern Michigan Press, 2018).

Crawford, Barbara, *Earl and Mormaer* (Inverness: Groam House Museum, 1995).

Crawford, Barbara, *Scandinavian Scotland* (Leicester: Leicester University Press, 1987).

Crawford, Barbara E., and Thomas Owen Clancy, "The Formation of the Scottish Kingdom," in *The New Penguin History of Scotland: From the Earliest Times to the Present Day*, ed. R. A. Houston and W. W. J. Knox, 28–95 (London: Penguin, 2001).

Crawford, Deborah K. E., "St. Joseph in Britain: Reconsidering the Legends, Part I," *Folklore* 104, no. 1–2 (1993) 86–98.

Crawford, Deborah K. E., "St. Joseph in Britain: Reconsidering The Legends. Part 2," *Folklore* 105 (1994) 51–59.

Crawford, Ian, "War or Peace? Viking Colonization in the Northern and Western Isles of Scotland," *Proceedings of the Eighth Viking Congress–Århus* (Odense, 1981).

Crawford, Robert, *Bannockburns: Scottish Independence and Literary Imagination* (Edinburgh: Edinburgh University Press, 2014).

Dalton, Paul, "Scottish Influence on Durham 1066–1214," in *Anglo-Norman Durham: 1093–1193*, ed. David Rollason, Margaret Harvey, and Michael Prestwich, 339–352 (Woodbridge: Boydell and Brewer, 1994).

Dickenson, W. C., *Scotland from the Earliest Times to 1603*, ed. A. A. M. Duncan (Oxford: Clarendon Press, 1977).

Ditchburn, David, *Scotland and Europe: The Medieval Kingdom and Its Contacts with Christendom c. 1215–1245* (East Linton: Tuckwell Press, 2001).

Selected Bibliography

Doherty, Charles, "Warrior and King in Early Ireland," in *Kings and Warriors in Early North-West Europe*, ed. Jan Erik Rekdal and Charles Doherty, 88–148 (Dublin: Four Courts Press, 2016).

Donaldsson, Gordon, "Scottish Bishops' Sees before the Reign of David I," *Proceedings of the Society of Antiquaries of Scotland* 87 (1952–1953) 106–117.

Drexler, Marjorie, "Fluid Prejudice: Scottish Origin Myths in the Later Middle Ages," in *People, Politics and Community in the Later Middle Ages*, ed. Joel Rosenthal and Colin Richmond, 60–76 (New York: St. Martin's Press, 1987).

Duffy, Seán, ed., *Robert the Bruce's Irish Wars: The Invasions of Ireland 1306–1329* (Gloucester: Stroud, 2002).

Duncan, A. A. M., *Scotland, the Making of the Kingdom*, Edinburgh History of Scotland I (Edinburgh: Edinburgh University Press, 1975).

Eccles, Mark, "Brief Lives: Tudor and Stuart Authors," *Studies in Philology* 79 (1982) 1–135.

Edmond, Mary, *Rare Sir William Davenant* (Manchester: Manchester University Press, 1989).

Edwards, Nancy, "The Decoration of the Earliest Welsh Manuscripts," in *The Cambridge History of the Book in Britain*, ed. John Barnard, D. F. McKenzie, David McKitterick, and I. R. Willison, 7 vols., i. 244–248 (Cambridge: Cambridge University Press, 1999–2019).

Edwards, Nancy, "11th-century Welsh Illuminated Manuscripts: The Nature of the Irish Connection," in *From the Isles of the North: Early Medieval Art in Ireland and Britain. Proceedings of the Third International Conference on Insular Art held in the Ulster Museum, Belfast, 7–11 April 1994*, ed. Cormac Bourke, 147–155 (Belfast: HMSO, 1995).

Egan, Simon, "A Playground of the Scots? Gaelic Ireland and the Stewart Monarchy in the Late Fourteenth and Fifteenth Centuries," *Fifteenth Century* 16 (2018) 101–121.

Enright, Michael J., "Further Reflections on Royal Ordinations in the *Vita Columbae*," in *Ogma: Essays in Celtic Studies in Honour of Próinséas Ní Chatháin*, ed. Michael Richter and Jean-Michel Picard, 20–35 (Dublin: Four Courts Press, 2002).

Evans, Nicholas, "Irish Chronicles as Sources for the History of Northern Britain, A.D. 660–800," *Innes Review* 69 (2018) 1–48.

Farrell, Jennifer, "History, Prophecy and the Arthur of the Normans: The Question of Audience and Motivation behind Geoffrey of Monmouth's *Historia regum Britanniae*," *Anglo-Norman Studies* 37 (2015) 99–114.

Farrow, Kenneth, "Historiographical Evolution of the Macbeth Narrative," *Scottish Literary Journal* 21 (1994) 5–23.

Farrow, Kenneth, "The Substance and Style of Hector Boece's 'Scotorum Historiae,'" *Scottish Literary Journal* 25 (1998) 5–25.

Findon, Joanne, "Supernatural Lovers, Liminal Women, and the Female Journey," *Florilegium* 30 (2014) 27–52.

Selected Bibliography

Foot, Sarah, *Æthelstan the First King of England* (New Haven: Yale University Press, 2011).

Foot, Sarah, "Where English Becomes British: Rethinking Contexts for *Brunanburh*," in *Myth, Rulership, Church and Charters: Essays in Honour of Nicholas Brooks*, ed. Julia Barrow and Andrew Wareham, 127–144 (Aldershot: Hambledon Press, 2008).

Forsyth, Katherine, "Some Thoughts on Pictish Symbols as a Formal Writing System," in *The Worm, the Germ, and the Thorn: Pictish and Related Studies Presented to Isabel Henderson*, ed. David Henry, 85–98 (Balgavie, Angus: Pictish Arts Society, 1997).

Forsyth, Katherine, ed., *Studies on the Book of Deer* (Dublin: Four Courts Press, 2008).

Foster, Sally, "Before Alba: Pictish and Dál Riata Power Centres from the Fifth to Late Ninth Centuries AD," in *Scottish Power Centres from the Early Middle Ages to the Twentieth Century*, ed. Sally Foster, Allan Macinnes, and Ranald MacInnes, 1–31 (Glasgow: Cruithne Press, 1998).

Fraser, Antonia, *King James VI of Scotland and James I of England* (London: Random House, 1974).

Fraser, Ian, *Pictish Symbol Stones of Scotland,* (London: RCAHMS, 2008).

Freeman, Arthur, and Janet Ing Freeman, *John Payne Collier*, 2 vols (New Haven: Yale University Press, 2004).

Freud, Sigmund, "Some Character-Types Met with in Psycho-Analytic Work," in *The Standard Edition of the Complete Psychological Works of Sigmund Freud*, 24 vols. (London: Hogarth Press, 1953–1974).

Dewey Ganzel, *Fortune and Men's Eyes: The Career of John Payne Collier* (New York: Oxford University Press, 1982).

Gasquet, Francis, *A History of the VENERABLE ENGLISH COLLEGE, Rome* (London: Longmans, Green, 1920).

Gautier Dalché, Patrick, "Principes et modes de la représentation de l'espace géographique durant le haut Moyen Age," in *L'Espace géographique au Moyen Age*, ed. Patrick Gautier Dalché, Micrologus Library 57, 5–30 (Firenze, 2013).

Gautier Dalché, Patrick, "Tradition et renouvellement dans la représentation de l'espace géographique au IXe siècle," in *Géographie et culture: La représentation de l'espace du VIe au XIIe siècle*, ed. Patrick Gautier Dalché, Variorum Collected Studies Series 592, 121–165 (Aldershot: Hambledon, 1997).

German, Gary, "*L'Armes Prydein Vawr* et la "Bataille de Brunanburh": les relations géopolitiques entre Bretons, Anglo-Saxons et Scandinaves dans la Bretagne insulaire au Xe siècle," in *Landévennec, les Vikings et la Bretagne: En hommage à Jean-Christophe Cassard*, ed. Magali Coumert and Yvon Tranvouez, 171–208 (Brest: Université de Bretagne Occidentale/Centre de Recherche Bretonne et Celtique, 2015).

Gillingham, John, "Britain, Ireland, and the South," in *From the Vikings to the Normans*, ed. Wendy Davies, 202–232 (Oxford: Oxford University Press, 2003).

Goldberg, Jonathan, *James I and the Politics of Literature: Jonson, Shakespeare, Donne and Their Contemporaries* (Baltimore: Johns Hopkins University Press, 1983).

Selected Bibliography

Goldstein, R. James, "'I Will My Proces Hald': Making Sense of Scottish Lives and the Desire for History in Barbour, Wyntoun and Blind Hary," in *A Companion to Medieval Scottish Poetry*, ed. Priscilla Bawcutt and Janet Hadley Williams, 35–47 (Cambridge: Cambridge University Press, 2006).

Gransden, Antonia, *Historical Writing in England c. 550–c.1307* (Cornell: Cornell University Press, 1974).

Grey, James, "MacBeth or MacHeth," *Scottish Historical Review* 17 (1920) 338–339.

Grote, David, *Best Actors in the World: Shakespeare and His Acting Company* (Westport: Greenwood Publishing, 2002).

Guðmundsson, Finnbogi, "On the Writing of *Orkneyinga Saga*," in *The Viking Age in Caithness, Orkney and the North Atlantic: Select Papers from the Proceedings of the Eleventh Viking Congress, Thurso and Kirkwall, 22 August–1 September 1989*, ed. Colleen E Batey, Judith Jesch, and Christopher D. Morris, 204–211 (Edinburgh: Edinburgh University Press, 1993).

Halliday, F. E., *A Shakespeare Companion 1564–1964* (New York: Duckworth, rev. 1964).

Halloran, Kevin, "The Brunanburh Campaign: A Reappraisal," *Scottish Historical Review* 84 (2005) 133–148.

Hamilton, Donna B., *Anthony Munday and the Catholics, 1560–1633* (Burlington: Ashgate, 2005).

Hanna, Elizabeth, "'A Mass of Incoherencies,' John Mair, William Caxton, and the Creation of British History in Early Sixteenth-Century Scotland," *Medievalia et Humanistica*, new series 41 (2016) 137–155.

Hanning, Robert, "Inescapable History: Geoffrey of Monmouth's *History of the Kings of Britain* and Arthurian Romances of the Twelfth and Thirteenth Centuries," in Jon Whitman, *Imagining Time from the Medieval to the Early Modern Period*, 55–73 (Cambridge: Cambridge University Press, 2015).

Hansen, Steffen Stumman, "Viking Settlement in Shetland. Chronological and Regional Contexts," *Acta Archaeologica* 71 (2000) 87–103.

Hardinge, Leslie, *The Celtic Church in Britain* (London: SPCK, 1972).

Harikae, Ryoko, "Daunting the Isles, Borders, and Highlands: Imperial Kingship in John Bellenden's Chronicles of Scotland and the Mar Lodge Translation," in *Premodern Scotland: Literature and Governance 1420–1587*, ed. Joanna Martin and Emily Wingfield, 159–170 (Oxford: Oxford University Press, 2017).

Harikae, Ryoko, "Kingship and Imperial Ideas in the *Chronicles*," in *Fresche Fontanis*, ed. Janet Hadley Williams and J. Derrick McClure, 217–229 (Newcastle upon Tyne: Cambridge Scholars, 2013).

Harkel, Letty ten, "The Good, the Bad and the Fearless. De Vikingen en hun vijanden in Oudnoorse en Oudengelse oorlogspoëzie," *Madoc* 18 (2004) 2–10.

Harris, Oliver, "William Camden, Philomen Holland, and the 1610 Translation of *Britannia*," *Antiquaries Journal* 95 (2015) 279–303.

Helgason, Jon, *Eddadigte*, 3 vols. (København: Ejnar Munksgaard, 1962–1965).

Henderson, Isabel, "Understanding the Figurative Style and Decorative Programme of the Book of Deer" in *Studies on the Book of Deer*, ed. K. Forsythe, 32–66 (Dublin: Four Courts Press, 2008).

Henry, F., *Irish Art during the Viking Invasions (800–1020 A.D.)* (London: Methuen, 1973).

Herbert, Máire, *Iona, Kells, and Derry: The History and Hagiography of the Monastic Familia of Columba* (Oxford: Clarendon Press, 1988).

Herbert, Maire, "Sea Divided Gaels," in *Britain and Ireland, 900–1300*, ed. B. Smith (Cambridge: Cambridge University Press, 1999).

Higgitt, John, ed., *Scottish Libraries, with an Introductory Essay by John Durkan*, Corpus of British Medieval Library Catalogues 12 (London: British Library, 2008).

Hindmarch, Erlend, and Richard D. Oram, "Eldbotle: The Archaeology and Environmental History of a Medieval Rural Settlement in East Lothian," *Proceedings of the Society of Antiquaries of Scotland* 142 (2013 for 2012) 245–299.

Hoenselaars, J., *Images of Englishmen and Foreigners in the Drama of Shakespeare and His Contemporaries: A Study of Stage Characters and National Identity in English Renaissance Drama* (Rutherford, NJ: St. Martin's Press, 1992).

Holzknecht, Karl, *Background of Shakespeare's Plays* (New York: American Book, 1950).

Houston, R. A., and W. W. J. Knox, *The New Penguin History of Scotland* (London: Penguin, 2001).

Howlett, D., "Rhygyfarch Ap Sulien and Ieuan Ap Sulien," in *Cambridge History of the Book in Britain*, gen. eds. John Barnard, D. F. McKenzie, David McKitterick, and I. R. Willison, 7 vols., i. 701–706 (Cambridge: Cambridge University Press, 1999–2019).

Hudson, B., "*Auld Inimys*? Favorable Perceptions of the Scots by the English," *Scotia* 33 (2009) 3–11.

Hudson, B., "The Changing Economy of the Irish Sea Province," in *Britain and Ireland 900–1300; Insular Responses to Medieval European Change*, ed. Brendan Smith, 39–66 (Cambridge: Cambridge University Press, 1999).

Hudson, B., "Cnut and the Scottish Kings," *English Historical Review* 107 (1992) 350–360.

Hudson, B., "Duncan I," in *A Reader's Guide to British History*, ed. D. Loades, 408 (London: Bloomsbury, 2003).

Hudson, B., *Familia and Household in the Medieval Atlantic World* (Phoenix: AMRS, 2011).

Hudson, B., "Historical Literature of Early Scotland," *Studies in Scottish Literature* 25 (1992) 141–155.

Hudson, B., *Irish Sea Studies 900–1200* (Dublin: Four Courts Press, 2006).

Hudson, B., *Kings of Celtic Scotland* (Westport: Greenwood, 1994).

Hudson, B., "Kings and Church in Early Scotland," *Scottish Historical Review* 73 (1994) 145–170.

Hudson, B., "Literary Culture of the Early Scottish Court," in *The European Sun*, ed. Graham Caie, Roderick Lyall, Sally Mapstone, and Kenneth Simpson, 156–165 (East Linton: Tuckwell, 2001).

Hudson, B., "Marianus Scotus," in *Encyclopedia of Medieval Ireland*, ed. S. Duffy, 320 (New York: Garland, 2004).

Hudson, B., *The Picts* (Oxford: Wylie Blackwell, 2014).

Hudson, B., "The Practical Hero," in *Ogma*, ed. M. Richter and J. M. Picard, 151–164 (Dublin: Four Courts Press, 2002).

Hudson, B., "Roll of the Kings in *Saltair na Rann*," *Peritia* 31 (2020) 125–146.

Hudson, B., "Schools in Early Scotland," *Scotia* 41 (2019) 1–27.

Hudson, B., "Scottish Gaze," in *History, Literature, and Music in Scotland, 700–1560*, ed. R. A. McDonald, 29–59 (Toronto: University of Toronto Press, 2002).

Hudson, B., "Senchus to Histore: Traditions about King Duncan I," *Studies in Scottish Literature* 25 (1990) 100–120.

Hudson, B., ed., *Studies in the Medieval Atlantic* (New York: Palgrave Macmillan, 2012).

Hudson, B., "Time Is Short," in *Last Things, Death and the Apocalypse in the Middle Ages*, ed. Caroline Walker Bynum and Paul Freedman, 101–123 (Philadelphia: University of Pennsylvania Press, 2000).

Hudson, B., Tracing Medieval Scotland's Lost History," in *Fil súil, A Grey Eye Looks Back, a Festschrift in honour of Colm Ó Baoill*, ed. Sharon Arbuthnot and Kaarina Hollo, 63–72 (Ceann Drochad: Clann Tuirc, 2007).

Hudson, B., *Viking Pirates and Christian Princes* (Oxford: Oxford University Press, 2005).

Hughes, Kathleen, "The Book of Deer (Cambridge University Library MS. Ii.6.32)," in *Celtic Britain in the Early Middle Ages: Studies in Scottish and Welsh Sources by Kathleen Hughes*, ed. David Dumville, Studies in Celtic History 2, 22–37 (Woodbridge/Totowa: Boydell and Brewer, 1980).

Hughes, Kathleen, *Celtic Britain in the Early Middle Ages* (Woodbridge: Boydell and Brewer, 1980).

Hughes, Kathleen, "The Irish Church, 800–c. 1050," in *A New History of Ireland, 1: Prehistoric and Early Ireland*, ed. Dáibhí Ó Cróinín, 635–655 (Oxford: Oxford University Press, 2005).

Humphery-Smith, Cecil, "The Legend of Macbeth," *Family History* 24 (2008) 368–373.

Hunt, Tony, "The *Roman de Fergus*: Parody or Pastiche?" in *The Scots and Medieval Arthurian Legend*, ed. Rhiannon Purdie and Nicola Royan, Arthurian Studies 61, 55–69 (Cambridge: D. S. Brewer, 2005).

Jackson, K. H., *Language and History in Early Britain* (Edinburgh: Edinburgh University Press, 1953).

Jaski, Bart, "King and Household in Early Medieval Ireland," in *Familia and Household in the Medieval Atlantic Province*, ed. B. Hudson, 89–122 (Tempe: ACMRS, 2011).

Johnson, Nora, "Spectacle and the Fantasy of Immateriality: Authorship and Magic in John A Kent and John A Comber," in *Spectacle and Public Performance in the Late Middle Ages and Renaissance*, ed. Robert Stillman, 105–126 (Turnhout: Brepols, 2006).

Johnston, A. W., "MacBeth or MacHeth," *Scottish Historical Review* 18 (1921) 155 and 236

Kapelle, W. E., *Norman Conquest of the North* (Chapel Hill: University of North Carolina Press, 1979).

Kassell, Lauren, "Forman, Simon (1552–1611), Astrologer and Medical Practitioner," *Oxford Dictionary of National Biography*, https://doi-org.ezaccess.libraries.psu.edu/10.1093/ref:odnb/9884.

Keene, Catherine, "The Dunfermline Vita of St. Margaret of Scotland: Hagiography as an Articulation of Hereditary Rights," *Arthuriana* 19 (2009) 43–61.

Keene, Katie, "Margaret of Scotland and Monastic Traditions in the Eleventh Century," *Annual of Medieval Studies at CEU* 14 (2008) 65–80.

Kelleher, John V., "The Pre-Norman Irish Genealogies," *Irish Historical Studies* 16 (1968) 138–153.

Kelly, Fergus, *Early Irish Law* (Dublin: Dublin Institute for Advanced Studies, 1988).

Kennedy, Edward Donald, "The Antiquity of Scottish Civilization: King-lists and Genealogical Chronicles," in *Broken Lines: Genealogical Literature in Medieval Britain and France*, ed. R. L. Radulescu and E. D. Kennedy, 159–174 (Turnhout: Brepols, 2008).

Kenney, James F., *Sources for the Early History of Ireland: Ecclesiastical*, ed. Ludwig Bieler (Dublin: Pádraic Ó Táillúir, 1979).

Kermode, Lloyd, *Aliens and Englishness in Elizabethan Drama* (Cambridge: Cambridge University Press, 2009).

Kewes, Paulina, Ian W. Archer, and Felicity Heal, eds., *The Oxford Handbook of Holinshed's Chronicle* (Oxford: Oxford University Press, 2013).

Kinney, Arthur F., *Lies like Truth. Shakespeare, Macbeth and the Cultural Moment* (Detroit: Wayne State University Press, 2001).

Knight S., "The Borders and Their Ballads," in *Jacobean Poetry and Prose*, ed. C. Bloom, 57–77 (London: Springer, 1988).

Kratzmann, Gregory, *Anglo-Scottish Literary Relations 1430–1550* (Cambridge: Cambridge University Press, 1980).

Kristjánsson, Jónas, "Isländische Handschriften," in *Wikinger, Waräger, Normannen: Die Skandinavier und Europa 800–1200*, ed. Else Roesdahl, Kunstausstellung des Europarates 22, 218–219 (Mainz, 1992).

Kulikowski, Michael, "Barbarians in Gaul, Usurpers in Britain," *Britannia* 31 (2000) 325–345.

Lacey, Brian, *Cenél Conaill and the Donegal Kingdoms* (Dublin: Four Courts, 2006).

Lagorio, Valerie M., "The Evolving Legend of St Joseph of Glastonbury," in *Glastonbury Abbey and the Arthurian Tradition*, ed., James P. Carley, Arthurian Studies 45, 55–81 (Cambridge: Cambridge University Press, 2001).

Lamb, Sally, "Knowledge about the Scandinavian North in Ninth-Century England and Francia," *Quaestio Insularis* 8 (2008 for 2007) 82–93.

Selected Bibliography

Lapidge, Michael, "The Welsh-Latin Poetry of Sulien's Family," *Studia Celtica* 8/9 (1973/4) 68–106.

Lawlor, H. J., and R. I. Best, eds., "The Ancient List of Coarbs of Patrick," *Proceedings of the Royal Irish Academy* 35 C, 316–362 (1918–1920).

Levack, Brian P., *The Formation of the British State: England, Scotland, and the Union, 1603–1707* (Oxford: The Clarendon Press, 1987).

Lockyer, Roger, *The Early Stuarts* (New York: Longman, 1989).

Lyall, R., "Lost Literature of Medieval Scotland," in *Bryght Lanternis*, ed. J. D. McClure and M. R. G. Spiller, 33–47 (Aberdeen: Aberdeen University Press, 1989).

Macbeth, John, *Macbeth: King, Queen and Clan* (Edinburgh: J. W. Hay, 1921).

Macbeth, John, "MacBeth or MacHeth," *Scottish Historical Review* 18 (1921) 153–155.

Mac Cana, Proinsias, *Learned Tales of Medieval Ireland* (Dublin: Dublin Institute for Advanced Studies, 1980).

MacDiarmid, M. P., "Metrical Chronicles and Non-alliterative Romances," in *History of Scottish Literature*, gen. ed. Cairns Craig, 3 vols., i. 27–38 (Aberdeen: Aberdeen University Press, 1988).

Mac Donncha, "Dáta Vita Tripartita Sancti Patricii," *Éigse* 18, no. 1 (1980) 125–142, and *Éigse* 19 no. 2 (1983) 354–372.

MacFarlane, Walter, *Geographical Collections Relating to Scotland Made by Walter Macfarlane*, ed. Sir Arthur Mitchell and James Toshach Clark, Scottish History Society vol. 53 (Edinburgh, 1906).

Macgregor, Martin, "Genealogies of the Clans: Contributions to the Study of MS 1467," *Innes Review* 51 (2000) 131–146.

Maclean, Lorraine, ed., *The Middle Ages in the Highlands* (Inverness: Inverness Field Club, 1981).

MacMillan, Somerled, *Vindication of Macbeth and His Claims* (Ipswich: Private Printing, 1959).

Mac Niocaill, Gearóid, *Medieval Irish Annals*, Medieval Irish History Series, 3 (Dublin, 1975).

Macquarrie, Alan, "The Kings of Strathclyde, c. 400–1018," in *Medieval Scotland: Crown, Lordship and Community: Essays Presented to G.W.S. Barrow*, ed. Alexander Grant and Keith Stringer, 1–19 (Edinburgh: Edinburgh University Press, 1993).

MacQueen, John, "The Literary Sources for the Life of St. Ninian," in *Galloway. Land and Lordship*, ed. Richard D. Oram, and Geoffrey P. Stell, 17–25 (Edinburgh: Edinburgh University Press, 1991).

Maguire, Laura, *Shakespeare Suspect Texts. The "Bad" Quartos and Their Contexts* (Cambridge: Cambridge University Press, 1996).

Marner, Dominic, "The Sword of the Spirit, the Word of God and the Book of Deer," *Medieval Archaeology* 46 (2002) 1–28.

Marsden, John, *Kings, Mormaers, Rebels: Early Scotland's Other Royal Family* (Edinburgh: John Donald, 2010).

Mason, Roger A., "From Chronicle to History. Recovering the Past in Renaissance Scotland," in *Building the Past: Konstruktion der eigenen Vergangenheit*, ed. Rudolf Suntrup and Jan R. Veenstra, Medieval to Early Modern Culture/Kultureller Wandel vom Mittelalter zur Frühen Neuzeit, 7, 53–66 (Frankfurt am Main, 2006).

Mason, Roger A., "Kingship, Tyranny and the Right to Resist in Fifteenth Century Scotland," *Scottish Historical Review* 66 (1987) 125–151.

Mayeski, Marie Anne, "Clothing Maketh the Saint: Ælred's Narrative Intent in the *Life of Saint Ninian*," *Cistercian Studies Quarterly: An International Review of Monastic and Contemplative Spirituality* 44 (2009) 181–190.

MacDonald, A. D. S., "Iona's Style of Government among the Picts and Scots: The Toponymic Evidence of Adomnán's *Life of Columba*," *Peritia* 4 (1987 for 1985) 174–186.

Mac Donncha, Frederic, "Dáta *Vita Tripartita Sancti Patricii*," *Éigse* 18 (1980) 125–142.

Mac Donncha, Frederic, "Dáta *Vita Tripartita Sancti Patricii*," *Éigse* 19 (1983) 354–372.

MacDonald, Alasdair A., "Allegorical (Dream-). Vision Poetry in Medieval and Early Modern Scotland," in *Himmel auf Erden, Heaven on Earth*, Medieval to Early Modern Culture / Kultureller Wandel vom Mittelalter zur Frühen Neuzeit, ed. Rudolf Suntrup and Jan R. Veenstra, 12, 167–176 (Bern: Peter Lang Verlag, 2011).

MacDonald, Alasdair A., "William Stewart and the Court Poetry of the Reign of James V," in *The Stewart Style, 1513–1542: Essays on the Court of James V*, ed. Janet Hadley Williams, 179–200 (East Linton: Tuckwell, 1996).

McDonald, R. A., ed., *History, Literature, and Music in Scotland, 700–1560* (Toronto: University of Toronto, 2002).

McDonald, R. A., *Kingdom of the Isles* (East Linton: Tuckwell, 1997).

McDonald, R. A., "Matrimonial Politics and Core-Periphery Interactions in Twelfth- and Early Thirteenth-Century Scotland," *Journal of Medieval History* 21 (1995) 227–247.

McDonald, R. A., *Outlaws of Medieval Scotland* (East Linton: Tuckwell, 2003).

McDonald, R. A., "Rebels without a Cause? The Relations of Fergus of Galloway and Somerled of Argyll with the Scottish Kings, 1153–1164," in *Alba, Celtic Scotland in the Middle Ages*, ed. E. Cowan and R. A. McDonald, 166–186 (East Linton: Tuckwell, 2000).

McDonald, R. A., "Soldiers Most Unfortunate": Gaelic and Scoto-Norse Opponents of the Canmore Dynasty," in R. Andrew McDonald, ed., *History, Literature, and Music in Scotland, 700–1560* (Toronto: University of Toronto Press, 2002) 93–119.

McDonald, R. A., "Treachery in the Remotest Territories of Scotland:" Northern Resistance to the Canmore Dynasty, 1130–1230," *Canadian Journal of History* 34 (1999) 161–192.

McDonald, R. A., "Wimund (fl. c.1130–c.1150)," *Oxford Dictionary of National Biography*, https://www-oxforddnb-com.ezaccess.libraries.psu.edu/view/10.1093/ref:odnb/9780198614128.001.0001/odnb-9780198614128-e-50011.

Selected Bibliography 279

McGavin, John J., "Faith, Pastime, Performance and Drama in Scotland to 1603," in *The Cambridge History of British Theatre: Origins to 1660*, ed. Jane Milling and Peter Thomson, 70–86 (Cambridge: Cambridge University Press, 2004).

MacGregor, Martin, "Genealogies of the Clans: Contributions to the Study of MS 1467," *Innes Review* 51 (2000) 131–146.

McIlwain, C. H., ed., *Political Works of James I* (Cambridge, MA: Harvard University Press, 1918).

McMullan, Gordon, "Fletcher, John (1579–1625)," in *Oxford Dictionary of National Biography*, http://www.oxforddnb.com/view/article/9730.

McNamara, Martin, "Psalter Text and Psalter Study in the Early Irish Church (A.D. 600–1200)," *Proceedings of the Royal Irish Academy* 71 C (1973) 201–298.

McSparron, Cormac, and Brian Williams, "'And They Won Land among the Picts by Friendly Treaty or the Sword': How a Re-Examination of Early Historical Sources and an Analysis of Early Medieval Settlement in North Co. Antrim Confirms the Validity of Traditional Accounts of Dál Riatic Migration to Scotland from Ulster," *Proceedings of the Society of Antiquaries of Scotland* 141 (2011) 145–158.

Meehan, Bernard, "The Siege of Durham, the Battle of Carham and the Cession of Lothian," *Scottish Historical Review* 55 (1976) 1–19.

Mikhailova, Tatiana, and Natalia Nikolaeva, "The Denotations of Death in Goidelic: To the Question of Celtic Eschatological Conceptions," *Zeitschrift für celtische Philologie* 53 (2003) 93–115.

Mill, Anna Jean, *Mediaeval Plays in Scotland* (New York/London: B. Blom, repr. 1969).

Milne, John, *Celtic Place-names in Aberdeenshire: With a Vocabulary of Gaelic Words Not in Dictionaries; the Meaning and Etymology of the Gaelic Names of Places in Aberdeenshire; Written for the Committee of the Carnegie Trust* (Aberdeen: Aberdeen University Press, 1912).

Moisl, Hermann, and Stefanie Hamann, "A Frankish Aristocrat at the Battle of Mag Roth," in *Ogma: Essays in Celtic Studies in Honour of Próinséas Ní Chatháin*, ed. Michael Richter and Jean-Michel Picard, 36–47 (Dublin: Four Courts Press, 2002).

Morrison, Ian A., "*Orkneyinga saga*, Jarlshof and Viking sea routes," *Northern Studies* 2 (1973) 22–26.

Muir, Kenneth, "Macbeth," in *Shakespeare's Sources*, vol. 1, *Comedies and Tragedies*, 167–186 (London: Methuen, 1957).

Murray, Kevin, "'Ticfa didiu rí aili foræ': Prophecy, Sovereignty Narratives and Medieval Irish Historiography," in *The Medieval Imagination: Mirabile dictu. Essays in Honour of Yolande de Pontfarcy Sexton*, ed. Phyllis Gaffney and Jean-Michel Picard, 111–122 (Dublin: Four Courts Press, 2012).

Murray, Kylie, "Dream and Vision in Late-Medieval Scotland: The Epic Case of William Wallace," *Proceedings of the Harvard Celtic Colloquium* 29 (2009) 177–198.

Nelson, Alan H., "George Buc, William Shakespeare, and the Folger George a Greene," *Shakespeare Quarterly* 49 (1998) 74–83.

Newton, Norman S., "Excavations at the Peel of Lumphanan, Aberdeenshire 1975–9," *Proceedings of the Society of Antiquaries of Scotland* 128 (1998) 653–670.

Nicolaisen, W. F. H., *Scottish Place-Names* (London: B. T. Batsford, 1976).

Nicoll, Josephine, and Allardyce Nicoll, *Holinshed's Chronicle as Used in Shakespeare's Plays* (London; J. M. Dent, 1943).

Ní Dhonnchadha, Máirín, "The Law of Adomnán: A Translation," in *Adomnán at Birr, AD 697: Essays in Commemoration of the Law of the Innocent*, ed. Thomas O'Loughlin, 53–68 (Dublin: Four Courts Press, 2001).

Nieke, Margaret R., and Holly B. Duncan, "Dalriada: The Establishment and Maintenance of an Early Historic Kingdom in Northern Britain," in *Power and Politics in Early Medieval Britain and Ireland*, ed. Stephen T. Driscoll, and Margaret R. Nieke, 6–21 (Edinburgh: Edinburgh University Press, 1988).

Nieuwenhuijsen, Kees, "De Komeet uit het jaar 1018," *Terra Nigra* 188 (2015) 37–41

Ní Mhaonaigh, Máire, "Friend and Foe: Vikings in Ninth- and Tenth-Century Irish Literature," in *Ireland and Scandinavia in the Early Viking Age*, ed. Howard Clarke, Máire Ní Mhaonaigh, and Raghnall Ó Floinn, 381–402 (Dublin, Four Courts Press, 1998).

Norbrook, David, "Macbeth and the Politics of Historiography," in *Politics of Discourse. The Literature and History of Seventeenth-Century England*, ed. Kevin Sharpe and Steven N. Zwicker, 78–116 (Berkeley: University of California Press, 1987).

Ó Cathasaigh, Tomás, "The Rhetoric of *Scéla Cano meic Gartnáin*," in *Sages, Saints and Storytellers*, ed. D. Ó Corráin, L. Breatnach, and K. McCone, 233–250 (Maynooth: An Sagart, 1989).

Ó Cathasaigh, Tomás, "The Theme of *ainmne* in *Scéla Cano meic Gartnáin*," *Celtica* 15 (1983) 78–87.

Ó Corráin, Donnchadh. "Creating the Past: The Early Irish Genealogical Tradition," *Peritia* 12 (1998) 177–208.

Ó Cróinín, Dáibhí, *Early Medieval Ireland* (New York: Longman, 2nd ed. 2016).

Ó Cróinín, Dáibhí, "Ireland, 400–800,"in *A New History of Ireland, 1: Prehistoric and Early Ireland*, ed. Dáibhí Ó Cróinín, 182–234 (Oxford: Oxford University Press, 2005).

Ó Cróinín, Dáibhí, "Who Was Palladius, 'First Bishop of the Irish'?," *Peritia* 14 (2000) 205–237.

Ó Cuív, Brian, *Catalogue of Irish Language Manuscripts in the Bodleian Library at Oxford and Oxford College Libraries*, 2 vols. (Oxford: Oxford University Press, 2001).

O'Dwyer, Peter, *The Céli Dé: Spiritual Reform in Ireland, 750–900* (Dublin: Editions Tailliura, 1981).

O'Loughlin, Thomas, "The Library of Iona at the Time of Adomnán," *The Cambridge History of the Book in Britain*, ed. Richard Gameson, i. 570–79 (Cambridge: Cambridge University Press, 2011).

Ó Maille, Tómas, *The Language of the Annals of Ulster* (Manchester: Manchester University Press, 1910).

Ó Maolalaigh, Roibeard, "The Property Records: Diplomatic Edition including Accents," in *Studies on the Book of Deer*, ed. Katherine Forsyth, 119–130 (Dublin: Four Courts Press, 2008).

Ó Muraíle, Nollaig, "The Irish Genealogies as an Onomastic Source," *Nomina* 16 (1992 for 1992) 23–46.

Ó Muraíle, Nollaig, "Irish Genealogical Collections: The Scottish Dimension," in *Celtic Connections: Proceedings of the 10th International Congress of Celtic Studies*, vol. 1, *Language, Literature, History, Culture*, ed. Ronald Black, William Gillies, and Roibeard Ó Maolalaigh, 251–264 (East Linton: Tuckwell, 1999).

O' Neill, Pamela, "The Political and Ecclesiastical Context of Scottish Dalriada," *Journal of the Australian Early Medieval Association* 1 (2005) 119–132.

Oram, Richard D., "David I and the Scottish Conquest and Colonisation of Moray," *Northern Scotland* 19 (1999) 1–19.

Oram, Richard D., "Fergus, Galloway and the Scots," in *Galloway. Land and Lordship*, ed. Richard D. Oram, and Geoffrey P. Stell, 117–130 (Edinburgh: Edinburgh University Press, 1991).

Owen, D. R. R., "Guillaume le Clerc: The Romance of Fergus," *Arthurian Literature* VIII (1989) 79–183.

Oxford Dictionary of National Biography, ed. H. C. G. Matthew and Brian Harrison (Oxford, 2004), online edition, ed. David Cannadine (Oxford: Oxford University Press, 2006).

Paul, Henry Neill, *The Royal Play of Macbeth: When, Why, and How It Was Written by Shakespeare* (New York: Macmillan, 1950).

Peck, Linda L., ed., *The Mental World of the Jacobean Court* (Cambridge: Cambridge University Press, 1991).

Pinkerton, John, *An Inquiry into the History of Scotland Preceding the Year 1056*, 2 vols. (London: John Nichols, 1789).

Porter, James, "From Solo Bard to Runrig: The Entertainer in the Scots Gaelic World, Medieval and Modern," in *The Entertainer in Medieval and Traditional Culture: A Symposium*, ed. Flemming G. Andersen, Thomas Pettitt, and Reinhold Schröder, 133–148 (Odense: Odense University, 1997).

Prideaux-Collins, William, "'Satan's Bonds Are Extremely Loose': Apocalyptic Expectation in Anglo-Saxon England during the Millennial Era," in *The Apocalyptic Year 1000: Religious Expectation and Social Change, 950–1050*, ed. Richard Landes, Andrew Gow, and David C. Van Meter, 289–310 (Oxford: Oxford University Press, 2003).

Purdie, Rhiannon, "Malcolm, Margaret, Macbeth, and the Miller: Rhetoric and the Re-Shaping of History in Wyntoun's *Original Chronicle*," *Medievalia et Humanistic*, new series 41 (2016) 45–63.

Rees, Alwyn, and Brinley Rees, *Celtic Heritage. Ancient Tradition in Ireland and Wales* (London: Thames and Hudson, 1961).

Rekdal, Jan Erik, "*Betha Coluimb Chille*: The Life as a Shrine," in *Saltair Saíochta, Sanasaíochta agus Seanchais: A Festschrift for Gearoíd Mac Eoin*, ed. Dónall Ó Baoill, Donncha Ó hAodha, and Nollaig Ó Muraíle, 407–414 (Dublin: Four Courts Press, 2013).

Rennie, Elizabeth B., "A Possible Boundary between Dal Riata and Pictland," *Pictish Arts Society Journal* 10 (1996) 17–22.

Rickard, P., *Britain in Medieval French Literature 1100–1500* (Cambridge: Cambridge University Press, 1956).

Ritchie, R. L. Graeme, *The Normans in Scotland* (Edinburgh: Edinburgh University Press, 1954).

Roberts, J. *Lost Kingdoms: Celtic Scotland and the Middle Ages* (Edinburgh: Edinburgh University Press, 1997).

Roberts, Peter, "Business of Playing and Patronage of Players," in *James VI and I: Ideas, Authority, and Government*, ed. Ralph Houlbrooke, 81–105 (Aldershot: Hambledon, 2006).

Robertson, E. W., *Scotland under Her Early Kings*, 2 vols. (Edinburgh: Edmonston and Douglas, 1862).

Rollason, David, and Lynda Rollason, eds., *Durham Liber vitae: London, British Library, MS Cotton Domitian A.VII: edition and digital facsimile with introduction, codicological, prosopographical and linguistic commentary, and indexes including the Biographical Register of Durham Cathedral Priory (1083–1539) by A. J. Piper*, 3 vols, (London: British Library, 2007).

Salmon, Pierre, "La composition d'un libellus precum a l'epoque de la reform gregorienne," *Benedictina* 26 (1979) 285–322.

Sams, Eric, *Shakespeare's Edward III: An Early Play Restored to the Canon* (New Haven: Yale University Press, 1996).

Samson, Ross, "The Reinterpretation of the Pictish Symbols," *Journal of the British Archaeological Association* 145 (1992) 29–65.

Scharf, Ralf, "Die Kanzleireform des Stilichs und das römische Britannien," *Historia* 39 (1990) 461–474.

Scott, J. G., "The Partition of a Kingdom: Strathclyde 1092–1153," *Transactions of the Dumfriesshire and Galloway Natural History and Antiquarian Society* 72 (1997) 11–40.

Scott, Sir Lindsay, "The Norse in the Hebrides," in *The Viking Congress–Lerwick,* ed. W. D. Simpson (Edinburgh: Edinburgh University Press, 1954).

Sellar, W. D. H., "Marriage, Divorce and Concubinage in Gaelic Scotland, in *Transactions of the Gaelic Society of Inverness* 52 (1978–80) 464–493.

Shapiro, Michael, *The Children of the Revels: The Boy Companies of Shakespeare's Time and Their Plays* (New York: Columbia University Press, 1977).

Sharpe, Richard, "The Thriving of Dalriada," in *Kings, Clerics and Chronicles in Scotland, 500–1297: Essays in Honour of Marjorie Ogilvie Anderson on the Occasion of Her Ninetieth Birthday*, ed. Simon Taylor, 47–61 (Dublin: Four Courts Press, 2000).

Selected Bibliography

Sheehan, Sarah, "Giants, Boar-Hunts, and Barbering: Masculinity in *Culhwch ac Olwen*," *Arthuriana* 15 (2005) 3–25.

Shepherd, Ian A. G., "The Picts in Moray," in *Moray: Province and People*, ed. W. D. H. Sellar, 75–90 (Edinburgh: Scottish Society for Northern Studies, 1993).

Simpson, G. G., ed., *Scotland and Scandinavia 800–1800* (Edinburgh: John Donald, 1989).

Skene, William Forbes, *Celtic Scotland, An History of Ancient Alba*, 3 vols. (Edinburgh: Edmonston and Douglad, 2nd ed., 1886–90).

Skene, William Forbes, "The Coronation Stone," *Proceedings of the Society of Antiquaries of Scotland* 8 (1869) 68–99.

Smallwood, T. M., "The Prophecy of the Six Kings," *Speculum* 60 (1985) 571–592.

Smith, A. H., *The Place-Names of the East Riding of Yorkshire and York*, English Place-Name Society 14 (repr. 1970).

Stancliffe, Clare, "Christianity amongst the Britons, Dalriadan Irish and Picts," in *The New Cambridge Medieval History*, ed. Paul Fouracre, i. 426–61 (Cambridge: Cambridge University Press, 2005).

Stringer, Keith J., "Acts of Lordship: The Records of the Lords of Galloway to 1234," in *Freedom and Authority: Scotland c. 1050–c. 1650. Historical and Historiographical Essays Presented to Grant G. Simpson*, ed. Terry Brotherstone and David Ditchburn, 203–234 (East Linton: Tuckwell, 2000).

Stringer, Keith J., "Reform Monasticism and Celtic Scotland: Galloway, c. 1140–c. 1240," in *Alba: Celtic Scotland in the Middle Ages*, ed. Edward J. Cowan and R. Andrew McDonald, 127–165 (East Linton: Tuckwell, 2000).

Strong, Roy, *Tudor and Stuart Monarchy, Pageantry, Painting, Iconography*, 3 vols. (Woodbridge: Boydell and Brewer, 1995–1997).

Sykes, H. Dugdale, "Robert Greene and *George A Greene, the Pinner of Wakefield*," *English Studies* 7 (1931) 129–136.

Tanaka, Miho, "Iona and the Kingship of Dál Riata in Adomnán's *Vita Columbae*," *Peritia* 17–18 (2004 for 2004) 199–214.

Tannenbaum, Samuel A., *Shakespearian Scraps and Other Elizabethan Fragments* (New York: Columbia University Press, 1933).

Tatlock, J. S. P., *The Legendary History of Britain* (Berkeley: University of California Press, 1950).

Taylor, A., "Karl Hundason, King of Scots," *Proceedings of the Society of Antiquaries of Scotland* 71 (1936–1937) 334–340.

Taylor, Gary, "Middleton, Thomas (bap. 1580, d. 1627), playwright," *Oxford Dictionary of National Biography*, https://doi-org.ezaccess.libraries.psu.edu/10.1093/ref:odnb/18682.

Taylor, Rupert, *The Political Prophecy in England* (New York: Columbia University Press, 1911).

Taylor, S., and G. Márkus, *The Place-Names of Fife*, 5 vols. (Donington: Shaun Tyas, 2006–2012).

Selected Bibliography

Terry, C. Sanford, "MacBeth or MacHeth," *Scottish Historical Review* 17 (1920) 155 and 338.

Thomas, Charles, *Early Christian Archaeology of North Britain* (Oxford: Clarendon Press, 1971).

Thomas, Charles, "The Pictish Class I Symbol Stones," *British Archaeological Reports. British Series* 125 (1984) 169–187.

Thomas, David, *Shakespeare in the Public Records*, text and selection of documents by David Thomas; section on the will and signatures by Jane Cox; photographs by John Millen (London: HMSO, 1985).

Thrupp, Sylvia, "Aliens in and around London in the Fifteenth Century," *Speculum* 32 (1957) 251–272

Thrupp, Sylvia, "A Survey of the Alien Population of England in 1440," in *Studies in London History Presented to Philip Edmund Jones*, ed. A. E. J. Hollaender and William Kellaway, 262–273 (London: Hodder and Stoughton, 1969).

Tristam, Hildegard L. C., "Mac Bethad mac Fin mic Laig XVI(I). annis regnavit," in *Mündlichkeit, Schriftlichkeit, Weltbildwandel: literarische Kommunikation und Deutungsschemata von Wirklichkeir in der Literatur des Mittelalters* (Tübingen: Narr Francke Attempto, 1966) 196–222.

Tyler, Elizabeth M., "Crossing Conquests: Polyglot Royal Women and Literary Culture in Eleventh-Century England," in *Conceptualizing Multilingualism in England, c. 800–c. 1250*, ed., Elizabeth M. Tyler, Studies in the Early Middle Ages 27, 171–196 (Turnhout: Brepols, 2011).

Van Rij, Hans, and Anna Sapir Abulafia, *Alpertus van Metz: gebeurtenissen van deze tijd; een fragment over bisschop Diederik I van Metz; De mirakelen van de heilige Walburg in Tiel* (Nederlands: Middeleeuwse Studies en Bronnen, 1999).

Wadden, Patrick, "Dál Riata c. 1000: Genealogies and Irish Sea Politics," *Scottish Historical Review* 95 (2016) 164–181.

Wallace-Hadrill, J. Michael, *The Vikings in Francia: The Stenton Lecture 1974* (Reading: University of Reading, 1975).

Watkin, Aelred, "The Glastonbury Legends," in *Arthurian Literature* 15 (1997) 77–91.

Watson, W. J., *The History of the Celtic Place-names of Scotland* (Edinburgh: William Blackwood & Sons Ltd, 1926).

Webster, Bruce, "John of Fordun and the Independent Identity of the Scots," in *Medieval Europeans: Studies in Ethnic Identity and National Perspectives in Medieval Europe*, ed. Alfred P. Smyth, 85–102 (Basingstoke: Palgrave Macmillan, 1998).

Wiles, David, *Shakespeare's Clown; Actor and Text in the Elizabethan Playhouse* (Cambridge: Cambridge University Press, 2005).

Wilmart, A., "La Trinité des Scots à Rome et les notes du Vat. Lat. 378," in *Revue bénédictine* 41 (1929) 218–230.

Wilson, C. Anne, *Food and Drink in Britain* (Harmondsworth: Penguin, 1976).

Wilson, Dover H., *King James VI and I* (New York: Oxford University Press, 1958).

Wingfield, Emily, "'Qwhen Alexander Our Kynge Was Dede': Kingship and Good Governance in Andrew of Wyntoun's *Original Chronicle*," in *Premodern Scotland: Literature and Governance 1420–1587. Essays for Sally Mapstone*, ed. Joanna Martin, and Emily Wingfield, 19–30 (Oxford: Oxford University Press, 2017).

Wood, Juliette, "Where Does Britain End? The Reception of Geoffrey of Monmouth in Scotland and Wales," in *The Scots and Medieval Arthurian Legend*, ed. Rhiannon Purdie and Nicola Royan, Arthurian Studies 61, 9–23 (Cambridge: Brewer, 2005).

Wooding, Jonathan M., "Cargoes in Trade along the Western Seaboard," in *External Contacts and the Economy of Late Roman and Post-Roman Britain*, ed. Kenneth R. Dark, 67–82 (Woodbridge: Boydell and Brewer, 1996).

Woolf, Alex, *From Pictavia to Alba* (Edinburgh: Edinburgh University Press, 2009).

Woolf, Alex, "Geoffrey of Monmouth and the Picts," in *Bile ós Chrannaibh: A Festschrift for William Gillies*, ed. Wilson McLeod, Abigail Burnyeat, Domhnall Uilleam Stiubhart, Thomas Owen Clancy, and Roibeard Ó Maolalaigh, 439–450 (Ceann Drochaid: Clann Tuirc, 2010).

Woolf, Alex, "Macbeth," in *The Oxford Companion to Scottish History*, ed. Michael Lynch (Oxford: Oxford University Press, 2001).

Woolf, Alex, "The 'Moray Question' and the Kingship of Alba in the Tenth and Eleventh Centuries," *Scottish Historical Review* 79 (1998) 145–168.

Wormald, Patrick, "Anglo-Saxon Law and Scots Law," *Scottish Historical Review* 88 (2009) 192–206.

Index

For the benefit of digital users, indexed terms that span two pages (e.g., 52–53) may, on occasion, appear on only one of those pages.

Aberdeen, 4–6, 35–37, 98–113, 116–17, 122, 145, 146, 152–53, 154, 156, 162, 163, 207–8, 209–10

Abernethy, church, round tower, 66–67, 89

Abthane, 117–18

Adomnán, head of church of Iona, 11–12, 22–23, 63–64, 135–36

Áedán son of Gabrán, king of Dál Riata, 19–21, 22, 30–31, 65, 76.

AEthelstan son of Edward the Elder, king of the English, 11, 12, 30

Affrica, daughter of Fergus of Galloway, 102–3

Andrew of Wyntoun, 54–55, 73, 120, 124–25, 126, 127–28, 129–30, 134, 135, 142, 144, 147–50, 152, 153–55, 207, 209–10, 219.

Angus son of Fergus, king of Fortriu, 28

Anne of Denmark, queen of Scots, 190–91

Anthony Munday, 178, 191

Antonine Wall 11, 12

Arnórr jarlaskáld Þórðarson, Arnórr "Jarls' Poet," 49–50, 56–57.

Balliol, Edward, 111

Banais, 18, 170–71,

Banquo, 2, 8–9, 147–48, 150, 151–53, 156–57, 158, 160–61, 162–63, 167–68, 169, 175, 201–2, 209–10

Barbour, John, *The Bruce*, 8, 110, 122, 136–37, 152, 203–4, 207–8

Bede, 11, 19, 37–38

Bellenden, John, 155–56, 157–59, 209–10

Berach, saint, 19–20, 65.

Berchán, saint, 23

Bethoc, 41, 53, 105, 147–48

Birnam Wood, 10, 124, 128, 130, 140, 148, 168–69, 187, 209, 228

Black, Henry, 202

Boats, 20, 92–93, 225

Buite/Boite/Bode son of Buite/Bode's son, 52–53, 74*f*

Buite/Boite/Bode son of Kenneth III, 52–53, 74*f*

Bolgyn son of Thorfinn, land of, 70–71, 130–31, 214

Book of Deer, 6–8, 37–38, 45–46, 47, 60–61, 62–63, 81, 89, 98, 214, 215

Border Ballads, 176–77

Brechin, round tower, 66–67

Bruce, Edward, 110–11, 117

Bruce, Marjorie, 111–12

Buchanan, George, 5–6, 154–55, 158–62, 163–64

288   *Index*

Butter. Joanne, 190–91

Camden, William, 174–75
Catroe, saint, 23–24, 60–61, 69
Cecil, Robert, 1st Earl of Salisbury, 190–92
Cecil, William, 1st Baron Burghley, 152–53, 166
Cenél Loairn, 17–19, 21–24, 28–29, 30–31, 32–33, 35, 47–48, 50, 80, 83–84, 89, 97, 102, 122
Cenél nGabráin, 17–18, 19, 22–23, 28–29, 30–31, 41–42, 80
Chambers, David, also known as David Chalmers, of Ormond, 107, 163
Chettle, Henry, 182, 184, 187
Children of the Chapel Royal, 180–81, 193
Children of the Queen's Revels, 193
Churchyard, Thomas, 180
Climate change, 24–25, 59–60, 105
Clontarf, battle of, 33, 40–41, 44, 139, 141
Cnut, king of the English and Danes, 10, 39–40, 41, 43, 48–50, 51, 55, 56–57, 67, 76–77, 108, 167–68
Cock of the North, prophecy, 171
Collier, John Payne, 198–99, 202–3
Columba, head of church of Iona, 11–12, 21–23, 27, 30–31, 37–38, 55–56, 89, 135–36
Coming of Dál Riata into Britain, 16
Coming of the Picts from Thrace to Ireland, 16
Complaynt of Scotland, 133
Constantine II son of Aed, Causantín mac Áeda, king of Scots, 18, 30, 105
Constantine Macduff, *mórmáer* Fife, 114
Constantine son of Dungal, Causantín mac Dúngal, king of Scots, 24f, 29–30, 122
Constantine son of Fergus, king of Fortriu, 28
Constantine son of Kenneth, Causantín mac Cináeda, king of Scots, 29

Copland, William, 176
Cormac son of Airt, Irish king, 105, 138–39
Cormac son of Macbeth, 214–15, 216
Creede, Thomas, 197–98
Crinán, 10, 18

Dál Riata, kingdom of, 6, 13–19, 23, 24–25, 27, 28, 29, 32, 65, 76, 89, 106, 149–50
David I son of Malcolm Canmore, king of the Scots, 85–86, 97, 102–3, 108, 112, 118–19, 149–50, 215, 216
David II son of Robert I, king of the Scots, 111–12, 119, 122, 134, 186
David II, son of Robert I, king of Scots, 111–12, 119, 122, 134, 186
Dekker, Thomas, 178, 182, 187
Diarmait mac Máel na mBó, 75–76, 77
Dícuil, 25
Doada, 41, 147–48, 149
Donald I son of Alpin, Domnaill mac Alpin, king of Scots, 149–50
Donald son of Constantine, Domnall mac Causantín, king of Scots, 30
Donne, John, 172, 173
Dunadd, 18
Duald Mac Firbis, 23
Dunbar, William, 176
Duncan, king of Scots, 4, 5, 9, 10, 20–21, 39f, 41, 53, 54–56, 58, 64–65, 70, 76, 83, 84, 86, 89, 90–91, 96, 105, 106–7, 108, 113, 115, 118, 119–20, 126, 129–30, 147–48, 149, 153–54, 155, 156–57, 158, 160, 161, 162–63, 167–68, 206–7, 229.
Dundee, 119, 145,
Dunkeld Litany, 29, 66,
Dunnottar Castle, 30, 31, 79–80, 103–4
Dunollie, 19
Dunsinane, 10, 127–28, 130, 140, 148, 150, 160–61, 168–69, 201–2, 222, 223, 224, 228, 229

Index

289

Eastward Ho, 193–94

Echmarcach, 48–50.

Edinburgh Psalter, 61

Edinburgh, 12–13, 31, 43, 44–45, 61, 94, 95–96, 120, 157–58, 169–71, 191–92, 203–4

Edward I, play, 181–82, 185–86

Edward I, son of Henry III, king of the English, 71–72, 83, 101, 107–9, 110, 117–18, 174, 207–8

Edward II, son of Edward I, king of the English, 55–56, 107, 110, 136–37

Edward III, son of Edward II, king of the English, 111

Edward son of AEthelraed, Edward "the Confessor", king of the English, 4, 10, 44–45, 66, 76–78, 85, 116, 160–61, 168–69, 205–6, 222

Einar son of Rögnvald, "Turf" Einar, jarl of the Orkneys, 27–28, 30, 32–33

Eithne, mother of Jarl Thorfinn of the Orkneys, 32–33, 39–40

Elizabeth I, queen of England, 191

Eochaid son of Rhun, king of Scots, 122

Essie, 84, 105

Fantasy Women, 138–40

fer léighinn, 60–61

Fergus of Galloway, 102–4, 122–23

Fergus of Galloway, Romance of, 102–4

Finlay son of Rory, Findláech mac Rhuidrí, king of Scots, 6–7, 39–41, 43, 44, 46, 52, 56–57, 58, 64–65, 70, 89, 105

Fleance, 148, 151–53, 156–57, 168, 201

Forman, Simon, 198, 201–4

Fortriu, 13, 23, 28, 58

Froissart, Jean, 116–17, 173

Gawdy, Philip, 172

George a Greene, 182, 185

Giric son of Dungal, Giric mac Dúngal, king of Scots, 122

Godfrey Haraldsson, lord of the Isles, 32

Godfrey Hardacnutsson, Guðrøðr Uí Imhar, king of York–Dublin, 30

Greene, Robert, 179–80, 182, 183–84, 185

Gruffudd ap Llwywellyn, 152–53

Gruoch/Lady Macbeth, 7–8, 10, 39f, 52–53, 54, 57, 69–70, 71–72, 73–75, 80, 99, 124–26, 130, 142, 144–45, 147–48, 156–57, 187, 201–2, 213–16, 220,

Hadrian's Wall, 11, 12, 36–37, 85–86

Hardacnut son of Cnut, king of the English and Danes, 51

Harrison, William, 165–66

Henry II, king of the English, 91–92, 95, 98–99, 102–3, 107–8

Henry son of David I, earl of Huntingdon, 44–45, 108

Henry VIII, king of England, 133, 145, 156, 166, 171, 173, 175–76, 177

Henry, Lord Darnley, 175–76, 180, 181–82

Henry, son of King James VI & I, 190–91

Henryson, Robert, 176

Henslowe, Philip, 187, 199–200

History of Norway, 25–27

History of the Men of Britain, 18–19, 20

Holinshed, Raphael, 157–59, 165–66, 167, 174–75, 182, 209–10

Holinshed's Chronicles of England, Ireland, and Scotland, 157, 165, 166, 167, 169, 171, 172, 173, 174–75, 177, 188–89, 190–91, 195, 197–98, 200–1, 203

Holland, Richard, 176

Honourable Company of the Stationers of London, 165, 173, 179, 182, 185, 188, 190–91, 197–98, 199, 210

Index

Hooker, John, 166–67
Hunnis, William, 180–82

Idulb son of Constantine, Idulb mac Causantín, king of Scots, 30, 31, 43
Ieun, son of Suilen, 60–61
Immigration, 174, 175–76
Ingibjorg daughter of Finn, wife of Malcolm Canmore, 86, 90–91
Inverness, 11–12, 22, 36–37, 153–54, 158, 160
Iona, 21–24, 27, 32, 106, 135–36, 146

James I of Scotland, 165, 168, 169–70
James IV of Scotland, 132–33, 140, 142, 145, 155–56, 176
James IV, Scottish Historie of King James the fourth, 181–84, 187, 188–89, 197–98
James V, king of Scots, 8–9, 133, 146, 155–56, 157–58
James VI of Scotland and James I of England, 1, 135, 146, 156, 166, 170–72, 177, 187, 193
Jarlshof, 25–27
John à Kent and John à Cumber, 178–79, 180
John Balliol, king of Scots, 81, 107, 109, 185–86, 188
John Major or Maer, 149, 155–56, 159, 174
John of Fordun, 4–5, 8, 16–17, 55, 58–59, 63, 74–75, 76–77, 105–20, 122–23, 124, 128–30, 132, 142, 144, 147–48, 154–55, 157, 196–97, 200, 207, 208–9.
Jonson, Ben, 174–75, 184, 193, 194
Joseph of Dál Riata, head of church of Armagh, 13–14

Kemp, Will, 9, 172, 173, 184, 195–98, 210–12

Kenneth I son of Alpin, Cináed mac Alpin, king of Scots, 28–29, 63–64, 66, 89, 104, 106, 122,
Kenneth II son of Malcolm I, Cináed mac Máel Coluim, 30–31
Kenneth III son of Dub, Cináed mac Duib, king of Scots, 42, 54, 74–75, 114
Kings Quair, 169–70

Lady Macbeth *see* Gruoch
Learned Tales: "The Coming of Dál Riata into Britain," 16–17
"The Coming of the Picts from Thrace to Ireland and their coming from Ireland to Britain," 16
Leges inter Scotos et Brittos, 214
Leslie, John, 5–6, 154–55, 158–59, 162–63
Life of St. Columbkill, 22–23
Lindsey, Sir William, 176
Lochquhaber , 147–48, 152, 167, 175
Lulach, king of Scots, 7, 38, 39f, 52–53, 64–65, 74–75, 74f, 80, 83–85, 89, 90, 99–100, 104, 105, 106, 115, 148, 213, 214, 216–17
Lumphanan, 35–38, 45, 62–63, 79–80, 105, 106, 114, 115–17, 128, 130, 148, 163, 168–69, 229

Macbeth, historical person: ancestry, 23–24, 24f, 35–38, 39f, 39, 41
name, 44–45
early career, 47–48, 51–53, 55–57
relations with Cnut, 47–49
relations with Thorfinn of the Orkneys, 49–51
reign, 58–59, 64–65, 67–68, 78–80
grants, 70–71, 76–77
Macbeth, in literature: king lists, 89, 104–5, 106, 108
in chronicle of John of Fordun, 113, 115
in chronicle of Walter Bower, 120

Index 291

in chronicle of Andrew of Wyntoun,
124, 125–27, 128, 129–30, 142
in history of Hector Boece, 147–48
in writings of George
Buchanan, 160–61
in writings of John Leslie, 162–63
in Holinshed's chronicles, 167–69
in Kemp's "Nine Days Wonder," 196–98
in *Malcolm Kynge of Scottes*, 200
in Warner's *Albion's England*, 200–1
legend used by Shakespeare, 3, 4, 200–
1, 203
Macduff, 76–77, 109, 113–15, 117–18, 120,
124, 127–28, 142, 148, 150, 155, 160–
61, 162–63, 168–69, 201–2, 208–9,
222, 223, 225, 226, 227, 228
Macduff, Lady, 124, 127, 142
Macduff's Law, 129, 175
Máel Doun son of Macbeth, 114,
214, 215–16
Magnus Haraldsson, lord of the Isles, 32
Magnús III Óláfsson, Magnus "Barefoot,"
king of the Norse, 100
Magnús Óláfsson, Magnus "the Good,"
king of the Norse, 51
Malcolm I son of Donald, Máel
Coluim mac Domnaill, king of
Scots, 30–31
Malcolm II son of Kenneth II, king of
Scots, 35, 41–43, 47, 48, 49–50, 53–
54, 64–65, 73–74
Malcolm III son of Duncan, Malcolm
Canmore, Máel Coluim mac
Donnchada, king of Scots, 10, 12–13,
30–31, 54–55, 58–59, 70, 72, 76–77,
78–81, 83–88, 89, 90–93, 96–97
Malcolm IV son of Henry, king of Scots,
44–45, 98–99
Malcolm IV, Malcolm "the Maiden," king
of Scots, 44–45, 98–99, 102–3
Malcolm son of Donald, Máel Coluim
mac Domnaill, king of Scots, 30–31

Malcolm son of Máel Brigte, king of Scots,
32–33, 38, 39*f*, 40–41, 47–48, 50–51
Malcolm Kynge of Scottes, 199–200
Margaret daughter of Edward the
AEtheling, St. Margaret, queen of
Scots, 7–8, 72, 86
Margaret Tudor, 155–56, 157–58, 170–
71, 175–76
Mary "Queen of Scots," 133, 180
Massey, Charles, 199–200
Millington, Thomas, 197–98
Minstrels/Musicians/Performers, 134,
137, 207
Monmouth, Geoffry of, *History of the
Kings of Britain*, 92, 94, 108, 136,
141, 144, 207,
*Mr. William Shakespeare's Comedies,
Histories, & Tragedies, First
Folio*, 3–4

Nennius, 11, 93–94, 151

Óláfr Haraldsson, St. Olaf "the Stout,"
king of the Norse, 6–7, 27, 48–49,
51, 56–57, 86
Olaf son of Godred "Crovan," king of the
Isles, 99, 102–3
Óláfr Tryggvason, king of the Norse, 32,
39–40, 48
Orkney Islands, 4, 6–7, 25, 27–28, 32–33,
39–41, 48, 49–50, 176
Orkneyinga Saga, 39–41, 49–51, 205–6
Osbern Pentecoste, 77–79

Perth, 102–3, 119, 127, 129–30, 140,
152, 158
Picts, 6, 15–17, 23, 24–27, 28, 29, 33, 45–
46, 65–66, 87, 89, 92–93, 94, 106,
122, 149–50
*Pleasant Conceited Comedy of George a
Greene, the Pinner of Wakefield*, 185,
Powel, David, 152–53

292 *Index*

Prophecy Of Berchán, 18, 23, 28, 29–30, 41–42, 44, 47–48, 54, 58, 63, 79–80, 81, 90–91, 105–6, 135–36, 170–71, 216
Prophecy of the Six Kings, 137
Prophecy, 13, 65, 128, 130, 134–40, 150, 151, 153–54, 160–61, 167–68, 170–72, 179, 209–10, 228

Raigne of Edward III, 182, 186–87
Raven Banner, 33, 39–40
Ravenspur Point, 117–18, 208–9
Rögnvald Hardaknútsson, Reginald Uí Imhar, king of York–Dublin, 30
Register of the Priory of St. Andrews, 69–70, 130–31
Robart the second, 182, 187
Robert Greene, 182, 183–84, 185
Robert I son of Robert, earl of Carrick, Robert "the Bruce," king of the Scots, 55–56, 107, 110–12, 119, 153, 207–8
Robert II son of Walter "the Steward," king of the Scots, 111–12, 122, 126, 134, 152
Robert III son of Robert II "the Steward," king of the Scots, 81, 119, 126, 129–30
Robert of Burgundy, 114, 215–16
Robert of St. Andrews, bishop, 131–32

scollog, 60–61
Scottish Historie of James the fourth see *James the fourth*
Senachie, 16, 105–6, 132
Sigurd son of Hlovi, jarl of the Orkney Islands, 32–33, 36*f*, 39–41, 48.
Sigvatr the Black, 48–49.
Sitryggr Hardacnutsson, Sigtryggr Uí Imhar, king of York–Dublin, 30
Skye, Isle of, 15, 20–21, 146

St. Andrews, Cathedral, 8, 28–29, 30, 60–61, 66, 87, 88, 96–97, 103, 124–25, 130–31, 169
St. Andrews, Priory of the Canons Regular of the Order of St. Augustine, 131–32, 140
St. Andrews, University, 120, 147, 155, 157–58, 159
St. Serf at Loch Leven, church of, 24–25, 28–29, 45, 52–53, 69–70, 71, 80, 124–25, 130–32, 213, 214–16
Stewart, William, 155–57, 210
Stow, John, 166–67, 173
Strathclyde, 12–13, 23, 29, 30–31, 43, 49, 54–55, 61, 71–72, 95–96, 214
Sulien, bishop of St. David's, 60–61

Tale of Cano son of Gartnán, 15, 20–21
Tara, 18, 65
Thorfinn son of Sigurd, jarl of the Orkney Islands, 6–7, 12, 30, 32–33, 39–41, 49–51, 56–57, 66, 86.
Todde, William, 171–72
Tragedie of the King of Scottes, 180–82
Trees, 140–42
Tres Sibyls, 2
Trio of women, 169–70
Tudor, Margaret, queen of Scots, 155–56, 157–58, 169–70
Turgot, bishop of St. Andrews, 87, 147

Uí Néill, confederation of, 14–15

Veremond, Richard, also known as Richard Vairmont, 106–7, 147
Verse Chronicle, 104, 105–6, 122–23, 130–31
Vikings, 25–27, 32

Walter Bower, 112, 116–17, 120, 129, 155, 209
Warner, William, 200–1

Weston, William, 171
William I son of Robert of Normandy, William "the Conquer", duke of Normandy and king of the English, 12, 85–86, 90–91
William II son of William I, duke of Normandy and king of the English, 11–12, 86, 90–91
William Malvoisine, bishop, 103
William of Malmesbury, historian, 115–16, 122–23, 183
William of Newburgh, historian, 95–96, 99
William of Touris, 176
William Shakespeare, 3, 9, 10, 123, 145, 151–52, 169–70, 178, 184, 185, 187, 192, 195, 200–1, 205, 209
William son of Henry of Huntingdon, William "the Lion," king of Scots, 98–99, 103, 104, 107–8, 119
William Wallace, Guardian of Scotland, 109–10, 203–4
Wimund, bishop of the Isles, 74f, 96, 99
Wolfe, Reyne, 165–66
Woodes, Nathaniel, 179–80